Final Solu

To Hugh & Adah
With best wishes,

Sally

16th June 2019

Final Solutions

Human Nature, Capitalism and Genocide

Sabby Sagall

PlutoPress
www.plutobooks.com

First published 2013 by Pluto Press
345 Archway Road, London N6 5AA

www.plutobooks.com

Distributed in the United States of America exclusively by
Palgrave Macmillan, a division of St. Martin's Press LLC,
175 Fifth Avenue, New York, NY 10010

British Library Cataloguing in Publication Data
A catalogue record for this book is available from the British Library

ISBN   978 0 7453 2654 2   Hardback
ISBN   978 0 7453 2653 5   Paperback
ISBN   978 1 8496 4891 2   PDF eBook
ISBN   978 1 8496 4893 6   Kindle eBook
ISBN   978 1 8496 4892 9   EPUB eBook

Library of Congress Cataloging in Publication Data applied for

This book is printed on paper suitable for recycling and made from fully managed
and sustained forest sources. Logging, pulping and manufacturing processes are
expected to conform to the environmental standards of the country of origin.

10 9 8 7 6 5 4 3 2 1

Typeset from disk by Stanford DTP Services, Northampton, England
Simultaneously printed digitally by CPI Antony Rowe, Chippenham, UK and
Edwards Bros in the United States of America

For Hilary

Contents

Acknowledgements   ix

Introduction: Capitalism and Genocide   1

PART ONE: THE ORIGINS OF HUMAN DESTRUCTIVENESS

1   Why Do People Kill People?   13
2   Killers On the Couch   38
3   What Makes Killers Tick?   64
4   Killing 'Things'   89

PART TWO: FOUR MODERN GENOCIDES

5   Native American Genocide   111
6   The Armenian Genocide   158
7   The Nazi Holocaust   183
8   The Rwandan Genocide   222

Summary and Conclusion   247

Notes   249
Bibliography   285
Index   298

Acknowledgements

A number of colleagues, comrades and friends have read different parts of the manuscript and made valuable comments or else directed me to important sources and texts. I would like to thank Professor Alex Callinicos, Dr. Alison Sealey, Andrew Enever, Professor Bob Carter, Dave Renton, Hilary Westlake, Professor Iain Ferguson, Dr. Jacqueline Fear-Segal, Professor Joel Kovel, Professor John Docker, John Rees, John Rose, Ken Muller, Professor Kevin Kenny, Dr. Kurt Jacobsen, Lindsey German, Dr. Marci Green, Professor Mike Gonzalez, Assistant Professor Murat Paker, Dr. Rainer Funk, Professor Roy Foster, Professor Stephen Frosh and Dr. Tirril Harris. My partner Hilary Westlake and my friend Kurt Jacobsen read the entire manuscript: their ideas and suggestions, at times critical but always constructive, gave me great encouragement, and helped to sustain me during a long and difficult writing process. Naturally, any errors of fact or judgment remain my responsibility. Many thanks also to Kurt Jacobsen for compiling the index. Hilary developed a good impersonation of a badger in her constant exhortation to complete the work as quickly as possible. My friend John Rose's pressure was also helpful and important. My friends Dr. George Paizis, Gerry Norris and Mel Norris also expressed interest and provided encouragement.

I would also like to thank the staff at Pluto Press for their patience and encouragement. Roger Van Zwanenberg, my original editor at Pluto, supported my project from the earliest stage and has been particularly helpful throughout the years it has taken me to complete it. My editor, David Shulman, has also been most supportive during that time. Robert Webb, production editor, has ably helped me cope with editing difficulties and delays. I am also grateful to my friend Dr. Ghada Karmi for the original introduction to Roger Van Zwanenberg. Thanks also to Melanie Patrick for the cover design. Tim Clark, copy-editor, and Dave Stanford, typesetter, are to be commended for their skill and efficiency.

Introduction:
Capitalism and Genocide

Certain historical events seem to defy all attempts at rational explanation. How is it possible that one group of human beings should have consciously planned, or at least visibly intended, to exterminate another group? Despite innumerable books having been written on the subject, there is no general consensus. The experts continue to engage in fierce debate, or else to ignore each other's contributions if they fall in an alternative discipline.

Apart from humankind, no animal species destroys large numbers of their own kind without any rational socio-economic or biological benefit. Yet in the American continent, between 1492 and 1890, possibly 80 million Native Americans died at the hands of the European colonists or from diseases brought from Europe – perhaps 95 per cent of the pre-Columbian population – arguably the greatest genocide in world history. In Turkey, between 1915 and 1922, up to one and a half million Armenians were slaughtered on the orders of the Young Turk regime. During the Second World War, six million Jews, but also tens of thousands of Gypsies, homosexuals and the mentally ill were massacred in Nazi-occupied eastern Europe in a programme of industrial genocide. And during the Rwandan crisis in 1994, some 800,000 Tutsis were slaughtered by Hutus. In the twentieth century alone, over 70 million people have been killed through ethnic conflict, a figure 'dwarfing that of previous centuries'.[1]

The term 'genocide' was coined by the jurist Raphael Lemkin in his book *Axis Rule in Occupied Europe*, published in the US in 1944. He defined it as 'the destruction of a nation or of an ethnic group'. The new word, denoting 'an old practice in its modern development', is made up from the ancient Greek word *genos* (race, tribe) and the Latin *cide* (killing). Lemkin went on, however, to argue that 'it does not necessarily mean the immediate destruction of a nation, except when accompanied by mass killings of all members of a nation'. The term signified 'a coordinated plan of different actions aiming at the destruction of essential foundations of the life of national groups, with the aim of annihilating the groups themselves'.[2] As Leo Kuper points out, the term was initially used in the indictment of the Nazi war criminals at the Nuremberg Trials in 1946, the first formal recognition of the crime of genocide.[3]

In 1946, two years after the publication of Lemkin's book, and thanks to his unflagging lobbying efforts, the United Nations General Assembly passed a resolution which stated that 'many instances of such crimes ... have occurred, when racial, religious, political and other groups have been destroyed, entirely or in part ... The punishment of the crime of genocide is a matter of international concern.'[4] Finally, the Genocide Convention of the UN was adopted unanimously and without abstentions in 1948.

However, Martin Shaw argues in his very useful book *What Is Genocide?* that the Geneva Convention's definition of genocide unduly narrowed Lemkin's original broad meaning by restricting it to the physical extermination of a group. Killing is, of course, the ultimate means of genocide, the one which 'trumps all others', but it is not its primary meaning. For Lemkin, as indicated above, this lay in the annihilation of a group's way of life, its social networks, its economic, cultural and political institutions.[5] There is a vast and growing literature on genocide, ethnic violence and ethno-nationalism. The lion's share of this endeavour has been given over to analyses of the Nazi Holocaust. In recent years, however, there has been increasing interest in the other modern genocides. A number of universities have set up special departments or programmes devoted to the study of genocide, Yale in the US and Southampton in the UK being two examples.

There are three points here. First, at an obvious level, this is undoubtedly to be welcomed. The deeper our understanding of human violence, the greater our chances of preventing it. A cliché, no doubt, but one to cherish.

Second, the burgeoning interest in genocides other than the extermination of the Jews – for example, that of the Armenians – represents an implicit challenge to the notion of the uniqueness of the Nazi Holocaust. This has been the focus of an important debate in recent years.

A third important, if obvious, point: we need to adopt a theoretical approach that is capable of accounting for the phenomenon of genocide. Without theory or a set of theories, there can be no understanding of human history and society. For example, without theory, we cannot explain the origins of Nazism or why the Holocaust occurred between 1941 and 1945 and not in 1923. Similarly with the Turkish genocide of the Armenians in 1915. The question is, which theory or set of theories is most adequate to the task of explanation?

Most of the work produced in the last three decades adopts an external, objective approach, analysing the historical, social or economic factors involved in the Nazi and other holocausts – the effects of war, colonisation, economic crisis, the class background of the perpetrators or the relationship between the state and civil society. There is neglect of the subjective factors involved.

In addition, most of the work published since the 1970s has been couched within a liberal perspective, one that emphasises the role of leaders, the structure of the state, or cultural factors – for example, Prussian militarism. The debate in the late 1980s and 1990s between German historians adopting either an intentionalist or a functionalist position is an example of such a liberal approach. Briefly, the debate was between those arguing that the Nazis had intended from the very beginning to exterminate the Jews, but had to wait for the right opportunity, and as against those who claimed that deteriorating circumstances radicalised the Nazis, driving them to perpetrate the Holocaust.

Furthermore, most work on modern genocide has been undertaken from within the confines of a single discipline, reflecting the fragmentation and specialisation of the existing social sciences. Thus, most books and articles are written by professional historians, sociologists, political scientists, economists or social psychologists, each adopting a conceptual approach derived from their specialism. Rarely do we find an attempt to forge links between the different fields, to grasp the inner ties that unite the partial aspects of what is, after all, a single social and historical reality.

Though many crucial insights have been developed from within these specialisms, in the end their separation amounts to confinement within an intellectual straitjacket, one that allows for no more than a partial explanation. Only by organically linking elements from history, social theory, economics and psychology will it be possible to approach an understanding of the Nazi death-camps and the killing fields of North America, Turkish Armenia and Rwanda.

To illustrate the point: it is, arguably hard to understand the Nazi Holocaust without examining the failure of the German middle class to overthrow feudalism and autocracy in the 1848 revolution, and the manner in which German capitalism subsequently developed. From there, it's on to the economic crises that beset Germany following defeat in the First World War and the Great Depression, and the effects of these crises on the urban and rural middle classes. Also crucial are the skilful manipulation of the despair of these strata by the Nazi Party and, finally, the mentality and family background of those who joined it.

Dori Laub makes a similar point, though from a different position. Referring to the wars and genocides of the twentieth century, he argues that 'disciplines in dialogue with one another are better suited to capturing the phenomena of massive psychic trauma, the raw data of genocidal events, than one scholarly discipline by itself'. Historians found themselves in the unprecedented situation of having to analyse 'events of an "unfamiliar and overpowering nature" ... that could not be articulated in the customary categories of traditional historiography'.[6]

There is one intellectual tradition, however, that has always insisted on the need to view the world as a totality, its parts organically interrelated, our perceptions of its separate aspects fused into an integrated vision. To follow the footpath of this tradition is to discover a large garden segmented into different sectors, each of which is, however, linked to every other, and from each of which one sees the garden as a whole. In other words, no garden wall separates our history from current social and power relations. Nor does any artificial boundary split off our past from the ideas and emotions that govern or accompany human actions and decisions in contemporary society.

The tradition that has always sought to link these different aspects is Marxism. As the Marxist philosopher Georg Lukács described the concept of 'totality' in Hegel and Marx:

> In Marx, the dialectical method aims at understanding society as a whole. Bourgeois thought concerns itself with objects that arise ... from the process of studying phenomena in isolation ... In the last analysis, Marxism does not acknowledge the existence of independent sciences of law, economics or history, etc.: there is nothing but a single, unified – dialectical and historical – science of the evolution of society as a totality.[7]

So, Marxism is at once a philosophy of humankind and of human history, a theory of society, that is, of social stability and change, and an economic theory of crisis, not just under capitalism but under pre-capitalist societies as well. These phenomena, and the theoretical approaches to them, do not fall into separate compartments but are aspects of a single, revolutionary view of our world, one that is, moreover, an integral part of our striving to change it. I therefore want to argue that Marxism, not liberal theory or postmodernism, is the theoretical approach to history and society best suited to deal with the question of genocide.

Nevertheless, to gain a fuller understanding of such extreme human violence, I believe that we do need, in addition, to get to grips with its subjective side. How do we account for hatred and destructiveness on such an enormous scale? What motivated the principal perpetrators, what 'made them tick'? As Freud put it, 'human behaviour implies a readiness to hate, an aggressiveness whose roots are unknown and that one would be inclined to characterise as elemental'.[8] Jacqueline Rose points out that this question is at the heart of all Freud's writings on collective life. We must, therefore, complement the objective analysis with an understanding of the perpetrators' motivation, their inner world.[9] Or as Mark Levene expressed it: 'Understanding genocide ... is very dependent on probing the mindset of the perpetrator's regime ... in order to tease out the anxieties, phobias and obsessions which ... drive it to act in often ... deeply irrational ways.'[10] The question is, where do such destructive urges come from? Are genocide and war expressions of the same basic destructiveness? Is it a 'genetic' human death instinct or drive, as Freud argued in the aftermath of the First World War, echoed later by Melanie Klein? Or do we need to analyse the relevant family and character structures and their historical development? Linked to this is the issue of human nature: is there a set of human features present in all societies, a bundle of universal needs, drives and capacities without which we cannot understand the phenomenon of genocide?

Let us be clear. All human actions, even those representing the most rationally devised means to an end, carry an emotional element. Analysing this dimension of feeling, grasping its links to rational aspects of action, is not, therefore, a dispensable after-thought, but an inescapable part of our task if we are to understand our history. We cannot comprehend such psychic or emotional phenomena through the application solely of economic, political or even ideological concepts. This is true not only at the individual level but also at the collective level. It is a point well brought out by Ramsay MacMullen: 'What I suggest is ... nothing new, but only long out of fashion: a way of searching out the emotions that determined behaviour; and entering into them ... representing them in all their colours, so as *more accurately* to reveal the past, or re-feel it, and so to understand it.'[11] In other words, there is an area of human existence that is irreducibly subjective, that cannot be flattened out by the weight of our objective social relations or understood simply as their mirror-image.

Marx and Engels themselves didn't have much to say on the individual, subjective aspect of history. There is a reference in *The German Ideology* to personality being conditioned by class relationships.[12] This is a start but, on its own, doesn't get us very far. They are not to blame for this. The modern psychological sciences could only emerge out of other sciences such as medicine or the social sciences. Rooted in the Enlightenment, Marx and Engels always followed with avid interest new scientific developments, enthusiastically welcoming, for example, the publication of Darwin's *On the Origin of Species* or of Morgan's anthropological studies of Native American communities, books about which Engels wrote important works. Unfortunately, Engels died in 1895, the year in which Freud and his colleague Breuer published *Studies on Hysteria*. Freud's chapter on psychotherapy is generally regarded as marking the inception of psychoanalysis.[13] Arguably, Engels would have greeted Freud's work with equal interest, and possibly enthusiasm, though no doubt critically. Indeed, Engels himself wrote:

> Ideology is a process accomplished by the so-called thinker consciously ... but with a false consciousness. The real motive forces impelling him remain unknown to him ... He works with mere thought material, which he accepts without examination as the product of thought, and does not investigate further for a more remote source independent of thought.[14]

Indeed, in the 1920s, Trotsky pleaded for tolerance towards psychoanalysis in the face of virulent attacks by many Bolsheviks who dismissed it as incompatible with Marxism due to its alleged anti-materialism and over-emphasis on sex.[15] 'He protested against the disparagement of Freudism all the more strongly because he held that Freud's teaching, like Pavlov's, was inherently materialistic.'[16] In 1923, Trotsky asked: 'Can [psychoanalysis] be reconciled with materialism, as, for instance, Karl Radek thinks (and I also), or is it hostile to it?'[17] And in 1926 he wrote: 'it would be too simple and crude to declare psycho-analysis incompatible with Marxism ... We are not obliged to adopt Freudism ... Freudism is a working hypothesis. It can produce, and it does produce, deductions and surmises which point to a materialist psychology.'[18]

I don't wish to ignore the work of academic and experimental social psychology in the area of modern genocide: there have been important contributions to our understanding of patterns of obedience and conformity. But the question remains: conformity to what? Where does the hatred, the urge to destroy, come from? I do, therefore, want to argue that psychoanalysis – because of its dynamic approach, its appreciation of the way the past casts its shadow over the present, its materialist focus on the family and hence on society, and because of its understanding of unconscious sources of motivation – is the psychological theory best equipped to dealing with the subjective factors at the heart of political and social action, in this case, genocide. As Erich Fromm observed: 'Freud did not simply state the existence of unconscious processes in general (others had done that before him), but showed empirically how unconscious processes operate by demonstrating their operation in concrete and observable phenomena: neurotic symptoms, dreams, and the small acts of daily life.'[19]

The fact remains that there was a gap in classical Marxism, one created by the absence of a theory of subjectivity, of the way external, material conditions become translated into the psyche of the individual, not just as ideology but as their overall emotional life. As Otto Fenichel wrote: 'the economic conditions do not just influence the individual directly, but also indirectly, via a change in his psychic structure'.[20] Nor did vulgar Marxists of the Stalinist and social-democratic traditions help, with their fear of psychologism, their mechanical belief in the automatic translation of economic crisis into class consciousness.

Their refusal to acknowledge the reality of the subjective factor, to admit the need for mediation between objective and subjective, resulted in a failure to understand fully the 'manner and mode by which ideology is translated in the everyday life and behaviour of the individual', including the presence or absence of revolutionary consciousness.[21]

More recently, Stephen Frosh has argued that 'The potential value of psychoanalysis for people concerned with politics lies in its ability to provide an account of subjectivity which links the "external" structures of the social world with the "internal" world of each individual.'[22] This is important for Marxists. It suggests they should take seriously the potential ability of psychoanalysis to help us understand how external structures of exploitation and oppression are internalised in the mind of the individual. Joel Kovel wrote in similar vein: 'psychoanalysis has discovered in each of us a spontaneous well of subjectivity that simply does not contain in any immediate sense the categories of political economy yet plays a powerful determining role in social life'.[23]

Jacqueline Rose likewise upholds the fruitfulness of psychoanalysis in its understanding of the individual in society: 'psychoanalysis remains for me the most powerful reading of the role of human subjects in the formation of states and nations, subjects as driven by their unconscious ... in thrall to identities that will not save them and that will readily destroy the world'.[24] Dori Laub, too, stresses the need to acknowledge 'the presence of the irrational, the unconscious, and the roles they play in the control of the rational mind, an alternative that calls for the involvement of the psychoanalyst who has become familiar with these processes through clinical work'.[25] He quotes Walter Benjamin's description of the psychological aftermath of the First World War: 'Was it not noticeable at the end of the war that men returned from the battlefield grown silent – not richer but poorer in communicable experience?'[26]

However, most psychoanalytical approaches deal with the effects on the victims or else investigate the emotional background of the perpetrators without linking this to the broad historical experience of their class. In short, they divorce psychology from history. Arguably, most psychoanalytical explanations of genocide are of this kind, reducing historical phenomena to the psychology of the protagonists and, conversely, failing to locate their individual psychology within the wider society and its politics.

We need to firmly reject such psychological reductionism, which is in no way inevitable. It is not part of the intellectual essence of psychoanalysis, even if, in practice, most psychoanalytical writers have based their work on such a psychologistic approach. (The real problem in most contemporary debate about genocide is the opposite – sociological reductionism.) In sum, we need a psychoanalysis that sets out to trace the character and family structures back to their historical roots and class backgrounds. This cannot, on its own, amount to a sufficient analysis, but it is an indispensable link in the overall chain of explanation. To quote Lukács again: 'what is decisive is whether this process of isolation is a means towards understanding the whole and whether it is integrated within the context it presupposes and requires, or whether the abstract knowledge of an isolated fragment retains its "autonomy" and becomes an end in itself'.[27]

To my knowledge, however, no work attempting to link the objective and the subjective reasons for genocide has been done since the 1970s. We need, therefore, to rejuvenate this dual approach, and to revisit the contribution of the two generations of psychoanalytic Marxists who consciously struggled to develop ideas that lent themselves to integration within a Marxist framework. The first generation consists of the early Wilhelm Reich and certain members of the Frankfurt School of Critical Theory, such as Herbert Marcuse and Erich Fromm. The psychologist Oliver James has stressed Fromm's role in highlighting the link between the materialism of modern capitalism and emotional distress, an argument put forward by Fromm in his classic work, *The Sane Society*.[28] James quotes the work of psychologists Tim Kasser and Richard Ryan, whose studies established that American students who put materialist aspirations ahead of emotional well-being suffered more depression and anxiety than those who did not.[29] However, it was Reich who first argued in a paper published in 1929 that Marxism and psychoanalysis were compatible: 'Just as Marxism was sociologically the expression of man *becoming conscious* of the laws of economics and the exploitation of a majority by the minority, so psychoanalysis is the expression of man *becoming conscious* of the social repression of sex.'[30] As John Rickert put it in a perceptive article: 'Marxism originally turned to psychoanalysis in an attempt to understand the role of psychological factors in social phenomena. Specifically, it sought an account of the origin and power of ideology, the subjective conditions for social change, and the processes by which society enters the individual psyche.'[31]

The failure of the Russian Revolution to spread, together with the rise of fascism in Europe, led a number of Marxist writers – in particular, but not only, the founders of the Frankfurt School – to attempt to deepen their understanding of the subjective obstacles to revolution. In Germany, following the failure of the revolution ushered in by the military collapse in 1918, most Marxists correctly stressed the absence of revolutionary leadership. For Karl Korsch, however: 'In the fateful months after November 1918, when the organised political power of the bourgeoisie was smashed and outwardly there was nothing else in the way of the transition from capitalism to socialism, the great chance was never seized because the socio-psychological preconditions for its seizure were lacking.'[32] Why did the working class fail to overthrow the decaying capitalist order with its perennial crises and wars and replace it with an alternative system – a revolutionary democracy? On the contrary, workers seemed to absorb not only capitalist ideology but capitalism's image of them as passive and ineffectual, its need for them to be accommodating and self-suppressing. Was it enough to talk about the failure of leadership, important as this was, or was there another factor, one that could perhaps explain why, in Lichtman's words, 'people come to want what is destructive of their need',[33] why workers not only remained imprisoned within the jail of alienation but had become their own jailers?[34]

The early Reich, Fromm and Marcuse set about trying to answer these questions. To understand them might provide some clues as to the psychological conditions for change. For Reich and the members of the Frankfurt School, Freud, with his notions of repression, unconscious motivation, defence mechanisms and the internalisation of authority, was a necessary starting point, promising to illuminate 'how human beings could come "willingly" to participate in their own dismemberment'.[35] As Reich expressed it, 'psychoanalysis, by virtue of its method, can reveal the instinctual roots of the individual's social activity, and by virtue of its dialectical theory of instincts can clarify, in detail, the psychological effects of production conditions upon the individual...' And most importantly, 'psychoanalysis proves that the economic structure of society does not directly transform itself into ideologies "inside the head"'.[36] Put another way, Freud stressed that there was more to human suffering than could be explained by oppressive, external economic conditions.[37] As Russell Jacoby wrote: 'The efforts of Lukács and Korsch, and after them others such as the Frankfurt School, were toward salvaging this lost dimension of Marxism: subjectivity.'[38]

Moreover, if the family is the crucial mediator between society and the individual, the indispensable conveyor-belt of authority and repression, both Marx and Freud are found wanting. For Marx, the family was seen as 'reflecting' the existing social relations of production rather than as an incubator of pathology.[39] Or, as Max Horkheimer put it: 'The family as one of the most important agents of education concerns itself with the reproduction of human character ... and largely imparts to human characters the authoritarian attitudes on which the bourgeois order depends.'[40] Freud, on the other hand, 'ignores the manner in which the family acts as the *mediation* of larger social-historical processes'.[41] The answer had to lie in some amalgamation of the two, more precisely, the integration of psychoanalysis into Marxism.

Periods of radical upheaval inevitably generate a preoccupation with a whole range of political and social issues, including that of personal alienation. Crucially, the liberation of society is seen to include the liberation of the human personality from the stultifying effects of capitalist alienation. So it was in the 1960s and the years following that most inspiring of decades. In the late 1960s, and during the 1970s and 1980s, a second generation of psychoanalytic Marxists made further important contributions to this debate – in chronological order, Reuben Osborn, Reimut Reiche, Michael Schneider, Joel Kovel, Richard Lichtman and Eugene Wolfenstein.[42] Andrew Samuels is a psychoanalyst who has examined the links between politics and psychoanalysis from a Jungian perspective.[43] Most of these writers will be examined or referred to in the appropriate context in the chapters that follow. The current period that has been witnessing the emergence of new international movements will hopefully encourage fresh debate around these vital issues. Exploring these writers will, perhaps, throw light upon the tangled question of human destructiveness.

It is also crucial for this analysis to appreciate the contribution of post-Freudian psychoanalysis – in particular the work of Melanie Klein and the object-relations school. Too often writers outside the field of psychoanalysis write as though it began and ended with Freud, as if modern physics began and ended with Newton or Kepler.

There is, however, one potential intellectual obstacle to this project: the ongoing legacy of postmodernism. Around 1979–80, politics in the UK and the US moved sharply to the right. As always, politics both reflects and influences social and intellectual developments. The effect of this political shift was felt throughout the cultural and academic spheres of the Anglo-Saxon world. In social theory, the result was a decline of interest in theories purporting to offer total views of society and history and the place of the individual within them. Postmodernism, with its narrow subjectivism, its denial of objective reality and of the possibility of all-embracing theory, came to dominate the intellectual scene. Postmodernist influence still prevails in many, if not most, sociology departments. However, there are a number of sociologists, historians and others who are unhappy with this dominance.

An important factor in my analysis is a distinction between different kinds of genocide. Michael Mann argues that genocide is essentially a modern phenomenon, inexplicable outside the rise of ethnic consciousness, whereas in ancient times class tended to 'trump' ethnicity.[44] Moreover, in earlier years, anthropologists adduced several arguments to back up their claim that tribal or pre-'civilisation' communities, that is, hunter-gatherer or early agricultural societies, did not experience the equivalent of mass murder.[45] In more recent debates, however, this claim has been subject to question.[46] What is clear is that, as regards the ancient and medieval worlds, in Greek, Roman or biblical societies, and also, say, the Middle Eastern world of the Crusades, brutal mass murders took place. It is, however, open to doubt whether these can be placed in the same category as modern genocides. More sensible would be to separate out the different kinds of genocide, analysing them in terms of their various sorts of economic and political contexts and the different kinds of motivation at their heart.

One can, therefore, distinguish between, on the one hand, economic and political genocides, which do have a 'rational' or utilitarian basis, and, on the other, those that have little or no instrumental explanation, and can therefore be deemed 'irrational', explicable if not only, then largely, in psychological terms. As regards 'political genocide' or political mass murder, what Mann calls 'classicide', examples would be Stalin's murder by summary execution or deliberate starvation of some ten million of the better-off peasant kulaks and other dissidents, or Pol Pot's murder of some 1.7 million Cambodians.[47] Both of these had a terrible 'rationale' as far as the economic and political objectives of the respective regimes were concerned. But they need to be distinguished from those genocides where no visible benefit accrued to the regime or perpetrator group, where, on the contrary, a preoccupation with the extermination of particular groups was against their interests, as they perceived them, and indeed set back the attainment of their objectives.

This issue is distinct from the question of whether the liquidation of an entire class, ethnic, national or religious group was planned or intended, as opposed to being the result of spontaneous mass anger. Both 'rational' and 'irrational' genocides have been planned – for example, Stalin's and Pol Pot's liquidation of those perceived as enemies of the state, and, of course, the Nazi Holocaust. Some have been 'semi-planned', or at least the result of an intention discernible over time, as in the case of the genocide of the Native Americans and other colonial peoples.

As for the second category of genocide – those without any 'rational' explanation – they can be further sub-divided into genocides that are 'spontaneous', motivated by rage or the desire for revenge, and those that can be related to social character. As I shall argue, all four 'irrational' genocides examined in this book are rooted in the perpetrators' social character. Some modern genocides will be found to contain both 'rational' and irrational elements, again, for example, colonial genocides such as that of the Native Americans or the Australian Aborigines.

The point of all this, as already stated, is to devise a psychological explanation that is compatible with, or rather in part derived from, a Marxist understanding of history. These arguments will be taken up in Part One. Part Two, containing the remaining four chapters, will offer case-studies of the four modern 'irrational' or character-based genocides.

These debates are not solely of academic interest. Theoretical clarification, enlarging our understanding of the history of humankind, grasping where we came from and who we are, helps us forge the intellectual tools that we need for the transformation of society. Understanding the roots of human destructiveness can only be, at best, a modest contribution to forging those tools. Without them, however, we shall be unable to transcend a society based on individual greed and competitiveness, political domination, the alienation of human labour and the commodification of human beings and their relationships. We need to understand in order to effect change. But underpinning a desire to understand is our imagination, and the vision of an alternative possible world in which individual and collective autonomy and our potential for cooperation, mutual care and democratic self-government will be maximised. It is not unreasonable to hope that such a society will perhaps, if not eliminate human destructiveness, then at least have the potential to minimise it.

PART ONE

THE ORIGINS OF
HUMAN DESTRUCTIVENESS

CHAPTER ONE

Why Do People Kill People?

What impels one human being to kill another, not because the latter has harmed him in any way, but simply because s/he is a member of a certain ethnic, religious or national group? I would argue that no explanation of human action is complete unless it adduces, not only its causes or the conditions under which it occurs, but also its reasons or motives. Experts from different fields, academic and clinical, have offered diverse explanations. In this chapter I shall, firstly, outline some of the theoretical approaches to the question of genocide and ethnic cleansing – those of political sociology, sociology, history and social psychology, including the non-psychoanalytical version of the authoritarian personality. I don't mean to suggest that the exemplars I quote deal fully with the contributions of these disciplines, merely that they represent good examples of their different approaches. I shall attempt to assess the extent to which they fulfil the criterion of providing reasons for genocidal behaviour. Secondly, I shall suggest, where possible, how insights arising out of these diverse methods might be integrated organically into a psychoanalytic Marxist view of history.

Towards Understanding Genocide

Political sociology

To what do we ascribe human destructiveness on such a scale? Recent work in the field of political sociology offers us one kind of answer. Michael Mann's book, *The Dark Side of Democracy* (2005), on ethnic cleansing and genocide, suggests eight general theses that purport to give us a collective explanation of these murderous phenomena.[1] To summarise briefly the main points:

Firstly, murderous cleansing is a modern phenomenon: conventional warfare has increasingly targeted civilian populations; moreover, amid the multi-ethnicity of modern societies, the ideal of rule by the people or 'demos' has often been entwined with 'ethnos' to produce the dominance of a particular group.

Secondly, ethnic hostility arises 'where ethnicity trumps class as the main form of social stratification'.[2] In the past, ethnic conflict was rare since most big societies were divided along class lines, dominated by an aristocracy or other elite that rarely shared a common culture with the people. Where the modern struggle for democracy involved an entire people struggling against rulers defined as foreign, an ethnic sense of identity arose, for example in Ireland or Poland.

Thirdly, ethno-nationalism is strongest where it becomes enmeshed with a sense of exploitation: for example, the Nazis felt exploited by the Jews, the Turks by the Armenians, the Hutus by the Tutsis. The danger zone of murderous cleansing is reached when movements claiming to represent two ethnic groups both lay claim to their own state having all or part of the same territory, as in colonial genocides. The brink of murderous cleansing is reached when the stronger side believes it has overwhelming military power and ideological legitimacy, as in Yugoslavia. Going over the edge into murderous cleansing occurs when the state exercising sovereignty over the contested territory has been factionalised and radicalised in an unstable geopolitical environment that usually leads to war.

Of course, ethnic mass murder is not usually the initial intention of the perpetrators of violence, not even in the case of Hitler. When they reach that point, it is usually Plan C, Plan A being a compromise or straightforward repression, Plan B 'a more radically repressive adaptation to the failure of Plan A'.[3] Plan C, involving murderous cleansing, is adopted after the failure of A and B. Genocide is certainly deliberate but not premeditated. Moreover, there are three main levels of perpetrators: the radical elites running the party and state; the bands of militants forming the violent paramilitaries; and the core constituencies providing mass if not majority popular support.

Finally, it is ordinary people living in normal social structures who carry out murderous cleansing. Mann quotes the psychologist Charny: 'the mass killers of humankind are largely everyday human beings – what we have called normal people according to currently accepted definitions by the mental health profession'.[4] Indeed, in Bosnia, some of them were psychiatrists! Placed in similar situations, anyone might commit ethnic murder. 'To understand ethnic cleansing, we need a sociology of power more than a special psychology of perpetrators as disturbed or psychotic people – though some may be.'[5]

These theses certainly provide significant insights insofar as they shed light on the conditions under which acts of ethnic cleansing and genocide have occurred in the modern world. However, in the end, they are a series of descriptions of factors, some of which, though not all, have been present in each of the events. Moreover, they refer exclusively to external factors – political, economic, territorial, and so on. Mann's analysis remains incomplete in that his theses do not offer us an *explanation* of genocide that includes the internal reasons or motives that drove groups of people to commit such crimes. And surely we need to understand what forces of hatred and destructiveness are unleashed by the various precipitating factors. The perpetrators of genocidal violence may well be 'ordinary people', and not clinically diagnosed homicidal psychotics, but at the very least certain situations have produced drastically altered mental states, characterised by a high level of destructiveness. Mann identifies *necessary* conditions, but these do not contain, in addition, *sufficient* conditions: a complete explanation requires both.

Furthermore, Mann writes as though pathology were a purely individual phenomenon. Yet surely we can legitimately posit the notion of social pathology, a situation in which a high proportion of members of a society or of certain groups or classes display identifiable symptoms of emotional malfunction, of being severely out of touch with reality. The middle class in Nazi Germany – and currently Israeli society – arguably fall within this category. If so, then individuals would not stand out from the pathological group to which they belong. As group psychoanalyst Wilfred Bion described it: 'no individual, however isolated in time and space, can be regarded as outside a group or lacking in active manifestations of group psychology'.[6] Or again: 'diseases manifest themselves in the individual but they have characteristics that make it clear that it is the group rather than the individual that is stricken'.[7]

This is the position espoused by Erich Fromm in his much-admired *The Sane Society* (1956) in which he argues that 'many psychiatrists and psychologists refuse to entertain the idea that society as a whole may be lacking in sanity: the problem of mental health is that of "unadjusted" individuals, not ... of a possible unadjustment of the culture itself'. He proposes, therefore, to deal 'not with individual pathology but with the pathology of normalcy ... the pathology of contemporary Western society'.[8]

Fromm invokes the authority of no less a figure than Freud himself, who wrote: 'would not the diagnosis be justified that many systems of civilisation – or epochs of it – possibly even the whole of humanity – have become "neurotic" under the pressure of the civilising trends'.[9] Freud underpinned this view with an insistence on the social nature of human beings, a challenge to the common interpretation of Freud as irredeemably individualistic. I will return to this argument in Chapter 2.

Psychoanalytic Marxist Michael Schneider offers a further example of group pathology. He argues that the traditional bourgeoisie, that of the pre-imperialist, pre-monopoly capitalist era, once it lost its independent, entrepreneurial role as the creator of new, revolutionary means of production, became prone to specific forms of mental illness. This collective neurosis expressed the loss of its historical role and its new powerlessness, its inability to defeat the emerging depersonalised structures of corporate power and its state ally.

> By destroying its social and economic foundation, developing monopoly capitalism not only transformed the classic bourgeois family into a breeding ground of psychic crises and disturbances; but through its elements of immanent social and political crisis, it created a social 'atmosphere' which favoured the massive creation of neurosis.[10]

Mann's theses are useful insofar as they refer to the sum of necessary external conditions for the occurrence of genocide. But, as already suggested, explanations both of natural phenomena and of human behaviour need to identify sufficient conditions as well. Moreover, Mann's necessary conditions refer to certain indispensable precipitating factors. But again, we need in addition to know if there are any predisposing factors, an inner proclivity or receptiveness, that becomes activated under the right precipitating conditions. Both predisposing and precipitating factors are necessary if we are to provide a fully rounded explanation, one that is both theoretically valid and empirically plausible. In other words, we need to establish the existence of the following historical situation: the presence of subjective predisposing factors which, however, lack precipitating factors such as economic crisis or social breakdown, intensifying military or territorial conflict between rival ethnic or national groups, favourable strategic moments, and so on. The converse would be historical situations which contain such precipitating factors but which do not slide into murderous cleansing. Can we establish that these situations do not result in genocide because of the absence of the necessary predisposing, subjective factors? Clearly, in both these situations, it would be hard to draw conclusions in the absence of relevant historical or empirical research.

Taking the second category first – the presence of objective precipitating factors with no genocidal outcome – there have, of course, been many such situations in the post-war world, for example, the numerous conflicts in sub-Saharan Africa in which hundreds of thousands have perished but which fall short of a Rwandan-type exterminatory genocide. The conflict in Bosnia in the 1990s would perhaps be another, despite the Srebrenica massacre. Eight thousand men and boys were murdered but women and girls, around 16,000, were escorted to Tuzla by the Bosnian Serbs.[11] But clearly such war zones do not provide fertile ground for conducting the kind of scrupulous research necessary to establish the presence of the subjective factors that are an essential ingredient of irrational genocide.

Sociology

As we saw in the Introduction, Martin Shaw aims to restore Lemkin's original sociological definition of genocide by seeing it as involving more than the physical extermination of a group. Important though this is – and genocide always involves mass killing – the core meaning of the term refers, in addition, to the use of legal and military power to destroy a group's social, economic, political and cultural life and institutions.[12]

Shaw therefore criticises the proliferation of concepts intended to refer to 'other forms of violence' – for example, ethnic cleansing, but including the many '-cides' of genocide, such as ethnocide, classicide, politicide, etc.[13] These are taken to refer to phenomena separate from 'full-blown genocide', in particular situations in which there is cultural or political suppression of a group but no attempt to physically destroy it. But Shaw insists that where 'deep, extensive cultural and linguistic suppression leads to violent attacks on a group ... this tips over into genocide'.[14] So the concept of 'ethnocide', often used to distinguish 'cultural genocide' from exterminatory genocide, is misleading, since it refers to the 'cultural dimension of genocide', a process integral to every genocide. Shaw prefers the terms 'cultural suppression' for the pre-genocidal denial of culture, and the 'cultural dimension of genocide' for suppression that is 'part of a broader genocidal process'.[15]

Similarly, 'politicide', or the killing of political groups, appears to be different from the genocide of ethnic, national or religious groups insofar as membership of the latter is ascribed (one is born into them), whereas one chooses to join the former. However, since genocide usually develops out of military conflict – a precipitating factor – rather than just prejudice – a predisposing factor – political elites are often the first target of genocidal killers.[16] There are two famous examples in which the destruction of a political group actually defines the mass slaughter: the massacre of half a million Communist Party members by the Indonesian army in 1965, and Stalin's murder of thousands of political opponents in the 1930s. In general, however, politicide is a variant or sub-category of genocide, and political targeting should be seen as a 'general dimension of genocide' in which 'political enemies are targeted alongside ... ethnic, class or other social enemies'.[17]

Similarly, 'classicide' is a term invented by Mann to refer to the liquidation of peasant classes by despotic state-capitalist regimes such as Stalin's Russia and Mao's China as part of the creation of powerful centralised industrial economies. In Russia between 1929 and 1933, the kulak class of rich peasants was destroyed as a class through deportations, killings and state-induced 'terror-famine', in preparation for the collectivisation of agriculture. Some 10 million peasants died. In China's Great Leap Forward between 1959 and 1961, over 30 million died under similar circumstances. However, for Shaw, the idea that entire social classes were enemies that had to be liquidated is only a variation on the more common theme of destroying ethnic or national groups. And it is not really separate: 'anti-peasant "classicides" were combined with and followed by similar murderous campaigns against other social groups – both other classes and ethnic or national groups'. So Stalin's terror-famine was not simply intended to destroy the peasants as a class: focused on Ukraine, its secondary target was Ukrainian national identity.[18]

In sum, Shaw disagrees with Mann's attempt to view these various forms of political oppression and violence as different kinds of phenomena. While it is necessary to adopt 'flexible language' to analyse the various forms of genocide, Shaw argues that the invention of new terms risks distorting reality by viewing as separate certain types of action that in fact belong to the same category. He concludes that 'we need concepts and theories that link them rather than set them apart'.[19] However, there is the opposite danger in Shaw's approach, namely that we lump together phenomena that do contain important differences, so that we obscure the social-historical contexts within which they occur, and fail to grasp the different kinds of motives that impelled the perpetrators. So, in the first case, the concept of genocide can usefully be taken to describe completely irrational acts of destruction, ones that actually set back the interests and goals of the perpetrators; whereas, in the second case, 'classicide' describes acts of violence that did advance those goals and interests. Hence the Nazi genocide of the Jews actually made their military defeat more likely, as we shall see in Chapter 7. On the other hand, Stalin's massacre of the kulaks, and the consequent forced implementation of the collectivisation of agriculture, did facilitate the rapid industrialisation of Russia (though, of course, Trotsky was right to oppose Stalin's strategy and to put forward his alternative internationalist and democratic path to socialism).

Shaw follows Weber in wanting to provide explanations of social action based on two criteria: any explanation must include the actor's intentions, taking into account the meaning the action has for him or her, but it must also analyse the structure of social relations of which the action is a part. In other words, an adequate sociological explanation must both grasp the subjective meaning of actions, how they appear or feel to the actor, understanding their intentions, but also be 'causally adequate', that is, place these actions in a wider context of social relations. Now, the first stage – understanding subjective intentions – leads to the second – elaborating a broader sociological framework that explains them in terms of certain key concepts or model. This model is created by extracting the most crucial or pure elements from the actors' meanings, a model that Weber called an 'ideal-type'. Shaw provides such an ideal-type or 'generic concept' of genocide: 'violent conflict, in which the armed, organised side engages in intentional social destruction of the unarmed group side'.[20] He criticises contemporary genocide studies for 'its overriding concern with establishing intentionality' and for being stuck at this first stage. A genuine sociology of genocide must include analyses of the interaction between perpetrators, victims and bystanders. Only such a 'relational' approach can provide us with an account of the social structure of genocide, the 'general "structuring of social relations across time and space" in which recurring patterns of social action are reproduced'.[21] In the case of genocide, this is a structure of conflict, primarily the 'qualitatively asymmetric conflict of armed power and unarmed civilian society, but also entailing the possibility of armed resistance and alliance with other armed powers'. Genocide is therefore best understood in relation to other structures of conflict, that is, from its distinctiveness visible through its differences from these other types – especially war, with which it shares many common features. In sum, genocide, for Shaw, is 'a structural phenomenon ... a recurring pattern of social conflict, characterised by particular kinds of relationships between actors, and with typical connections to other conflict structures in society'.[22]

This sociological approach can be criticised on two counts: first for its formalism. Shaw theorises genocide in terms of social action comprising intention and structure. But these concepts provide us only with a definition: they do not in themselves explain any particular genocide, nor do they lead to any general analysis of the causes of genocide, or rather of its reasons (where human social action is concerned, 'reason' is a better concept than 'cause'). Secondly, because of this formalism, Shaw's formulae, while useful in themselves, do not amount to an explanation specifically of genocide. The idea of 'a recurring pattern of social conflict' applies to other phenomena – for example, revolutionary movements, war, civil war. The notion of an 'asymmetric conflict of armed power and unarmed civilian society' applies also to punitive attacks that fall short of genocide – for example, the bombing of Dresden in the Second World War or the punitive expeditions in the Low Countries by Spain's Duke of Alba in the sixteenth century.[23] What we need is an analysis of the subjective, motivational factors impelling a group of perpetrators to commit genocide, together with an explanation of how these factors are rooted in objective social and historical conditions.

History

Ben Kiernan's *Blood and Soil* is an engrossing, all-encompassing historical account of genocides 'from Sparta to Darfur'. It is, moreover, an illuminating attempt to link the objective with the subjective, though by the latter he refers not to psychological causal factors but to key ideological concomitants. The three main 'common ideological features of genocides' are racism, the cult of antiquity, and the cult of cultivation, or what he also describes as 'the romance of agrarianism'.[24] Racism implies belief in the inferiority of, or threat posed by, a people or group. It becomes genocidal 'when perpetrators imagine a world without certain kinds of people in it'.[25]

Kiernan's theses undoubtedly represent valuable insights into the phenomenon of genocide, and specifically into the mentality of its perpetrators. He has indeed identified key factors accompanying the lurch into genocide. But what is unclear is the link between these ideological factors and such ultimate human destructiveness. Why should the cults of antiquity and agriculture, even racism, be at the heart of genocide? More concretely, under what socio-economic and psychological conditions does racism become genocidal? Missing from this account is an analysis of why these ideological factors should appeal to the perpetrators, *of precipitating factors which activate the predisposing ones*. Again, Kiernan suggests necessary conditions, but we need, in addition, sufficient conditions.

Another important historical work full of valuable insights is Mark Levene's *Genocide in the Age of the Nation State*. Levene argues that modern genocide must be understood as the product of the transformation of pre-modern human societies into the international system of interlocking nation states. It generally occurs within the context of 'latecomer states' striving to assert their independence or sovereignty, to emulate, catch up with or challenge established rivals. But it represents a systemic dysfunction of that international system, a fundamental disequilibrium usually brought about by major societal dislocations such as war. It can't, therefore, be dismissed as solely 'the aberrant or deviant behaviour of rogue regimes since it results from their struggle for development or empowerment'.[26] As for the perpetrators of genocide, there are, for Levene, three models, or aspects. The first is that of modernity, or rather the modern, rational state. Here, genocide is seen as the product of a highly organised, coordinated state machine, whose foundation is a technically advanced, scientifically oriented society. The most obvious example of this model is the Nazi Holocaust. The second model is that of the 'ideologically driven elite'. The core-perpetrators of modern genocide are often an ideologically inspired group who have assumed control of the state and are committed to the transformation or improvement of their society or the world as a whole. Theirs is an almost messianic vision of an alternative, redeemed world: one, however, that they themselves will create, 'as if they were gods'. Members of this elite, moreover, have lived through massive socio-economic upheavals, but alone possess the 'visionary insight as to both cause and cure of that malady', thus seeing themselves as the indispensable mediators of this vision of renewal, the creators of the new world, of a society 'dramatically reborn for ... a perfected future without end'.[27]

As for the carrying out of genocide, members of the core group generally feel the need to set up secret, informal structures based on the party, and run by loyalists. Decisions taken by the leadership will then be transmitted to the inner sanctums of the party-controlled state and implemented through them. So, the core-perpetrators feel entitled to appropriate key organs of state power in order 'to actualise their vision of a cleaner, safer, more just and sound world society'.[28] In this application of state power to the fulfilment of their vision, we see a conjoining of models one and two. However, the perpetrators are generally 'outsiders', people with a background of social exclusion, whose mentality reflects this upstart, outsider status. In short, they are people with 'unsatisfied or suppressed feelings of existential envy and hatred'. This means the core-perpetrators are not a small, isolated group, and that their message is likely to have a resonance with broader layers of society. It is impossible that they could have conceived of or carried out genocide without the explicit support, assistance or 'motivated engagement of many thousands of like-minded cadres'.[29] This comes out most clearly in the genocides perpetrated by the Ottomans and the Nazis.

This leads directly to the third model or aspect: the people. The question here is whether genocide is defined and implemented solely by an elite and their cadres, or whether wider layers, of whose disaffection and aspirations the elite are the voice, are incorporated. The most clearly affirmative answer is provided in the Rwandan case, but also in that of the Native American and other colonial genocides.

Finally, Levene emphasises that genocide cannot be fully understood without probing the mindset of the perpetrator regime, 'in order to tease out the anxieties, phobias and obsessions which ... drive it to act in often highly conspiratorial and even deeply *irrational* ways'.[30] Perpetrators usually fear their victims, if not physically, then in some other much less concrete but conceivably more frightening way.[31] The targeted community are seen as powerful and dangerous, able to and intent on undermining or destroying the regime's agenda. This is despite the vast disparity of real power and resources separating the perpetrators from the targeted community. Levene adopts psychoanalytical language in stressing the need to understand what perpetrator groups project on to their victims, the malevolent power the latter are felt to possess, which, in the mind of the regime, justifies their extermination. He argues that we cannot fully understand genocide without 'engagement with issues of collective human psychopathology', and again that 'projective tendencies seem to be intrinsic to the human condition'.[32]

Levene has provided us with an analysis that is comprehensive and persuasive, but there is a twofold weakness to his argument. First is the failure to develop more fully the link between genocide and genocidal pathology, and social class. He briefly mentions the petty-bourgeois background of the perpetrators but doesn't see their paranoia as a class pathology. However, as will be argued throughout this study, genocidal perpetrators are largely of middle-class background, and this is central to the analysis of their ideology and pathology. Secondly, to his great credit, Levene stresses the psychopathological element in genocide but then doesn't develop this crucial factor through a socio-psychoanalysis of the perpetrators. This study aims to cover that ground.

Social psychology

In 1950, Theodor Adorno and his colleagues published the groundbreaking, psychoanalytically oriented *The Authoritarian Personality*, which attempted to analyse the personality type of the potentially fascist individual.[33] (This work will be examined further in Chapter 2.) However, in recent decades, the mantle of leading protagonist of research into authoritarianism passed from Adorno on to the shoulders of Canadian psychology professor, Bob Altemeyer. In a series of works published between 1981 and 2006, he developed his version of the concept of Right-Wing Authoritarianism (RWA). He outlines three features of RWA:

(1) a high degree of submission to the established, legitimate authorities in their society;
(2) high levels of aggression in the name of their authorities; and
(3) a high level of conventionalism.[34]

There is, in addition, a high correlation between RWA as defined by the three criteria above and right-wing, conservative attitudes.

Regarding the first feature – a high level of submission – high RWAs will insist that we submit to authority in all situations. For example, asked whether it is right to steal an expensive drug to save someone's life, they are more likely to answer: 'The law is the law and must be obeyed.'[35] High RWAs show much stronger respect for their fathers or the presidents of the companies where they work. During the Watergate crisis, high RWAs believed Nixon was innocent for longer and more strongly than most people.[36] As Altemeyer puts it, 'authoritarian followers have a "Daddy and Mommy know best" attitude toward the government'.[37] Also, authoritarians have a volcano of hostility bubbling away inside them, seeking a safe, approved channel along which to erupt.[38] High RWAs are more punitive than most people, ready to send almost anyone to jail for a longer time than most people would, from rapists to those who spit on the sidewalk. By contrast, they are more lenient towards the crimes of the rich and powerful than most people. They are likely to support a law banning communists, homosexuals and other outgroups. They would support outlawing the Ku Klux Klan if the government decreed it, and, more than others, would even uphold a law banning RWAs, that is, themselves.[39] As for conventionalism, high RWAs didn't simply choose to follow society's prevailing norms and customs but insisted that everyone had to do so.[40]

Altemeyer devised a psychometric system of measuring authoritarianism, reminiscent of Adorno et al's F scale, which he calls the RWA scale. It consists of a range of scores running from −4 to +4 which measure the strength of negative or positive attitudes towards key political and social issues.[41] Seven features characterise the authoritarian's mode of thinking: illogical thinking, highly compartmentalised minds, double standards, hypocrisy, blindness to their own faults, profound ethnocentrism, and dogmatism.[42]

As for the origins of RWA, Altemeyer rejects the Frankfurt School's Freudian approach which, for him, following Karl Popper and others, remains unscientific due to its alleged untestability and, therefore, its lack of predictive power. So, there is 'no way of discovering whether it is right or wrong, because it ... involves deeply unconscious defense mechanisms which the defending mechanic knows nothing about, and so will quite honestly deny'. As for Freud's manifestations of unconscious mechanisms observable through introspection or memory, such as dreams and fantasies, these, according to Altemeyer, are 'a mishmash that can be interpreted however you wish'.[43]

Altemeyer prefers the social learning theory of Albert Bandura, according to which parental teaching about the outside world reinforced by one's own life-experience are the key factors determining whether or not one becomes an RWA. Children from authoritarian homes are more likely to become authoritarian, and those with unauthoritarian parents to become unauthoritarian. But ultimately 'the experiences do most of the shaping'.[44]

There is no space here to pursue this debate other than to say that this conclusion seems to be contradicted by Altemeyer's own evidence about the deep dogmatism of RWAs, their rock-like resistance to objective evidence presented to them by the outside world.[45] Moreover, according to Bandura, there are two stages in the making of an RWA: first, some bad feeling like anger or envy arouses hostility, but an angry individual who wants to attack someone may anticipate getting punched back, or being jailed. So, the second stage involves overcoming these inhibitions, allowing the aggression to erupt.[46] However, neither Altemeyer nor Bandura seem to offer any explanation of where the hostility comes from in the first place, assuming there is no obvious, rational, external reason. In that case, we have to look for alternative sources, such as hatred of a punitive parent that has been repressed but remains active in the unconscious.

Moreover, Altemeyer does not correlate his scale of RWA with sociological variables such as social class. His analysis can, therefore, be subjected to criticism similar to that which has been made of the Adorno study, namely, psychologism, that is, reducing social phenomena to individual, psychological factors (though, as will be argued in Chapter 2, in the latter case this would seem to be somewhat unfair).

Altemeyer's analysis is, nevertheless, of great interest. According to him, 'hard-core, right-wing authoritarians' appear to make up roughly 20 to 25 per cent of the American public.[47] This finding would seem to offer convincing proof that Hitler's Germany was not unique. A predisposition to accept fascist ideology could have been, and can be, found in a number of other societies, including Britain and the US, given the necessary precipitating factors such as economic depression and social breakdown, growing resentment towards other states or outgroups and a divided left. Under the right combination of predisposing and precipitating conditions, there would have been enough volunteers to staff a Nazi-type party, or a mass-killing organisation such as the SS, in societies other than Germany. This is, of course, on the assumption that the left fails to offer an alternative, socialist, way out of the crisis.

Another important contribution to the debate from a non-psychoanalytical social psychologist is to be found in James Waller's *Becoming Evil: How Ordinary Men Commit Genocide and Mass Killing* (2007).[48] He obviously doesn't deny the importance of psychological factors in genocide or mass killing, but he does reject the notion that the perpetrators are pathological people different from the rest of us; for example, that there was some kind of homogeneous personality that unified the Nazis as a group. They were, he argues, as different from each other as like each other. Going through a number of analyses of Nazi or SS members, mainly studies using the Rorschach inkblot tests, and scrutinising some psychoanalytical works, Waller concludes that the Nazis were ordinary men (and women). There is no evidence, he insists, that they were drawn to the Nazi movement or participated in genocide because of a prior, predisposing authoritarian or other pathological character.

There are, however, three initial problems with Waller's approach. First, his over-reliance on and uncritical approach to the Rorschach tests. One example: one study examined Nazi defendants awaiting trial. Arguably, most would have had a sufficient sense of self-preservation and cunning to make sure that their answers did not reflect the slightest suspicion of sadism or even undue aggression. Second, Waller's definition of 'pathological' as a condition pertaining solely to individuals, and his refusal to countenance the notion that groups, such as classes or indeed entire societies, can be pathological. Third, and flowing from the second objection, the absence of any definition of 'normality' in Waller's argument. Now this is clearly a complex and contentious issue, the resolution of which depends on one's moral and philosophical position. No doubt most Nazi killers were 'normal' in the clinical sense of not manifesting overt symptoms of mental ill-health such as the inability to function in an everyday context, lack of adjustment to immediate external reality, symptoms of severe depression or anxiety, and so on. But is this clinical definition sufficient? Wouldn't one want to suggest a deeper 'human' definition of 'normal', one that emanates from our conception of humans as social beings whose need for the other is at the heart of their existence? Again, Fromm put it very well:

> Mental health is achieved if man develops into full maturity according to the characteristics and laws of human nature. Mental illness consists in the failure of such development. From this premise, the criterion of mental health is not one of individual adjustment to a given social order, but a universal one, valid for all men, of giving a satisfactory answer to the problem of human existence.[49]

The latter criterion of 'normal' is no doubt based on the idea of a universal ethic rooted in Marx's view of human nature as essentially social. This gives rise to our human potential for creating a system of social relations in which, under Kant's moral law, we treat other human beings as ends rather than means, a prescription that every human being is capable of implementing.[50] On this definition of 'normal', the Nazi killers were anything but normal.

Moreover, is there not a sound case for arguing that many of the top Nazi leaders did in fact manifest symptoms of abnormality in, for example, their clearly paranoid feelings about Jews? Indeed, Douglas Kelly, a psychiatrist at the Nuremberg Jail where the leading Nazi war criminals were held during their trial, described Hitler as 'an abnormal and a mentally ill individual, though his deviations were not of a nature which in the average individual would arouse the serious concern of others'.[51] And in November 1941, Goebbels wrote of the way Jewry 'is now suffering the gradual process of annihilation which is intended for us', a fairly clear case of 'splitting' and paranoid projection.[52] In May 1943, he wrote of the Jewish plans for the 'total destruction' of the German people. This feeling was paranoid even if it was the norm among sections of

German society.[53] Hannah Arendt's view of the Nazis as dedicated bureaucrats obeying orders will be examined in Chapter 7.

Waller distinguishes two levels of analysis in the explanation of genocide. First, the 'proximate' or immediate causes of 'how' we behave now, such as hunger and desire as factors prompting us to eat and to have sex. Second, an 'ultimate' cause referring to deeper influences from our evolutionary past – 'why' a form of behaviour evolved through natural selection, facilitating our survival and reproduction. Waller goes on to describe a model containing three sets of proximate conditions under which ordinary people become genocidal. They are, first, the 'cultural construction of worldview'; second, the 'psychological construction of the other'; and third, the 'social construction of cruelty'.

'The *cultural construction of worldview* examines the influence of cultural models ... that are widely shared by members of a perpetrator group.'[54] It in turn has three aspects. Firstly, such groups generally adhere to *collectivist values* of obedience, conformity, tradition and order.[55] Collectivist cultures also generally carry a tendency for members to define themselves not as individuals but as members of a group.[56] Secondly, *authority orientation* describes a cultural model which 'orders the social world and relates to people according to their position and power in hierarchies'. In a culture that instils strong authority attitudes, it is less likely that individuals will challenge leaders who scapegoat, or encourage violence against, a particular group. Indeed, in most cases of genocide and mass killing, a crucial feature of the culture has been a strong authority orientation.[57] This attitude to authority is inculcated through various socialisation practices inherent in child rearing, schools and other social institutions. Waller quotes the sociologist D.N. Smith who argues that 'intense violence occurs with significantly greater frequency in cultures where children are routinely physically or emotionally abused or denied affection'.[58] This is obviously a central point to which we will return. Thirdly, such groups manifest a need and desire for *social dominance*. According to Waller, evolutionary psychology suggests that hierarchies or pecking orders arise in both animal and human communities as a means of mitigating conflict between individuals competing for limited resources.[59]

The second set of proximate conditions under which ordinary people can become genocidal is described as the *psychological construction of the other*. This, in turn, is sub-divided into three further aspects: *us-them thinking*, *moral disengagement*, and *blaming the victims*. For Waller, *us-them thinking*, or ethnocentrism, is a universal phenomenon of human social life and from an evolutionary perspective serves a useful function or 'adaptation' – reinforcing our sense of community, our collective self-image or social identity, thus furthering our survival and reproduction. However, it can assume a negative aspect, as in xenophobia, or the 'complementary tendency to fear outsiders or strangers'.[60] *Moral disengagement* refers to the process by which victims are placed outside the circle of those to whom we have moral obligations. One expression of this is the dehumanisation of victims by portraying them as animals or subhumans. Exclusion from the human family leads to exclusion from the moral universe of rights and duties.[61] The third aspect of the psychological construction of the other involves *blaming the victims*. Studies showed that blaming victims for their suffering reduced the perpetrators' guilt: 'the victims must have done something to bring it on themselves'.[62]

The third set of proximate conditions for the commission of genocide, *the social construction of cruelty: the power of the situation*, bases itself on a central notion of mainstream social psychology: what matters is not *who* you are but *where* you are. It is the external situation rather than our internal disposition that conditions our thoughts, feelings and behaviour. Such a context makes each perpetrator believe that anyone could do what he or she is doing.[63] Again, there are three sets of sub-factors of the social construction of cruelty that are relevant in explaining how ordinary people commit genocide: *professional socialisation*, *group identification*, and *binding factors of the group*.

In the process of professional socialisation, new recruits learn which forms of behaviour are acceptable and which not. They may be socialised into accepting the perpetration of even extraordinary evil. One important mechanism here is the merger of role and person: 'when one performs the behaviours appropriate for a given role ... one often acquires the attitudes, beliefs, values, and morals consonant with that role and behaviours'.[64] Waller describes a progression of stages of acceptance of social influence – compliance, identification and internalisation. In *compliance*, one obeys authority in order to receive a positive response. In *identification*, one behaves according to a prescribed role without believing in it or the values it implies. In *internalisation*, one accepts authority because it has come to be 'congruent with' one's own values.

The second set of sub-factors of the social construction of cruelty is *group identification*. This refers to our emotional attachment to a group – clearly a potent influence on an individual's ideas, emotions and behaviour. According to Waller, there are two mechanisms that deepen the process of group identification: the *repression of conscience*, and *rational self-interest*. In the repression of conscience, 'outside' values gradually cease to prevail, to be replaced by 'locally generated' ones. Evidence from different genocides testifies to the way in which 'the repression of conscience had a progressively desensitising effect on the perpetrators'.[65] Although they were at first shocked by the atrocities they were committing, these actions gradually became 'routinised and habitual for all but the most sensitive of perpetrators'.

However, Waller himself quotes from accounts of the brutalities committed by SS physicians and the Einsatzkommandos. According to the autobiography of Auschwitz commander Rudolf Hoess, many Einsatzkommandos, unable to continue wading through blood, committed suicide, others went mad, and most had to rely on alcohol when carrying out their atrocities.[66] An important factor in the repression of conscience is the diffusion of responsibility. We are familiar with this defence from the infamous phrase 'I was only obeying orders'. Waller describes the division of responsibility among many individuals and departments in large and complex groups, so that no one is to blame for the horrors. Another factor in the repression of conscience is *deindividuation* – a person cannot be identified, and does not identify her/himself, as an individual but only as a member of a group. According to Waller, experiments have revealed that 'people show an increased tendency towards aggressive behaviour in deindividuated conditions'.[67] A deindividuated person is less worried about self-evaluation or evaluation by others.

The second category of sub-factors within *group identification* is personal self-interest. This simply refers to acts that are carried out from motives of material benefit or professional advancement, or to satisfy ego-needs such as status or power.[68] Waller quotes a study by Baumeister whose research led him to argue that the link between self-esteem and aggression is best captured by his theory of 'threatened egotism':

> [Narcissistic or] grandiose views of personal superiority, an inflated sense of entitlement, low empathy towards others, fantasies of greatness, and so on – is the specific form of self-regard most closely associated with violence ... narcissists have high ego needs ... they will behave aggressively against the specific people who undermine their flattering self-portrait.

Extreme nationalism consists precisely of such threatened collective egotism, a belief in the superiority of one's own nation that has been dented by defeat or crisis.[69] The relevance of this factor will become clear when analysing the perpetrators of the genocides of the Armenians, the Jews and the Tutsis.

The third and final set of sub-factors in the social construction of cruelty is described as *binding factors of the group*. This again sub-divides into three categories: *conformity to peer pressure*, *kin recognition cues*, and *gender*. As Waller puts it: 'the influence of our peers leads us to conform in order to be liked and accepted by them'.[70] He refers to Browning's study (*Ordinary Men*, to be examined in Chapter 7) of non-Nazi police reservists who were inducted into the programme of mass murder of Jews in Poland in 1940.

Waller has adduced some important preconditions of genocide as well as some key, no doubt universally present, accompanying factors. There are two initial problems with his theoretical framework. First, he approaches our inner world as though it were a tabula rasa, a blank screen on which the external situation – other people, difficult circumstances – inscribes its text. This view treats human beings as totally pliable, without any prior, interior world, without any set of pre-existing features – needs, drives, capacities – that interacts with the external world. But the question then arises (as we shall see when examining the determinist view of human nature, seen as the product of society) – who created the society and its culture, for example Waller's 'authority orientation', that shape individual human beings? In other words, there can be no adequate theory of genocide without an underlying theory of human nature.

Secondly, the three sets of proximate conditions tell us much about the *manner* in which genocide takes place – for example, the rationalisations by which perpetrators justify their brutality – but they do not provide the reasons for it. They do not explain the hatred, the rage, that perpetrators feel towards their chosen targets, where these feelings came from, their particular socio-historical sources, and how they were translated into destructiveness. Waller has given us a set of necessary conditions, factors without which genocide would not occur, or at least conditions that generally accompany genocide, but this is far from a satisfactory overall explanation. It does not contain the bundle of necessary and sufficient conditions that constitutes a valid explanation of motive and behaviour. The preconditions Waller adduces are a set of universal, concomitant factors that are always or usually present in the perpetration of genocide. But because his analysis remains abstract and ahistorical, those factors cannot explain particular, historically specific events. His theory answers the question 'how' but not 'why'.

According to Waller, however, beyond these proximate causes of genocide – those operating in the immediate here-and-now situation – lies an ultimate cause, a set of psychological mechanisms that have been genetically transmitted from our earliest history as humans, a bundle of features that defines our human nature as it evolved during our development as a distinct species. The relatively new discipline of evolutionary psychology, developed within a Darwinian framework, 'seeks to apply theories of evolutionary biology in order to understand the human mind'.[71] Since aggressive or war-like behaviour solved our problems of survival in the earliest period of human evolution, we have inherited a tendency to reproduce that behaviour. But these instinctual mechanisms are a hangover from the past, solutions to problems in a world that no longer exists.[72] So, we have the capacity for altruism, cooperation and caring, without which society would not hold together, but also the potential, shaped by natural selection, for extraordinary evil.

There are three further criticisms of Waller's arguments. First, he assumes that hunter-gatherer communities were largely based on mutual aggression. However, at the end of this chapter, the views of Fromm and other writers who question this view of constant warfare will be examined. Secondly, Waller slips too easily from an emphasis on our capacity to commit evil to its actual perpetration. Clearly a capacity for murderous aggression is a necessary condition of genocide, but there is no automatic route from the potential to the actual. Waller leaves out the mass of social and historical factors without which specific genocidal events cannot be explained. Thirdly, his view of human nature, with its genuflection towards human cooperation but overwhelming stress on aggression, is open to question. Allied to this is the absence of a theory of human need, without which we surely cannot understand human violence. In general, evolutionary psychology has been criticised both for its unreliability, the untestability of its hypotheses, and for its neglect of the social roots of behaviour. Another important, earlier work in the area of social psychology is Ervin Staub's *The Roots of Evil: The Origins of Genocide and Other Group Violence*.[73] It will be referred to at various points in the text.

Behaviourism

Whereas psychoanalysis focuses on instinct as the source of destructiveness, an alternative tradition, one that has dominated mainstream academic psychology, is that of behaviourism. According to this school, aggressiveness is not the product of any innate factors rooted in a non-observable, hence pre-scientific, notion of human nature. Scientific psychology must not, therefore, concern itself with subjective factors such as feelings or impulses, goals or intentions. The subject-matter of psychology is the behaviour or activities of human beings, that is, external, observable – social or cultural – factors. According to B.F.

Skinner, a high priest of behaviourism, aggression is the result of conditioning, and psychology is therefore 'the science of the engineering of behaviour'. Its goal is to study what kinds of 'reinforcements' tend to shape behaviour, and, from a practical point of view, how to apply the reinforcement most effectively and beneficially. (According to Fromm, 'Skinner has shown that by the proper use of positive reinforcement, the behaviour of animals and humans can be altered to an amazing degree, even in opposition to what some would loosely call "innate" tendencies.'[74])

In a famous series of experiments, carried out by Stanley Milgram in the early 1960s, 40 volunteers were instructed to administer increasingly painful electric shocks to a group of people who, unbeknown to the volunteers, were part of the experiment and merely pretended to feel pain. Milgram thus claimed to have proved that human beings who had authority could condition others to obey any orders, however much these conflicted with the latter's ethical code.[75] However, fourteen subjects of the experiment (35 per cent) were unable to complete the task, refusing at various points in the ascending scale of electric shocks to carry out orders to inflict increasing pain. The obedient subjects 'often did so under extreme stress ... and displayed fears similar to those who defied the experimenter'.[76] Fromm concludes that

> the most important finding of Milgram's study is the strength of the reactions *against* the cruel behaviour. To be sure, 65 per cent of the subjects could be 'conditioned' to *behave* cruelly, but a reaction of indignation or horror against this sadistic behaviour was clearly present in most of them ... The main result of Milgram's study seems to be one he does not stress: the presence of conscience in most subjects, and their pain when obedience made them act against their conscience.[77]

According to Fromm, a further criticism of Milgram's experiment, and of a similar one carried out by Zimbardo,[78] is the failure to distinguish between behaviour and character. It is one thing to follow the rules by behaving in a sadistic way, and another to want to do so, and to derive enjoyment from it, as a result of certain character traits.[79] And character is not the product of external conditioning, but of the society and its impact on the structure of human needs, drives and capacities. It is often said that the basic cause of aggressive behaviour is frustration. However, individuals react differently to the same frustration, depending on their character structure. The starting point of any investigation of destructive or conformist behaviour is the interaction between external events and the character structure of individuals as this has been shaped by the society.[80] I will return to these arguments in subsequent chapters.

The Problem of Human Nature

Is there a human nature?

This discussion leads directly to a further question that has taxed the minds of many social theorists, both Marxist and non- or anti-Marxist: is there a human nature, and if so, what are its key features? Or is the human mind simply an empty screen, on to which the existing society projects its key features? We need to re-visit this broad debate before moving on to the more specific questions of human destructiveness and genocide.

Explanations of genocide are generally tied to an explicit or implicit theory of human nature, or else to the view that the latter does not exist. Ever since the dawn of European thought, most philosophers have asserted their belief in the notion of an essential human nature. From the Greeks onwards, thinkers have put forward various views about what constitutes the essence of humankind. But there was general agreement that such an essence exists, whether it is 'defined as a rational being, as a social animal, an animal that can make tools or a symbol-making animal'.[81]

However, in recent times, this notion has been challenged. One reason has been the blossoming of historical research in the twentieth century. Another has been the spread of cultural anthropology, especially in the US. Both these disciplines have resulted in a huge increase in our knowledge of other societies, especially pre-modern or at least pre-twentieth-century societies. Anthropology in particular has unveiled 'such a diversity of customs, values, feelings and thoughts that anthropologists arrived at the concept that man is born as a blank sheet on which each culture writes its text'.[82]

In the 1960s and 1970s it became fashionable in social theory, even among many who professed to be Marxists, to claim that there was no such thing as a universal human nature. Human beings were the product of society, which changed its institutional forms as it progressed from one historical epoch to another. These changes determined the thought and behaviour of successive groups of human beings, none of which, therefore, remained constant. It seemed consonant with the idea of freedom that human beings created themselves afresh in each epoch without being burdened with the baggage of the past, as Sartre argued.

But even if we accept the idea of a blank sheet, a *tabula rasa*, we can still ask where the culture that is doing the writing comes from. And then it is hard to avoid the concept of some kind of human nature, some bundle of characteristics, with both physical and psychic components, that interacts with or is shaped by the social and natural environment.

Secondly, whether or not we accept the notion of human nature, don't we want to understand the mentality of the perpetrators of extreme violence? Shouldn't we therefore also probe the mind of the individual perpetrator so as to discover whether there is a personality structure, an inner world, however it is shaped, that constitutes, not the sole cause, but one causal factor among several predisposing elements? If we accept the idea of such a personality type or structure as one link in the chain of explanation, then surely two other links are the type of family produced by a society in crisis, and that society itself. A key theme running through the historical case-studies that follow will be the role of the family as the mediating link, the 'workshop' in which a destructive predisposition is created. As Vamik Volkan put it: 'the group draws the mental representation of a traumatic event into *its very identity*. It passes the mental representation of the event – along with associated shared feelings of hurt and shame, and defences against the perceived shared conflicts they initiate – from generation to generation'.[83]

Marx's concept of human nature

Richard Lichtman and Norman Geras were two Marxist writers who in the 1980s affirmed Marx's commitment to the idea of a human nature, opposing the claim that he believed that 'human beings are totally malleable and derive whatever nature they possess from their concrete social-historical environment'.[84] According to Lichtman, Marx adduces four basic features of human nature.

First, humankind's capacity for self-creativity: human beings transform themselves in the course of historical development. 'By thus acting on the external world, and changing it, he [man] at the same time changes his own nature.'[85]

Second, as social, self-transformative beings, we create ourselves in the course of history through the process of labour. 'The practical construction of an objective world, the manipulation of inorganic nature, is the confirmation of man as a conscious species-being.'[86] As Lichtman says, 'for Marx, the basic human characteristic is our ability to transform our original nature by creating the objective world in which we acquire our specific nature'.[87] As Marx also put it: 'By thus acting on the external world and changing it, he [man] at the same time changes his own nature.'[88] For Marx, moreover, humankind has a dual character: we are part of nature but also transcend nature insofar as we are capable of reason, imagination and will.[89]

Thirdly, human labour is a collective activity that results in a historical succession of different 'modes of production' or types of society – tribal, ancient, oriental despotic, feudal and capitalist. In general, social change is the transition from one mode of production to another, and history as a whole, apart from early tribal communities, is the succession of different types of class society. So, in humanity's 'pre-history', that is from the end of the early tribal community until the creation of socialism, the specific historical manifestation of labour is one or other form of class domination. And the particular form of this domination is expressed in a specific kind and extent of the alienation of labour. Closely linked to this concept of the succession of class societies is Marx's unique blend of freedom and determinism: 'Men make their own history, but they do not make it just as they please; they do not make it under circumstances chosen by themselves, but under circumstances directly encountered, given and transmitted from the past.'[90]

Fourthly, and this is the conclusion to be drawn from the first three features, we are inherently social beings. Human nature is constituted by, and is to be found in, the links we forge with each other through the processes of transforming nature, both external nature and our own human nature, and of expressing our human selves. 'The essence of man is no abstraction inhering in each single individual ... it is the ensemble of social relations.'[91] There is no duality between or division separating the individual and society. This point applies in two senses: firstly, individuals do not exist apart from society, and, secondly, society is not an entity over and above its members but exists within the totality of relations that bind human beings in myriad ways. 'Man is not an abstract being, squatting outside the world. Man is the world of men, the State and society.'[92]

In sum, there seems to be no question, as Norman Geras also insists, that Marx did affirm the notion of human nature, of a set of universal human features present in some form in every society. However, Geras wants to distinguish between two senses of human nature found in Marx: 'human nature in general', and 'human nature as manifested in each historical epoch'. Geras also describes the latter as 'the nature of man'. This enables us to avoid characterising features found in a specific society – for example, selfishness and competitiveness under capitalism – as part of a permanent human nature.[93] As Callinicos points out, the latter simply become part of the nature of man under capitalism.[94] The first – human nature in general – consists of fixed drives, needs and capacities such as hunger or the sexual urge, which we share with the rest of the animal world, but also those such as the need for clothing which are specifically human. But in each case, the forms of its manifestation depend on the type of society, which is a historical and cultural product. As Geras says,

> what we mean by human nature ... is never found in pure form. It is always 'socially mediated'. Even the way we experience the most basic of all needs, hunger, is socially conditioned. As Marx says: 'Hunger is hunger, but the hunger gratified by cooked meat eaten with a knife and fork is a different hunger from that which bolts down raw meat with the aid of hand, nail and tooth.'[95]

However, it is the need and capacity to engage in labour – an essentially collective endeavour – that defines our most essential nature as social beings. And it is our nature as social beings that gives rise to other needs – the need and the ability to communicate through language, to devise moral codes that regulate our social behaviour, to create forms of art through which we orient ourselves in our social world and, in general, to build society through our scientific understanding of the forces of nature and our ability to harness them to our needs through the application of science to technology. Of course, this human capacity for physical and mental labour depends on our advanced evolutionary stage of development.

In short, these drives, needs and capacities define us as human beings who need to collaborate in these different ways in order to develop society and ourselves as individuals. Marx's notion of alienation would not make sense unless it was set against some notion of human essence or potentiality from which we are alienated.

This brings us to those other needs, which Marx calls 'relative appetites', and Geras 'the nature of man', which we might also describe as a specific mode of orientation to others. These 'appetites' are not part of the 'essence' of human nature but 'owe their origin to certain social structures and certain conditions of production and communication'. Marx berates Bentham for taking 'the modern shopkeeper, especially the English shopkeeper, as the normal man'.[96] For example, individual ambition, competitiveness and achievement, in terms of their importance both as the basis for a sense of individual fulfilment and as criteria for the assessment of human value, could be said to be features of human character that were ushered in by the rise of capitalism. They are, of course, the features most commonly referred to as constituting the essence of human nature by cynics affirming our inherent, irredeemable selfishness and, therefore, the futility of struggling for a better world. But, as Geras has pointed out, it is this narrow approach to human nature that led some theorists, including a structural 'Marxist' such as Althusser, to reject the notion.[97] As Callinicos puts it: 'Such a distinction [between 'human nature' and 'the nature of man'] removes a traditional Marxist objection to the notion of human nature, namely that forms of behaviour arising within specific social relations (say, egoism and competitiveness under capitalism) are treated as "permanent human characteristics".'[98]

Support for this view of human beings as essentially social comes from an unlikely source: experimental psychology. A team of neurobiologists at the University of Groningen, Holland, undertaking research into the human brain, confirmed, as have other research groups, the existence of 'mirror neurons' in both monkeys and humans. These neurons enable us to empathically share other people's feelings. 'Whenever we see what happens to others, we not only *understand* what they experience, but also often empathically share their states.'[99]

'Rational' and 'irrational' genocide

Let me return to the distinction suggested in the introduction between 'rational' and 'irrational' genocide, the first category comprising genocides motivated by economic or political considerations. There is an overlapping distinction, namely that between ancient massacres and modern genocides.

This in turn raises the question of whether a similar amount and kind of violence was manifested in historically distinct types of society. In this way, we are led back to the three issues: first, is genocide to be found in all historical societies or, on the contrary, is it a specifically modern form of ultimate violence? Second, can we distinguish between genocides that express a spontaneous as opposed to a character-based destructiveness?* Third, if we can, does this distinction correspond to that between 'rational' and 'irrational' genocide, since, given that in pre-modern times class usually trumped ethnicity, there was little ethnic cleansing? Or does the 'irrational' category contain both the spontaneous and the character-based types?

Pre-Modern Massacres

Clearly, humans have carried out horrific massacres in their history, including in ancient or pre-modern societies. However, as Mann argues, few early historical regimes intended to wipe out or expel whole civilian populations, or 'to cleanse particular identities'.[100] So is genocide, as he believes, a peculiarly modern phenomenon, involving the notion of 'ethnos' or a group linked by kinship, an

---

*   These terms, used by Fromm, are explained in Chapter 2, pp. 55–6.

idea or type of identification lacking in pre-modern society?[101] We move on to examine the violence characteristic of the different historical types of society.

Tribal society

Firstly, tribal society. In the post-war period, the prevalent view among scholars was that in hunter-gatherer or early agricultural communities war was rare and atypical. Fromm articulates this position, drawing on evidence adduced by anthropologists such as M.J. Meggitt, E.R. Service and D. Pilbeam. There are two basic economic arguments: Firstly, in early hunter-gatherer society, economic resources are at such a low level of development, and economic activity at such a basic level of productivity, that there is little to fight over or to gain by plunder. According to Meggitt, 'there was little reason for all-out warfare between communities ... Portable goods were few ... and the territory seized in a battle was virtually an embarrassment to the victors ... Slaves would be useless, given the low productivity of the economy ... they would have difficulty producing more than enough food to feed themselves'. Meggitt believes that small-scale wars of conquest against other tribes did occur occasionally, but differed only in degree from internal tribal conflicts.[102] Secondly, the demographic argument. As Service says:

> the birth-death ratio in hunting-gatherer societies is such that it would be rare for population pressure to cause some part of the population to fight others for territorial acquisition. Even if such a circumstance occurred, it would not lead to much of a battle. The stronger, more numerous, group would simply prevail, probably even without a battle, if hunting rights or rights to some gathering spot were demanded.[103]

A third argument expressed by Pilbeam emphasises 'the principle of reciprocity and generosity, and the central role of cooperation'.[104] For example, in such early tribal communities, food-sharing was the norm.

In recent times, however, several writers have taken issue with what they describe as 'the myth of the peaceful savage'. Kiernan ventures the opposite thesis. 'Some prehistorians suspect that ancestors of modern humans exterminated Europe's archaic Neanderthal population.' Later archaeological evidence suggests that during the Stone Age 'competing local communities may have resorted to annihilation of one another'.[105] Lawrence Keeley, too, argues that there is ample evidence in Western Europe and North Africa of wholesale killing of the final hunter-gatherers of the Mesolithic period (10,000 to 5,000 years ago). He gives a gruesome example of the Ofnet Cave in Germany, where two caches of 'trophy' skulls were found, arranged 'like eggs in a basket', consisting of the severed heads of 34 men, women and children, with holes knocked through their skulls by stone axes. Keeley concludes: 'There is simply no proof that warfare in small-scale societies was a rarer or less serious undertaking than among civilised societies.'[106]

Now, it seems we don't have the evidence by which to judge whether the aggression committed against rival communities was of a purely instrumental kind, carried out in order to achieve specific practical ends – for example, the conquest of farming land – or whether the destructiveness contained an 'irrational' element – for example, revenge. The discovery of the skulls of children suggests the possibility of an element of the latter. And, of course, we have no way of knowing whether and to what extent these attacks were planned. However, on the evidence available, there does not seem to have been any element of character-based destructiveness.

The ancient world

Secondly, the ancient world – the so-called classical era of the Greek and Roman slave societies. Casting a dark shadow over the dawn of ancient Greece is the Greek invasion of Troy and the massacre of all its citizens. This was sparked off by the abduction of the Athenian queen Helen and the resulting anger on the part of her husband Menelaus. According to the Greek philosopher Aristotle, there is a difference between hatred and anger. We hate a person or a group of people because of certain negative traits we perceive to be present in their character – because they represent 'a certain kind of person'. But we feel anger because of a particular act of aggression, injustice or treachery. Normally, we feel anger towards an individual whereas the object of our hatred is a group or class of people.[107] However this distinction isn't always strictly observed. It is rage rather than hatred that Agamemnon and his fellow Greeks feel towards the Trojans for the abduction. 'The antagonism characteristic of war is intensified to the point of extermination because of a particular act of treachery, not an ingrained character trait.'[108] What Agamemnon feels is a wish to punish Troy, to be avenged, rather than any deep or permanent hatred towards the Trojans.[109] The massacre of the Trojans therefore falls into Fromm's category of 'spontaneous' rather than 'character-based' destructiveness.[110] Or, as Geoffrey de Sainte Croix put it in his epic work: 'The Greek and Roman gods could be cruel enough ... but at least their devotees did not seek to represent them as prescribing genocide.'[111]

Again, Konstan argues that attacks on cities and towns could be motivated by the wish to capture potential slaves and other forms of wealth, but enslavement was not usually justified in terms of the evil character of the population, rather in terms of self-interest or the right of the victor.[112]

A different analysis applies to the Roman sacking of Carthage in 146 BC, described by Ben Kiernan as the first genocide. In the course of a three-year siege of the world's wealthiest city, out of a population of a quarter of a million, at least 150,000 Carthaginians died. Kiernan argues that Rome's policy of 'extreme violence', the 'annihilation of Carthage and most of its inhabitants', ruining 'an entire culture', fits the modern legal definition of the 1948 UN Genocide Convention: the intentional destruction, 'in whole or in part, of a national, ethnical, racial or religious group as such'.[113]

However, Kiernan also points out that the war against Carthage was not one of racial extermination. 'The Romans did not massacre the survivors, nor the adult males ... Though the Romans also destroyed six allied African cities of Punic culture, they spared seven other towns which had defected to them.'[114] Cato, the influential Roman senator, had visited Carthage in 152 BC and was shocked at the recovery the city had made from previous defeats. It was once again a 'thriving mercantile metropolis, "burgeoning with an abundance of young men, brimming with copious wealth, teeming with weapons"'.[115] The threat from this rival had to be destroyed. And after its destruction, Rome ruled the Mediterranean.[116]

So, the conclusion would appear to be that Rome's sacking of Carthage was undertaken out of fear of its economic and military rivalry, not because of the eruption of spontaneous anger or of some deep-seated irrational, character-based destructive urge. In that sense, it bears an affinity to all wars fought for land or for economic or geopolitical superiority. Apart from Troy, which was a war of spontaneous anger, the wars of ancient times are not intrinsically different from, say, the two world wars of the twentieth century, fought between competing imperialisms for economic and military superiority, and in the second of which millions of civilians died.

Neil Faulkner describes this type of society as 'ancient military imperialism', a prime example of which was ancient Rome. This was a system of robbery with violence whose aim was the seizing of ever greater plunder, including captives for enslavement. The appropriation of such surpluses from defeated enemies increased the capacity of the Roman ruling class to wage even more wars and acquire even greater surpluses.[117]

Ancient wars and the killing of large numbers of the populations of conquered cities were thus an expression of 'instrumental aggression', examples of what I have described, however bizarrely, as 'rational' destructiveness, not irrational, character-based destructiveness.

Feudal violence

Fast-forwarding to medieval European society based on the feudal mode of production, we find a high level of violence in the frequent wars of conquest between rival kingdoms or in massacres perpetrated against urban populations, including many Jews, during campaigns for the seizure of booty – for example, during the Crusades. Now, Jews were regarded as 'Christ-killers'; however, before the First Crusade in 1096, many Crusaders became indebted to Jewish money-lenders out of a need to purchase weapons and equipment for their expedition, given that Western Christianity banned usury. Also, 'for many crusaders the loot taken from the Jews provided the only means of financing such a journey'. No doubt killing Jews was conveniently rationalised as part of their Christian mission.[118] But in no way are we talking about a twentieth-century-style industrial genocide.

If we compare feudalism to modern capitalism, it is a familiar part of the Marxist analysis that the twin pillars of capitalist society are exploitation and competition, and at some point these spill over into the international arena, and economic competition transmutes into military competition, that is, war between nation states. In other words, warfare is an inevitable outcome of capitalist competition.

Neil Faulkner argues that pre-capitalist societies were similarly driven by competition. Both the ancient and medieval worlds were divided into rival 'states' or polities that were frequently at war. 'No pre-capitalist ruling class could afford to be complacent about military preparedness if it wished to hold on to its property and power.' Faulkner argues that in the absence of rises in labour productivity, that is, given the long periods of economic stagnation, the only method open to a ruling class bent on increasing surplus appropriation – and therefore military capacity – was conquest.[119] The power of states was based on the territories under their control and the number of soldiers these could support. Hence, states were engaged in a fierce struggle for geopolitical superiority and the consequent ability to build up military capacity by accumulating surpluses. War was the principal method for increasing surplus appropriation, hence the central role of the state. Through the state, rival ruling classes increased their wealth and power at each other's expense. As Faulkner says: 'a stable global economy with fixed output made the struggle for surplus a zero-sum game – one ruler's gain was necessarily another's loss. Thus the history of pre-capitalist class societies was dominated by the state, war-making and eternal geopolitical struggle for empire.'[120]

Faulkner also applies this analysis to European feudalism and the medieval Islamic states. Under Western feudalism, all the land was vested in the ruler who parcelled it out to a number of lesser noble 'tenants'. In return for these estates or fiefdoms, the knights owed a duty of loyalty to the ruler, in particular, to provide him with soldiers in times of war. Civil and foreign wars were frequent, given the economic and military rivalry, for example, the competition for land. On the one hand, the aristocratic rulers needed more land and knights to pursue their struggles with rival states. On the other, the younger sons of the warring, landholding nobility required more land and plunder to boost their power and consumption. To prevent domestic rivalry reaching the point where the aristocracy tore itself apart in deadly fratricide, the feudal elite sought to export the military conflicts. Faulkner describes the system as 'feudal imperialism', concluding that 'violence was inherent in the system – something for which the peoples of medieval Europe and the Middle East paid a heavy price'.[121]

In conclusion, it seems that pre-modern massacres – during the Crusades, in the ancient Greek and Roman slave empires, or those described in the Old Testament – were largely of the 'rational' kind, that is, they were undertaken for the sake of land, slaves or booty. Yet in many cases there does seem to have been an 'irrational' element, of the 'spontaneous' rather than character-based kind. Apart from anything else, these massacres lacked the huge planning effort present in modern genocides – in the Nazi Holocaust or the Armenian genocide, or the intention, discernible over four centuries, to exterminate the Native Americans. The attacks on Troy and Carthage were certainly planned, but there is no evidence that the massacres of their citizens were planned. These two would seem to contain elements of both 'rational' and 'irrational' (that is, spontaneous rather than character-based) destructiveness. The sacking of Troy possibly contains a 'rational' element, given that Helen's abduction may have been a useful pretext for an attack motivated at a deeper level by the desire for Greek imperial expansion. As John Docker notes in his study of ancient massacres, quoting Thucydides' *The History of the Peloponnesian War*, 'children in the ancient classical world along with women were routinely sold into slavery after a siege lost by a city's defenders'.[122] In sum, there are grounds for accepting Mann's argument that genocide, including ethnic cleansing, are specifically modern phenomena. In the next chapter, I shall examine psychoanalytical approaches to human destructiveness.

CHAPTER TWO

Killers On the Couch

Freud on Human Nature

Freud believed, contrary to Marx, that human nature is to be discovered within the boundaries of the individual psyche. Humankind has a universal and immutable mental structure: all human beings have fixed psychic drives which are rooted in our instinctual, biological make-up. This universal, unchanging psychic structure is the result of society stepping in via the family to control our drives. Hence, what we are as human beings is the effect of society on biology. His four key concepts are the unconscious, sexuality, neurosis, and the Oedipal family.

Freud assumed that the chief principle of psychic activity is the 'pleasure principle', that is, the urge to discharge instinctual tensions so as to maximise pleasure. But the pleasure principle is modified by the 'reality principle': taking external reality into account leads us to renounce or postpone pleasure in order to avoid greater discomfort or to gain even greater pleasure in the future. He argued that these two types of instinct or drive were the motive force behind psychic life: the drive for self-preservation and the sexual drive. He described the energy in the sexual drive as 'libido'.[1]

But in the final phase of his work, beginning in 1920, in a mood of deep pessimism brought on by the unprecedented violence of the First World War, Freud developed a new classification of instincts or drives and a new theory of the structure of the mind. Instead of the division between the libido and the self-preservative instincts, he assimilated the latter into the former and the central duality becomes that between our libidinal instincts (life instincts) and the newly discovered death instinct – Thanatos. Eros versus Thanatos is the decisive conflict in human nature and human affairs: 'now ... we describe the opposition as being, not between ego-instincts and sexual instincts but between life and death instincts'. As Freud also put it:

> The aim of the first of these basic instincts is to establish ever-greater unities ... to bind together; the aim of the second is ... to undo connections and so to destroy things. In the case of the destructive instinct ... its final aim is to lead what is living into an inorganic state. For this reason, we also call it the death instinct ... In their biological functions, the two basic instincts either operate against or combine with each other. Thus, the act of eating is a destruction of the object with the final aim of incorporating it, and the sexual act is an act of aggression with the purpose of the most intimate union.[2]

Freud also described our instinctual duality: on the one hand, Eros aims to bind together individuals, then families, then tribes, races or nations into one overarching, common humanity. But this can only be achieved libidinally: material need, the advantages of common work, wouldn't hold people together. So, on the other hand, humankind's instinct of aggressiveness, our mutual hostility, pits each one against all and all against each one, nullifying civilisation's programme. 'This aggressive instinct is ... the main representative of the death instinct ... alongside of Eros.'[3]

Yet another essential Freudian theme embedded in the notion of 'death drive' is that of repetition or return. For Freud, 'there really does exist in the mind a compulsion to repeat which over-rides the pleasure principle'. As Frosh puts it: 'repetition becomes the defining motif of life itself, both in the sense of the death drive's "desire" to return to an earlier state of inorganic activity, and in the way traumatic moments plague the mind and drive it to actions aimed at mastery or self-defence'.[4]

Freud, moreover, saw the human psyche as divided into three 'sectors' – the id, ego and super-ego – which combine and interact with each other in varying ways. The 'id' is the source of our instinctual drives, while the 'ego' is the rational part of the mind attuned to external reality that 'negotiates' between the 'id' and the outside world. Finally, the 'super-ego', to quote the familiar metaphors, is the censor, the prohibitor of our biological drives, the 'rider who keeps in check the superior strength of the horse', the garrison watching over the conquered city, the 'dam' that prevents the instinctual flow from breaking through. Freud recognises its social origins: 'the superego – the demands of conscience – ... is simply a continuation of the severity of the external authority, to which it has succeeded'. For Freud, this internal policing authority is indispensable for the existence and survival of civilised society: 'civilisation is built up upon a renunciation of instinct ... the non-satisfaction (by suppression, repression or some other means?) of powerful instincts. This "cultural frustration" dominates the large field of social relationships between human beings.' In other words, the cost of civilisation is the abandonment by the individual of the full satisfaction of pleasures. There is an inherent conflict between the individual's search for instinctual gratification and the needs of society as expressed in morality. Without the super-ego, and 'in consequence of this primary mutual hostility of human beings, civilised society is perpetually threatened with disintegration'. Moreover, since aggressiveness is part of our nature, it 'was not created by property. It reigned almost without limit in primitive times, when property was still very scanty.'[5]

Freud mostly regarded this organisation of the mind as unchanging through history. 'Are we wrong in carrying this differentiation between ego, super-ego and id back into ... early times? The differentiation ... must be attributed not only to primitive man but even to much simpler organisms for it is the inevitable expression of the influence of the external world.'[6] Freud, moreover, had a fixed view of the process of childhood in any society: every individual goes through three phases: the oral, anal and genital.[7]

Freud's thought was rooted in the twin traditions of philosophical liberalism and nineteenth-century biological determinism. The theoretical heart of liberalism, derived from Hobbes, is that society is a collection of competing individuals who agree to tone down their mutual conflict out of enlightened self-interest. We are thus primarily isolated beings whose physical and emotional needs drive us into relationships with others.

> [For] men are not friendly, gentle creatures wishing for love, who simply defend themselves if they are attacked ... a powerful ... desire for aggression ... [is] part of their instinctual endowment ... Their neighbour is ... not only a possible helper or sexual object but also a temptation ... to gratify their aggressiveness on him, to exploit his capacity for work without recompense, to use him sexually without his consent ... to torture and kill him.

By the same token, 'the psychological premises on which the [communist] system is based' are an 'untenable illusion'.[8]

The other root of Freud's theory was biological determinism with its concomitant hedonistic individualism. Because civilisation and social harmony demand a massive sacrifice of instinctual gratification, the most we can expect is the reduction of suffering – achieved through the sublimation of instincts into creative or socially useful outlets. So, implicit in Freud's theory of innate human destructiveness is a generally pessimistic view of human nature and human existence.

Psychoanalytic Marxist Criticisms of Freud

Erich Fromm

According to psychoanalytic Marxist Erich Fromm, for Freud, the human individual is primarily an isolated being driven by biological needs into relationships with others. That is, our relationships are the secondary effects of our primary biological drives. The individual needs others to satisfy 'his libidinous drives as well as those of self-preservation. The child is in need of mother ... the adult needs a sexual partner. Feelings like tenderness or love are ... phenomena [that] result from libidinous interests.'[9] Fromm therefore argues that Freud's theory is pervaded by the spirit of the market economy. His human being 'is the self-sufficient man who has to enter into relations with others in order that they may mutually fulfil their needs'. It is a vision that closely resembles the Enlightenment view of economic man whose needs are satisfied by mutual exchange on the commodity market. For Fromm, Freud developed important insights into the psychic functioning of alienated humankind under capitalism but, in the end, he misidentified alienated humanity with natural humanity and divorced psychology from history. In general, psychoanalytic Marxists depart from orthodox Freudianism by emphasising social or cultural factors in the growth of the individual.

Jacqueline Rose takes issue with this interpretation of Freud as supreme individualist, arguing that, for him, 'from the earliest moment of our lives ... we are peopled by others. Our "psyche" is a social space.' Rose argues that, contrary to the general assumption, Freud insisted on the human being's social nature, on each individual's need for the Other.[10] In the first paragraph of *Mass Psychology and the Analysis of the 'I'*, Freud writes:

> The antithesis between individual and social or mass psychology, which at first glance may seem very important to us, loses a great deal of its sharpness on close examination ... In the mental life of the individual, the other comes very regularly into consideration as model, object, aid and antagonist ... from the outset, the psychology of the individual is also social psychology.[11]

So, Freud asks, 'what may be the nature of the ties that exist in groups', binding them together into cohesive groups? He believes that, 'as with the individual, so too in the development of mankind as a whole, only love has had effect as a civilising factor in the sense of a turning away from egoism towards altruism'.[12] He also describes this binding as 'love drives ... deflected from their original goals'.[13] Freud specifies two libidinal aims: a narcissistic love of oneself and the sex drive directed at potential objects of libidinal satisfaction. For the group to cohere, both drives must be renounced or mitigated, their energy sublimated into libidinal ties to others. The mechanisms that create these emotional ties are the various kinds of identification. The most basic occurs as 'the emotional tie with another person', for example, the boy who wants to grow up like his father. Secondly, it is expressed through the internalisation of the object, in which 'the ego ... assumes the characteristics of the object', for example, the boy absorbing the father's ideas and values. Thirdly, identification arises with 'the perception of a common quality shared with some other person', the latter helping to explain the ties that bind group members to their leader. 'Love' of the leader ties them to each other as well as to him.[14]

However, there is a certain ambivalence in Freud. As Rose points out, he returns to the theme of *Totem and Taboo* (1913) according to which society originated in the murder by the sons of the father who controlled the women of the tribe. None of the sons could replace their father, and if one tried to do so, 'the fighting resumed until they realised that they must all renounce their father's inheritance. They then formed the totemic brotherhood, all enjoying equal rights and bound together by the totem bans that were to keep the memory of the murder alive and atone for it'.[15] Freud retains the notion of a primordial instinct which is then 'diverted from its original aim', bringing about 'a change from egoism to altruism'. As Paul Roazen pointed out, he resorted to a kind of social contract: 'driven by guilt over their aggressiveness to accept society, [men] did so in a rationalistic way for purposes of self-preservation'.[16] There is an echo of Hobbes' 'state of nature' here: selfish individuals, at risk of mutual destruction through 'a war of all against all', attenuate their conflict by accepting a body of rules out of enlightened self-interest.

There would thus seem to be a difference between Freud's conception of the individual as a biological unit, mitigating his/her drives and relating to others for the satisfaction of their needs, and a notion of the individual whose being is permeated by the external society, who seeks the other from the moment of birth, as in Kleinian or object-relations theory. For all three – Freud, Klein and object-relations theory – the individual, with his/her needs, capacities, and outlook, is shaped by and in turn shapes the other, the outside social world. Yet for Freud, the individual retains an identity that is separate, somewhat like the cream at the top of the bottle that is part of but separate from the milk, as compared to its permeation of the milk when the bottle is shaken. Moreover, Freud's own examples of binding within a group are the Catholic Church and the army, particular organisations rather than the wider society, social classes or ethnic groups. Despite this, Freud does seem to have modified his position around 1921, placing human beings' social nature closer to the heart of his theory.

Michael Schneider

As noted in Chapter 1, Michael Schneider criticised Freud for universalising a type of neurosis rooted in specific historical conditions – the rigid taboos of the Victorian period. He charges Freud with ignoring 'the specific class character of his clinical material which formed the empirical foundation of his theoretical structure'.[17] His clients were largely from the Viennese upper (74 per cent) and middle classes who had been 'hystericalised' by the decline of the Austro-Hungarian empire.[18] In contrast, Freud's early disciple and eventual rival, Alfred Adler, analysed patients not only from the middle class (38 per cent) but also from the working class (36 per cent). The latter's very different class situation resulted in dissimilar emotional disturbances. For the mostly proletarian and uprooted (déclassé) patients of Adler, the core of their neuroses was the 'inferiority complex', the unconscious rejection of their under-privileged position rather than sexual repression. Like Freud with his Oedipus complex, however, Adler made the mistake of making the inferiority complex the universal source of neurosis.[19]

Schneider analyses Freud's ideal ego: the rational, adult 'genital character', who is neither overwhelmed by instinctual libidinal drives nor represses them, but is capable of sublimating them into alternative creative outlets. This ideal, of course, 'presupposes not only a sunny childhood but also a luxurious economic and social situation'.[20] This ego reflects the self-image of the classical bourgeois man in his most heroic and innovative phase. It is the capitalist class in 'its liberal stage of ascendancy', the class of small and medium businessmen who carried out the great bourgeois revolutions of the seventeenth and eighteenth centuries, fought against the feudal aristocracy for the rights of private property, for their parliamentary representation, and for the bourgeois freedoms of assembly, speech and expression.

For the wage-labourer, in Georg Lukács' description, 'the separation of labour-power from the personality of the worker, its transformation into a thing, into an object, which he sells on the market', his/her subjugation to capital, renders wage-labour incompatible with Freud's rational, potent, self-determin-ing 'genital' ego-ideal.[21] Even for the capitalist, the social and economic situation of competition and endless accumulation militates against the development of a rational ego-ideal. The capitalist typically develops a social character based on 'phallic narcissism',[22] a self-esteem expressed through extreme egotism, authori-tarianism, vanity and arrogance. As Schneider says, this type flourishes primarily in that class which considers itself something special. Its roots are not located in individual psychology and early childhood experience, as Freudians would claim, but in the socio-economic situation of the small businessman, though clearly mediated through the family. Schneider concludes that 'claims that Freud made for narcissism are valid in particular for the psychology of the bourgeoisie'.[23] In 1927, Malinowski wrote: 'It is obvious that the infantile conflicts will not be the same in the lavish nursery of the wealthy bourgeois as in the cabin of the peasant, or in the one-room tenement of the poor working man.'[24]

Richard Lichtman

Richard Lichtman argues that whereas for Freud human nature is 'centripetal', with the individual attempting to draw the world towards the body and its physical needs, for Marx, it is 'centrifugal', with the individual always enmeshed in a web of social relations.[25] As we saw in Chapter 1, the self is constructed by the social process and can never exist apart from it. In contrast to bourgeois thought, which regards thought or self-consciousness as an individual capacity, we are shaped by our community, so that even rebels define themselves in relation to the socially dominant set of ideas. Equally, our emotional life is formed by the social relations into which we are inserted at the moment of birth, and which we internalise as children.

Lichtman acknowledges that Freud's theory connecting conscious and unconscious processes represented a monumental discovery.[26] The problems arise, however, with Freud's contradictory views of the origin and nature of the unconscious. At times he describes it in 'topographical' terms, as a distinct region of the mind, the highest system, with its own content and organisation. At other times, it is a receptor sense organ having no content. A related problem is that according to Freud's own criteria for distinguishing the conscious from the unconscious, key mental phenomena such as dreams or fantasies cannot be placed in a single location. 'By one criterion, they belong to the unconscious, by another to the ... conscious.'[27] Moreover, Lichtman takes Freud to task for his overlaying dualisms: the separation between individual and society, the split within human nature between the functions of the 'ego', 'super-ego' and the 'id', and the 'topographical' division between the unconscious and the conscious. Freud recognises that individuals are greatly affected by their social existence. But he retains an Enlightenment view of 'natural man', whose structure of instincts and individual character exist outside of and prior to society and are unchanging through history. The centrepiece of Freudian psychoanalysis is the moulding of the infant's structure of primal instincts by the moral forces of the external culture so as to convert him/her into a civilised member of society. Society itself is no more than the agglomeration of individuals whose original nature does not change through history.[28]

Freud thus replaced the Enlightenment's 'rational man' with his own 'irrational man', reaffirming Hobbes' 'war of all against all' – an inherently destructive social order that can only be controlled by a repressive social morality. Yet if all historical societies are fundamentally the same, inherently antagonistic and repressive, it is hard to see how humanity could achieve any progress –

indeed, any social change – and how any kind of mutual solidarity is possible: human love and friendship, trade unions, mutual aid societies. If civilisation is essentially antagonistic and repressive, no 'social or political transformation can do more than modify the most extreme instances of its pathology'.[29] Of course, as Lichtman acknowledges, Freud went further than any previous bourgeois thinker by revealing how this split between individual and society was reproduced within the individual.

Secondly, Lichtman criticises Freud for his dualism of mental functions: the rational calculating 'ego' that transmits to the individual the demands and restrictions of society, and the system of instinctual drives known as the 'id'. Part of the 'ego' splits off to become the 'super-ego' or repressive force. The ego is the politician whereas the super-ego is a combination of judge and policeman. The ego/super-ego are society's representatives within the individual, whereas the id is in a sense the 'real' individual. The problem with this dichotomy of separate structural compartments is that the instinctual drives are themselves shaped by society. In all human societies, 'both the repressed desire and the repressing counterforce [are] socially determined'.[30]

However, Lichtman's critique can itself be criticised on four counts. He interprets Freud's 'geographical' division of the mind into conscious/unconscious or ego/super-ego/id literally instead of as metaphorical descriptions of key mental or emotional functions. Secondly, he assumes (as do a number of writers, especially from the US) that psychoanalysis begins and ends with Freud, as if physics began and ended with Newton or Kepler. Lichtman and others ignore post-Freudian developments within psychoanalysis, schools of thought and of therapy of particular importance in the British context – Klein and the 'object-relations' school, for example – which seem to represent an advance over orthodox Freudianism. He dismisses the 'object-relations' school in one sentence: 'Nor does the extension of Freud's paradigm to contemporary theories of object relations ... adequately approach a social dimension.'[31] Lichtman has here thrown out the 'psychoanalytical baby' with the 'Freudian bathwater'.

Thirdly, Lichtman rejects Freudian psychoanalysis on the basis of a philosophical critique of its biological individualism. However, one may question the epistemological validity of renouncing psychoanalysis, not only as a theory of the mind but also as clinical practice, on the basis purely of a philosophical critique. Finally, Lichtman's approach implies that the individual is merely a reflection of alienated social relations and possesses no autonomy or element of freedom. So 'every "permanent" structure is rooted in a comparably "permanent" disposition in individuals'. He claims that this is not 'isomorphism', that is, the features literally mirroring each other. But it is hard to see how else it is to be interpreted. In Lichtman's deterministic analysis, the individual does appear simply as bearing the stamp of alienated social relations, which leaves him without an analysis of inner motivation, of the world of subjectivity that results from individual members of society internalising that outer world of alienation. He states: 'the social necessity, under capitalism, for mindless obedience to media self-definition, bureaucratic estrangement of means and ends, state domination and mystification, and corporate brutality and deceit must be rooted in character in a process begun at birth'.[32] Given this all-powerful social order, it is hard to account for individual character variation, and also how any kind of social creativity or rebellion becomes possible.

Anthropological Studies

Left-wing critics of Freud also used anthropological studies to throw fresh light on the Freudian 'topographical' scheme, his division of the mind into fixed sectors of id, ego and super-ego. These 'psycho-ethnological' investigations seemed to reveal that not every society produced identical psychic features. In particular, in early societies based on collective ownership of property and a social mode of production, in which the institution of private property had not developed, there were marked differences with Western capitalist societies. Not only were the typical kinds of instinctual gratification and levels of repression different, but even the instinctual structures. All elements were shown to be strongly influenced by social factors.

Margaret Mead described three New Guinea tribes all of which had different and complicated methods of enforcing an incest ban. But none had any process comparable to the Western Oedipus Complex, which lays the basis for the formation of later genital sexuality. Also, their experience of the anal phase was completely different. In capitalist society the anal phase has a direct relationship to what, in adult life, is thought of as an individual's capacity for being clean, orderly and punctual (emptying one's bowels punctually as a child makes for a disciplined adult). Infantile anal pleasure is repressed and transformed into orderliness and punctuality, virtues conducive to the smooth fulfilment of tasks in work and production. In these New Guinea tribes, individuals do go through a childhood phase in which sexual sensations are chiefly derived from the anal parts. But for them, it doesn't become linked to a set of cultural attitudes and norms basic to society. If anything, the culture of these tribes is 'stuck' at the oral level: they immediately consume what they have, apparently incapable of even the most elementary storage of property, or of any form of primitive accumulation.[33] In Malinowski's study of the Trobriand Islanders, in which he challenged Freud's universal Oedipus complex, the society was matrilineal, with kinship and inheritance determined through the mother's line of descent. The child belongs to the mother's family or clan; the boy inherits the social position and responsibilities of the mother's brother, from whom he inherits his possessions. The father is not recognised as such due to ignorance about physical paternity. He is a benevolent friend of the child, but has no authority over him or her. Authority is vested again in the maternal uncle. There is a general absence of Western-style repression: after a period of sexual play in childhood, adolescents are allowed general licence, after which lovers live together before settling down to a matrimony which is generally monogamous.[34] There is no period in which what Freud called 'pre-genital', 'anal-erotic' interest predominates.[35]

In contrast, under capitalism, as an advanced commodity society, the typical forms of instinctual drives and objects of desire assume, or rather are shaped into, the form of commodities, that is, 'the form of possessions, alienation and competition'. Lukács observes how the 'commodity relation stamps its imprint upon the whole consciousness of man; his qualities and abilities are no longer an inorganic part of his personality, they are things which he can own or dispose of like the various objects of the external world'.[36] One conclusion is that much of the psychoanalytical tradition regards war and destructiveness as an inherent and ineradicable part of the essence of humankind, whereas the Marxist tradition sees it as rooted in the social system, an inevitable outcome of class society, its poverty and inter-imperialist rivalry. It is, therefore, in principle eradicable through the creation of a classless, socialist world.

Klein and the Object–Relations School

Freud's theory of the death drive attracted much criticism. However, as we saw, one counter-criticism is that many critics of Freud argue as though psychoanalysis begins and ends with Freud. This leads directly to the question whether post-Freudian psychoanalysis is better able to illuminate the key processes of personal development and historical change than orthodox Freudianism. For traditional Freudian psychoanalysis, human beings are driven by the need to satisfy instinctual drives: this prompts them to seek to form relationships with others. However, according to the British post-war 'object-relations' school of psychoanalysis (W.R.D. Fairbairn, D.W. Winnicott, Harry Guntrip and Michael Balint), this sequence is reversed: our essence as human beings is the drive to form relationships.[37] This is the vital feature of human activity from the moment of birth. There is an initial psychic unity, so that our libido is fundamentally 'object-seeking' rather than narrowly pleasure-seeking, and it is this drive to relate to external 'objects' that creates the context within which our psychic structures are created. Object-relations theorists thus view the key psychic developmental stages according to patterns of relating rather than parts of the infant's body, as in Freud.

The object-relations school was inspired by Freud's pupil Melanie Klein (1878–1960), although many disagree with her inclusion in the school due to her acceptance of the death instinct.[38] Klein posits the ego as fundamentally split between life and death instincts, whose projections onto external objects, specifically the mother's breasts, result in their being split between good and bad features, arousing, on the one hand, envy and destructiveness, on the other, love and gratitude. The external world is also in reality a bundle of contradictory elements, both frustrating and gratifying. Within the individual psyche lies the potential to advance from the initial 'paranoid-schizoid' position, where destructive impulses threatening to overwhelm the ego are projected outwards, to the 'depressive position' whose key characteristic is reparation. Here the ego, mourning and guilt-ridden towards the good object destroyed in its phantasy, attempts to make good the damage. Michael Rustin suggested that the 'depressive position' underscores the human capacity for recognising the pain of others, which, in turn, is a vital element in the human capacity for relatedness. In general, object-relations theory, with 'its commitment to the values of life, of relationship, of membership in a social community' has an affinity with a 'socialist conception of man'.[39] However, according to Frosh, for the object-relations school, destructiveness is a 'fall from grace that can be overcome by a reparative relationship which assumes the existence of an integrated psyche at birth that then becomes split because of frustration and loss. In contrast, the Kleinian view is that destructiveness is a basic force that ... can never be fully resolved'.[40]

Robert M. Young argues for a view of human nature that chimes with Kleinian and object-relations theory, and echoes a Marxist view of humans as fundamentally social. He writes that

> to be human is to have perpetually ongoing object relations, however painful and fraught, and to have object relations is to partake of a recognisably shared human nature – 'human' in having interpersonal relationships which are not reducible to a pre-symbolic or purely animal set of interactions, and 'nature' in the sense that there is no denial of our link to our biological origins and the social, political and economic determinations at work in our lives.[41]

Judith Butler also puts forward a view of human nature as social. Basing her account on the work of French psychoanalyst Jean Laplanche, she argues that there is a 'sociality at the basis of the "I"'.[42] The individual self is constituted or formed by others, who thus penetrate to the deepest level of our psyche. In Frosh's words: 'identity is not "owned" but is shared'.[43] It follows that our ethics can be, and need to be, based on our relations with others. As Frosh puts it: 'Ethics is always forged in relationality.'[44]

Psychoanalysis: The Authoritarian Personality

This category – in which the existence of subjective, predisposing factors in the absence of precipitating ones can be established – is a more fruitful area of research. In fact, since the Second World War, much psychological research has been conducted into the 'authoritarian personality'. *The Authoritarian Personality* by Theodor Adorno, Else Frenkel-Brunswik and other researchers at the University of California was published in 1950, in the shadow of the Holocaust and the defeat of Nazism.[45] The authors posited the existence of such a personality, so defined because of its receptivity to authoritarian appeals and a display of traits such as submission to authority, hostility towards outgroups, dogmatism, destructiveness, and so on. The researchers developed a psychometric instrument measuring 'fascism' (the F-scale) and allied this to a Freudian analysis of the origins of this personality type. Despite much methodological criticism (issues of sample size, sample bias, etc.), the book remains a classic, spawning enormous research in social psychology, political socialisation, and so on. Adorno and his colleagues argued that establishing the presence of these traits in an individual enabled one to predict their potential for fascist or anti-democratic leanings or behaviour.

They linked this personality type to early childhood experiences, in particular the internalisation of the values and norms of the father. This process results in the emergence within the child's burgeoning unconscious of their super-ego or conscience. However, if the father's character is particularly harsh and authoritarian, the child develops an unusually strong super-ego that represses instinctual drives – sexual desires or the drive to self-assertion. Lifelong unconscious conflicts are unleashed which the person 'solves' by projecting forbidden drives, or their anger and hatred, on to outgroups. Ethnic or religious minority groups often become the screen onto which these drives or this repressed anger are projected, since in this way individuals keep themselves in line with the prevailing social prejudices. Adorno and his colleagues developed the notion of Right-Wing Authoritarianism (RWA), a theoretical psychological construct made up of a cluster of attitudes. Unlike Reich and Fromm, for whom the authoritarian personality was specific to the German middle class, Adorno and his colleagues did not relate it to a particular social class.

Fred Greenstein illuminatingly pointed out that three types of phenomena were relevant for the understanding of a personality type: first, its phenomenology, that is, the observable psychological characteristics that make up the type. In the authoritarian type, an obvious pair of related features are 'authoritarian aggression' and 'authoritarian submission', which together form 'the dominance-submissiveness tendencies of the authoritarian ... Such an individual ... abases himself before those who stand above him hierarchically, or whom he perceives to be powerful, and lords it over whomever seems to be weak, subordinate or inferior.'[46] Secondly, the dynamics. The authoritarian has a powerful but ambivalent attitude towards authority figures. The negative aspects are feelings of anger and hatred which, of course, have to be concealed through massive repression. This involves suppressing critical thoughts about authority and exhibiting compensatory and exaggerated praise and obedience. But repressed impulses seek alternative outlets, and the hostility is channelled towards weak groups seen as outsiders. Influenced by classical psychoanalysis, this 'ego-defensive' theory of the origins of authoritarianism stresses the irrationality of the self. The latter tries to maintain an inner equilibrium and thus needs to defend itself against being swamped by repressed hostile feelings by channelling anger against approved weaker groups. Frosh describes how this linked in to anti-Semitism:

> the figure of the Jew has usefully been the subject of cultural and historical abuse and so constitutes a ready-made container for the destructive urges of the anti-Semite. Adorno et al hold to a view that individuals are systematically misled by ideology into misreading their own sense of frustration as having a specific external cause rather than as embedded in the social order; faced with psychological pressure leading to breakdown, their balance is maintained if they can find somewhere for their aggression to go.[47]

Thirdly, the origins of authoritarianism. The authors argued that these feelings and attitudes were rooted in childhood experiences. Studies of children suggested that 'warmer, closer and more affectionate interpersonal relationships prevail in the homes of the unprejudiced children'.[48] Prejudice was associated with 'strictness, rigidity, punitiveness, rejection vs. acceptance of the child.' In other words, authoritarians tend to come from families in which 'relationships are characterised by fearful subservience to the demands of the parents and by an early suppression of impulses not acceptable to the adults'.[49] At a later stage, 'the displacement of a repressed antagonism toward authority may be ... the principal source of his antagonism toward outgroups'.[50]

Some psychologists attempted to jump from such analyses of the links between political attitudes and childhood experience to conclusions about the origins of broad historical phenomena such as the rise of Nazism or Japanese militarism. Greenstein believes that despite the scientific value of a work like *The Authoritarian Personality*, it is 'shot through with psychologism'.[51] However, Adorno et al were fully aware of the links between prejudice and socio-economic factors: 'This does not mean that group memberships and social forces are unimportant ... it would appear that sociological factors play an essential but *complex and indirect* psychological role.'[52] And in the interview schedule, key socio-economic factors are adduced as necessary to determine the sources of prejudice: for example, the parents' national origins, the parents' ingroup membership (for example, trade union), the family's socio-economic status and their standard of living. Adorno later re-emphasised this: 'We have never doubted the primacy of objective factors over psychological ... We saw socio-psychology as a subjective mediation of an objective social system: without its mediation the subject would not be able to be held on the leash.'[53]

Attachment Theory

Attachment theorists, working within the psychoanalytical tradition but inspired by John Bowlby,[54] also reject Freud's aggressive individualism, arguing instead for a view of humans as social beings. In common with Klein and the object-relations school, they see object-seeking and the need for attachment as the basic feature of human nature. In this respect, they are closer to Marx than to Freud. In *From Pain to Violence*, Felicity de Zulueta rejects Freud's drive-based or instinctual approach, and indeed Klein's view insofar as the latter accepts a genetically derived death instinct.[55] De Zulueta argues, instead, for a 'relational model', believing that the need for the 'other' is 'of paramount importance for our psychological and physical well-being. Human beings cannot exist outside society. Unsatisfactory relations lead to frustration, self-destruction and violence, because we are essentially sociable animals.'[56]

Bowlby described 'attachment behaviour' as 'any form of behaviour that results in a person attaining or maintaining proximity to some other clearly defined individual who is conceived as better able to cope with the world'.[57] For de Zulueta, 'it is through this attachment behaviour that the first attachment bond with mother is formed. Although this behaviour is most obvious in childhood, it can be observed throughout life, especially at times of crisis. Attachment behaviour is ... an integral part of human nature and one we share with many other species.'[58] An early 'attunement' between infant and caregiver is 'the precursor and instigator of the attachment bond that becomes fully developed in the human infant at about the age of seven months'.[59] In general, 'our need for significant relationships is ... established at a "psychobiological" level: we are interacting organisms, albeit thinking individuals too; we need one another to maintain ourselves physiologically as well as emotionally'.[60] As de Zulueta points out, 'research on the attachment bond has increasingly established our intrinsic need for one another'.[61] The infant internalises the relationships with the adult caregivers. 'Through the internalisation of repeated interactions with the caregivers, the infant appears to create psychic structures that in some way recreate the experiences lived through his/her important relationships.' These are 'working models', a concept of Bowlby's that has an affinity with the notions of internalised good and bad objects developed by Klein and the object-relations theorists.[62] According to de Zulueta, violence is a 'by-product of psychological trauma and its effects on infants, children and adults ... Trauma can be processed into rage ... memories, which are "split off" within our minds can re-emerge ... when triggered off by the appropriate environmental stimuli.'[63] Violence is 'the extreme expression of human rage, due to overwhelming narcissistic injuries to the self, and as the expression of a disrupted attachment system'.[64]

Anna Freud: Identification with the Aggressor

In an important contribution to our understanding of human aggression, Anna Freud describes the case of a schoolboy who habitually made strange faces when admonished by the teacher.[65] It emerged that the schoolboy was imitating the facial expressions of the teacher when angry. Through his grimaces, the schoolboy was allaying his anxiety by identifying with the teacher – its external source.[66] This mechanism has a dual nature. On the one hand, it is a normal stage in the development of the super-ego. The child introjects the adults' criticisms of its behaviour, so that over time, s/he internalises their qualities and opinions, 'all the time providing material from which the superego may take shape'.[67] However, at times, external criticism is not immediately transformed into self-criticism but is dissociated in the child's mind from its reprehensible behaviour and turned back on the outside world. 'By means of a new defensive process, identification with the aggressor is succeeded by an active assault on the outside world.'[68] Here, 'the mechanism of identification with the aggressor is supplemented by another defensive measure, namely, the projection of guilt'.[69] For Anna Freud, when this stage of intolerance of other people occurs, it generally precedes the ego's severity towards itself, and is, therefore, a 'preliminary phase of morality'. She concludes that 'identification with the aggressor represents, on the one hand, a preliminary phase of superego development and, on the other, an intermediate stage in the development of paranoia'.[70] It is this development of paranoia that is important for understanding genocide. We return to this notion later when examining Fromm's concept of the destructive social character.

Heinz Kohut: Healthy and Pathological Narcissism

In the Greek legend of Narcissus, a beautiful young man rejected the love of the nymph Echo, who died of a broken heart. Nemesis punished him by making him fall in love with his own image in the lake: overcome by self-admiration, he fell into the lake and drowned. 'Primary narcissism', as the psychoanalytical tradition defines it, is the normal focus on the self by the infant from around six months up to six years. For Freud, it is the investment of libidinal energy in the ego, a defence mechanism that protects the child during the formation of its self. The foetus, then the baby, experiences 'normal', or, in Freud's term, 'self-sufficient' narcissism where there is no distinction between the outside world and the self. The baby experiences external objects, such as its mother, as part of itself. Heinz Kohut describes this as 'narcissistic cathexis'.[71]

A child needs to be allowed to express a healthy narcissism: it is a precondition for psychic growth and for separation from the parent and the development of individual identity. As Alice Miller describes it, a baby is fortunate if its mother allows herself to be its 'mirror', to be 'cathected narcissistically', that is, 'allows herself to be "made use of " as a function of the child's narcissistic development ... then a healthy self-feeling can gradually develop'.[72] In other words, the baby needs to feel that its drives, its feelings, its needs, are recognised, accepted and responded to positively. If so, then it can slowly develop a sense of itself as a separate being and of its potency and effectiveness. Only after some months does the infant begin to perceive the external world as 'not me'. As Fromm and Maccoby put it: 'Individual narcissism is hammered into "object-love" by the many blows to the child's narcissism caused by his ever-increasing acquaintance with the outside world and its laws.'[73] 'Secondary' narcissism is the more 'normal' kind in which older children and adults seek personal gratification rather than the achievement of social goals and values. As Freud, emphasised, 'a human being remains to some extent narcissistic even after he has found external objects for his libido'.[74]

So, the 'normal' person is one 'whose narcissism has been reduced to the socially accepted minimum without ever disappearing completely'.[75] It becomes pathological when the narcissist lacks normal empathy and uses others ruthlessly in the pursuit of their own goals.[76] Sadly, too often the mother (or father) fails to create an emotional framework within which the baby's drives and feelings are acknowledged and validated, mainly because their own narcissistic needs remain unsatisfied. Instead, the child's needs are subordinated to those of the parent, who reflects back to the child the demand that it play the role that their own mother failed to fulfil. But if the object behaves in a manner the child does not want or expect, it feels disappointed or angry, as though an arm failed to function. Then, as Miller puts it, 'the narcissistic needs appropriate to the child's age ... cannot be integrated into the developing personality. They are split off, partially repressed, and retain their early, archaic form, which makes their later integration still more difficult.'[77] For Freud, this narcissistic libido is not just love for the self, but love which covers up a loss.[78] Kohut describes patients who are

overly enthusiastic, dramatic, and excessively intense in their responses to everyday events ... In cases of narcissistic personality disorder, it is not difficult to discern the defensive nature – a pseudovitality – of the overt excitement. Behind it lie low esteem and depression – a deep sense of uncared-for worthlessness and rejection ... a yearning for reassurance.[79]

As Miller put it: 'Behind manifest grandiosity, depression is constantly lurking, and hiding behind a depressive mood there are often unconscious (or conscious but split off) fantasies of grandiosity. In fact, grandiosity is the defence against depression and depression is the defence against real pain over loss of the self.'[80] Miller describes the frequent result: 'This sudden loss of control may also lead to an intense narcissistic rage.'[81] De Zulueta defines narcissistic rage as 'the deeply held need for revenge, for undoing a hurt by whatever means, and a deep unrelenting compulsion in the pursuit of those aims'.[82] For Kohut, 'narcissistic rage is at the origins of some of the most gruesome aspects of human destructiveness, often in the form of well-organised activities in which the perpetrators' destructiveness is alloyed with absolute conviction about their greatness and with their devotion to archaic omnipotent figures'.[83] The need for relational bonds is a fundamental human need in both infants and adults. When this need is thwarted, through neglect or abuse, through deprivation or loss, we feel helpless, mortified and paralysed by fear. A need to matter to someone, even a delusional 'other', 'seems at the core of human psychic existence. For those individuals who cannot be valued for being good, being bad is preferable to not being at all.'[84] As Ernest Wolf put it:

> The origin of narcissistic rage must be sought in the childhood experience of utter helplessness vis-à-vis the humiliating self-object parent ... Such experiences of helplessness are unbearably painful, because they threaten the very continuity and existence of the self and they therefore evoke the strongest emergency defence of the self in the form of narcissistic rage.[85]

High self-esteem is important for the capacity for empathy, since the latter is in part an 'extension of the self to other people'. As Staub points out, 'a poor self concept makes it difficult to extend the boundaries of the self in benevolent ways. Racism, nationalism and prejudice are inevitable consequences.'[86] However, to fully understand violence, specifically genocide, we must add the phenomenon of dissociation or, in Kleinian terms, splitting. Infants, enraged with and in fear of abusive or neglectful or rejecting carers, will also be terrified of these dangerous feelings. 'They need to maintain their attachment in order to survive and they will do this by resorting to "splitting", that is, creating different representations of themselves and their caregivers.' This is reminiscent of Klein's description of 'good and bad object-relations'.[87] As de Zulueta puts it:

> when subject to deprivation, loss or abuse, such people can only survive by doing violence to their feelings. Pain and rage must be suppressed or denied in order to remain close to those on whom our lives depend ... These destructive feelings can then also be projected and subsequently attacked in the 'other'.[88]

Such feelings of rage and destructiveness, together with memories of them, remain unconscious for as long as the person's psychological defences are able to keep them split off. But they can be expressed indirectly, generally through displacement on to a 'culturally approved object'.[89]

The relevance of this analysis to genocide is that we need to view the mechanisms of splitting, projection and destructiveness as collective psychic phenomena, processes that affect an entire class or at least a majority of its members. This is not a preposterous claim, given that most members of a class will be so defined by their having undergone similar historical experiences through sharing a broadly common relationship to that society's means of production and to other class forces within the social formation. It is that historical experience which forms the ground out of which arise the psychic forces that govern the inner life of a class. De Zulueta gives as an example the Nazi projection onto the Jews of their own hatred and destructiveness, an example we return to in Chapter 7.[90] The next task is to attempt to integrate attachment theory with Fromm's concept of social character. As we saw, there are, for Fromm, two types of destructiveness – spontaneous and character-based. In this case we are dealing with the longer-term, deeper-rooted, character-based version. Moreover, an important part of the content of character-based destructiveness, or indeed of the authoritarian social character, is the split-off and projected element of destructive rage.

The Death Instinct

Early Psychoanalytic Marxism

The first generation of psychoanalytic Marxists was divided over the death instinct. Reich was first into the fray, rejecting Freud's notion in an article entitled 'The Masochistic Character', first published in 1932, later incorporated into *Character Analysis* (1933). Reich repudiated Freud's theory of culture, namely that its precondition was instinctual renunciation. If this were so, then it followed that sexual liberation spelt the end of art and culture. Reich went on to argue that destructiveness was not the result of an innate drive but of repressed sexuality. 'It is the inhibition of sexuality ... which makes aggression a power beyond mastery, because inhibited sexual energy turns into destructive energy.'[91] Marcuse was more inclined to accept the death instinct, but echoed Reich's view of the link between sexual repression and destructiveness. Marcuse distinguished between 'basic repression' and 'surplus repression': the former was the minimum 'modification' to our erotic impulses which any human civilisation would have to impose for survival and perpetuation; the latter was the additional restriction imposed for the purpose of social or class domination.[92] According to Marcuse and Otto Fenichel (a disciple of Freud's and leading left-wing figure in the history of psychoanalysis),[93] Freud believed in the common origin of the life and death instincts. Freud assumed a 'displaceable energy, which is in itself neutral, but is able to join forces either with an erotic or with a destructive impulse' – with the life or the death instinct.[94] As Freud put it: 'After sublimation, the erotic component no longer has the power to bind the whole of the destructive elements that were previously combined with it, and these are released in the form of inclinations to aggression and destruction.'[95] So sublimation, required under a repressive 'reality principle', redirects sexual energy down alternative, socially useful channels. However, Marcuse writes:

> Culture demands continuous sublimation; it thereby weakens Eros, the builder of culture. And desexualisation, by weakening Eros, unbinds the destructive impulses. Civilisation is thus threatened by an instinctual de-fusion, in which the death instinct strives to gain ascendancy over the life instincts. Originating in renunciation ... civilisation tends towards self-destruction.[96]

In other words, only when sexuality remains unrestricted, our libido unsublimated, can human destructiveness be kept in check. But modern 'civilised society', operating under the aegis of the 'performance principle' (the form that the reality principle takes under capitalism), requires the suppression of Eros and therefore 'tends towards self-destruction'. Robinson believes that Marcuse felt the need for some grand, overarching concept to deal adequately with the enormous destruction of the twentieth century, qualitatively different from that of any previous era.[97]

Is there a death instinct?

There seem to be seven main objections to the theory of the death instinct: three psychological objections, plus biological, cultural, political and historical ones. The first psychological objection was expressed by W.R.D. Fairbairn, a founder of the object-relations school: 'What Freud describes under the category of "death instinct" would thus appear to represent for the most part masochistic relationships with bad objects.' In other words, the libido is attached to bad as well as good objects, for example, a mother who frustrates her baby, and this relationship to the bad object can take either a sadistic or a masochistic form. Either way, it is then internalised and repressed.[98] As noted, a different psychological objection was expressed by Reich who argued that destructiveness was the result, not of any death instinct, but of sexual repression. Finally, a third psychological objection is that much of the aggression which the 'instinctual' school analyses in terms of the death instinct can be attributed to defensive behaviour.[99]

Regarding the biological objection, Fenichel argued that 'instinct' implies a biologically based drive or stimulus seeking satisfaction in the outside world. Instinct would be expressed through a disturbance of the cells causing painful tension which can be eliminated by a physical process which returns the cells to their original condition. For example, the sexual instinct is aroused by the 'chemical sensitising of the erogenous zones' which impels the person to seek sexual gratification, a process that restores the cells to their previous stability. There is no comparable process of chemical excitation which can be said to be at the root of a destructive urge. 'It seems ... as if aggressiveness were originally no instinctual aim of its own, characterising one category of instincts in contra-distinction to others, but rather a mode in which instinctual aims sometimes are striven for, in response to frustrations or even spontaneously.'[100]

Fifth, the cultural objection put forward by Erich Fromm in his final work, *The Anatomy of Human Destructiveness*, is that Freud mistakenly believed that tension reduction is the aim of human life. Freud argued this, not as a result of his clinical investigations but rather due to his rather dogmatic adherence to nine-teenth-century mechanical materialism, according to which human beings are machines. On the contrary, both clinical and everyday observation establish that 'man at all ages seeks excitation, stimulation, relations of love and friendship ... to increase his relatedness to the world ... man seems to be motivated just as much by the principle of tension increase as by that of tension reduction'.[101] Fromm himself attributes destructiveness to the thwarting of basic human needs such as those for unity, rootedness and effectiveness. He makes another, related point, that many societies in fact reveal a virtual absence of destructiveness. (Regarding early societies, this has been challenged, as we saw in the Introduction.[102])

Sixth, the political objection: Reich argued that 'the theory of the death instinct, that is, the theory of self-destructive biological instincts, leads to a cultural philosophy of human suffering.'[103] This view would render futile any attempts by human beings to create a better world. Seventh, the historical objection: Freud and Klein left unanswered a crucial question: given that the human destructive 'instinct' lies dormant, or under control most of the time, otherwise social life would be impossible, under what circumstances is it unleashed? Why did the First World War break out when it did? Why was the Nazi Holocaust decided on some time in 1941 and not in 1938? Why did certain groups in German society and not others follow the Nazis? That which explains everything explains nothing. So for example, if we wish to analyse the causes of the First World War, Lenin is more useful than Freud.

Also, crucially, to attempt to deal with these questions in purely psychological terms is to fall prey to cross psychological reductionism. These questions need concrete historical answers. Shouldn't we therefore abandon Freud's and Klein's Thanatos as too abstract? Shouldn't we speak instead of a destructiveness that is part of the life-assertive drive, in other words, an aggressive potentiality present in all life forms, which exists in latent form within the human psyche and is converted into actual aggression or violence under specific social and personal conditions? It is the latter which we need to analyse to understand the particular expressions of destructiveness such as war or genocide.

Most social theorists reject the idea of a destructive drive, arguing more vaguely about the strain that unbearable social or economic conditions puts on human relationships. In this vein, they conjure up the notion of scapegoating brought about by the extreme frustration, anxiety and anger caused by economic or social crises. But it is not enough to refer simply to economic and social conditions: a comprehensive analysis must include psychological factors. So we need to search for the answer to the question, Why Genocide?, in the interface between social theory and that psychological theory which provides the clearest in-depth understanding of the human psyche, that is, psychoanalysis.

Fromm's Theory of Destructiveness

Fromm, like Reich, rejected the death instinct. Destructiveness is not an inherent, ineradicable feature of human nature or of our social life, but the consequence of the repression or frustration of fundamental human needs. Whereas Reich attributed destructiveness to the frustration of our libidinal impulses, Fromm ascribed it to a thwarting of the 'drive to life', to the aloneness and powerlessness that are expressions of such a suppression of life. Fromm believes that our basic human psychic needs – for unity, rootedness and effectiveness, for example – can be met in one of two ways, either by solidarity, love and productive work or by sadism and destructiveness.[104] These will be explored further in Chapter 4.

As we have seen, Fromm distinguished between spontaneous and character-based destructiveness. The former refers to outbursts of 'dormant ... destructive impulses ... activated by extraordinary circumstances, in contrast to the permanent, although not always expressed, presence of destructive traits in the character'.[105] Destructive outbursts are not spontaneous in the sense of not having reasons. They can be, and usually are, explained in terms of external events such as war, economic, political or religious conflict, poverty and the threat of sudden impoverishment. Such violence should not be explained as an unavoidable expression of human nature, or as rooted in a particular social character, but as the enactment of a potential for destructiveness unleashed in response to extraordinary circumstances without which it would lie dormant.[106]

According to Fromm, there are two main kinds of spontaneous destructiveness – 'vengeful' and 'ecstatic'. Vengeful destructiveness is a spontaneous reaction to the suffering experienced by an individual or the group with which they identify. It differs from defensive aggression in two ways: first, it occurs after damage has been sustained, so is not a defence against a perceived threat; secondly, it is of greater intensity, being often cruel and insatiable. Vengeful aggression is widespread among both individuals and groups. The examples Fromm adduces are the blood revenge practised all over the world – 'the sacred duty that falls upon the member of a family, clan or tribe who has to kill a member of the corresponding unit if one of his people has been killed'.[107] The second kind, 'ecstatic destructiveness', occurs when groups act out rituals or achieve trance-like states aiming at transcending or overcoming deep fears of isolation or powerlessness, thus achieving a new unity within oneself or with nature. Often, such rituals give vent to concealed feelings of rage and hatred, and allow for the expression of destructiveness normally prohibited in everyday social existence.[108] Quite different is the destructiveness rooted in social character, which Fromm describes as 'a constantly flowing source of energy'.[109] This character-based destructiveness has, in turn, two forms: sadism and necrophilia, or love of the dead, which are explored in the next chapter.

Žižek and Butler

The psychoanalytically influenced thinker Slavoj Žižek focuses not on 'subjective violence' such as acts of assault, murder and terrorism, but on two distinct modes of objective violence: first, one which is embodied in language ('symbolic' violence), and second, the hidden, institutional violence of the system ('systemic' violence').[110] For Žižek, a 'neighbour' is primarily an intruder, someone with different ideas and a different way of life whose intrusion is something to be feared, the opposite of the benign image of someone who drops in to borrow sugar. When the neighbour comes too close, that closeness suggests the Thing with its alien, threatening character, and there is a risk of an aggressive reaction to repel the intrusion.[111]

Žižek argues that European civilisation's ability to tolerate different ways of life is predicated on this maintenance of distance from the 'neighbour', of alienation from others. 'One of the things alienation means is that distance is woven into the very texture of social life. Even if I live side by side with others, in my normal state I ignore them. I am not allowed to get too close to others ... Sometimes alienation is not a problem but a solution.' In this context, he considers the Danish cartoons caricaturing Mohammed that aroused a storm of protest across the Muslim world in 2005. He says Muslims were reacting not to the caricatures themselves but to what they interpreted to be Western images of and attitudes to the Prophet. 'A torrent of humiliations and frustrations were condensed into the caricatures.'[112]

Žižek argues that this condensation is a basic feature of language, the way it constructs and imposes a 'certain symbolic field'. Language doesn't simply reflect the outside world but simplifies it, reduces it to a single feature. 'It dismembers the thing, destroys its organic unity, treating its parts and properties as autonomous. It inserts the thing into a field of meaning which is ultimately external to it.'[113] Žižek challenges the conventional pairing of language and harmony or reconciliation: as long as people can talk to each other, peace is more likely than war ('jaw-jaw better than war-war'). For Žižek, language itself can be the problem: 'What if, however, humans exceed animals in their capacity for violence precisely because they speak?'[114]

One must question the way Žižek's jumps from his analysis of the manner in which language condenses or even mutilates reality to the claim that this is a reflection of human reality. This is an ahistorical approach to violence. Language is a distinguishing mark of humankind, and has always contained these 'violent' features, but humans have not always related to each other with the same degree or type of violence. So again, what explains everything explains nothing. There is here an echo of the poststructuralist analysis of language as the only medium through which we can grasp the external social or natural world, so that analyses of nature and society become analyses of the various independent 'discourses' through which we describe and interpret them. Alex Callinicos makes a similar point regarding Saussure: 'For Saussure, the crucial distinction is not that between word and object, but that between signifier (word) and signified (concept).'[115] In other words, we can't grasp nature or society in themselves but only through language, that is, the symbolic. As Callinicos notes: 'Lacan and Žižek equate the Symbolic and the social.'[116]

Philosophically, this represents a return to Kant, for whom we cannot grasp the world, or nature, as it is in itself but only through the categories or concepts of the human mind. It is 'pre-Marxist' in that Marx overcame the earlier dualism between mind and matter, or thought and nature, by seeing the relationship between them as a practical one. We understand the external world insofar as we act upon it and transform it according to our needs.[117] Hence language is not a super-medium through which alone we can relate to the external world, but a tool by means of which we act on and transform that world, including our relations with each other. Language is not so much a phenomenon that explains other phenomena as one itself in need of explanation. It is a feature of human existence created by human beings themselves acting collectively as they evolved from the ape. Language arose from the very nature of humans as social beings. In Marx's words, 'language is practical consciousness that exists also for other men ... language, like consciousness, only arises from the need, the necessity, of intercourse with other men'.[118]

Žižek also approaches violence in terms of 'institutional violence', the violence done to human beings through the very nature of the social system, including the violence inherent in the economic system. Žižek pillories philanthropists such as Bill Gates, tearing off the mask of benevolence that conceals the underlying violence of the manner in which they acquired the wealth that allows them to become lavish donors to charity. However, what Žižek does is re-define the meaning of violence, re-chart its territory in the direction of 'institutional violence'. He has not offered us any new explanations, fresh ways of understanding the reasons why human beings commit acts of violence against each other. Nevertheless, he does offer us a clue in his view of the neighbour not as a person to love as oneself, as ordained by the Judaeo-Christian tradition, but as someone from whom one should keep one's distance. This reflects a view of society as made up of separate individuals engaged in permanent, mutual competition, a Hobbesian 'war of all against all'. If relative peace and harmony are to prevail, we need a powerful state to adjudicate between rivals, holding them apart if necessary. Individuals do not have common, collective goals but cooperate out of enlightened, mutual self-interest. Žižek, therefore, asserts the need for 'ethical violence', which is 'the most precious and revolutionary aspect of the Jewish legacy'. This is the Mosaic Law, 'experienced as something externally, violently imposed'; 'the pronouncement of the Decalogue on Mount Sinai is ... ethical violence at its purest'. He believes we need this 'violent imposition of the Law' because of the danger 'of an even more fundamental violence, that of encountering a neighbour: far from brutally disturbing a preceding harmonious social interaction, the imposition of the Law endeavours to introduce a minimum of regulation on to a stressful "impossible" relationship'.[119]

A key influence on Žižek is French psychoanalyst Jacques Lacan. Žižek argues that Freud and Lacan 'insist on the problematic nature of the basic Judaeo-Christian injunction to "love they neighbour"', believing in 'the incompatibility of the Neighbour with the very dimension of universality. What resists universality is the ... *inhuman* dimension of the Neighbour.'[120] And in 'Neighbours and Other Monsters' Žižek writes: 'beneath the neighbour as ... my mirror image, there always lurks the unfathomable abyss of radical Otherness, of a monstrous Thing that cannot be "gentrified"'.[121] According to Lacan, we don't relate directly to the 'other', but only through language – the symbolic order which alone can 'render our co-existence with the Thing minimally bearable ... There is no intersubjectivity ... without the impersonal symbolic Order', acting as the 'pacifying mediator'.[122] But is there not a contradiction between Lacan's notion of the symbolic order as 'pacifying mediator' and Žižek's view of language as an expression of violence?

However, the symbolic order is also the big Other, the realm of prohibition into which the infant is initiated by the father.[123] The father within the Oedipal situation represents the law and it is his role, through prohibition of desire and the imposition of the incest taboo, to initiate the child into the cultural and symbolic order. Humans are alienated in the 'normalisation' of their sexual and aggressive instincts by the symbolic order.

> It is here that the origin of human aggression is to be sought. Obliged to fashion himself with reference to and in rivalry with the other, obliged to wait for recognition from or judgment by the other, man becomes inclined to a whole range of aggressive behaviour, from envy, morbid jealousy and real aggression to mortal negation of self or other.[124]

This dependence on the Other results in a lack of being that is also the source of the death instinct. Lacan's idiosyncratic view of the death drive is thus revealed in the way he links it to the unconscious and the related notions of being and non-being. The subject is dependent on the Other, highlighting his/her lack of being, a 'negativity to be overcome', a state akin to Freud's death drive, which strives to return the living being to the inorganic state.[125] And 'language represents that "margin beyond life" where the being of the individual is *only represented* ... the subject is always caught up in language's function of representing something inaccessible, the margin beyond life, and the ultimate, inaccessible experience of death'.[126]

However, it's not clear whether for Lacan aggression is instinctive or socially produced. Either way, it seems inevitably present in all human social arrangements. We seem to be back to some version of Freud's view of the ineradicable conflict between desire and civilisation – or indeed Freud's and Klein's theory of the death instinct, a psychological force we cannot eliminate but only control through various socio-cultural restrictions. But, as with Freud, this notion is of little use in explaining specific historical expressions of destructiveness such as war or genocide. Lacan's ahistorical approach is also shown up in his view of the eternal nature of the 'phallic' law or law of the father, neglecting an important school of anthropology according to which patriarchy has not always dominated human communities but that at the dawn of humanity matriarchal societies were the norm.

Žižek (and Lacan) also display a grievous lack of historical perspective by assuming that the way humans behave and relate to each other under capitalism are universal features to be found in all historical societies. In fact, the kind of competitive individualism Žižek refers to in describing our relations with our neighbour is characteristic of capitalism. In previous class societies, human relationships and institutions were considerably more collective in outlook and behaviour. If we look at tribal or feudal social formations, the predominant mode of identification was not as an individual but as a member of a tribe, family or estate. This doesn't mean that those societies were less oppressive, just that human beings didn't think of themselves as individuals, rather as members of a collective.

In addition, Žižek contradicts himself since he puts forward the view of society as a 'war of all against all' whereas in his book on violence he argues that, for most of the time, 'it is difficult for the majority to overcome their revulsion at torturing and killing another human being. The large majority of people are spontaneously "moral": killing another human being is deeply traumatic for them.'[127] If we are spontaneously 'moral', how come the neighbour is essentially a threat, someone to be avoided rather than engaged with? On the other hand, as Stephen Frosh has pointed out, Žižek is a critic of capitalism. He wants to adapt Lacan's concepts of the Real and big Other for the purpose of social critique.[128] Lacan's notion of the Real seems to have two possible meanings, weighed down, as is so much of Lacan, by ambiguity and obscurity. Sometimes, it appears to refer to the domain outside the symbolic order, the realm of fantasy and dreams, that is, of the unconscious. As Benvenuto and Kennedy describe it: 'Lacan stated that what does not come to light in the Symbolic Order appears in the real, the realm outside the subject, for instance as a hallucination.'[129] As Callinicos put it recently: 'The Real is the limit of symbolization ... where the incoherence of the Symbolic becomes visible.'[130] In the second sense, 'psychoanalysis ... tries to deal with something that knowledge belonging to the Real can never reach'.[131] Here Lacan appears to mean by the 'Real' that which is outside our imagination, knowledge and language, the ultimate reality which resists any kind of mediation by human endeavour, reminiscent, again, of Kant's unknowable 'thing-in-itself'. The impenetrability of the Real is a major source of anxiety. Žižek applies the notion to the ways in which capitalism attempts to impose ideological hegemony. So, we view society not in terms of its actual material and social relations but through 'the inexorable "abstract" spectral logic of capital that determines what goes on in social reality'.[132] Frosh argues that Žižek's radicalism is revealed in his application of Lacan's concept of the big Other to the contemporary political scene. 'The subject is always constructed according to the desire of the Other, always answerable to a "big Other" that is over and beyond itself and can perhaps be thought of as "society" (amongst other things).'[133]

Another writer who engages with the issue of violence is the poststructuralist philosopher Judith Butler. As with Žižek and Lacan, the reader faces the daunting task of negotiating their way through some fairly opaque, indigestible prose to tease out its meaning. Butler develops a theory of the formation of the subject – the 'I' – as occurring through one's relation to the community – others. 'The infant enters the world given over from the start to a language and to a series of signs ... that begin to structure an already operative mode of receptivity and demand.'[134] She gives credence to the object-relations approach to subject-formation, where the 'other' is described as the 'condition ... of my affective life, installed within me as an object-source that gives rise to the drives and desires that are mine. From within the object-relations perspective, the primary impressions constitute objects ... to which an emergent self might attach itself to satisfy basic needs.'[135] As she also puts it: 'There is ... a sociality at the basis of the 'I' ... from which one cannot – and ought not to – escape.'[136] So far, this would seem to be unexceptionable. Indeed, it ties in with a Marxist view of humans as social beings.

Her analysis takes on a darker hue insofar as she argues that the process by which I become myself is one of dispossession by the other. She quotes French psychoanalyst Jean Laplanche for whom 'man is not at home with himself in himself, which means that in himself, he is not the master and that finally, he is decentred'.[137] According to Butler, this 'decentering follows from the way in which others, from the outset, transmit certain messages to us, instilling their thoughts in our own, producing an indistinguishability between the other and myself at the heart of who I am'.[138] Butler concludes: 'A formation in passivity, then, constitutes the prehistory of the subject ... prior to any possibility of its own acting. The scene is persecutory because it is unwilled and unchosen.'[139] According to Frosh, Butler's interpretation of 'ethical violence' involves 'the promulgation of a version of the other that forces the other to become something it should not be'.[140]

The final stage of Butler's argument concerns the possibility of moral action despite the 'human condition' – that the opaque nature of our 'prehistory' results in our inability to give a full ethical account of ourselves. This is 'my final "irresponsibility", one for which I may be forgiven only because I could not do otherwise. This not being able to do otherwise is our common predicament.'[141] Nevertheless, Butler insists on the possibility of ethical action despite the limits of our self-knowledge. An ethical life, one characterised by responsibility to the other, cannot be based on my transparency to myself or on the visibility of the 'other': 'the very meaning of responsibility must be rethought on the basis of this limitation; it cannot be tied to the conceit of a self fully transparent to itself'.[142] As Butler also puts it: 'my very formation implicates the other in me, my own foreignness to myself is, paradoxically, the source of my ethical connections with others'.[143] In our very formation, we are susceptible to others in a manner we have not willed or chosen. In other words, we can act ethically towards others because others are within us: 'None of us is fully bounded, utterly separate, but, rather, we are in our skins, given over, in each other's hands, at each other's mercy.'[144]

There are two points here. Firstly, it seems that for Butler, the presence of others 'in us' creates the potential for ethical behaviour and responsibility towards others. This renders redundant or even counter-productive the imposition of an external law such as Žižek advocates. Secondly, surely the entire psychoanalytical tradition points to a certain relationship between ethics and psychoanalysis: namely that the opacity of our deep-seated emotional life means that while we cannot be held responsible for our feelings, we are certainly responsible for our actions, unless the severity of our mental illness requires us to be sectioned.

Butler's approach is abstract and ahistorical. She describes the dispossession of the subject by the Other as virtually an assault. For her, this is a universal feature of human experience, unchanging through history which inevitably takes such a form. An alternative view is that one needs to distinguish between the manner in which different societies produce different relationships between 'self' and 'other' in infancy and adulthood. No doubt, the more repressed a society, the more 'dispossessed' the subject during its 'prehistory', and the more alienated the social relationships of that society will be. But not all historical societies produce the same level of 'dispossession', and consequent repression and alienation. And, arguably, one cannot arrive at an understanding of these differences without introducing the concepts of class and exploitation. However, in her later *Frames of War*, Butler describes approvingly Klein's and Winnicott's shared position that 'even if aggression is coextensive with being human ... the way destructiveness is lived and directed varies enormously'.[145] Butler also compares their different approaches to destructiveness: 'For Winnicott, the question is whether the object of love can survive our love, can bear a certain mutilation and still persist as an object. But for Klein, the effort to preserve the object against our own destructiveness reduces finally to a fear for one's own survival.'[146] It seems that Butler is rooting guilt in the drive to survival, a view that negates the thrust of Klein's view of humans as object-seeking with a strong reparative capacity.

Butler relies considerably on the notion of primary trauma offered by Laplanche, whose account she prefers to those of the object-relations or Kleinian schools. 'For Laplanche ... the primary experience for the infant is invariably that of being overwhelmed ... profoundly clueless about the impingements of the adult world ... as a consequence of trauma, an originally external object becomes installed as a source or cause of sexual drives.' In general, 'drives (life drives and death drives) are not ... primary – they follow from an interiorisation of the enigmatic desires of others'.[147] In short, 'the primary address overwhelms: it cannot be interpreted or understood. It is the primary experience of trauma.'[148] Butler's acceptance of Laplanche's view of trauma and drives has three consequences. Firstly, Laplanche's account is no doubt one side of the picture of the infant's induction into the world. But it assumes that an infant is an empty vessel into which the adult world pours its needs and desires, an infant that has no prior elements of human nature which it brings to the situation. And this gives rise to the problem examined in Chapter 1: if human beings begin life as a blank sheet on which each culture writes its text, then who wrote that text, where does that culture come from?

Secondly, Laplanche leaves us with the same abstract analysis of destructiveness we find in Freud and Klein – a universal death drive that cannot explain actual instances of war or genocide. Thirdly, if this is the whole, or at least the preponderant, story, then it is hard to see how ethical life and responsibility emerge. Ethics then surely becomes moralism, preaching to the non-converted rather than the construction of moral relationships related to and grown organically out of our nature as social beings. Buttressing this view of ethics is the other side of the story of affectionate bonding, of the infant's object-seeking and its attachment to a primary caregiver. This is surely the earliest, 'pre-historic' expression of Marx's view of human nature as 'the ensemble of social relations'.

Why War?

War or civil war is nearly always the context in which genocide takes place. We have examined the debate around the death instinct. Interestingly, Freud himself, in his letter to Einstein 'Why War?' (1932), did not adduce the death instinct or a general human destructiveness as the main cause, attributing to it a subordinate role. At best, it is a predisposing factor, in Fromm's paraphrase, 'facilitating people's readiness to go to war once the government has decided to wage war'.[149] Freud did not here abandon the notion of a death drive pervading human relations, but sought, at least initially, to explain it more concretely in terms of a realistic conflict of interests, in particular, disputes over ownership. The conclusion would be that war has nearly always been a 'rational' undertaking, embarked on for specific, calculable gains, even when large numbers of civilians get killed. To argue that it stems from innate human destructiveness is, in addition, dangerous, since it would follow that human intellectual endeavour to understand its causes and consequent political action to eliminate it are doomed to fail.

Fromm argues that war is simply the most important case of 'instrumental aggression'. One might also call it 'rational' or 'utilitarian' aggression, a collective act that those undertaking it use as a means of achieving their practical ends. From ancient times, through medieval feudalism down to modern capitalism, those who went to war did so occasionally for revenge but more typically for the sake of land for cultivation, slaves, riches, raw materials and markets, pre-empting enemy attacks. Fromm's argument suggests that we should add a third form of destructiveness to the two he puts forward (that is, spontaneous and character-based) – namely, 'instrumental' or 'utilitarian' or 'rational' destructiveness.[150]

In these last two chapters, I have explored the debate between those who affirm that destructiveness is an ineradicable part of human nature as against those who seek its roots in social conditions. I have argued that the latter view of course carries with it the implicit notion of a potential for destructiveness. But I also suggested that this is best seen as part of the life drive of human beings, one, however, that is only activated at times of stress emanating from specific social and personal conditions. We are back to Freud's notion of the common source of the life and death instincts. Perhaps it helps to understand this if we compare the mutation from life to death to a normal cell which becomes cancerous under certain external and internal conditions. To return, in conclusion, to the insights provided by the attachment school: in general, violence is seen as 'a by-product of psychological trauma and its effects on infants, children and adults'.[151] The question raised by Marcuse and Fromm is whether it is civilisation as such which is the source of destructiveness or its specific capitalist form.

CHAPTER THREE

What Makes Killers Tick?

Destructiveness and Social Character

Social theories may be said to fall into one of two categories, depending on their approach to the issue of human agency. The key debate is between those theories that emphasise social structure as determining human thought and behaviour, and those that stress the independent, self-creative aspect of human beings. The concept of 'social character', in both social theory and psychoanalysis, has been developed and transformed as an attempt to bridge the gap between structure and agency, between society and individuals or groups, to see human behaviour as both determined by and in turn determining social structures.[1]

Meisenhelder traces the development of the notion of social character from its classical sociological beginnings in Marx and Durkheim, followed by an account of how it was taken up by psychoanalysis, that is, Freud and Fromm (omitting Reich's contribution). He concludes with an analysis of how it found a place in American social science via Abram Kardiner, Hans Gerth and C. Wright Mills, and David Riesman, and in the work of French sociologist Pierre Bourdieu. Margaret Archer has also discussed the concept from a non-psychoanalytical perspective.[2] The notion of social character is arguably the most significant theoretical contribution of the first generation of psychoanalytic Marxists. With the failure of the Russian Revolution to spread to other countries, and the subsequent rise of fascism, their objectives were to explain the power and origin of ideology, how social and political factors are internalised within the individual psyche, and to understand the subjective conditions for radical social change.[3]

As developed in different ways by Reich and Fromm, the notion of character was the crucial link mediating between external society and individual psyche. As we have seen, Freud was the first to mention the concept in his analysis of the 'anal-compulsive' character. In 1908 he drew attention to this type, arguing that 'the traits of parsimony, obstinacy, and orderliness do not occur together by chance; rather they constitute a syndrome of traits rooted in a common libidinal source'.[4] By 'social character' one isn't referring to 'national character' in the conventional meaning of a set of traits fixed and unchanging over time, which is generally not discussed in relation to historical origins and social change. Rather it is a phenomenon closely bound up with the class conflicts of the various societies and is, therefore, subject to historical change.

Reich's concept of 'character structure' was closely related to Marx's theory of ideology. Reich stated that:

> every social organisation produces those character structures which it needs to exist. In class society, the existing ruling class secures its position with the

help of education and the institution of the family, by making its ideologies the ruling ideologies of all members of the society. However it is not solely a matter of implanting the ideologies in all members of the society ... [of] attitudes and opinions ... but of a far-reaching process in every new generation of a given society, the purpose of which is to effect a change in and mould psychic structures (and this in all layers of the population) in conformity with the social order.[5]

Basing himself on Freud's notion of the primacy of the libido, Reich argued, contrary to Freud, that sexual repression was not the necessary price of civilisation but was the product of a repressive class society, one for which sexual repression was a key weapon of class rule. The ruling class needed to instil sexual renunciation as a means of securing control over society. As Ollman put it, 'life in capitalism is not only responsible for our beliefs ... but also for ... all our spontaneous reactions which proceed from our character structure ... emotions as well as ideas are socially determined'.[6]

Reich noted that sexual impotence was accompanied by specific ways of fending off instinctual impulses. These defensive reactions he labelled 'character structure' or 'character armour', which referred to the unconscious means whereby an individual protects him/herself from the repressive techniques of parents in early childhood. However, if character structure begins as a form of self-protection against attacks from the family environment, it ends up by closing off the flow of instinctual impulses. The result is a generalised dulling effect, which affects every aspect of the individual's life. It means he/she is conditioned to accept the boring, repetitive work that modern capitalism requires its workers to carry out unquestioningly.[7] But Reich warns us that the blocking off of sexual energy by these external and internal repressive forces means that energy seeks alternative outlets. It then becomes available for various neuroses and, as we saw in Chapter 2, for destructiveness.[8]

Reich's notion of character structure echoes Marx's concept of alienation. Character is the form that self-alienation takes through the repression of sexual activity, through the alienation of our sexuality. The damning-up of sexual energy is described by Ollman as the 'objectification of human existence that has acquired power over the individual through its formation in inhuman conditions. Its various forms, the precise attitudes taken, are reified as moral sense, strength of character, sense of duty, etc.'[9] In other words, the ruling class and its various ideological agencies (family, school, media, church, etc.) instil fear into the individual and use his/her character structure to build support within the mind for the external institutions and practices that oppress them.[10] People are thus prisoners not only of those external conditions but also of themselves.

Reich attempted to apply his concept of character structure to the political situation prevailing in Germany when Hitler became chancellor in 1933. This materialised in his principal political work, a study of the psychology of Nazism, published in 1933.[11] This work contains another early systematic formulation of character structure. Reich argues, following Marx, that ruling classes don't normally resort to brute force in order to consolidate their rule. They do so by instilling into the subordinate class not only the ruling ideology but also character forms which guarantee acquiescence to capitalism. They do so by means of sexual repression, a process that begins in early childhood. So, 'the authoritarian family ... becomes the factory in which the state's structure and ideology are moulded'. Hence, 'the family is the authoritarian state in miniature, to which the child must learn to adapt himself as a preparation for the general social adjustment required of him later'.[12] We will return to Reich's analysis in Chapter 7.

Of course, in the post-'60s era, sexual repression is no longer the means by which the ruling class instils conformity or represses awareness of alternatives to its rule. Sexuality has been unshackled but only to be re-moulded into an instrument of the corporations. Marcuse described this as 'repressive desublimation', a concept that links Marx and Freud. For Freud, sublimation was the process that diverted repressed sexual energy into alternative, socially acceptable channels. Desublimation means permitting the satisfaction of instinctual drives but on condition that they are subordinated to capitalism's need for mass consumption, for profit. As Reimut Reiche put it: 'sexuality is given a little more rein and thus brought into the service of safeguarding the system'.[13] The methods adopted under late capitalism thus have more to do with the heightened role of the market and the mass media, but also with the strengthening of the command structure and the increasing remoteness of the global corporations and the state. These huge institutions intensify workers' feelings of insignificance and impotence, inducing deeper passivity. Of central importance in the recent strengthening of these institutions were the defeats inflicted on the labour movement in the 1980s in Britain and the US.

Jeffrey Weeks has mounted a general critique of 'Freudo-Marxism'. Firstly, like the Freudianism it claims to replace, it depends on a theory of sexuality which is rigidly biological and, therefore, ahistorical. Though differing on the nature of the sex drive, Reich and Marcuse agree about an identical instinctual structure common to all cultures: sexuality is shaped not within society but outside it. For Weeks, this means they are unable to overcome the dualism between man and society.

This led, secondly, to an identification of sexual and social liberation. While this provided an important corrective to a socialist tradition that tended to ignore issues of sexuality, it also led to a moral position emphasising heterosexual 'genital normality'. The problem is that constructing the major opposition as that between society and an undifferentiated sex drive leads to a neglect of different gendered sexualities. Weeks claims that, unlike the later Freud, none of the Freudo-Marxists showed an interest in female sexuality: 'masculinity and femininity are active and passive forms of the same sexual drive'.[14] However, this is to ignore Fromm, who criticised Freud's 'patriarchal bias': 'For Freud, only the male is really a full human being. Woman is a crippled, castrated man. She ... can be happy only if she finally overcomes her "castration complex" by the acceptance of a child and husband.'[15]

Finally, according to Weeks, Freudo-Marxism made a vital contribution by stressing the importance of sexual change to wider social change. However, by conflating the social and the sexual into a single process of repression, seeing them as merely different aspects of the same subjugation, it ignores the complexity of the ways in which sexuality is shaped culturally and the diversity of wider forms of social conflict and means of resistance such as those of class, race or ethnicity. Here Weeks also ignored Fromm's criticism of orthodox psychoanalysis for 'focusing mainly on sexual needs, or, later, on destructive needs, in addition to the needs for survival' and ignoring 'the wider range of needs'. This is implicitly also a criticism of Reich's and Marcuse's dominant focus on instinctual needs.[16] I will argue that, suitably modified, Fromm's concept of social character goes a long way to overcoming the separation between the objective and subjective, human nature and society.

Slavoj Žižek has also referred to class factors that are partly ideological but clearly also partly characterological. He quotes with approval George Orwell's description of the individual's difficulty in ridding themselves of their class attributes: 'Here am I, a typical member of the middle class. It is easy for me to say that I want to get rid of class-distinctions, but nearly everything I think or do is the result of class distinctions ... I have got to alter myself so completely that at the end I should hardly be recognisable as the same person.'[17] Žižek adds:

> My notions – of good and evil, of pleasant and unpleasant, of funny and serious, of ugly and beautiful – are essentially *middle-class* notions; my taste in books and food and clothes, my sense of honour, my table manners, my turns of phrase, my accent, even the characteristic movements of my body, are all matters of habit. Smell could usefully be added.[18]

Fromm's Concept of Social Character

The most intellectually sophisticated version of the concept of social character is that developed by Erich Fromm. Character, for him, is the human equivalent of animal instincts, that is, an enduring or historically relative system of feelings, needs and drives that conditions us to deal in certain ways with our natural and social worlds, but which doesn't determine our behaviour in the manner of instincts.[19] Character structure replaces the animal's instinct. It is the means by which human energy is organised in the pursuit of different goals. It enables us to respond to external events in a more or less coherent and effective manner. Since the emergence of homo sapiens some 40,000 years ago, human beings have not been dominated by their genetic inheritance, so that different environmental conditions required them to develop alternative methods of dealing with them. To quote Heraclitus, character is man's fate.

Fromm's exposition of the notion of social character is found in *The Fear of Freedom* (1942) and *Man For Himself* (1949). In the latter, he outlines his difference from Freud for whom the fundamental basis of character is 'various types of libido organisation', whereas for Fromm it is 'specific kinds of a person's relatedness to the world'.[20] In *The Fear of Freedom*, Fromm described social character as the 'essential nucleus shared by members of a group which has developed as a result of the basic experiences and mode of life common to that group'. It is the 'specific form in which human energy is shaped by the dynamic adaptation of human needs to the mode of existence of a given society'.[21] So, for Fromm, *social* character is the sum of more or less fixed traits shared by members of a group that impels them to orient their psychic energy in a manner conducive to the fulfilment of their goals. It is the mediating mechanism that facilitates 'the process of transforming general psychic energy into specific psychosocial energy'. Social character 'internalises external necessities and thus harnesses human energy for the tasks of a given economic and social system'.[22]

Character is what drives or at least conditions us to act in specific, at times predictable, ways. The miser doesn't reflect on whether to save or spend but is driven to hoard; the exploitative character is driven by the urge to exploit; and the sadistic character cannot help but take pleasure in controlling and hurting.[23] Fromm also describes the productive character who strives to share, to look after, to love. Of course, these are all abstract schemes and real human beings are formed of different and contradictory mixes of these basic psycho-social ingredients. In his later work, *Man For Himself*, Fromm describes what he takes to be the main types of social character in the modern industrial-capitalist world. In general, social character makes us 'want to do what we have to if the society is to function properly'.[24] The concept means that each type of society requires its members to internalise certain values, norms and ideas, the modes of thought and feeling, of action and relatedness, necessary for that group to fulfil its goals and function as it should. Social character is transmitted through the agency of the family and the education system, and reinforced by the mass media and the political system and, crucially, by individuals' work situation.

In Fromm's later work, *Social Character in a Mexican Village*, he gives the concept a more 'evolutionist' formulation: social character is described as 'a syndrome of character traits which has developed as an *adaptation* to the economic, social and cultural conditions common to that group' (my emphasis).[25] Fromm also believes that ideologies and culture are rooted in the social character. 'Ideas can become powerful forces, but only to the extent to which they are answers to specific human needs prominent in a given social character.'[26] He takes issue with those who believe that thinking is an 'exclusively intellectual act and independent of the psychological structure of the personality'.[27] The same analysis applies to our characteristic actions.

Fromm goes on to argue that 'while man is moulded by the necessities of the economic and social structure of society, he is not infinitely adaptable ... there are certain psychological qualities inherent in man that need to be satisfied and that result in certain reactions if they are frustrated'.[28] The 'character-system'

> has been formed in response to the total social configuration; however, this response is not an arbitrary one but conditioned by the nature of man, which determines the ways in which human energy can be channelled. The system-character is the relatively permanent form in which human energy is structuralised in the process of relating to others and of assimilating nature.[29]

Fromm is stressing that the 'nature of man' imposes certain constraints on the possible variation of character traits or types of social character. This refers back to the previous chapters where I argued that the most basic feature of humankind is that of a social being.

In his early work Fromm describes the relationship between character and society as a two-way process: 'man reacts to changing external situations by changes in himself, and ... these psychological factors in their turn help in moulding the economic and social process'. In this way, the dominant character traits become productive forces shaping the social process.[30] Fromm and Maccoby take this a step further, using the Marxist term 'mode of production'. They believe that the most important conditioning factor in the creation of social character, the context in which it is shaped, is the mode of production. The aim of their Mexican study is 'to analyse the interrelations and interactions between [the peasant's] emotional attitudes rooted in his character and the socio-economic conditions under which he lives ... the peasant's mode of production is highly individualistic'.[31] The authors argue that 'there is no "society" in general ... there exist only specific social structures ... each society and class demands different kinds of functions from its members. The mode of production varies from society to society and from class to class.'[32] In Part Two, I suggest how we may apply the notion of 'social character' to the specific cases of genocide.

Two initial criticisms: quite often, Fromm and Maccoby slip into mechanistic or dualistic formulations, writing as though the mode of production and social character are external to each other, the one determining the other, like cause and effect. One can agree that social character is part of the mode of production, a productive force in its own right. However, like the other productive forces, it is shaped by human beings acting collectively through their labour, in this case at least partly unconscious. It is the product of the formation and maintenance of a particular society or class within it. Arising out of this problem is the second criticism: Fromm doesn't make clear the class origins and class nature of social character, its roots in the self-activity of a rising class or of one that resists oppression. To say it is a product of the mode of production smacks of 'structural' Marxism, according to which institutional structures are independent of the human beings that created them. The implication is that the social character of a class develops automatically in response to given or changing socio-economic conditions, behind the backs of real, living human beings. We need to remind ourselves of Marx's third thesis on Feuerbach: 'The materialistic doctrine concerning the change of circumstances and education forgets that circumstances are changed by men and that the educator must himself be educated.'[33]

Non-Productive Social Characters

Fromm differentiates between 'productive' and 'non-productive' social characters or 'character orientations'. The non-productive orientations are of four types: the receptive, the exploitative, the hoarding, and the marketing.[34]

(a) In the receptive orientation, the 'person feels the source of all good to be outside' and that the only way of getting what they need, whether it be a material item, affection, knowledge, pleasure is to receive it from the outside.

Such a person feels a certain optimism about the world, and has a strong sense of loyalty. But they are plagued by a sense of powerlessness.

(b) In the exploitative orientation, there is a similar sense that the source of all good is outside, not in oneself. Such people share with those having a receptive orientation a dependence on the outside world, but they differ from them in their lack of belief in its benevolence. They don't feel they will be given the things they need, and they therefore have to steal them, whether it is love, ideas or material things.

(c) Whereas the two previous orientations resemble each other in believing that the source of all things good is outside themselves, the hoarding orientation is based on the opposite feeling. There is nothing positive to be obtained from the external world. Hence, their sole security lies in hoarding and saving, with spending felt to be a threat. Key character features here are obsessive cleanliness and orderliness.

(d) The marketing orientation, omitted from the study of the Mexican village, is a specifically modern type of social character. The modern market differs from its pre-modern ancestor. The latter was characterised by barter between sellers and buyers enjoying a face-to-face relationship at the local level. The former 'is no longer a meeting-place, but a mechanism characterised by abstract and impersonal demand. One produces for this market, not for a known circle of customers; its verdict is based on laws of supply and demand; and it determines whether the commodity can be sold and at what price.'[35] The impersonal market has had a profound influence on the social character of the middle class, and, through their cultural influence, on the working class. In today's globalised world, one sees the overwhelming domination of the abstract market affecting the character orientation of the controllers of industry and finance. The celebrity culture we suffer from today is a further symptom of the same phenomenon.

This market concept of value, the predominance, in Marx's terms, of exchange-value over use-value, has profoundly affected our experience of ourselves. In recent decades, we have seen the huge growth and intensification of the 'personality market'. To sell the product, one is simultaneously required to sell oneself. It is not enough to possess the skill and equipment necessary to carry out a given task. The need to project one's personality in competition with many others fundamentally shapes our attitude towards ourselves. With the rise of modern capitalism, human beings increasingly experience themselves as commodities, as both the seller and the object to be sold.[36] As Fromm explains: 'if one feels that one's own value is not constituted primarily by [one's] human qualities ... but by one's success on a competitive market with ever-changing conditions, one's self-esteem is bound to be shaky and in constant need of confirmation by others'.[37] Moreover, the way we experience ourselves shapes the way we perceive others. They, too, are seen as commodities to be bought and sold. In an echo of Marx's concept of 'reification' – the reduction of human beings and their relationships to things – Fromm argues that 'the difference between people is reduced to a merely quantitative difference of being more or less successful, attractive, hence valuable'.[38] I will develop this theme to see how it relates to the analysis of genocide in the next chapter.

The Destructive Character

In his final work, Fromm provides a detailed analysis of the destructive social character. As indicated in Chapter 2, it appears in two forms, sadism and necrophilia. Sadism is 'the passion to have absolute and unrestricted control over a living being'. One manifestation, though not the only one, is that of forcing someone to endure pain or humiliation without them being able to defend themselves.[39] Fromm also describes sadism as 'the transformation of impotence into the experience of omnipotence ... the religion of psychic cripples'.[40] There is, of course, a close connection between sadism and masochism, though one or the other will be dominant in a particular individual. This psychological character also finds expression as a political attitude, when it becomes 'the authoritarian character': 'control of those below and submission to those above'.[41]

Fromm describes the necrophiliac character as the 'passionate attraction to all that is dead, decayed, putrid ... the passion to transform that which is alive into something unalive; to destroy for the sake of destruction'.[42] 'It is the passion "to tear apart living structures."'[43] Clinical data, including dream analysis, indicate an affinity between the anal-hoarding character and necrophilia, given the latter's preoccupation with faeces, the symbolic expression of decay. However, there is a difference between sadism and necrophilia: where necrophiliacs want to destroy, sadists want total control.[44] Theweleit argues that Fromm overstates the link between necrophilia and corpses, for example in his description of Hitler as 'a necrophiliac character'.[45] According to Theweleit, quoting Canetti, Hitler 'loves his own life ... for its ability to survive'.[46] 'Corpses piled upon corpses reveal him as a victor, a man who has successfully externalised that which is dead within him, who remains standing when all else is crumbling.'[47] Hence, 'a corpse is not necessarily the most important thing'.[48] Theweleit describes the case of a 28-year-old medical student who fantasised about having sex with a dead or dying woman, believing 'I can do anything I want with her.'[49] However, Theweleit is here surely conflating necrophilia and sadism: on the one hand, the urge 'to tear apart living structures' expressing the perversion of the drive to life, and, on the other, the desire for total power. Arguably, Hitler suffered from both. Finally, as we noted in Chapter 2, Anna Freud's concept of identification with the aggressor helps us understand the unconscious, paranoid process by which destructive urges are projected on to the victims.

The Productive Social Character

In contrast to non-productive character orientations, the 'productive' social character has an affinity with Freud's concept of the genital stage of development where a person has developed the capacity for natural production: the union of sperm and egg results in the creation of new life. As regards personality, the productive character refers to our ability to use our powers and to realise the potentialities inherent in us. It means that we experience ourselves as the embodiment of our powers, that they are not masked or alienated from us. As Rainer Funk describes it: it 'is to be a *social* being and thus to be related to others and to oneself in a way that is oriented towards the development of love, reason, and productive work'.[50]

Moreover, as early as the 1930s Fromm contributed to the development of a new psychoanalytical paradigm based on the notion of 'intersubjectivity' – seeing 'the individual in the context of his prior relationship to others ... [transcending] a view that the individual is a self-sufficient being only secondarily related to others'.[51] According to this 'relational' approach, 'society is nothing but living, concrete individuals, and the individual can live only as a social human being'.[52] There would appear to be an affinity with the object-relations school and possibly with the Kleinian school, though Fromm would certainly disagree with the idea of a universal death instinct.

Rainer Funk, Fromm's literary executor, distinguishes between two kinds of aggression: firstly, the kind that is necessary for the self-preservation of the individual, whether this be defence against threats or the kind of 'aggressive behaviour ... crucial to the psychic development of the human being', the kind that has 'a life-preserving and growth-promoting function'; and, secondly, the kind where there are perpetrators and victims, that is, violence against those who cannot defend themselves, 'directed toward a defenceless victim or pursuing the aim of making a person defenceless'.[53] It is clearly the second kind which is relevant to human cruelty and destructiveness, since making a person defenceless is part of what is involved in reducing them to an object, or commodifying them, an important element in genocide, as we shall see in Chapter 4.

Assimilation and Socialisation

There are two processes forming social character: the process of assimilation of things and that of socialisation. Human beings relate to the world in two ways, firstly, by acquiring and assimilating things (assimilation), and secondly, by relating to other people and ourselves (socialisation). Both modes of relatedness to the world, to nature and society, are 'open' in the sense of not being instinctively determined. Regarding the first, humankind 'can acquire things by receiving or taking them from an outside source or by producing them through [their] own efforts. But [they] must acquire and assimilate them in some fashion in order to satisfy [their] needs.' Humans also have 'to associate with others for defence, for work, for sexual satisfaction, for play, for the upbringing of the young, for the transmission of knowledge, and for material possessions'. In general, we need others. 'Complete isolation is unbearable and incompatible with sanity.'[54]

As for the process of socialisation, the ways we relate to others, Fromm and Maccoby distinguish four types: (1) symbiotic relatedness, (2) withdrawal-destructiveness, (3) narcissism, and (4) love. In symbiotic relatedness, 'the person ... loses or never attains his independence; he avoids the danger of aloneness by becoming part of another person, either by being "swallowed" by that person or by "swallowing" him'. The former is described as the core of clinical masochism. The latter, the 'sadistic' impulse to completely dominate another person, is 'the essence of symbiotic relatedness'. Crucially, 'it is rooted in and compensates for deep – and often unconscious feelings of ... powerlessness'.[55]

The second type of relatedness is withdrawal-destructiveness: 'the feeling of individual powerlessness can be overcome by withdrawal from others who are experienced as threats ... Its emotional equivalent is the feeling of indifference toward others, often accompanied by a compensatory feeling of self-inflation.' Destructiveness, which is qualitatively different from sadism, 'is an extreme form of withdrawal; the impulse to destroy others follows from the fear of being destroyed by them and from a hatred for life'.[56] The authors, however, don't explore the roots of these forms of relatedness within the family and society, or their psychological nature, such as the extent to which the fear of others is the result of projection, as in Klein's 'paranoid-schizoid' position (see Chapter 2, pp. 46–7). Also, it is not clear why withdrawal and destructiveness are lumped together, as though they were two aspects of a single type of non-productive relatedness. Arguably, there is a form of destructiveness that is not an expression of withdrawal but has different emotional roots and a different objective. Narcissism is described as a third type of withdrawal, which has both normal and pathological manifestations. Nor do they examine the relationship between these types of relatedness and the different social characters. Arguably, each social character contains within itself, or is made up of, a specific mode or modes of relating to others. Taking the exploitative character as an example, the relationship between a capitalist and the workers he/she exploits is likely to be one of emotional detachment or withdrawal.

In contrast to non-productive forms of relatedness – symbiosis, withdrawal, destructiveness, narcissism – there is one type of productive relatedness: love, both of others and of oneself. Love 'implies responsibility, care, respect, and knowledge, and the wish for the other person to grow and develop. It is the expression of intimacy between two human beings under the condition of the preservation of each other's integrity.'[57] In addition to Klein, Anna Freud's work is important for illuminating the unconscious mechanisms, such as projection, by which victims of destructiveness are targeted. As we saw, the latter's concept of 'identification with the aggressor' (see Chapter 2, p. 50) indicates how oppressed groups identify with their persecutors and the latter's destructiveness, and seek to project it and the accompanying guilt onto new victim groups.[58]

Socio-Political Orientations

Closely related to the forms of relatedness just discussed are four 'socio-political orientations' – the authoritarian, traditional, democratic, and revolutionary. Firstly, the authoritarian character orientation is that of

> a person whose sense of strength and identity is based on a symbiotic subordination to authorities, and at the same time, a symbiotic domination of those submitting to his authority ... The authoritarian character feels himself strong when he can submit and be part of an authority which ... is inflated ... and when ... he can inflate himself by incorporating those subject to his authority.[59]

Fromm and Maccoby stress that there are differences within the range of the authoritarian character depending on the degree of sadism (or masochism) it contains.

They relate these various degrees of authoritarianism to social class, in particular to the socio-economic functions of different classes. When a class has a productive role in a society, such as the Western middle classes in the nineteenth century, or the peasant class in twentieth-century Mexico, there is a low admixture of sadomasochistic authoritarianism. In contrast, when a class has lost its productive function, and, moreover, is being destroyed economically and socially, such as the German middle class after the First World War, or the poor whites in the American Deep South, there is likely to be a high admixture of sadomasochism.

In contrast, the 'traditional authoritarian' is not sadomasochistic but conforms to traditional patterns in his or her emotional outlook and behaviour. The traditional person accepts the existing social system, including the notions that those in power deserve respect, that children should obey their parents, and so on. However, he or she does not accept that might is right, nor is his or her identity based on an identification with the rich and powerful. Fromm and Maccoby describe the kind of middle path trodden by the 'traditionalist': 'The traditional pattern of relationships gives him a sense of ... security and meaning, but he could probably accept a new social consensus as long as it did not threaten his life or livelihood.'[60]

The third socio-political orientation is the democratic. The democratic person believes in respect for human rights, his or her own and those of others, because we are all equally human. S/he wants freedom to pursue his or her own goals and desires that others should have the same freedom. Decisions affecting the community should be made by all its members, taking into account their needs and wishes.[61]

Finally, the main impulse of the revolutionary orientation (seen as a characterological, not a political concept) is to seek to liberate life and society from the obstacles that block their growth and ability to flourish. Fromm distinguishes the revolutionary from the rebel: the latter is motivated by hatred and seeks vengeance, whereas the former seeks to create a better world and is able to criticise the existing one from the standpoint of reason and humanity.[62]

All these forms of relatedness and social characters are 'ideal-types', arguably in Max Weber's sense. One constructs a theoretical model and then assesses how far it conforms to reality. Actual individuals are not made up of a single character but are usually a blend, with perhaps one character dominant.[63] Fromm does make clear that these character orientations describe the emotional outlook of specific cultures or social classes and emerge under certain historical conditions. So, for example, the exploitative character goes back to piratical and feudal ancestors and from there to the robber barons of the nineteenth century who exploited the natural resources of the continent.[64] Strangely, Fromm does not mention the new class of industrial capitalists, the Gradgrinds of nineteenth-century Britain who herded the workers into the new factories, setting them to work in the new context of socialised mechanical labour. Moreover, his analysis of the origins of the hoarding character is not quite accurate: its roots lay in the early capitalist need to accumulate, to re-invest, and refrain from excessive consumption. Without this, and given the level of development of society's productive forces at that historical juncture, there would not have been sufficient funds to reinvest so as to develop industrial production. As Marx put it: 'Accumulate, accumulate. That is Moses and the prophets.'[65]

Exploitation and hoarding were inextricably intertwined – without exploitation, there would have been no economic surpluses for reinvestment, and without investment funds, there could have been no exploitation. So while Gradgrind typifies the exploitative character, Scrooge exemplifies the hoarding orientation. But each contains an element of the other and both were necessary to the development of industrial capitalism. More generally, Fromm doesn't relate these social character types to the individualism of modern capitalism, seen as both ideology and psychology. Arguably, however, the possessiveness, competitiveness and ambition at the heart of the individualist personality that emerged in sixteenth- and seventeenth-century Europe were the essence of the exploitative and hoarding character traits. But there was surely an admixture of productiveness in the early capitalist character, without which the rising middle class would not have been able to create a new social order. Fromm concludes that a 'combination of a stable world, stable possessions, and a stable ethic gave ... the middle class a feeling of belonging, self-confidence and pride'.[66]

The marketing social character is a more modern orientation. Today, in the age of globalisation, we are used to social commentators bemoaning the marketisation of life, the importance of packaging, the projection of the brand name. Fromm pointed to this phenomenon in the late 1940s. Under monopoly capitalist conditions, particularly as these developed after the Second World War, there are few opportunities for the lone individual to succeed through their own efforts in the economic marketplace. Overwhelmingly, the ambitious person has to become part of a large organisation, to fit into its structure and ambience, cooperate smoothly, play the expected role. Fromm described this type succinctly: 'What is the "social character" suited to twentieth century capitalism? It needs men who cooperate smoothly in large groups; who want to consume more and more, and whose tastes are standardised and can be easily influenced and anticipated.'[67] Fromm's marketing character could thus also be described as the 'commodity or commodifying character'. But 'the depersonalisation, the emptiness, the meaninglessness of life, the automatisation of the individual result in a growing dissatisfaction and in a need to search for a more adequate way of living'.[68]

Empirical Verification

The notion of 'social character' is empirically verifiable. 'Just as psychoanalysis studies the character of an individual in terms of analysing the underlying forces which in a structuralised form make up his/her character and motivate him/her to feel and think in certain ways, the character common to a whole group, *social character*, has the same function and can be studied empirically.'[69] The method adopted by Fromm and Maccoby was the interpretative questionnaire. In the conventional questionnaire, 'the answers are taken as raw material or coded according to behavioural categories, and the task is to analyse them statistically, either simply in terms of the frequency of each single answer or ... by factor analysis, which shows clusters of answers found together with significant frequency'. The authors stress that in the interpretative questionnaire there is an additional element. This is the interpretation of the answers in psychoanalytical terms, that is, attempting to grasp their hidden, unintended or unconscious meaning by attending to 'the very small details of his expressions and formulations, the precise words he uses, or in the contradictions, unconscious to him, between the various statements, or in the unwarranted over-emphasis of the one or the other feeling'.[70]

On the basis of their empirical approach, Fromm and Maccoby conclude that the social character of the Mexican villagers is of three kinds. The most frequent is the non-productive-receptive, whose key element is that 'security and individual progress is not gained primarily on the basis of achievement and competence, as in modern society, but rather on the basis of total loyalty to the superior in return for the hope that the superior will do favours for and protect the inferior'.[71] This orientation is rooted in, and is a hangover of, the semi-feudal hacienda which dominated the Spanish empire, and before it the Aztec empire, for hundreds of years. In this system, serfs or peons were fixed in the socio-economic structure for life, totally dependent on their masters, and powerless to change their circumstances. This peasant remains submissive, feeling hopeless and ground down by life.[72]

Secondly, the productive-hoarding orientation makes up 30 per cent of the villagers – 22 per cent of the men, 39 per cent of the women. This character is typically independent, resourceful, creative even, but also cautious, methodical and tenacious.[73] The agricultural labour undertaken by the free peasant allows for, even requires, a degree of activeness and thought missing from, for example, assembly-line work. The peasant must decide which crops to plant and in caring for his animals he must respond to life and to nature.[74]

Thirdly, 10 per cent of the villagers belong to the dominantly exploitative character type, but this number increases to 25 per cent when one adds in those with secondary exploitative traits. This category divides into two sub-groups: the productive-exploitative entrepreneurs and the unproductive-exploitative individuals. The latter are the small number of aggressive, egocentic peasants, that is, those with a destructive character – the men who get into fights. The former are 'the modern entrepreneurs who have been the first to exploit the new opportunities of capitalism.'[75] Fromm and Maccoby stress that

> each main character type is moulded by and adaptive to distinctive socio-economic conditions. The receptive character was formed by the conditions of the hacienda. The productive-hoarding character is adapted to traditional, small-scale agriculture. The productive-exploitative character is adapted to the new, industrialising society and to capitalism.[76]

Productive-hoarding is the character best suited to the village mode of production. We have already pointed to the somewhat mechanical view implied by this formulation: 'socio-economic conditions' are not created by God or nature but are the product of human activity, conscious or unconscious. Fromm and Maccoby make clear that the incubation of social character takes place within the family. There are three main periods of emotional development when the child adapts to the conditions of life, especially the parents' socio-economic class, and to their psychological pressures and cultural expectations. These are infancy (roughly birth to two), early childhood (two to six), and middle childhood to adolescence (six or seven to 13 or 14). 'By the age of 13 or 14, the process of adaptation – to the parents and the requirements of work – has resulted in the formation of the child's mode of assimilation, in the degree of productiveness, and in the quality of submissiveness.'[77] Fromm and Maccoby studied children's emotional development by questioning them at the different stages of growth. The key finding was that productive children 'are more likely to have parents who are loving, productive and economically successful. Unproductive children are more likely to have unproductive parents.'[78]

In summary, there are four kinds of evidence for the existence of social character:

(a) Sociological or socio-psychoanalytical survey evidence: Fromm's studies of the German working class and of the Mexican village; McKenzie's analysis of the English working class deference voter; Goldthorpe and Lockwood's studies of 'bourgeoisification' among car workers; and Altemeyer on the authoritarian personality.[79]

(b) Psychoanalytical: the works of Wilhelm Reich, Theodor Adorno et al., Erich Fromm, Henry Dicks and Heinz Kohut.

(c) Historical: studies of Puritanism, E.P. Thompson on Methodism.[80]

(d) Literary: realist novels which identify individual characters that are also social types – Dickens, Balzac, Dostoevsky's *Crime and Punishment*. Also Moliere's play *L'Avare* (*The Miser*).[81]

As regards the evidence for the existence of specific social character types that are a crucial part of the analysis of 'irrational' genocide, these will be looked at in the various case-studies in Part Two.

Others have similarly written about the modern experience and the ways in which it affects individuals' perceptions of themselves, their social character and relationships with others. The experience of modernity is that of constant change, of everything being in flux, of openness, possibility and excitement. Marx and Engels described how the bourgeoisie broke the traditional boundaries of the old, pre-capitalist society and dissolved the barriers preventing individuals and groups from developing a new world and realising a new potential: 'All that is solid melts into the air.' (This is the title, in addition, of Marshall Berman's important book.[82])

So the experience of modernity is that of unceasing change, while the only thing that is certain is uncertainty, the only thing that is stable is instability. The modern individual's experience is that of isolation, being cut off or alienated from others, being crushed by powerful, uncontrollable forces such as large corporations or an oppressive state, buffeted by the fluctuations of an impersonal, global market, terrorised by destructive military forces, unable to make sense of an absurd, bureaucratic and bewildering world. It is the world so graphically described in Franz Kafka's novels. Excitement and terror are the twin experiences of modernity. As Frosh writes:

> Modernity is characterised by uncertainty, rapidity of change and kaleidoscopic juxtapositions of objects, people and events. Finding our uncertain way through these uncertainties is a prime task of contemporary existence, for individuals as well as for cultures as a whole ... Specific patterns of existence may be linked with this modern state of affairs ... problematic structures in which the self is experienced as fragile and precarious.[83]

The effect of modernity on the individual is twofold. Firstly, alienation from others: individuals experience great difficulty establishing links with other people. Secondly, self-alienation: a sense of being cut off from any secure, stable inner self.

Freud's theory of the repression of biological drives was partly based on his experience of his patients' psychology. His middle-class neurotics had a sense of being controlled by passions they could barely perceive, let alone accept, a powerful flow of inner desires constantly threatening to burst their dams. But, for Frosh, the modern experience is quite different. For Freud, although society makes people unhappy by denying them their deepest wishes, it is nevertheless benevolent since it protects the individual against the dangers posed by nature, by what would otherwise be the uncontrolled impulses of others. However, self-control is no longer the issue. The real problem that has emerged is not what happens at a purely personal level but the gap between the individual and others. Controlling one's passions doesn't bear on the central difficulty of modern society. This is, as Frosh puts it:

> moving out from oneself to make real links with others ... The contemporary perception seems to be not that people's desires are too deep and powerful to be fully controllable, but that people are too shallow to feel anything much at all − neither desire nor responsibility. The great 'getting in touch with oneself' fashions of the 1960s gave way to despair when ... it became clear that there was nothing much with which to get in touch. Nothing, that is, except a terrifying sense of personal dissolution and an anger at the conditions that had produced this universal, inner desert. So society is experienced not just as repressive ... but also as ... a mirage; the relationship between self and other is non-existent, a gap reflecting both a lack of social ties and an internal, alienated absence.[84]

One derives a strong sense of this inner and outer alienation from the plays of Harold Pinter. Frosh, writing in 1991, argued that most psychoanalytical work in the US and the UK had been dominated by the object-relations approach, in which the focus is the object-relational quality – or lack of it – of the patients' relationships.[85]

The Culture of Narcissism

Christopher Lasch writes that every age develops its peculiar forms of pathology, which express in exaggerated form its underlying character structure. Our age's pathology is that of narcissistic and borderline (psychotic) states.[86] As we saw in Chapter 2, for Kohut as for Freud, 'narcissism is a normal developmental phase and the grandiose and idealising tendencies that inform narcissism have a respectable place in every infant's life. However when these tendencies are not negotiated successfully, the self grows in a distorted or partial way, stuck in part or whole at the infant phase.'[87]

For Kohut, parental failure is rooted in social conditions, in particular in the breakdown of those family structures the mother needs in order to empathise with her infant's grandiose needs. Frosh concludes:

> in a society in which everyone's selfhood is undermined by the rapidity of cultural, economic, and technological change, by uncertainty over who controls what (accompanied by a sense that someone or something is in control of each of us), by fascination with fantasies centred on interchangeable images, and by a severing of roots and traditions in the context of an increasing sameness of culture – in such a society it must become increasingly difficult to offer a stable and still point around which the personality of a child can be formed.[88]

Moreover, the child will be aware of the parent's anxiety and sense of alienation and thus internalise a parental image or self-object that is fragmented and incapable of providing the basis for a secure, stable, self-loving and loving self. An oppressive and narcissistic culture produces empty, alienated individuals who, in turn, reinforce the social pathology.

An interesting example is provided by Erik Erikson in his 'play cure' of a girl of three who had been having nightmares and violent anxiety attacks in her play group.[89] It emerged that her father was worried over a possible disruption of his work status, and had dealt her sexual curiosity a blow by telling her to stop her customary morning visits to him in the bathroom.[90] Erikson was able to help her act out through play her anxiety about her father's rejection as a result of which her nightmares ceased and there was a revived play relationship with her father. Erikson comments about the father that 'threatened loss of status, threatened marginality, often result in an unconscious attempt by more stringent self-control and by purified standards to regain the ground lost'.[91] This made the father frighten and offend his daughter by rejecting her sexual exploration. Erikson concludes: 'Thus do children reflect ... and ... carry over into their own lives, the historical and economic crises of their parents.'[92]

'Normal' everyday narcissists thrive in environments that reward the manipulation of others whilst penalising the more personally expensive formation of intimate and caring relationships. These environments are characteristic institutions of contemporary capitalism. Narcissistically disturbed individuals are but exaggerations of the normal successful 'type' in Western capitalism, revealing extreme versions of the contemporary alienated character. As we saw in Chapter 2, and as O. Kernberg explains: 'The main characteristics of these narcissistic personalities are grandiosity, extreme self-centredness and a remarkable absence of interest in and empathy for others in spite of the fact that they are so eager to obtain admiration and approval from other people.'[93] In all analytic descriptions of narcissistic pathology, accompanying this emphasis on grandiosity and mirror-fixation is a need to have this inflated image of self constantly reinforced by others. Underlying it, though, isn't self-confidence, but a desperate sense of emptiness and fragility, of a self always in danger of dissolution. The cost of such personal functioning is great: it both derives from and deepens distortions in the self that are experienced as painful or terrifying.

Culturally, 'narcissism' refers to the egocentricity and rampant individualism of modern capitalist consumer culture. Psychoanalytically, it results from a deep sense of emptiness at the heart of both contemporary culture and the individuals who are part of it.[94] According to this view of the modern state of mind, superficiality and the avoidance of intimacy are fundamental attitudes. The outside world is experienced as meaningless and our inner selves similarly as without depth, as a surface. So, narcissism takes off from its clinical base[95] and is used as a diagnosis of our collective experience and our culture: contemporary capitalism is a 'culture of narcissism'. The struggle to form a stable self and meaningful and trusting relationships with others can be extended. The conflicts we are all familiar with – road rage, for example – are part of a broader cultural trend and reflect the organisation of contemporary capitalism.

The problem again becomes that of whether it is legitimate to extrapolate from individual to social pathology. Can we speak of a social class, an ethnic group, or an entire society as suffering from a narcissistic (or other) disorder, for example, narcissistic rage? I want to put it the other way round, to argue, as in Chapter 1, that there are historical situations in which we can ascribe such a pathology to whole groups, indeed that individual pathology can only be explained in terms of the wider social pathology; moreover, that such social pathology is an essential component of our explanation of genocide. This (narcissistic) mode of personal functioning both reflects and deepens those cultural conditions that emphasise the image, the superficiality of things (including relationships) and the inter-changeability of objects. The latter is typical of a society based on commodity production, in which human labour power is also a commodity (I analyse Marx's concepts of commodity and commodification in Chapter 4).

Joel Kovel describes his narcissistic patients as feeling hatred for their parents but being too dependent to express it. The child was regarded by parents as an adornment, not a creature in his or her own right. This parental concern had a quality of capital invested for future yield.[96] Kovel argues that neither early tribal societies nor feudal nor nineteenth-century capitalist societies revealed this social type. It appears with the bourgeois family of late capitalism. The bourgeois age is the one in which childhood emerges for first time in history as a distinct category of existence. Pathological narcissism is what happens when the family is not merely centred on children but collapses on them as well, crushing them beneath its emotional weight. It is the specific disorder of late capitalism. Oliver James is another writer who has documented the destructive emotional effects of the narcissistic personality.[97] And a recent study reveals how 'narcissistic managers ... tend to rise to management positions ... in disproportionately large numbers. Being particularly self-absorbed, they are known to use (and abuse) their subordinates and play up to their superiors to assure their own personal career success.'[98]

What emerges from Fromm's analysis is that different, historically specific social characters fall into that branch of human nature which Marx describes as 'relative appetites'. We also saw that Fromm's analysis of the genesis of social character was in terms of a class or a whole society 'being impelled' to act in certain ways or 'adapting to' specific socio-economic conditions. However, because these formulations have a slightly mechanical or perhaps evolutionist ring, they don't quite grasp the true nature of these modes of behaviour as the actions or reactions of different classes within the historical contexts in which they find themselves. To re-visit Marx's famous quote: 'Men make their own history, but ... not ... under circumstances chosen by themselves.'[99] To fully understand Fromm's four social characters, and to use them as one important foundation stone of a Marxist psychoanalysis, they must be seen not just as the 'adaptations' by specific classes to, or the products of, the historical contexts in which they find themselves. These classes must also be viewed as creators or co-creators of those contexts. In other words, the origins and development of the different social characters must be seen in terms of the social and economic goals that specific classes set themselves, consciously or unconsciously, within the historical process, and of other classes' reactions to those goals. I want to argue, therefore, that Fromm's notion of social character needs expansion in three directions: human social creativity; the inculcation of a new social character; and class resistance and social character.

Human Social Creativity

As human beings, we create and transform ourselves through the process of labour. As we transform and develop our society and our relationship to nature, we also change our own human nature. Rising or emerging classes set themselves new goals, which include the creation of new tools or work equipment and a new labour process. But this process also includes the creation of new psychic forces capable of developing new productive forces and new ideas — ideas, therefore, not tied to the previous social order. Above all, it involves the creation of a new type of personality, one that fits the new labour process. New social forces, as they emerge through collective struggle, are potentially the bearers not only of a new ideology but also of a new psyche and social character, geared to the fulfilment of historically innovatory tasks in the social and economic spheres. Fromm and Maccoby expressed it well:

there is no society in general ... only specific social structures ... each society and class demands different kinds of functions from its members. A serf, a free peasant, an industrial worker in the nineteenth century and one in an automated society, an independent entrepreneur of the nineteenth century and an industrial manager of the twentieth century have different functions to fulfil ... The different social context demands that they relate themselves in different ways to equals, superiors and inferiors ... the industrial worker has to be disciplined and punctual, the nineteenth century bourgeois had to be parsimonious, individualistic and self-reliant; today, members of all classes, except the poor, have to work in teams, and they must wish to spend and to consume new products.[100]

The exploitative and hoarding social characters developed as the emotional underpinnings of the rising bourgeoisie as they created the new industrial capitalist society. To guarantee the process of capital accumulation undertaken by the rising middle classes from the seventeenth to the nineteenth centuries, a specific type of social character had to be produced, one that willingly subordinated consumption to saving and accumulation, and in which an 'anal-hoarding' emphasis, to use Fromm's description, predominated within their psychic formation.

Inculcation of a New Social Character

In order to guarantee their social supremacy, new social classes instil into the new or existing subordinate classes not only a specific ideology but also a new set of emotional features, that is, a new social character. This is necessary if they are to preserve and consolidate their rule. In other words, ruling classes, whether emerging or established, have to create and maintain, first, a ruling ideology, that is, a culture including a system of values, but also a psychic structure and social personality that they are able to impose on society as a whole. This is necessary if the purposes of their class are to be carried out and their political hegemony safeguarded. Reich and Lichtman emphasise this point. Jacoby put it slightly differently: 'the form of individuality that prevails in the bourgeoisie is not confined to the bourgeoisie; rather it seeps into the proletariat and cripples the process of the proletariat which seeks to constitute itself as the historical subject'.[101] To express it more concretely, we need to understand how ruling classes, through their conscious and unconscious political, ideological and psychological activities, are able to inculcate submission.

However, the new social character which the rising or dominant class create in themselves is not necessarily the same as that which they instil into the exploited or subordinate class. As we saw earlier, the exploitative and hoarding orientations were typical of the rising industrial capitalist class, but hardly of the new working class who had nothing to hoard. The new classes of exploiters and exploited were both expected to exercise discipline, but in the case of the latter – until they entered into struggle, formed trade unions, and so on – their emotional life would fluctuate between the passivity that flows from religious millenarianism and outbursts of rage as expressed, for example, in the Gordon Riots of 1780. E.P. Thompson, in his classic work *The Making of the English Working Class*, helps us understand how a new work discipline was imposed on the burgeoning working class. He identified Methodism as the key factor mediating between class and psyche, the ideological mechanism by which a new, authoritarian social character was instilled into them. 'This weakened the poor from within, by adding to them the active ingredient of submission; and they [the Methodist leaders] fostered within the Methodist Church those elements most suited to make up the psychic component of the work-discipline of which the manufacturers stood most in need.'[102] Thompson also takes a leaf out of Fromm: 'men came to be driven to work not so much by external pressure but by an internal compulsion ... The inner compulsion was more effective in harnessing all energies to work than any outer compulsion can ever be ... man was turned into his own slave-driver.'[103]

In pre-Weimar Germany, the old ruling class transmitted part of its social character – its authoritarianism – to the old middle class. As Fromm argued, before 1914,

> the social character of the old middle class was markedly different from that of the working class, of the higher strata of the middle class, and of the nobility ... their love of the strong, hatred of the weak, their pettiness, hostility, thriftiness with feelings as well as with money, and essentially their asceticism. Their outlook on life was narrow ... their whole life was based on the principle of scarcity – economically as well as psychologically.[104]

But the old ruling class did not succeed in inculcating its authoritarianism into the German working class to anything like the same extent. In 1929–30, Fromm supervised a research project into the social character of a group of manual and white-collar workers. The result was a landmark study of social attitudes, and of the way these reveal character orientation. Fromm writes:

> To say that the social character of the lower middle class differed from that of the working class does not imply that this character structure was not present in the working class also. But it was *typical* for the lower middle class, while only a minority of the working class exhibited the same character structure in a similarly clear-cut fashion ... in a less intense form ... enhanced respect of authority or thrift was to be found in most members of the working class too.[105]

Fromm adds: 'Analysis of the responses of six hundred persons to a detailed questionnaire showed that a minority of the respondents exhibited the authoritarian character, that with about the same number the quest for freedom and independence was prevalent, while the great majority exhibited a less clear-cut mixture of different traits.'[106]

We need, then, to see a new society as the result of human collective labour and a new ideology, but also of a new social character. A new social character is not a product of *conscious* human effort. Rather does it occur as the product of what might perhaps be described as 'unconscious human labour'. (This notion would appear to echo aspects of Jung's work, but there is no space to explore this idea.)

Class Resistance and Social Character

An emerging or existing ruling class, however, is generally not wholly successful in inculcating the ideology and social character it requires the subordinate classes to possess. Subordinate classes fight back, and part of that resistance involves the creation of an alternative or opposing ideology and social character. There is a modification of the dominant social character as a necessary adaptation through the impact of the struggle of the exploited class. For example, the modern Western working classes organised themselves from the beginning of industrial capitalism into trade unions, at the heart of which lay values of solidarity and collective endeavour, in opposition to the bourgeois values of individual ambition and competition. Reformism is the ideological and political expression of this compromise. Arguably, through its struggles, the early industrial working class developed a more extroverted, 'other-directed' social character than that possessed by their capitalist masters.

Nevertheless, exploited and oppressed classes cannot be completely successful in their attempts to create alternative ideological and psychic structures. This can only be finally achieved with the overthrow of the old order and its replacement by a new one. But the class struggle results in the creation of a complex character type, obviously containing a substantial component of the old psyche, as witnessed by the survival of the old deferential 'they're born to rule' attitude among sections of the working class, but also throwing up something new, a mixed collective psychic force that challenges the existing rulers. Defeat can set back the struggle for a new society and a new social character, or simply for reforms – as witnessed by the defeats of the British and American working classes in the 1980s, defeats which resulted in less confident and less assertive labour movements. Thompson quotes Karl Mannheim in relation to the defeats of the 1790s: 'the Chiliastic optimism of the revolutionaries ultimately gave birth to the ... conservative attitude of resignation'.[107] And as suggested in the Introduction, the failure of German middle class to overthrow the feudal landed nobility during the 1848 revolution was a factor enabling the latter to impose their authoritarian character structure on the former with dire consequences during the massive social and economic crises of the twentieth century. (This will be explored further in Chapter 7.)

The success or failure of a class to break through the barriers of the old order results either in its creating a new social character or in its adoption or reinforcement of the old ruling class social character. The Russian workers who carried out the 1917 revolution transformed themselves in significant ways, as Trotsky, John Reed and Victor Serge attested. As Kovel notes, 'the so-called "mental apparatus" has to be something that is evolving as humanity itself evolves ... the psyche is as much a historical as it is a biological entity'.[108] Lichtman developed a similar theme with his concept of the 'structurally repressed unconscious', or 'Marxist unconscious'. He argues that social 'structures are the relations that men and women sustain and reproduce in regards to nature and the system of their own interdependence'. These become independent of their creators, standing over them as alien and malignant forces. Clearly, social structures are sustained not merely by the rules of the system, enforced externally, but through the tendency of the agents themselves 'to reproduce the deepest aspects of character necessary to the continued maintenance of the social system'.[109] Or as he describes it, echoing both Reich and Fromm, 'every system of production creates both the structure of value and the appropriate characterology to sustain and reproduce its particular condition'.[110]

Fromm has been criticised for being a moralist; in particular, that his concept of 'productive character' confuses analytical with ethical categories, perceiving and depicting our human reality not as it is, but as he would like it to be. The conflating of analysis and moral imperatives leads to a quasi-religious image of human beings. Now, in his later period, Fromm was increasingly drawn to Zen Buddhism as a non-theistic religion, and on the face of it, some of his pronouncements do smack of religious Messianism. Thus, Maccoby talks of the two voices of Fromm, the analytic and the prophetic. He argues that where Fromm is analysing social character orientations such as marketing or hoarding, he is being genuinely analytical; but when it comes to the productive character, analysis gives way to moral prescription or evaluation. Fromm is guilty of what, in philosophical parlance, is called the 'naturalistic fallacy', mixing *what is* with *what ought to be*.[111] In a similar vein, Paul Robinson, in his review of Fromm's *Anatomy of Human Destructiveness*, refers to his weakness for 'uplifting but unpersuasive generalisations about love, justice, creativity and life. He also posits fine-sounding but dubious psychological propensities, such as "the need for a goal" or "the need for a frame of orientation and devotion".'[112]

Yet there are two arguments against this line of criticism. First, analysis and evaluation are not nearly as distinct as philosophers, especially those schooled in the empiricist or positivist traditions, have made out. Scientists themselves select areas for investigation, or hypotheses for testing, on the basis of a personal evaluation, which can have various sources including subjective preference. Lucien Goldmann captured the spirit of such a dialectical method in discussing Marx's approach to religion: 'Marx condemns simultaneously the social order and the religion which is a part of it. He does not "blend" a judgment with an objective analysis, but, as throughout his work, makes a dialectical analysis in which understanding, explanation and evaluation are strictly inseparable.'[113] In the case of Fromm's 'productive orientation', it is perfectly legitimate to imagine or create social conditions which would facilitate the emergence of such a character, and then to seek verification of its existence in history or through social experiment or political innovation.

Secondly, these critics of Fromm have arguably failed to understand the dialectical character of his discourse. They argue from within an empiricist understanding of the world, thus failing or refusing to locate his ideas in the dialectical tradition established by Hegel and Marx. According to the latter, however, the real is not just what is out there, visible and testable, it is also the potential. Concepts such as 'the productive orientation' are thus derived from a particular philosophy of humankind, a view of the latter as social beings. Under capitalism, they are, in Marx's language, alienated from their 'species-being', but in a socialist world they are potentially capable of recapturing their social essence, or at least approximating to it. This potentiality is not something whose existence we can establish under laboratory conditions. We can nevertheless point to its reality through assessments of the almost infinite number of ways in which, historically, human beings have bonded with each other. In the end, however, such a potentiality can only be realised through political action.

There are two, more serious, criticisms of Fromm, put forward by Marcuse and his followers in a famous debate in the mid-1950s.[114] The first is that he abandoned Freud's libido theory and thus effectively psychoanalysis itself. On this view, in his attempts to create a Marxist social psychology, Fromm jettisoned Freud's notions of Eros, our biologically based sexual and life drives, and of unconscious motivation and repression, replacing them at the centre of his theory with his concept of social character. Since the latter is fundamentally shaped by the socio-economic environment, that is, by the emotional and ideological pressures derived from the family and society, it belongs more properly to social theory or political sociology. In short, by stripping away Freud's key concepts, Fromm 'sociologised' psychoanalysis out of the equation. As Marcuse put it: 'the weakening of the psychoanalytic conception, and especially of the theory of sexuality, must lead to a weakening of the sociological critique and to a reduction of the social substance of psychoanalysis.'[115] By rejecting Freud's most radical notions, Fromm objectively became a social conformist.

Secondly, Marcuse argues that Fromm's description of the 'productive character' is utopian and open to similar criticism. Fromm proclaims the need for

the optimal development of a person's potentialities and the realisation of his individuality ... [reviving] all the time-honoured values of idealistic ethics ... Fromm ... speaks of the productive realisation of the personality, of care, responsibility, and respect for one's fellow men, of productive love and happiness as if man could actually practise all this and still remain sane and full of 'well-being' in a society which [he] himself describes as one of total alienation, dominated by the commodity relations of the 'market'.[116]

It is true, as Rickert points out, that with the publication of *The Fear of Freedom* in 1941, Fromm did abandon the libido theory. He had grasped that 'an account of character formation based in libido theory is essentially incompatible with the basic tenets of the Marx–Freud synthesis'.[117] In the Appendix to *The Fear of Freedom*, Fromm argued that only by explaining character in terms of interpersonal relationships rather than libidinal fixations

can Freud's characterological findings become fruitful for social psychology. As long as we assume, for instance, that the anal character, as it is typical of the European lower middle class, is caused by certain early experiences in connection with defecation, we have hardly any data that lead us to understand why a specific class should have an anal social character. However, if we understand it as one form of relatedness to others, rooted in the character structure and resulting from the experiences with the outside world, we have a key for understanding why the whole mode of life of the lower middle class, its narrowness, isolation, and hostility, made for the development of this kind of character structure.[118]

Fromm is saying two things here. First, there is such a 'thing' as a group or social character which cannot be seen as an aggregation of individual characters. Secondly, therefore, we cannot understand the characterological traits shared by members of such a group by probing into their early childhood experiences. We can only grasp their social character by analysing the network of social relationships entered into by the members of the group, the impact on them of the external world. In other words, their social character is the product of shared experiences of the socio-economic world in which they live and work. As Rickert says, 'Freud's characterology had been developed within the framework of an individual psychology. Thus, while it could – in principle ... explain the individual's character structure in terms of libido theory, it found it much more difficult to give an adequate account of *social* character.'[119] In other words, Freud could not answer the question as to why a particular social class had developed a certain social character. Taking, for example, the anal character of the European lower middle class, Freud would have to assume that anal fixation had developed as a result of the ways in which defecation had been experienced in childhood. But there is no way that Freud's individual theory could explain how most members of a *class* had come to experience a similar fixation.

Similarly, his individual approach did not equip him to answer the question whether the shared fixation was rooted in the position of that class in the external social world. Freud did not have the theoretical means of dealing with the notion that social character was formed by the socio-economic situation of the class whose members had come to share these traits. His emphasis was exclusively on childhood influences and he never considered the impact on character formation of the mode of production.[120] Marcuse does seem to have a point insofar as Fromm did espouse some decidedly naive, utopian notions. He was rightly scathing about Fromm's suggestion that a National Council of 50 Americans of impeccable integrity be constituted as the Voice of America and, backed by local groups, be collectively charged with changing society.[121] One can just imagine such a loose network of well-meaning but powerless individuals trying to take on the corporate giants of the oil, defence or pharmaceutical industries. Jacoby describes this 'revolution of hope' as a Walt Disney production.[122]

Fromm, however, replied to these criticisms with two counter-arguments. Firstly, that Marcuse was being undialectical, that capitalist alienation developed its own contradiction, its opposite, from within itself. 'If Marcuse were right, then indeed we would have to arrive at the conclusion that there is no place for love and happiness whatsoever in capitalistic society.' But this was an untenable black and white position. While contemporary capitalism is an alienated society in which the 'humanistic goals of life', those of happiness and individuality, are rarely realised, it doesn't follow that these qualities exist in no one, or that to encourage their practice means preaching adjustment to the existing society.[123] Secondly, in *The Sane Society*, published the same year, Fromm made clear that the complete overcoming of alienation and the self-recreation of human beings, through the adoption of a productive social character, required a social transformation, that it was only achievable through the creation of a 'communitarian socialist' society. Fromm's vision is essentially that of a workers' democracy, despite his naivety and haziness about the means of achieving it.[124]

Wolfenstein also criticised the notion of character structure or social character as developed by Reich and Fromm. He argues that 'social character' is not a genuinely social concept, but merely an aggregate of individual traits, unlike, say, Marx's notion of 'commodity' which encapsulates the totality of relations that make up the capitalist social structure. However, Wolfenstein acknowledges that 'social character' can be interpreted as a Weberian-style ideal-type, by which one constructs a hypothetical concept or model, proceeding to judge its conformity to reality by empirical testing. And as we have seen, Fromm went to considerable trouble subjecting his hypothetical social characters to empirical validation.[125] In the light of this development of Fromm's notion of social character, that is, its integration into a Marxist theoretical framework of class and class struggle, a question arises. What remains of Freud's original structure of the mind, its compartmentalisation into three 'sectors' – ego, super-ego, id – and the underlying division into conscious and unconscious? And what is the connection, if any, between Freud's mental typology and the concept of social character? We shall suggest tentative answers in Chapter 4.

CHAPTER FOUR

Killing 'Things'

Freud, as we have seen, attributed the widespread creation of neurosis to the repressive culture of sexual morality. In modern capitalism, this repression is clearly the product of the Protestant work ethic, famously analysed by Max Weber and R.H. Tawney. It instilled in the minds of the aspiring bourgeoisie, or rather they unconsciously instilled in themselves, the compulsion for work and achievement, an essential ingredient in the anal-compulsive character, a notion, as we saw, originally described by Freud and later developed by Reich and Fromm.[1]

Protestantism saw the human mind as a duality: a pure world of reason and virtue and an impure world of base instincts and passions. Its repression of the instincts by the forces of reason in a sense reflects the division between use-value and exchange-value. For Marx, as we saw in Chapter 3, the commodity is split into its use-value, as an object for use, created by specific, concrete human labour, and its exchange-value, its saleability or money-value from which all notion of concrete labour has been removed. In order for an object to become a commodity, it is necessary to 'abstract' from its use-value, that is, its character as an object to be consumed and enjoyed.

Modern capitalism, therefore, represses the use-value of objects, including human relationships and the human personality. As Schneider reminds us, for Marx, 'psychological relationships between human beings ... assume the form of their economic relations in capitalist commodity society, that is, the form of "abstract" exchange relationships'.[2] As we also saw in Chapter 3, Schneider argues in a similar vein about the commodification of our human physical and psychological features – our instincts and needs – which become as abstract as money. Regarded in this light, Freud's theory of repression is the psychological complement of, is symmetrical with, Marx's theories of alienation and the commodity.[3]

This dichotomy between pure and impure, reason and instinct, exchange-value and use-value, finds its equivalent or echo in Freud's split between ego and id. For the individual under capitalism, part of his/her psyche, the ego, is subjected to the abstract rationality of the world of commodities, where intrinsic value or use-value is lost and everything is translated into the formal equality of exchange-value. The other part, the id, is the underworld of passions and instincts, which must be repressed if capitalism is to function and which, therefore, becomes the locus of rebellion against the reifying ego.[4] 'The pathic gap, the dysfunction between "ego" and "id", which is the basis of neurosis, therefore comes into existence only in the course of the development of a capitalist mode of production which compels a progressive subsumption of any kind of spontaneity, emotion or instinct under the rationalism of capital.'[5]

Barry Richards has argued that Schneider's analysis 'presents a too direct and simple reflection of the mode of production in the mode of psychic formation'.[6] Lichtman argues similarly that Schneider conflates abstraction and repression. So, on the one hand, we have the abstraction that capitalism imposes on society – the capitalist's disinterest in *what* he sells – that is, its use-value – so long as it makes a profit, that is, has exchange-value. On the other hand, we have repression – the unconscious censorship of our instinctual needs and drives by the super-ego. However, for Lichtman, 'Schneider has a tendency to derive the characteristics of individual life *directly* from the most abstract features of the capitalist system.'[7]

But Schneider stresses that the clinical phenomenon of repression isn't identical with the economic and political phenomenon of 'abstraction of use-values and of the usable needs and satisfactions related thereto'. The abstraction of use-values – seeing a useful object merely as a source of profit – is 'the germinal political-economic cell of those processes of "abstraction" which Freud described with his concept of "instinctual repression"'. And, as we saw, he believes that 'a necessary connection exists between the degree of abstraction which (capitalist) commodity society has reached in the course of its history and its degree of social instinctual repression'.[8] The connection is indirect since the family acts as mediator between society and the individual. Also, Schneider wants to broaden the concept of repression to include social instincts and needs, since the 'money structure not only has deformed and perverted the sexual structure but the entire structure of social needs'.[9] This would seem to have an affinity with the ideas of Fromm.

The word 'repression' is used here in both a political and a psychological sense. Neurosis can thus also be conceived as the upsurge of hidden forces which refuse to be abstracted or reified out of existence, a rebellion against not only the super-ego, but also the social power, capitalism, whose internal representative it is. As Schneider says: 'If social contradictions cannot be resolved "progressively", by taking on the form of a class struggle, then they must be solved "regressively" by being repressed from consciousness, that is, by assuming the rigid form of neurosis.'[10]

Therefore, both the class structure of capitalism, and the class struggle, are reproduced within the mind of the individual.[11] The forces of repression, Freud's super-ego, represent the state censor, keeping the working class, represented by the id, in its place, whereas the ruling class 'inhabits' the ego, formal rationality, society's official consciousness or ideology. As regards the ego, perhaps it would be more accurate to say that at times of heightened class struggle it becomes disputed territory, the terrain on which the official ideology and social character are challenged by those of the subordinate class.

How does this advance the discussion of Freud's typology? We know that the ruling class of any society control not only the material means of production but also the mental means of production. Generally this is interpreted to mean the ideological and intellectual forces of society – the dominant ideas and values, but also their means of dissemination and inculcation into the minds of the subordinate classes. But drawing conclusions from the debates around Marxist psychoanalysis enables us to suggest that the ruling class, if it is to solidify and perpetuate its rule, must control the 'emotional or psychic means of production'. Simply put, it has to control the emotional lives of those over whom it rules. Going back to Freud's categories, this means that the 'ego' and 'super-ego' are for the most part the preserve of the ruling class. As we know, the ego is the rational 'part' of the mind, the 'part' that relays back to the individual society's demands, its prevailing ideas and norms, as defined by the ruling class. The super-ego is, of course, the censor or conscience, the force repressing the outward expression, the acting out, of forbidden drives. The id is, then, the repository of those prohibited drives themselves. I have argued, following the Marxist view of human nature, that humans are essentially social beings, but that capitalist society requires human beings to be competitive and individualistic. So what has happened to our social nature? Has it shrivelled, so that its expression is limited to family life, to parents' love for their children, to the love of a man and a woman, or, perhaps, to organisations such as trade unions and charities? Isn't it the case that capitalism succeeds in distorting the human personality, in suppressing our inherently social nature? If so, how does it achieve this?

It is not outlandish to suggest that whereas the ego 'contains' or is the force that drives the ruling ideology and dominant social character elements, the id is the force that drives our most basic nature – our sociality. This, of course, leaves the super-ego as the censor that represses this sociality in the interests of the ruling class. For they require society's members to behave and feel towards themselves and others in the manner that promotes their interests. In other words, the role of the super-ego is to ensure that most members of society have a similar ego and to repress any counter-ideology or social character that conflicts with the dominant ones.

Returning to the issue of destructiveness, we need to address the dual nature of Freud's id. It is the source of our life drive, including both our sexuality and our sociality. On the other hand, pursuing the implications of Freud's notion of 'displaceable energy', our potential for destructiveness is also located in the id, which remains, however, mainly the repository of life-energy and life drives. On this model, destructiveness implies the overpowering of the ego and super-ego by the id. Should we not suggest, therefore, that there are two kinds of id, or rather that it can take two different forms? There is the 'normal', positive aggressivity of our life drive, including the sex drive, or our normal life-energy as displayed, for example, in work or love; but there is also the negative, destructive kind of aggression. These represent the dual nature of the id as it displays its capacity for morphing from the one type to the other, somewhat in the manner of Dr Jekyll turning into Mr Hyde and back, or a normal cell turning into a cancerous one. Under different historical conditions, one or the other will predominate. As suggested in Chapter 2, Freud has something similar in mind when he writes: 'We have reckoned as though there existed in the mind – whether in the ego or in the id – a displaceable energy, which, indifferent in itself, can be added to a qualitatively differentiated erotic or destructive impulse.'[12] Fromm and Maccoby also put it well: 'Destructiveness is the perversion of the drive to live; it is the energy of unlived life transformed into energy for the destruction of life.'[13]

Wolfenstein develops Schneider's notion that the class structure of capitalism is reflected within the mind of the individual. For Schneider, the structure of the capitalist commodity is reflected in the character structure or social character of the individual, which is split into consciousness and repressed desires.

> What matters ... on the one hand, is to pick up the beginnings, the seeds, of a materialist psychology and psychopathology that are strewn throughout Marx's *Capital* and to develop them further; and, on the other hand, to derive Freud's magnificent structural description of the 'bourgeois soul', especially as a theory of illness and neurosis, from the laws of economic movement of bourgeois society itself.[14]

In the earliest human communities, production was for use and, therefore, planned, based on collective ownership and a simple division of labour.[15] At a later stage, we have 'simple commodity production', where objects are produced for exchange by private producers engaging in different kinds of labour independently of each other. They satisfy each other's needs through this more advanced division of labour. In this earliest kind of commodity production, barter, there is individual ownership of production but 'the articles exchanged do not acquire a value-form independent of their use-value'.[16] That is, they are not measured against each other according to a universal criterion of value, for example, money. Now, Marx emphasises that 'from the moment that men in any way work for one another, their labour assumes a social form',[17] in at least two senses. First, as seen, they satisfy each other's needs through the division of labour, and, secondly, the value of their labour is measured according to the basic criterion of necessary labour-time.

However, even at this stage, the relations between human producers become 'reified'. That is, the real social relations between them assumes the form of a relationship between the objects of their production. Objects produced by independent producers to satisfy each other's consumption needs are related to each other according to the duration of labour. This is what determines their value. So, what is at a deeper level a social relationship between human beings comes to appear as a relationship between things: 'a definite social relation between men ... assumes, in their eyes, the fantastic form of a relation between things'.[18] Marx calls this the 'fetishism of commodities'.

> A commodity is ... a mysterious thing, simply because in it the social character of men's labour appears to them as an objective character stamped upon the product of that labour; because the relation of the producers to the sum-total of their own labour is presented to them as a social relation, existing not between themselves, but between the products of their labour.[19]

Commodity production makes its appearance at an early date in history, though it doesn't assume the same predominating and characteristic form as nowadays. However, at this early stage of simple commodity production, with social and economic relations relatively undeveloped, 'this mystification is as yet very simple', and its fetish character 'is therefore easily seen through'.[20]

At a later stage, with the development of the productive forces, and the increasing number and variety of commodities exchanged, money is introduced as the medium of exchange.[21] Money assumes the character of 'a general social equivalent'. Whether in the form of gold or silver, commodities find that they are represented by another commodity.

> These objects, gold and silver, just as they come out of the bowels of the earth, are forthwith the direct incarnation of all human labour. Hence the magic of money. In the form of society now under consideration, the behaviour of men in the social process of production is purely atomic. Hence their relations to each other in production assume a material character independent of their control and conscious individual action.[22]

The existence of commodities and the emergence of money illustrate the independence and separation of producers who now can only relate to each other by means of the exchange of their products.

Enter the merchant. As the production and exchange of commodities develops, a sufficient quantity of money accumulates in the hands of certain producers. They proceed to transform it into capital, whose value increases through the purchase and putting to work of labour-power. Labour-power thus becomes a commodity, to be bought and sold, the only one which has the capacity to expand its own value, that is, to produce more than the value of those commodities necessary for its reproduction, for example, food and shelter. It is only now that commodity production permeates the whole of society as a result of the intensifying alienation of labour. As Sweezy says:

> It is only when commodity production becomes so highly developed and so widespread as to dominate the life of society that the phenomenon of reification of social relations acquires decisive importance. This occurs under conditions of relatively advanced capitalism such as emerged in Western Europe during the seventeenth and eighteenth centuries.[23]

According to Schneider, 'the structure of social instincts and needs becomes, with the historical development of the structure of commodity and money, just as *abstract* as the latter'.[24] So, under capitalism, the abstraction of use-values inherent in the commodity is reflected in the repression and distortion of our social instincts and needs. The pressures of capitalist exploitation and commercialism, the extension of commodification to labour-power, results in the abstraction from our real human needs, drives and capacities. The commodification of the human spirit under capitalism corresponds to that of labour-power and the consequent reification of human relationships.

> The 'abstraction' of use values and of those useful needs and instincts which correspond to them and which lie at the root of the commodity and money form is ... to be regarded as the germinal political-economic cell of those processes of psychical 'abstraction' which Freud described with his concept of 'instinctual repression'.[25]

Wolfenstein sums up Schneider's argument: 'Commodity structure and character structure are isomorphic. Each involves a vertical split in which sensuousness is devalued.'[26] Just as commodities are produced in order to be sold at a profit, not to satisfy need, so this is mirrored in the unconscious where needs and drives are repressed. Closely bound up with commodification and reification is the alienation of labour, the separation of the worker from his/her product, from other human beings and from his own human essence, a process which reaches its climax under industrial capitalism. Indeed, alienation of labour, in which the worker does not recognise him/herself as the creator of objects, lies at the root of the fetishism of commodities. It is its precondition.

Wolfenstein develops Schneider's analysis, arguing that under the barter system, where each producer satisfies the other's needs through the exchange of the products of their labour, they, in a sense, 'recognise' each other. The same continues to apply with the introduction of money as the medium of exchange. 'A fair exchange, equivalent for equivalent, is mutual recognition in the world of commodities.' However, under commodity production, the subjectivity of human individuals is not recognised, since 'the value that they give to their commodities through their labour appears instead to be an attribute of the commodities themselves ... Thus, instead of self-recognition, we have money worship and the fetishism of commodities.'[27] Wolfenstein here seems to be confusing the fetishism of commodities with alienation, which is not the same, but also conflating simple commodity production and capitalism. Nevertheless, we can, perhaps, glean his meaning. Before labour-power became a commodity, that is, under simple commodity production, even with the introduction of money as the medium of circulation, there was an element of freedom for and equality between producers, of their mutual recognition.

However, with the emergence of full-blown capitalism, based on the buying and selling of labour-power, the capitalist constantly tries to suck more and more out of the worker. The working day is extended into the night. But this 'only slightly quenches the (capitalist's) vampire thirst for the living blood of labour'.[28] The capitalist labour contract looks superficially to be a free choice on the part of both parties, an agreement between equals. But it masks the real, underlying power relationship in which the capitalist's ownership of capital ensures his dominance. As Wolfenstein says: 'In accepting the labour contract, the worker has lost the battle for recognition and has accepted the position of bondsman.'[29] As Marx expressed it: 'He who was previously the money-owner now strides out in front as a capitalist; the possessor of labour-power follows as his worker. The one smirks self-importantly and is intent on business; the other is timid and holds back, like someone who has brought his hide to market and now has nothing else to expect but – a hiding.'[30]

Commodification and Social Character

Schneider presents a related Marxist analysis of the nature of pathology in capitalist society. Because it is a society based on the production and sale of commodities, in which labour-power itself is reduced to a commodity, human relationships become reified. This means that everything is presented to us, and we experience ourselves and others, as things, perceived and defined in terms of their exchange-value, their price or cost, not their usefulness or intrinsic value as individual persons or objects, that is, their use-value. We constantly seek to 'abstract' from, to peel off, the inherent or qualitative value from people, our relations with others, ourselves, things, nature and so on. As we have seen, this process of abstraction applies equally to our instincts and needs, as they have been shaped by the development of capitalism. Fromm undertook a similar analysis in *The Sane Society* in 1955, quoting a news item in the *New York Times*: 'B.Sc. + Ph.D. = $40,000': 'knowledge is experienced as the embodiment of a certain exchange-value on the personality market'.[31]

Schneider argues that Freud's theory of repression is the emotional equivalent of or counterpart to Marx's theory of commodities. Moreover, he believes that there is a necessary connection between the degree of abstraction that capitalism has reached in its extensive commodification of life and the extent of repression in the individual's emotional and instinctual life.

To return to our basic theme: how is such an external reality of lordship and bondage reflected in the players' psyche? Money is the universal equivalent of all commodities. But this extends to the inner world as well as the outer. 'But money may be equated with anything. And not just with objects but also with affects',[32] for example, love and hate. Hence, receiving (and paying) money may be subjectively experienced as bearing either love and/or hatred. In other words, since money is the measure of the man, psychic phenomena become commodities in the way that physical objects are. Both the ego and super-ego are commodified, with money, according to Wolfenstein, taking up residence in the super-ego.[33] So, as the child becomes an adult, the stages of his/her development are marked by the reward/punishment dual exchange system: 'praise in exchange for proper defecation, presents as rewards for good behaviour, grades in school as reward/punishment for academic performance, money for job performance'. Desires that do not have an exchange-value are downgraded, for example, infantile sexuality.[34]

Typical life crises, such as the loss of a job or the break-up of a relationship, evoke anger, but if this cannot be directed at the proper person(s), it is repressed and turned against the self, which results in depression and lowered self-esteem. In addition, the unconscious overlays the experience of contemporary setbacks with that of childhood emotional trauma. The adult relives the child's need for healing, for affirmative recognition. But that desire for recognition 'remains unrecognised'.

> It is repressed along with the individual's impotent rage ... All that the individual consciously experiences is worthlessness ... And because the link to the ego has been severed, these alienated desires have no direct outlet. But they do have an indirect one. The individual projects on to money the power of realising repressed desires.[35]

Wolfenstein then raises the question of the psychic meaning of the buying and selling of labour-power. Insofar as the worker is 'overpowered but not overawed, defeated but not persuaded', psychoanalysis has nothing to say. But insofar as the worker believes that his/her relationship with the employer is based on equality and fairness, then we have what he describes as a 'sado-masochistic contract'. 'It involves an objective situation of domination that is subjectively mediated by a surrender of freedom, an act of self-abnegation, a voluntary giving over of one's will to the other.' This notion has an affinity with Fromm's analysis of fascist authoritarianism and Jessica Benjamin's interpretation of *The Story of O*. At its most extreme, this 'contract establishes the roles of torturer and tortured, with the specific proviso that the torture victim is to love and identify with the torturer'. According to this model of commodity-character, the sadist's role is taken over by the super-ego, that of the masochist by the ego. The 'capitalist super-ego' comes to be seen by the worker as having legitimate authority, whereas the worker, confined to the ego, is felt to be morally devalued.[36]

This account might perhaps have rung true of the most backward, least conscious section of the working class. According to sociological studies popular in the 1950s, one third of the British working class were described as 'deference voters', the cap-doffing, bowing and scraping workers whose attitude to their upper-class rulers was that they were 'born to rule'. But even here, we need to be clear about the meaning of the term 'sadomasochistic'. Fromm does not use the term exclusively to denote inviting or inflicting physical pain. For him, 'masochistic' describes 'feelings of inferiority, powerlessness, individual insignificance ... these persons show a tendency to belittle themselves, to make themselves weak ... [they] show a marked dependence on powers outside themselves, on other people, or institutions'.[37] 'Sadistic' denotes three factors: (a) wanting to make others dependent on oneself, (b) wanting to exploit or steal from them, and (c) the wish to make them suffer, usually mentally but possibly physically too.[38] For capitalism to rule and to exploit, it has to instil into the psyche of working class people notions of inferiority, incapacity and the internalisation of an image of themselves as automaton conformists. This psychological process has to accompany ideological notions of capitalism as the only possible social order, with capitalists, and those who govern on their behalf, as the rightful rulers. An array of social and political institutions fulfil this role: the family, school, the mass media. As Orwell said: 'A thousand influences constantly press a working man down into a passive role.'[39]

Yet the working class under industrial capitalism has from its very beginnings sought to organise and resist. At least, its most conscious and confident sections have done so. E.P. Thompson described the earliest unions in the 1790s through which workers discovered their capacity to resist, and the utopian socialist organisations of the 1830s in which they developed the notion of an alternative society. In so doing, workers challenged capitalist authority and legitimacy and thereby transformed their social character from one based on dependence and submission to one founded on independence and self-creativity. It is the transition that Marx described as that from a 'class-in-itself' to a 'class for-itself'. To pursue the psychoanalytical concomitant of this process, what we have is the collective challenge to the capitalist super-ego by the previously submissive ego, an enlargement of the freedom-searching ego at the expense of the oppressive super-ego. In common with most academic Marxists, and despite his valuable insights, Wolfenstein sees the working class largely as an exploited class, not as one that also resists.

If we are essentially social beings who create ourselves through the collective process of labour, there is one kind of relatedness that most clearly and decisively expresses human nature. This is the need and the capacity for affective relationships, for human bonding, for love. Clearly the presence of the features constituting human nature discussed so far are dependent on certain physical and mental preconditions unique to human beings. Our physical evolution has facilitated the development of reason, imagination and self-awareness. Our reason enables us to understand the outer world of objects, including our own bodies. Our self-awareness renders us capable, not only of knowing, but of knowing that we know; also of reflecting on our inner selves, our physical weakness and inevitable death. As many writers have pointed out, these features disrupted the harmony with nature that characterises animal existence. We are aware of ourselves as separate from nature. As Fromm puts it, our reason and self-awareness have transformed us into an anomaly, a freak of nature. We are 'part of nature, subject to her physical laws and unable to change them, yet [we] transcend nature...' and have the capacity to subordinate her to our needs. Humans 'are set apart while being a part ... homeless yet chained to the home [we] share with all creatures'.[40]

So far, we have talked about human nature in the sense of a set of physical and mental characteristics which all human individuals possess, and which are present in some form in every society. Some writers, in particular certain existentialists and some 'humanist' psychoanalysts, have described what they call the human condition. This is described, again by Fromm, as the 'fundamental contradictions that characterise human existence and have their root in the biological dichotomy between missing instincts and self-awareness. Man's existential conflict produces certain psychic needs common to all men.' Humans are thus driven to try to overcome their fear of aloneness, of separateness and of powerlessness, by finding new ways of relating to the world so as to feel at home in it. Fromm describes these psychic needs as existential because they are 'rooted in the very conditions of human existence'.[41] Each of these needs can be fulfilled in different ways depending on social and historical conditions.

We have seen that Kleinian and object-relations psychoanalysis describe the human infant as seeking from the moment of birth to form relationships, as though born with a sense of its powerlessness. This notion would seem to fit in with the idea of human reason, imagination and self-awareness driving us to create a society through different kinds of relationships. From this standpoint, successive historical societies, embodying different social conditions, contain attempts at satisfying human existential needs (seen as among the needs embedded in human nature.)

Kovel developed his notion of 'Desire' referring to basic human emotional striving, the 'striving towards an object that cannot yet be named'. The newborn infant 'responds to the human voice, tracks objects visually, and engages in protoexpressive facial movements that form the raw material of dialogue'. From the outset of life, the baby shows an interest in the outside world even though there is no clear demarcation yet between 'I' or 'self' and 'other'. This absence of division between subject and object produces a kind of blurred continuum that envelops and binds the whole into a single reality. Nevertheless, we can say that the baby is 'prestructured at birth to respond to and join the human community'. Kovel points out that this echoes Marx's notion that the 'self is an ensemble of social relations'.[42]

Kovel's concept of 'Desire' is similar to Freud's concepts of the 'id' or unconscious drives, but even more to the 'object-seeking' at the heart of both the Kleinian and the object-relations schools. Desire is 'transhistorical', a universal feature of human nature, but 'exists within and is transformed by every historical situation'.[43] The form or mode of expression of Desire, however, depends on the character of a historically specific society. Desire arises in the earliest phase of babyhood but is present throughout life until silenced by death.[44]

Kovel also develops the notion of Other, defined as 'the hidden qualities of the self that we project outward in the act of desiring'.[45] Like Desire, the Other is a transhistorical feature of infantile life, present in all types of society. However, the objects to which it relates are shaped by different historical societies. Desire is inter-subjective, a relationship between human beings, a feature that 'follows from the fundamentally social nature of people ... Therefore, no subjectivity can occur without inter-subjectivity.'[46] Although Desire can never be totally fulfilled, even under favourable social and family circumstances, the individual, that is, the baby, can experience relative gratification, in other words, a 'state of goodness'. In contrast, the experience of 'relative ungratification' is 'the experience of badness'. The child invests the objects he/she constructs with Desire, which is as necessary as is a certain degree of repression. However, Desire only becomes problematical if the society in which it is expressed is alienated, or estranged from nature. In the case of capitalist society, the extreme 'time-binding' – that is, the rigid control of the worker's time-keeping by the capitalist – necessary for the accumulation of capital, results in the alienation of desire, its distortion into a force that oppresses the subject.[47]

However, returning to the issue of existential anxiety, two questions arise: has the fear of separateness and aloneness, and of powerlessness, described by Fromm, always existed, even in tribal or feudal societies with their emphasis on close family or kinship ties? Or is it a product of capitalism with its alienation and atomisation of individuals outside the productive process? Surely, humans in such pre-capitalist, collectivist societies were oppressed by scarcity and were terrified by the forces of nature, but not by a horror of separateness. There was little sense of a separate, individual identity, since human beings thought of themselves as part of the 'we'. But if this horror has always existed, perhaps it is a product of human imagination and self-awareness. In that case, couldn't our powers of reason and imagination be what propel us into social relationships? Social labour and the creation of society would then partly result from the need to overcome existential anxiety. But isn't this, in turn, to fall back on to a kind of Hobbesian individualism, for which social relationships are the product of our enlightened self-interest? There is an ambiguity here in Fromm's work, as the general tenor of his work contains a strong emphasis on sociality.

Fromm's view of our existential anxiety would seem to negate the Kleinian and object-relations view of the innate character of the infant's object-seeking, its genetic need and capacity for human relationships. Not wishing to get into a chicken-and-egg situation, let us concede that this existential anxiety, this fear of separation and isolation, is an element in the 'human condition', a factor that reinforces our need for other human beings with whom we engage in social labour. It is part of the cement that binds us to others, and, therefore, an aspect of human nature. Humans can also be said to satisfy their existential needs through their passions – love, the struggle for justice, the search for truth, but also negatively, through narcissism and destructiveness. This dichotomy will be seen to have a direct bearing on the issue of the roots of genocide. Fromm analyses these passions as rooted in character, 'the relatively permanent system of all non-instinctual strivings through which man relates himself to the human and natural world'. As we saw in Chapter 1, there are two aspects of character – first, those enduring aspects that result from human nature, the fact that humans have always engaged in labour, social construction, the creation of art and science and so on; and second, those traits that result from the different, historically specific ways human beings have dealt with socio-economic problems or natural barriers that confronted them, for example, Fromm's hoarding or exploitative characters. These two aspects of character correspond to Marx's distinction between 'human nature in general' and 'relative appetites' – what Geras calls the 'nature of man'.[48]

Four Existential Needs

Fromm discusses existential needs that arise out of our human condition. First is the need for a framework of orientation and devotion, some map of our social and natural world, including our place in it. Such a map needs to be cohesive and structured, providing a framework of understanding and orientation in the world – a picture of our universe containing elements of both art and science – that enables us to make sense of our world and facilitates the creation of meaningful goals and forms of action to fulfil them.[49] Every culture creates such a framework, a coherent system of ideas, goals and action, without which purposeful activity would be impossible. Fromm's analysis recalls Gramsci's view:

> There is no human activity from which every form of intellectual participation can be excluded ... Every man ... outside his professional activity, carries on some form of intellectual activity, that is, he is a 'philosopher', an artist, a man of taste, he participates in a particular conception of the world, has a conscious line of moral conduct, and therefore contributes to sustain a conception of the world or to modify it.[50]

Every human being engages in some set of ideological activities, whether explicitly or implicitly, whether consistently or with contradictions.

But human subjectivity is not exhausted by the ideological factor. We need, in addition, to see human beings as having an emotional life that intersects and overlaps with their intellectual life but is not commensurate with it. We have developed a language to express our emotional life that is separate from the language we use in intellectual life. Marx was right to affirm that 'social being determines consciousness' so long as we don't interpret this in a mechanistic sense, and include in 'consciousness' our conscious and unconscious emotional life.[51] Human beings have always devised some 'framework of devotion', a map or guide orienting us towards the fulfilment of our goals, even the most basic one of physical survival. Moreover, humans need objects of moral value that become the focus of their strivings. Animals have no such need as their instincts provide them with both a map and a set of goals. But humans, lacking instinctual determination of their actions – even the satisfaction of those instinctual needs is socially conditioned – need objects of devotion and commitment which help to organise their energies down certain routes, in those directions that help them to make sense of their world and to confer value and meaning on their lives.[52]

There are different routes open to human beings, different modes of satisfying our need for a devotional framework. We can either pursue objects of devotion and commitment that unite us with other human beings, that are life-enhancing, or others that are destructive. For example, we can either pursue the goal of amassing a fortune or accumulating power, or choose goals that elevate the lives of those around us. Of course, working-class people, the majority of society, have a much narrower range of choices. So we ought to speak of society's rulers seeking to impose choices that take us down the path of either productive or destructive endeavour.

Secondly, regarding our need for relatedness or rootedness, Fromm, like psychoanalysts in general, argues that the infant's separation from the mother creates a need to replace that connection with new affective ties, to put down fresh roots that embed us firmly in new, wider relationships. Hence, our sanity depends on our ability to form links with others. Without these, we would be overcome by our separation and isolation. But again, there are two ways of fulfilling this need – a productive and a destructive way. One can love another or others, or, if one's sense of freedom is lacking or is underdeveloped, relate to them symbiotically, that is, become part of them or make them part of oneself. 'In this symbiotic relationship, he strives either to control others (sadism), or to be controlled by them (masochism). If he cannot choose either the way of love or that of symbiosis, he can solve the problem by relating exclusively to himself (narcissism); then he becomes the world, and loves the world by "loving" himself.'[53] Narcissism is a dangerous form of relatedness – one usually mixed with sadism. Another malignant solution to the need for relatedness is the desire to destroy, again generally blended with extreme narcissism. 'If no one exists outside of me, I need not fear others, nor need I relate myself to them. By destroying the world, I am saved from being crushed by it.'[54] Again, this point is relevant to the issue of genocide.

Thirdly, tied to the need for rootedness is another aspect of the search for relatedness: the need for unity, both unity within oneself and unity with the natural and social world outside. This unity provides one with a sense of wholeness as an individual human being but also a sense of relatedness to nature and the social world. Capitalist society is clearly one that makes much harder, if not impossible, the achievement of these forms of relatedness. The experience of alienation, which is not simply a psychological experience but is part of the social structure of capitalism, ensures that the majority of individuals, that is, both individuals from oppressed classes and members of the ruling class, are largely unable to achieve the kind of roots and social relationships that can render their lives meaningful. The latter are alienated in that the system of exploitation from which they benefit cuts them off from the majority of their fellow human beings.

The related process of commodification whereby human beings and their relationships assume the character of relations between things, also described by Marx as commodity fetishism, undoubtedly plays a major role in destroying our sense of rootedness, unity and effectiveness. Human beings come to experience themselves and others as things and so treat themselves and others in this reified fashion. The link between commodification and cruelty is borne out empirically in Simon Baron-Cohen's interesting study.[55] A precondition of people treating others cruelly, inflicting physical or psychological damage on them, is the erosion of empathy, a breakdown of our human capacity to sense that they experience pain when we hurt them. And this 'erosion of empathy' involves 'people turning people into objects'. 'When our empathy is switched off, we are solely in the "I" mode. In such a state, we relate only to things, or to people as if they were just things.'[56] Individuals with zero degrees of empathy fall into three categories – borderline, psychopathic or narcissistic – but their roots in childhood emotional neglect, a failure of nurturing attachment to a loving object, are similar, though narcissism may also be caused by over-indulgence.[57]

This is highly relevant to genocide, since it is when human beings are oppressed by social and psychological conditions that make them feel powerless, alienated from any sense of their own value or effectiveness, that they are driven to seek that ultimate badge of supreme power over other human beings – killing them, reducing them to objects. And the more devalued or powerless they feel, the more they potentially seek fulfilment of their needs through acts of destruction.

Fourthly, there is the need for effectiveness. The awareness of oneself as weak and helpless in relation to the powerful forces of nature and society can lead to an overwhelming passivity. As Lichtman says, 'the mutual imposition of ... dependence and the pretence of independence produces exaggerated forms of helplessness, guilt and violence'.[58] To counteract such paralysis, we need to feel effective in pursuing whatever set of goals shape our lives. Both as individuals and as members of a group, we need to feel we are active, functioning human beings.[59] Winnicott makes a similar point: 'if society is in danger, it is not because of man's aggressiveness but because of the repression of personal aggressiveness in individuals'.[60] Storr interprets this to mean that 'if the individual's requirement to be recognised and appreciated as a person in his own right has not been met, the normal drive towards self-affirmation and self-assertion becomes intensified and transmuted into hostility'.[61] Referring to individuals who have not been able to achieve a sense of personal significance or self-appreciation, Storr comments that 'their violent acts represent the emergence of repressed aggression converted into destructive hatred'.[62]

Now, it would seem plausible to argue that the first three existential needs discussed by Fromm – a framework of devotion, relatedness and unity – are aspects or elaborations of the human need for the Other. They embody our search for relationships that express our potential nature as social beings.

However, we have seen that human beings have developed different means of fulfilling their needs. They can be realised by seeking ties of solidarity with others, by commitment to the values of justice and peace or by engaging in narcissistic or destructive modes of action. The fourth existential need – for effectiveness – is an important aspect of the way we express our life drive and reflects our capacity for self-assertion. It clearly differs from a similar need in animals in that we are aware of it and therefore able to consciously plan ways in which it can be materialised.

Are we justified in asserting the existence of such 'basic human needs', in this case psychic? What physical, social or historical reasons can provide such justification? So many so-called 'needs' have turned out to be demands or whims on the part of groups or individuals pursuing private agendas. Discounting these, there are surely, in Kate Soper's words, 'needs that are universal and basic in the sense that their satisfaction is essential to the health and well-being of any human individual, or that suffering will be the inevitable consequence of the pursuit of policies that ignore these determinations of nature'.[63] There are two criteria to be applied in order to assess whether a drive or type of activity represents or expresses a 'basic human need'. The first is universality. Have humans in all societies manifested this drive or undertaken this activity? The four needs described by Fromm fall into that category. But universality is not enough. Humans in every society so far have killed each other, but we surely wouldn't describe killing as a human need. The answer is perhaps an epistemological one. Can we explain a drive or an activity in terms of an anterior set of social or personal conditions, or does it represent an 'ultimate' factor, not explicable in terms of prior reasons or deeper causes? The urge to create a framework of devotion and orientation, to relate to others, to be effective in one's life, are activities or drives that humans have always carried out or expressed. If someone behaves charitably or lovingly to another, we don't normally ask for an explanation. This is simply the kind of activity which humans, at their best, carry out. On the other hand, when a person or group kills another, we do ask why, deeming it necessary to explain destructive behaviour.

Economic Development and Cultural Progress

So far, economic progress has depended on class exploitation, on surpluses appropriated by a minority ruling class from the labour of the majority, so as to be able to invest a portion of it in development rather than to consume it. On the other hand, Fromm argues that historical progress, specifically here moral and cultural progress, even in the pre-modern period prior to the rise of capitalism, has depended on the struggle for justice, liberty, truth and solidarity. However, it cannot be denied that human efforts in this direction have been stymied by existing social conditions. Human beings have the potential to achieve the fullest growth, physical and cultural, individual and social, but only so long as the external conditions are conducive to the 'life-furthering syndrome'. The presence of unfavourable conditions will entail the 'life-thwarting' syndrome. Of course, this doesn't mean that human beings are totally determined by their social environment and have a character-structure imposed from the outside. Because human beings possess reason, imagination and will, these faculties enable them to struggle for higher values. As already stressed, we are formed by history but we also create our history.[64] Marxists have always insisted on our human self-transformative capacity.

Fromm emphasises a point that Marxists have also argued, that for most of human history, the low level of development of productive forces meant that great cultural products, such as the pyramids or the great ancient temples, could only be achieved at the expense of the majority, through super-exploitation, slavery, war and conquest. Hence culture and freedom were incompatible, the one only achievable at the expense of the other.[65] Prior to the development of capitalist production, the low level of economic surpluses enabled ruling classes to hold down the consumption of the majority while preserving their wealth, a portion of which they used to develop cultural artefacts.

Fromm makes a further distinction between rational and irrational thought, feeling and behaviour. The former promotes the functioning and growth of the whole of which it is a part, whereas the latter weakens or destroys them. Regarding the passions rooted in our character, the life-enhancing ones are rational in that they advance the growth and well-being of the organism or personality. In contrast, the life-throttling passions are irrational in that they undermine them.

Now, under given circumstances, a person or group may be unable to do better, or may become destructive, because they lack the social, economic and psychological conditions for growth, for the development of solidarity and the striving for justice and peace. Society and history have set limits to the potential for growth, so that extreme circumstances – war, famine, etc. – are capable of unleashing destructiveness. To the extent that human beings are imprisoned within a historical structure of a low socio-economic level, they come under pressure to react with greater or lesser degrees of destructiveness. This is not inevitable, as we have already stressed, since alternative political choices are often available, at least in theory. The Nazi victory in 1933 was not inevitable. But the range of free choice open to human beings is greater or smaller depending on the external socio-economic conditions. We are back to Marx's dictum about human beings making their own history but in circumstances not of their choosing. The point here is that the life-thwarting passions and actions – hatred, destructiveness – are as much ways of meeting human social and existential needs as the life-enhancing ones.

'Rational' and 'Irrational' Destructiveness

As we saw in Chapter 2, and following the distinction between rational and irrational thought and behaviour, Fromm makes a useful distinction between 'rational' and 'irrational' destructiveness. The former can also be described as 'instrumental aggression' and is to be found throughout history, in numerous wars and massacres. Its precondition is the relatively low level of development of society's productive forces. Against that background, clans, tribes, city-states and kingdoms fought each other for a greater share of society's scarce material resources. Irrational destructiveness occurs where there are no material gains to be made from killing or where far more killing than is necessary to fulfil a group's material aims occurs. As we have seen, it can, in turn, be divided into spontaneous and character-based types. The former, as we also saw earlier, is the product of unusual circumstances and can in turn be 'vengeful' or 'ecstatic'.

The notion of the irrational has a direct bearing on our analysis of genocide. The four case-studies in this enquiry fall into the category of the irrational, primarily in the sense that even from the point of view of the perpetrators, the genocide of an entire people or ethnic or religious group seems to have been against their own objective interests. Storr makes some interesting points on this in his book *Human Destructiveness*: 'The behaviour of many anti-social individuals suggests that they live in a world they assume to be either actively hostile or else indifferent to their welfare.'[66] He adduces the frequent socio-economic context of violence: 'the majority of people who commit violent acts in peacetime come from the bottom of the social heap, where many individuals feel humiliated, inadequate, ineffective, helpless, and inconsequential'. His analysis aims at understanding the violent behaviour of individuals, but is surely valid when extended to groups, such as social classes whose historical experience has been one of exploitation, oppression and rejection. Such groups, moreover, most probably suffered major economic crises or political defeats or were unable to develop a significant capacity to resist. As we saw, Freud himself accepted the possibility of collective neurosis. Storr concludes by pointing to our society as bearing a major share of responsibility for modern violence: 'Competitive, capitalist, industrial societies have not begun to solve, or even to address, the problem of making the less gifted and the less competent feel valued or wanted.'[67]

Human Nature, Psychoanalysis and History

Freud and the post-Freudians are often viewed as having an ahistorical view of human nature and individual development. But Freud did recognise the possibility of historical variation, at least in the way individuals experienced the same basic mental structures. The Oedipus complex may be, like language, a universal phenomenon, an essential prerequisite of social life, but the form it takes differs according to the culture. He notes that 'the simple Oedipus complex is by no means the most frequent', and he argues elsewhere, comparing its manifestation in the two plays *Oedipus Rex* and *Hamlet*, that 'the changed treatment of the same material reveals the whole difference in the mental life of these two widely separated epochs of civilization: the secular advance of repression in the emotional life of mankind'.[68] The question is, however, why did a 'secular advance of repression' occur?

I would argue that certain key Freudian, or more broadly, psychoanalytic, categories need to be included as building blocks or 'psychic DNA' forming the structure of human nature. It is those which can be identified as possessing the greatest universality and which, therefore, link us as social beings across the ages. Concepts such as the unconscious, the Oedipus complex, Freud's triad of psychic 'sectors', the id, ego and super-ego, object-seeking, good and bad objects, the life drive, destructiveness, the paranoid-schizoid position, projective identification, and so on, form a useful initial psychic inventory.

Broad changes in psychic formation generally accompany the most crucial historical transitions. In each case, we need to ask about the applicability of these psychoanalytic categories or the relative weight that each new social formation, or rather its ruling class, assigns unconsciously to these concepts. We will see in each a different configuration of the above psychic elements. Lichtman makes a similar point that 'the ego and superego will be differently formed in the varying social circumstances in which one form of defence comes to prevail over another'.[69] Klein was no doubt putting the same argument when she suggested there was no super-ego in pre-ancient, pre-Hellenic tribal society.[70] Additional examples are perhaps Greek and Roman slave societies. Their ruling classes allowed the passions of the freemen, that is, the forces of the Freudian id, a freer rein than was the case under the subsequent class societies of feudalism and capitalism. These, on the contrary, with their emphasis on growing sexual renunciation, witnessed a strengthening of the super-ego at the expense of the id and its passions.

These psychoanalytical categories can be seen as the components of Fromm's social character or Reich's character structure. The problem with their concept of 'social character' is its lack of psychological content. To this extent, Fromm's critics, especially Marcuse, but also Fenichel, have a point: he did abandon or play down psychoanalysis for a kind of radical social philosophy. So the question remains: what is the subjective, psychic content of the 'authoritarian' or 'marketing' character? If we apply Freud's triadic structure or the 'dual' structure of Kleinian and object-relations theory to Fromm's notion, we arrive at certain possible syntheses. Clearly, the authoritarian character has an overdeveloped super-ego whereas individuals in late feudal and late capitalist societies have perhaps weaker super-egos, thereby giving greater rein to the forces of the id. The hoarding character is based on a strong super-ego. Moreover, 'splitting', the 'paranoid-schizoid' position analysed by Klein and the object-relations theorists, comes to dominate the psyche of certain groups where there is a high level of rage and, therefore, of routine aggression. The example of late feudalism and early capitalism, in which the traditional certainties and sources of security came under threat, provides, again, one example. Lawrence Stone illustrates this point in his book on the English family. Sixteenth- and early seventeenth-century England was 'a society in which a majority of the individuals ... found it very difficult to establish close emotional ties to any person. Children were often neglected, brutally treated and even killed; many adults treated each other with suspicion and hostility ... England between 1500 and 1660 was relatively cold ... and violence-prone.'[71] Social classes suffering sudden economic deprivation or a major political or military defeat can experience regression from a perhaps anxious but seemingly normal psyche to the paranoid-schizoid position. Here again, the example of the Nazi Party is relevant. As we shall see, defeat in the First World War pushed an already emotionally fragile German middle class further towards the brink. The hyperinflation of 1923 and the Great Depression sparked off by the 1929 Crash pushed them over the edge. In sum, to fully understand any particular society, we need to grasp how the predominant class has secured a specific arrangement of psychic elements which it then more or less successfully inculcates into the minds of the exploited. This set of arguments is relevant to the question of genocide insofar as the external social and economic crisis that forms the context of precipitating factors within which genocide occurs is also likely to see a configuration of elements of the social character that gives the greatest rein to destructiveness. In other words, we are also likely to find a highly developed predisposition to violence.

Levels of Sociality

Marx's dialectical notion of the historical development of human relationships can be approached in terms of higher and lower levels of sociality and of individuality. Early collective communities – tribal, ancient oriental despotic and feudal societies – were based on a strong community and a weak sense of individuality. The emergence of capitalism reversed this process, ushering in a society based on a high individuality and a low sociality. A future socialist society would overcome this opposition by synthesising the two opposites into a new unity, creating a high degree of sociality but at a much higher level of individuality. Can we integrate Freud's representation of the individual mental structure into this paradigm? We can perhaps say that the internal ego-superego-id structure looks different depending on the type of society we are examining.

Under capitalism, each individual structure looks to be quite distinct from the rest, with clear, hard boundaries separating each person from their fellow human beings. In more collective societies, these boundaries seem soft and blurred, the borders of each personality penetrating or intersecting with others, whether they be members of one's family, village, clan and so on. Moreover, the situation of the borders being hard and the individual more isolated seems to be accompanied by a stronger super-ego, its allotted task that of holding the psychic constituents together. In contrast, where the boundaries are looser or even interpenetrate, the individual psyches are held together by the concentric structures of collectivity – family, village/clan/fiefdom, kingdom/state bureaucracy.

Social Character and Human Need

Finally, we must look at the relationship between social character and human need. We examined notions of human nature defined in terms of a set of universal basic needs, drives and capacities, and suggested that Marx's notion of humankind as essentially a social being underlies the four basic needs suggested by Fromm as constituting the essential core of human nature. But we have also seen that social character intervenes as mediator between human nature and society. It is the psychological expression of the way different social groups set about fulfilling both their human needs and the historical tasks that confront them. In the case of dominant classes, it is the tasks they have set themselves or else inherited from their forbears, whereas in the case of subordinate classes, it is the manner in which they resist the imposition of these tasks.

If we look at the social characters that arose with the emergence and development of modern capitalism – productive, hoarding, exploitative, authoritarian, destructive, narcissistic – there is arguably a clash between them (except for the productive character) and the fulfilment of human needs. The evidence is surely to be found in the numerous studies of modern pathology – alcoholism, suicide, homicide and other forms of destructiveness, and mental illness in general. These expressions of pathology are, it seems, specific to modern society.[72]

The social character of greatest interest for a discussion of genocide is clearly the authoritarian-destructive character. Fromm differentiates between destructiveness and sadomasochism, though he argues that they are generally found together. Sadomasochism aims at an active or passive 'symbiosis' with the object, either submitting to an overpowering authority or forcing others into such a submission. Destructiveness, in contrast, aims at the elimination of the object. Both, however,

> are rooted in the unbearableness of individual powerlessness and isolation. I can escape the feeling of my own powerlessness in comparison with the world outside myself by destroying it ... The destruction of the world is the last, almost desperate attempt to save myself from being crushed by it ... Sadism tends to strengthen the atomised individual by the domination over others, destructiveness by the absence of any threat from the outside.[73]

In the first four chapters, I have suggested that modern genocide can be analysed in part as the 'irrational' destructiveness of communities or social classes that have either suffered major historical defeats at the hands of stronger, more ruthless (ideologically driven) social or military forces, or have felt threatened by the possibility of such defeats. The fear of defeat aroused by the onset of severe social stress or dislocation – economic crisis, impending or actual military defeat – can precipitate those groups with a predisposition to violence into mass destructiveness.

The resulting denial of the satisfaction of their human needs, the ensuing feelings of isolation and powerlessness, have propelled them in the direction of projecting onto outgroups the impotent rage, hatred and destructiveness engendered by these defeats or the threat of them. Part Two will explore the historical roots of these group pathologies with reference to four cases of genocide.

PART TWO

FOUR MODERN GENOCIDES

CHAPTER FIVE

Native American Genocide

The Native Americans are those peoples who migrated from East Asia to America across the Bering Straits. Some scholars estimate their arrival to have occurred 70,000 years ago while others argue it was around 13,500 years ago. Recent archaeological and genetic evidence suggests a figure of between 30,000 and 40,000 years ago.[1] There has also been much debate over the size of the American population prior to the arrival of Columbus on the island of Hispaniola in 1492. According to one source, most recent anthropological and archaeological evidence – since the mid-1960s – suggests it was between 75 and 100 million, with around 8 to 12 million living north of Mexico.[2] Dobyns put the numbers living north of the Rio Grande at 12.5 million.[3] Kirkpatrick Sale gives a figure of 15 million.[4] However, other scholars give lower figures: between 3 and 5 million in the present-day United States at the time of contact, and around 55 million south of the Rio Grande including the Caribbean.[5] According to Gary B. Nash, 'a conservative estimate might place the loss in the Indian population due to disease, war and enslavement during the first half century of English settlement at about 60%'.[6] By the end of the nineteenth century, no more than around 5 per cent of the original population had survived.

Several questions present themselves at the outset of any discussion about the fate of the Native Americans:

1. Didn't the vast majority die of diseases, admittedly introduced by the European colonists, but accidentally, and not as part of any plan or intention to exterminate the native population? The ravages of the numerous epidemics were caused by the natives' lack of immunity. Or was it genocide? Millions died, not from diseases, but as a direct result of war, murder and mistreatment by the colonists. But in that case, isn't it more accurate to describe their fate as ethnic cleansing rather than genocide, albeit that generally a thin dividing line separates the two? From the seventeenth century on, the Native Americans were systematically removed from the eastern side of Anglo America and gradually pushed westwards, first across the Appalachians and then across the Mississippi, finally into western states such as California. The objective was simply to vacate the land inhabited by the various Native American nations to make it available for the European frontiersmen and settlers who came over in waves of growing intensity from the end of the eighteenth century and throughout the nineteenth. But could there not have been an acculturation, a mutual accommodation or mixing of cultures, between the Native Americans and the Europeans, or even an assimilation of the former into the latter? Or were the societies of the Europeans too different from those of the Native Americans – the latter being nomads, hunter-gatherers, in contrast to the former who brought settled agriculture?

2. Following on from this issue is the question of whether the elimination of the Native Americans, accepting for now that it is best described as genocide, conformed to what might be called 'rational' or 'utilitarian' genocide.[7] The argument is that, however horrific and regrettable the genocide of the native Americans, it nevertheless advanced the economic or political interests of the perpetrators. If this was not the case, then it can legitimately be described as irrational – in which case a psychological level of explanation is appropriate, in addition to, not instead of, explanation at the economic and political levels.

If the disappearance of the Native Americans from their homelands was due to ethnic cleansing or 'rational' genocide as a result of a desire and need to acquire and develop their land, then the question 'who were the perpetrators?' becomes less important. They were simply men and women who escaped from a Europe ravaged by the erosion of the old order, the gradual disappearance of the stability and authority of traditional society, caught in the historical interstices that lay between the decline of feudalism and the rise of industrial capitalism. They were brave, enterprising people in search of a new land and a new life, men and women eager to work hard, and determined to build a new world based on freedom, equality and democracy, a career open to the talents and the rights of the individual.

However, the story is more complicated. Perhaps we are dealing with European men and women severely damaged by the sudden disappearance of their traditional security, traumatised by being driven off their land and out of their artisan workshops by a new class of enterprising landlords, capitalist farmers and merchants. Such people arrived in the new world with economic, social, cultural and psychological baggage. They had courage, determination and a spirit of independence, but were also filled with fear, anger and resentment. These attitudes found expression not only at the ideological but also the psychological level. European settlers viewed the natives amongst whom they now lived, not just in racist terms as 'savages', 'barbarians' or 'heathens' in need of conversion to the civilised culture of Christianity, but as a separate species, half-way between humans and animals, with whom no accommodation was possible. Ideally, they could simply be driven away from white society, but if that failed, then extermination became necessary, and the settlers' racism increasingly took on a genocidal form.

3. If so, then we can legitimately ask a third question: what was the perpetrators' mentality, the social character, that drove them to commit genocide? This last point is important also partly because the colonisation of the US by the European settlers opened the gates to the development of US capitalism, creating huge agricultural surpluses which fed the growing industrial cities, with rural America becoming itself a huge market for surplus capital and industrial goods. Thomas Jefferson, drafter of the American Declaration of Independence in 1775 and the second US president, came to believe that the removal of the natives 'was necessary for the opening of the vast American lands to agriculture, to commerce, to markets, to money, to the development of the modern American economy'.[8]

Moreover, from a strict Marxist standpoint, the relentless rise of American capitalism ensured the development of world industrial capitalism, itself a necessary precondition for the creation of a global working class capable of ushering in socialism. So the removal and destruction of the Native Americans was a regrettable but unavoidable step on the road to the eventual liberation of humanity. An alternative body of American scholarship has, however, argued the opposite thesis that there were many small, independent communities in which Native Americans and settlers did establish harmonious relations.[9] According to recent work, this became possible when both sides allowed themselves to be 'guided by their shared humanity' and were 'free from the pressures of imperial governments'.[10] An important book in this tradition is Richard White's *The Middle Ground*.[11] Over a period of 165 years, some natives and settlers, having started out regarding each other as alien and hostile, succeeded in constructing a world of mutual understanding based on common meanings and economic exchange. This mutual accommodation only broke down following the American War of Independence, with the natives once again seen as alien and unassimilable. Two books by Kevin Kenny and David Preston start from the same premise: that 'the violence of the revolutionary era was not inevitable and that seventeenth-century colonial enterprises offered a world of possibilities, including cross-cultural peace'.[12] This approach certainly chimes with my own argument to be developed in this chapter – that the genocide of the Native Americans was not the result purely of 'rational' land-hunger, and that a process of mutual adjustment akin to the Spanish model of proletarianisation would have been possible, but for the destructive, racist mentality of the settlers.

I will now explore these three key questions in detail.

Disease or Genocide?

Disease took a truly terrible toll. The victory of the Spanish conquistador Cortes over the Aztecs in 1521 was assisted by a smallpox epidemic that possibly halved their population just before the Spanish attack on Tenochtitlan (modern Mexico City).[13] In the eastern United States, hardly a Native American tribe escaped the ravages of European diseases in the sixteenth and seventeenth centuries. 'The Europeans' invisible ally had decimated the eastern Massachusetts tribes even before the Puritans arrived [1620] and struck hard again in the early years of White settlement.'[14]

In contrast, when black slaves were hit by disease, their white masters took immediate precautions: inoculation and treatment. Black slaves were valuable property, the source of great profits, to be looked after, therefore, as one would farm animals. But when disease swept through Native American villages, their white neighbours were gratified, regarding this as divine providence, God's intervention to ensure that Europeans replaced the natives on their land. There were also cases of Europeans in effect waging bacteriological warfare against Native Americans by infecting trade goods with smallpox.[15] In 1763, the English commander Lord Amherst, following defeat at the hands of an alliance of French and indigenous forces under the Ottawa leader, Pontiac, instructed a subordinate to infect the Indians by means of 'gifts' of smallpox blankets and 'to try every other method that can serve to extirpate this execrable race'.[16] This was not an isolated incident. In 1837, at Fort Clark, North Dakota, the US Army dispensed 'trade blankets' taken from a military infirmary in St Louis quarantined for smallpox to Mandans and other Indians. This ignited 'a pandemic which raged for several years', killing perhaps 100,000 natives. Whatever the figure, there is little doubt 'their "vanishing" made the subsequent US conquest of the entire Plains region, begun seriously in the 1850s, far easier than it would otherwise have been'.[17]

European settlers were thus not passive, unwitting and blameless carriers of disease, but actively fostered contamination of the native people. Moreover, European settlement not only robbed the Native Americans of their lands but also destroyed their environment. The building of roads and staging posts, and later the railroads, frightened the game away, but the colonists also hunted it to extinction, selling meat to the growing cities. The Native Americans' environment was gradually degraded, resulting in hunger and malnutrition, a major factor in disease and early death. The rest were impoverished and rendered dependent on government handouts for which they often unknowingly traded their lands. And over the four centuries between 1492 and 1890, the date of the last great battle – Wounded Knee – there was an accelerating tide of mass deportations, with many, particularly the sick and hungry, dying on the way. In the west, they were forced on to reservations, with increasingly small hunting grounds unable to guarantee their survival.

However, there is evidence that the Anglo-American native population, after collapsing in the first two centuries of colonial settlement, began to rise again. According to a study by Jeanne Kay of four Native American tribes living in a region stretching from the Great Lakes east to the Midwest and down to the Mississippi valley, these groups experienced a catastrophic population decline in the 130 years or so following contact with European settlers in the late sixteenth century. But their population began to recover around 1700 and rose steadily until 1840. Kay attributes this revival to the rise of the fur trade, whose system of exchange encouraged these tribes to develop other resources to sell and to consume themselves, for example, maple sugar. 'Fur traders provided economic incentives for Indians to develop previously little-used resources, and traded or donated food to ward off starvation.'[18] These products improved native levels of subsistence. Kay also indicates that after two centuries of being stricken by European diseases, Native Americans developed a degree of immunity: 'accounts of disease epidemics are comparatively infrequent between 1690 and 1830, suggesting that disease mortality diminished after the initial post-contact depopulation'.[19] Arguably, other regions would have witnessed a similar demographic revival in the eighteenth century.

Dobyns, however, argues that epidemics continued to decimate the Anglo-American native population from 1520 till 1900: 'A serious contagious disease causing significant mortality invaded North American peoples at intervals of four years and two and a half months, on the average, from 1520 to 1900.'[20] In contrast, the native population in Spanish America did not experience the same disastrous population loss after the early period, a factor which emphasises the role of biological warfare, famine, poverty and so on in Anglo America. According to Charles Gibson, the Native American population of the Spanish colonies collapsed in the sixteenth century, falling from 50 million at the beginning to 25 million in 1519 and to just over 1 million in 1605. After that, it began to rise again, reaching 4 million in the course of the seventeenth century, and 7.5 million by the end of the colonial period.[21]

Finally, the Europeans induced alcoholism among natives, whereas black slaves were only occasionally allowed alcohol during holiday periods. The conclusion must surely be that disease, devastating though it was to begin with, is not a factor sufficient to account for the virtual disappearance of the Native Americans from Anglo America.

Anglo-American Genocide

In Anglo America, by the end of the nineteenth century, there were no more than a few hundred thousand natives compared with the 8 to 12 million of the pre-Columbian population. The early period witnessed neither the all-out offensive and enslavement by the Spanish conquistadors nor the subsequent assimilation of Native Americans into the white settler-colonies of the Spanish Empire. In Anglo America, it was the unrelenting pressure of the settler-farmers sweeping westwards in ever larger waves that pushed the Native Americans out of their traditional homelands, with ethnic cleansing gradually descending into outright genocide.

The early Anglo-American settlers also needed labour. Did they try to use Native Americans either as free labourers or as slaves? According to Mann, the colonists tried to press captured natives into farming, but centuries of life as hunter-gatherers did not facilitate a smooth transfer to settled agriculture.[22] An alternative view of the Anglo-American natives' level of agricultural development is provided by Nash, Zinn and others, as we shall see.

In the Americas, European settlers plundered the gold and silver mines of Mexico and Peru, and later, new sources of wealth such as sugar, rice, coffee, tobacco and indigo. At first, in areas such as Brazil and Mexico, Spanish and Portuguese colonists coerced native labour into working in agriculture and mining, but the native people were ravaged by disease. Moreover, 'the colonisers found that Indians, far more at home in their environment than white settlers, were difficult to subjugate'.[23] Moreover, in Anglo America, members of weaker native tribes were enslaved by the colonists in alliance with stronger tribes. 'In 1708, the population of the white settlements in Carolina included about 5300 whites, 2900 African slaves and 1400 Indian slaves.'[24] The Puritans of New England, apart from trying to employ the Native Americans, also made attempts to convert them to Christianity. But alongside these efforts at 'civilising the heathens' came the first genocidal atrocities: in 1622, carried out by the Virginian settlers, and in 1637 in New England.[25]

The Quakers

One group among the colonists adopted a different attitude towards the Native Americans – the Quakers of Pennsylvania and New Jersey. Their pacifism protected the local natives for several generations and also attracted large numbers fleeing from cleansing operations elsewhere. The Quakers tried to carry out assimilation by means of education, conversion, work and the abandonment of the hunter-warrior culture, the tribal order and native notions of collective rather than private property. Early on, Presidents Washington and Jefferson, several war secretaries, and federal 'Indian' agencies worked closely with missionaries and educational bodies in this assimilation project, to which, however, white settlers remained largely opposed.[26] The project did attract a few Native Americans, but was contradicted by the continuous economic, political and military pressure they were subjected to. 'Their experience of settlers was of greed, exploitation and betrayal.'[27]

Moreover, assimilation implied abandoning their institutions of tribal collectivism and egalitarianism, which had sustained them for centuries, and entering a society based on different values without any guarantees about their future welfare. To do so meant stepping into the unknown. A number did try to join white colonial society and were rejected. Understandably, many Native Americans chose to resist the relentless tide of European settlement. They raided farms, out of hunger as well as anger. Kenny quotes a letter from Benjamin Franklin explaining Indian attacks on small farming communities in Pennsylvania in the 1750s: 'The object of the attacks was to intimidate the settlers, drive them out, and turn them against the provincial government. In so doing, they hoped to recover lost land, or at least the land they occupied, as the basis of an equitable peace.'[28]

This provoked massive retaliation on the part of the colonists, guided by an ideology that justified such creeping genocide by depicting Native Americans as either savages or animals. According to Berkhofer, the early English or French idea of the natives as savage probably derives from the medieval legend of the 'wild man', 'a hairy, naked, club-wielding child of nature who existed halfway between humanity and animality'.[29] In the late eighteenth or early nineteenth century, there was a transition to racial labels derived from a pseudo-scientific classification of races as distinct species, akin to labels pinned on to the African slaves. As Mann says: 'God plus science reinforced economic, military, and political power to make it difficult for Europeans and Indians to live together.'[30]

From Ethnic Cleansing to Genocide

The southern Native Americans – the Cherokee, Creek, Chickasaw, Choctaw and Seminole tribes residing in Mississippi, Alabama, Georgia, Tennessee and Florida – had made considerable progress in adapting to the European way of life, to the extent that they were dubbed 'the five civilised tribes'. Many had become proficient artisans, and with the depletion of their game resources had replaced hunting with farming as the means of sustenance. Some had even developed large plantations, owning scores of slaves and herds of cattle, becoming more prosperous than their white neighbours. Their children went to school. 'The southern Indians were adapting to the white man's world at such a rate that there was every prospect that they might soon merge into the mainstream of American life as fully acceptable citizens.'[31]

These hopes were dashed by the removal decree passed in 1830 by a small majority in Congress at the behest of the Georgia state government, egged on by President Andrew Jackson. Perhaps the most poignant chapter in this shameful story was the impact on the Cherokees, whose acculturation to white society in the 1820s had advanced the furthest: they had adopted settled agriculture and private property, and developed a written language and permanent political institutions, including a democratic constitution modelled on that of the US.[32] Yet they too were rejected by the state of Georgia under pressure from the settlers. Of the country's 13 million people, 11 million lived in the north where there was widespread sympathy with the natives and disapproval of the removal of their legal rights. Despite protests, in 1830 Congress voted to deport the Cherokees westwards, the Senate ratifying the vote by 31 to 15. More than 8,000 died in the infamous Trail of Tears in 1838, the expulsion from their homeland across Tennessee, Kentucky Illinois and Missouri.[33]

Who was responsible for this genocidal cleansing? According to Van Every, there was a hierarchy of responsibility. Immediate blame for the natives' suffering lay with the motley crew of southern politicians, land speculators, contractors, lawyers and the local police who, acting in concert, personally visited aggression and cruelty upon the indigenous people. At another level were those southerners who no doubt experienced pangs of conscience but looked the other way. Also, in their unswerving support for the principle of states' rights, they continued to re-elect officials who had committed these crimes. Even greater shame lay with those Congress members who had voted not only against their own convictions but also, according to Van Every, against those of their constituents. But the main responsibility, he argues, lay with the American people as a whole. They had not been revolted by the spectacle of injustice. The failure of the government of the United States to dispense justice had not been due to any institutional breakdown of democracy but to the hypocritical 'unreadiness of the American people to rise to the demands democracy was making upon them'.[34]

For the south, the removal was a total victory which, Van Every suggests, encouraged them to hold out more firmly than they might otherwise have done on the issue of slavery that came to the boil in the brutal Civil War of 1860–4. According to Mann, there was a trajectory of genocide that began with 'Plan A of limited deportations plus partial assimilation, moving some Indians away, converting all to Christianity, and maintaining racial barriers against full assimilation.'[35] Confronted with continuing waves of European settlers, the federal government moved on to Plan B of forced deportations to reservations that they fondly hoped would enable the Native Americans to maintain their life and traditions. The federal government and Supreme Court might adopt a more conciliatory and humanitarian stance: the Court eventually ruled that properly constituted Indian governments had sovereign power to negotiate treaties over their lands. Since eastern politicians represented electorates for whom Native Americans 'were no longer salient', they could afford to adopt an attitude of 'disinterested enlightenment'. But the local state governments in the frontier areas were responsive to the interests and pressures of the settlers.[36] A cycle of land encroachment and resistance induced southern or western legislatures in the 1820s and 1830s to press for deportations and mostly to reject the idea of granting land or subsidies to the Native Americans to make segregated resettlement on reservations a viable proposition. Advocating deportation, accompanied by genocidal rhetoric, was more of a vote-winner than the idea of higher taxes to help the Native Americans.

Another example was California, whose constitution of 1850 provided full white male suffrage, the most advanced democracy of the time, but which also sanctioned the detention and placing in indentured labour of any Native Americans who fled from the reservations, including children. Between 1769, when the Spanish missions were established, and 1845, when the United States defeated Mexico to conquer California, the native population declined by 75 per cent. In the following 25 years under US rule, it would fall by a further 80 per cent. The California legislature opposed granting land rights to the Native Americans, but 'they then had to face the final consequences of such obduracy, since there was nowhere farther west to which the problem could be sent'.[37] This geopolitical reality drove successive governors to utter genocidal threats. Governor Burnett rejected the idea of conciliation through adequate reservations. In fact, the gold rush was attracting an avalanche of miners and ranchers who 'seemed to delight in killing Indians, miners and ranchers who rose to political power and prominence – and from those platforms not only legalised the enslavement of California Indians but, as in Colorado and elsewhere, launched public campaigns of genocide with the explicitly stated goal of all-out Indian extermination'.[38] The problem was that the settlers' continuing seizure of Indian land was increasing their resistance, leading Governor Burnett to declare: 'A war of extermination will continue to be waged between the two races until the Indian becomes extinct.' His successor, Governor McDougall, agreed: the war 'must of necessity be one of extermination to many of the tribes'. Not even Hitler dared to declare so openly his policy of extermination of the Jews.[39]

The US government moved finally to Plan C, issuing the threat of genocide if the Native Americans did not accept deportation. Presidents Washington and Jefferson are famous for proclaiming support for the Rights of Man. But these enlightened presidents forgot about the Enlightenment when the Native Americans fought alongside the British in the War of Independence (1775–83). Washington instructed his generals to attack the Iroquois and 'lay waste all their settlements ... that the country may not be merely overrun but destroyed', and not to 'listen to any overture of peace before the total ruin of their settlements is effected'. Indians were like wolves, he said, who must be driven west of the Mississippi, with any who remained being broken by force. Jefferson, too, during Indian wars, forgot about the Rights of Man, declaring his support for the 'root-and-branch destruction of hostile tribes', or else their deportation beyond the Mississippi. 'Nothing is more desirable than total suppression of their savage insolence and cruelties ... Their ferocious barbarities justified extermination.' As Mann points out, 'neither Washington nor Jefferson ever spoke about the civilized British enemy in exterminist language'.[40] Jefferson's first choice solution was assimilation, followed by deportation, but extermination was unavoidable if the Native Americans rejected these or offered resistance.

Andrew Jackson is sometimes depicted by revisionist historians as a pragmatist, 'bending to pressure from southern legislatures over deportations, prepared to defend Indians against white squatters ... but coming to believe that deportations were ultimately the only way to protect Indians from the white man'. Mann describes this account as whitewash. When the Native Americans resisted, Jackson was ferocious. When one white woman was taken prisoner by the Creeks, his response was: 'I shall penetrate the Creek towns until the Captive with her Captors are delivered up, and think myself Justifiable in laying waste their villages, burning their houses, killing their warriors and leading into Captivity their wives and children, until I do obtain a surrender of the Captive and the Captors.'[41] Jackson believed that '"fear is better than love with an Indian"; he urged his soldiers to kill women and children'.[42] As Remini says, 'Most white men in America had a long history of racism. They regarded other races as inferior and were not about to accept assimilation, no matter what the Founding Fathers hoped.'[43] Jackson's reputation is thus forever tarnished.

So, under Jackson, the great democratic leader of the American people, the tragic and horrible removal of the Indians began. Whatever the intentions of those responsible for the policy, the actual removal was a frightful injustice which brought sickness, starvation, and death to thousands of human beings.'[44]

Absence of a Plan

Twentieth-century genocides and politicides, such as the Jewish and Armenian holocausts, usually occurred at the behest of the existing state authorities and were planned in advance. In the case of the Native Americans, no such plan was drawn up by the state or elements within it. Ordinary settlers on the frontier, assisted by the army, did most of the killing, but with the encouragement of the federal state. Ethnic cleansing occurred in small rolling waves of local land dispossession and expulsion. After a series of such acts – a process lasting anywhere from five to 50 years – a large area had been rendered free of Native Americans and consolidated by European land-grabbers. The degree of violence accompanying each act of land seizure depended on the relative numbers of whites and Native Americans, the speed of the land seizure, and the capacity of the natives to resist.

Moreover, during hostilities the Europeans routinely engaged in the indiscriminate killing of all Native Americans, including women and children, in the vicinity. This 'was more than an atrocity. It was flatly and intentionally genocidal. For no population can survive if its women and children are destroyed.'[45] The sequence of plans A, B and C is not applicable to the settlers since 'local exigencies, the lack of a highly institutionalised local state, and their own greed and ideology would drive them quickly through varied cleansing means'.[46] Killers generally justified their actions in terms of self-defence or retaliation for Indian atrocities. But in reality it was escalation – massive retaliation – such as when a 36-strong militia unit looking for the killers of one white man found an Indian village and killed all but two or three of its 150 inhabitants.

Spanish America: Genocide or Exploitation?

According to Stannard, between 1492, when Columbus landed at Hispaniola, and 1518, the island's native population dropped from 8 million to less than 20,000,[47] wiped out by disease, enslavement and genocidal murder. The Spanish then turned to Mexico and Central America, extending their tentacles south.[48] They were hungry for gold and silver, and hundreds of thousands of Native Americans were enslaved in the mines. By 1542, half a million Nicaraguan natives were exported for slave labour – a death sentence – to distant lands whose population had been decimated. Enslavement went hand in hand with death from disease and mass murder, including unbelievably sadistic cruelty.[49] In central Mexico, within 75 years of the arrival of the European colonists under Cortes, the population fell by almost 95 per cent, from 25 million in 1519 to 1.3 million in 1595.[50] Across Mexico and Central America, the European invasion resulted in the sudden and almost total disappearance of peoples who had lived and prospered there for thousands of years.

Peru and Chile were home to the Incas, one of the wealthiest and largest empires in the world, with 9 to 14 million inhabitants. Here too 'conquistadors' diseases preceded them: smallpox and other epidemics swept down through Mexico and across the Andes in the early 1520s ... but also, as elsewhere, the soldiers and settlers who followed wreaked ... havoc and destruction themselves'. By the end of the century, some 94 per cent of the population had been killed, between 8.5 and 13 million people. As in Mexico and Central America, 'Indians were flogged, hanged, drowned, dismembered, and set upon by dogs of war as the Spanish and others demanded more gold and silver than the natives were able to supply.'[51]

Despite the colonists' barbarism, it was enslavement on the plantations and in the silver mines, together with starvation and disease, that killed most natives.[52] The irrationality of the slaughter can be gleaned from the fact that the Spanish, on entering the region, destroyed the Incas' roads and bridges, agricultural terraces and canals. They slaughtered thousands of llamas to eat the marrow-fat and to make tallow candles while the rest of the meat was wasted. They also carried out unbelievable destruction of agriculture. Natives were left with nothing to plant and, since they had no cattle, they died of hunger.[53] The life expectancy of natives working in mines or on plantations in Peru as slaves was around three to four months, roughly the same as that of a prisoner working in Auschwitz in the 1940s.[54]

Some friars and settlers eventually wrote to the Spanish king, asking him to moderate the genocide in case the disappearance of the natives ended their supply of labour.[55] The king consented with a decree in 1551 ordering labour to become voluntary, but in the 1560s this was countermanded by the viceroy who ordered that one-seventh of the native population be drafted to work in the mines. After four months, this group would be replaced by another. A century after the first encounter of the Andean population with the Europeans, between 94 and 96 per cent had been exterminated: along 2,000 miles of coastline, where once 6.5 million people had lived, almost everyone was dead.[56] By the end of the sixteenth century, some 200,000 Spanish had moved to the Indies, Mexico,

Central and South America. In contrast, somewhere between 60 and 80 million natives were dead. However, a lower figure was given by the great Jesuit reformer Bartolomé de las Casas who estimated that 'by 1542 "our Spaniards" in the Caribbean, Mexico and Central America had "devastated the land and exterminated the rational people who fully inhabited it", killing "more than twelve million men, women and children"'.[57]

Ben Kiernan also argues that 'direct killing caused only a minority of the Indian deaths ... From the outset, a major goal of their oppressors was enslavement.' From the day of his arrival, Columbus predicted that the Indians 'should be good servants'.[58] Las Casas was also clear that 'the motive of the Spanish slave-drivers was generally not to exterminate the Indians but to exploit their labour'. According to him, the settlers didn't kill the natives out of hatred. 'They kill them because they want to be rich and get a lot of gold ... through the labour and sweat of the tortured and the unfortunate.'[59]

Spanish Imperial Control

The conquistadors quickly established the *encomienda* system. This was a 'trusteeship labour system', a division not of the land but of communities, which enabled the governors or *encomenderos* to impose a kind of medieval feudal domination over the natives. The maximum size of an encomienda was 300 natives. Their *encomenderos* resembled feudal lords in that they exacted tribute from the people in kind or in taxes, seizing more and more of their land and ruthlessly exploiting those under their ostensible care. They used their power to drive many natives into a kind of slavery. As Stannard puts it: 'the result was an even greater increase in cruelty and a magnification of the firestorm of human devastation'.[60]

The conquistadores carried out numerous acts of barbarism against the natives in their bid to crush their resistance and subject them to forced labour in the mines and plantations. The result of the *encomienda* system in the West Indies was that it wiped out a major economic resource, namely the native population itself.[61] Indeed, the Spanish government set up a body of laws to govern its new empire, many of which were promulgated to protect the natives against the cruelty of the Spanish settlers. Only 20 years after Columbus landed, the first law designed to regulate relations between Spaniards and natives on Hispaniola decreed that 'no person ... shall dare to beat any Indian with sticks, or whip him, or call him dog, or address him by any name other than his proper name alone'.[62]

Bartolomé de las Casas

Much credit must go to the great Jesuit reformer Bartolomé de las Casas who rejected the common view that the Native Americans were an inferior type of humanity. Stretching 'out his hand to the American Indians with faith in the capacity for civilisation of all peoples',[63] he wrote a treatise on Indian culture in which he insisted that it must not be judged by Spanish criteria but on its own terms.[64] He campaigned tirelessly for justice and sought to clarify the ethical and legal basis on which Spaniards were entitled to wage war against the natives, to acquire land and to persuade them to accept Spanish civilisation.[65] According to J.H. Elliott, 'the theologians protested and the Queen's conscience rebelled, and enslavement of the Indians was formally prohibited in 1500'. Exceptions were made, however, and Cortes easily found pretexts to enslave men, women and children.[66] In 1542, the Cortes in Valladolid petitioned the emperor 'to remedy the cruelties which are committed in the Indies against the Indians'.[67] Also that year, Las Casas persuaded the Spanish authorities to pass the 'New Laws' which banned the enslavement of Native Americans and the encomienda system by which they were tied to Spanish masters.[68]

By the mid sixteenth century, moreover, the *encomiendas* had become sources of independent settler power. The unified monarchy had destroyed the power of the old feudal nobility in the late fifteenth and early sixteenth centuries. They were now concerned to prevent the growth of a hereditary feudal aristocracy in the New World. So the settlers were barred from creating their own Cortes or other representative institutions which might one day become a source of independent power. 'The officials of the Spanish Crown slowly asserted their authority over every aspect of American life, forcing *encomenderos* and cabildos to yield before them.'[69] As Elliott says: 'the crown was determined to impose its own authority at the earliest opportunity. Too much was at stake, in terms of both potential American revenues and the commitment entered into with the papacy for the salvation of Indian souls, to permit the kind of laissez-faire approach that would characterise so much of early Stuart policy towards the new plantations.'[70]

Native Autonomy and Integration

The *encomiendas* were replaced by *corregimientos* – districts with governors appointed by and responsible to the Crown. According to Spicer, 'this system was established as the mechanism for ensuring crown control of and direct benefit from Indian labour and tribute, and for bringing Indian communities, with the aid of the ecclesiastics, into the empire as fully functioning local governments and cultural units'. Again, native communities retained considerable local autonomy.[71] Magnus Morner gives a similar account of the Indians' legal status under the Spanish empire:

> The Indians were to be governed by authorities of their own and ruled partly in accordance with their ancient customs, but they were specially supervised and their liberty of movement was restricted. They had to pay tribute to the king or to the *encomendero* and they also had to perform labour. On the other hand, they were exempted from tithes and sales tax.[72]

The major preoccupation of the Spanish, given that they were intent not on genocide but exploitation, was the best means of integrating the natives into colonial society. According to Spicer, the Spanish adopted four approaches to the problem of assimilation. The difference between these methods was partly due to cultural variation among the native communities but also, more importantly, to the needs of the Spanish, facing, as they did, different ecological and demographic situations. Spicer argues that this variety indicates 'the wide adaptive potential of the Spanish social system'.[73]

Four Types of Assimilation

1. Among the Aztecs, their alienation from Spanish life impelled the colonists to create new rules to ensure a steady flow of native labour and tribute. The 'protective separation' of Spaniards, black slaves and mestizos (mixed European and native) from the natives meant Spaniards were restricted from residing in native communities: distances were established between native and non-native towns and land. The former were reorganised as political and ecclesiastical units with a high level of autonomy. This changed during the mid 1660s, following a major demographic shift: the Indian population began to rise after its catastrophic collapse over 150 years. The *hacienda* emerged as a privately owned plantation competing for land and labour. Indian life reoriented itself towards the *hacienda* and the economic security its rising wages offered. Many Indians became distant from their communities. At the same time, however, the *hacienda*'s intensifying exploitation drove the Indian communities to become more tightly integrated and oriented away from Spanish society.[74]

2. As for the Yacquis of north-west Mexico, the Jesuits entered their territory without military escort and proceeded to convert by persuasion, as advocated by Las Casas. The *encomienda* system was never introduced. Instead, the Jesuits developed the 'mission community', a political unit organised according to the principles of Spanish local government, without, however, channelling tribute or labour to the Crown. Instead, the Yacquis were persuaded to give a portion of their surpluses to the local mission. From 1617 until the 1730s, the missionaries controlled Yacqui towns by appointing Yacquis to local office. However, in 1740, they were provoked into rebellion by settlers moving to the edge of their country and the administration's attempt to undermine the Jesuits' authority, although the Yacquis did participate in the new mixed towns. The eighteenth century witnessed the rise of a new autonomous local organisation, with the Yacquis selecting and modifying those Spanish political and military elements which fitted with their life and community.[75]

3. The Pueblos of northern New Spain were integrated by a method closer to that adopted for the Aztecs, although culturally they were quite different. The first phase, from 1610 to 1692, witnessed the setting up of the standard institutions of Spanish rule: *encomienda*, tribute, *corregimiento*, mission and ecclesiastical tribunals, the Spanish town and 'the Spanish blueprint for the reorganisation of Indian communities'. However, the number of Spaniards was small and settlers tended to occupy land outside the traditional Indian areas.[76] Hence pressure on land was not intense. The major conflict was between church and state, rivals for Indian

labour, with the ecclesiastical authorities oppressing the natives more harshly than the civil.

At the outset of Spanish rule, Pueblo communities differed from Aztec ones in being politically autonomous areas of local government. There was no class of hereditary rulers or priests, indeed no system based on wealth or power. The missionaries established themselves in the Pueblo settlements and, with military back-up, forced the natives to build churches. However, the local native priests continued to function, and the towns were not reconstituted units as among the Yacquis, so the missionaries were not able to exercise authority. It was the missionaries' frustration with their inability to change this system that led them to try to suppress the indigenous religion, thus sparking the rebellion of 1680.[77]

The result of the rebellion was the passing of power from the ecclesiastical to the civil authorities. The Pueblos became allies of the Spanish against common enemies amongst other native tribes. There was less and less interference in their local government, so the Pueblo communities survived little changed since the conquest. The result was the co-existence of two distinct cultural systems, with 'neither a re-forming Indian culture like that of the Yacquis, nor a withdrawal from Spanish involvement as in the case of the Aztecs in the Valley of Mexico'.[78]

4. Finally, while the region of Bajio was devastated by the conquest it contained the largest silver mines in all of New Spain. Thousands of natives were therefore able to earn good wages from the mines and the Spanish settlements that sprang up in the area. This fourth method of incorporation involved the destruction of the native communities and the displacement of the population over 150 years. The result was a 'progressive cultural assimilation on the part of the Indians who had lost their territorial roots. The great majority took this route and became the foundation of Mexico's Mestizo population.'[79]

Anglo and Spanish America

There can be little doubt that the term 'genocide' is highly apposite as a description of the treatment meted out to the Native Americans by the European settlers in British colonial and post-revolutionary America. It does not, however, seem appropriate when applied to the Spanish and Portuguese empires. The problem with the two major works discussed here – by David Stannard and Ward Churchill, both published in the 1990s – is that they lump together the experience of the natives in Anglo and Latin America. According to their view, Native Americans throughout the continent were victims of an identical European genocide. However, closer analysis challenges this undiffer-entiated approach. There was, for example, a difference between the English and French approaches to the natives. As Charles Thomson (a Patriot leader of the American Revolution) noted regarding the Pennsylvania western Delawares: '"The English, in order to get their lands, drive them as far from them as possible, nor seem to care what becomes of them, provided they can get them removed out of the Way of their present settlements."' In contrast, the French, '"who enjoy the Friendship of the Indians, use all the Means in their Power to draw as many into their Alliance as possible"'. According to Thomson, by this means the French made friends of the Indians 'whereas the British excelled in turning them into their "most bitter enemies".'[80] However, Delaware leaders Shingas and his brothers made it clear that in wartime the French were no better than the British.

Perhaps the clearest illustration of the considerably different experience of the natives in Anglo and Latin America is the degree of intermarriage. In Anglo America, there were only a tiny number of intermarriages with native women, it being a practice towards which colonial and post-revolutionary society were deeply hostile. The state never attempted to regulate such relationships, as this would have been to accept intermarriage as a normal social institution. In contrast, the Spanish Crown recognised intermarriage between Europeans and natives and sought to regulate it. As Nash says, 'Latin America is known as the area of the world where the most extensive blending of the races in human history has taken place.'[81] Both psycho-cultural and socio-demographic reasons are adduced to explain this: firstly, prior to the European colonisation of the New World, the Spanish and Portuguese had a history of interaction with different cultures, particularly with darker-skinned people, whereas the English did not. As a result of centuries of war and trade with Middle Eastern and North African people,

> Iberian society had already absorbed new cultural and genetic elements and developed flexible attitudes about the sexual mixing of peoples. The English, by contrast, had remained within their island fortress, sheltered from other cultures and therefore disposed toward viewing interracial contacts with suspicion.[82]

Secondly, the Catholic Church had a permissive attitude towards non–Christian people. Thirdly, Roman law, on which Spanish law was based, protected the slave. These factors combined with the paternalistic attitude of the Iberian governments 'to make racial intermixture acceptable ... By contrast, English Protestantism was unusually rigid in admitting "savage" people to the church.'[83] Other historians emphasise material factors encountered in the New World, mainly the disproportionately male character of Spanish colonial society which led the men to take native women as sexual partners, both as mistresses and wives, whereas the population of Anglo America consisted far more of families. Other factors shaping the new cultural intermixing were the extent to which Native Americans could be pressed into forced labour, and the need to employ non-Europeans in positions of authority.[84]

In 1514, the Spanish government decreed that Spaniards were free to marry native women. Two kinds of intermarriage were promoted: between Spaniards and daughters of tribal chiefs (caciques), specifically where there was no male heir, and between native women and *encomenderos*. However, as James Lockhart explains:

> men in all ethnic categories from the Spanish down continued to produce children from informal matches with women in lower categories than

theirs, while for the middle categories and Indians-among-Spaniards, ethnic intermarriage was so prevalent as to become the norm ... Miscegenation did not occur because of any lack of Spanish women. The great multiplication of people in mixed categories comes in the later period, long after the short-lived under-representation of Spanish women in the conquest generation.

This was an essential part of the process of social change which Lockhart describes as 'the biological and cultural intermixing of the various ethnic groups'.[85]

Capitalism or Feudalism?

A debate between Andre Gunder Frank and Ernesto Laclau in the late 1960s and early '70s focused on whether Latin America was, from the time of the conquest, dominated by capitalist relations. Frank argued that it was, since even the local market in the Spanish empire was tied to the world market. Laclau, however, argued that if market relations were a sufficient criterion of capitalism, then most of the feudal period or of ancient Roman slave society should also be counted as capitalist. Laclau insisted on defining a society according to its dominant relations of production (the key factor in the mode of production), rather than to whether it is linked into a network of commercial relations with the outside world. He argued, against Frank, that the world economy was characterised by 'economic dualism', with some European metropolitan states embarking on the development of capitalist relations of production, while the satellite colonial economies, such as Spanish America, remained dominated by pre-capitalist, specifically feudal relationships. The relation between the two remained one of the dependence of the latter on the former. 'The expansion of industrial capitalism in the metropolitan countries necessarily depended on the maintenance of pre-capitalist modes of production in the peripheral areas.'[86]

State Feudalism

We have seen how the Spanish Crown exacted tribute from the native population, leading several writers to describe their economic relations as one of feudal dependence. But we also saw how the Crown fought hard, and largely successfully, to prevent the growth of a hereditary feudal class or caste. This leads one to conclude that the most accurate description of Spanish American society following the conquest is 'state feudalism'. We must recall, however, that while the relations of production between feudal lord and serf were exploitative, the nobility also had a duty of protection towards the peasants. We have seen how this played out in the protective approach of the Spanish monarchy towards the Indians. Moreover, the thousands of Crown bureaucrats in Spain and Spanish America would seem to have constituted a specific class in Spanish society. Lewis Hanke perhaps sums up best the dual nature, and contradictory character, of the Spanish conquest, as being not just a great military achievement but also 'one of the greatest attempts the world has seen to make Christian precepts prevail in the relations between peoples'. This attempt rested on two fundamental Christian principles: that 'all men are equal before God, and that a Christian has a responsibility for the welfare of his brothers no matter how alien or lowly they may be'.[87] As Hanke explains, the contradictions at the heart of Spanish Crown policy stemmed from its attempt to reconcile two conflicting aims: 'as Spanish rulers, the kings sought imperial dominion, prestige and revenue – in short, conquest and the fruits of conquest which involve war. As heads of the church in America, they were urgently committed to the great enterprise of winning the Indians to the faith – which requires peace.'[88] An accurate description of their social character would perhaps be 'authoritarian-paternalistic'.

To return to the contrasting experiences of Indians in Anglo and Latin America, there seems little doubt that the difference was that between labour exploitation – often brutal, but which required the exploited to remain alive – and a genocidal racism in which land theft and ethnic cleansing eventually led to holocaust. Interestingly, there was no equivalent in Anglo America of either Bartolomé de las Casas or Father Vieira. The closest would perhaps be William Penn.

Was Assimilation Impossible?

Is this contrast explicable solely in economic terms – in terms of the desire for land as opposed to the desire for wealth; the lower density of the native population in Anglo America compared to Latin America; or the superiority of Africans as slaves? Or do such explanations only go some of the way in accounting for the difference? Was assimilation and acculturation, whether one-way or two-way, impossible, as the majority of historians either argue or simply assume? Were the European and native cultures so distinct, located at such different stages of the evolution of human societies, that no mutual accommodation was possible? One fall-back position adopted by some scholars is to argue that the natives of Spanish America, and especially Mexico, had developed settled agriculture, while those of Anglo America remained 'small and wandering bands of nomads who inhabited [the] "virgin land" before it was discovered by Europeans'.[89]

Howard Zinn has questioned some of these assumptions, beginning with the belief that the Native Americans had not progressed beyond the economic stage of hunter-gatherers:

> Responding to the different environments of soil and climate, they developed hundreds of different tribal cultures, perhaps two thousand different languages. They perfected the art of agriculture, and figured out how to grow maize (corn) which cannot grow by itself ... They ingeniously developed a variety of other vegetables and fruits ... On their own, the Indians were engaged in the great agricultural revolution that other peoples in Asia, Europe, Africa were going through about the same time. While many of the tribes remained nomadic hunters and food gatherers in wandering, egalitarian communes, others began to live in more settled communities where there was more food, larger populations, more division of labour between men and women, more

surplus to feed chiefs and priests, more leisure time for artistic and social work and for building houses.[90]

Zinn concludes by questioning 'the excuse of progress in the annihilation of races, and the telling of history from the standpoint of the conquerors and leaders of Western civilisation'.[91]

According to Stannard, despite the diseases and massacres the natives had already endured, they maintained their ability 'to produce enormous amounts of food', impressing the earliest British explorers:

> Beans, pumpkins and many other vegetables, especially corn, which was greatly superior in its yield ... and in its variety of uses to anything Europeans had ever seen, were grown in fields tended with such care that they looked more like huge gardens ... than farmlands ... Some British, despite their general disdain for the Indians, initially praised their technological ingenuity.[92]

Indeed, the early Pilgrim Fathers were saved from starvation by the generosity and human solidarity displayed by local Wampanoags, Pequots and other Indians who shared their harvest with the English settlers. 'The following spring, these pitiful English hunter-gatherers were taught how to plant crops for themselves.'[93] Nash describes the relationship between Squanto, a Wampanoag native who survived the plague which had killed most of his tribe, and the Pilgrims to whom he gave valuable assistance.[94]

According to Nash, archaeologists estimate that the transition from hunter-gathering to settled agriculture in the New World began around 5000 BCE, roughly the same time that it spread from southwest Asia and Africa to Europe. The effects of producing domesticated plant instead of gathering it wild were threefold: first, it allowed settled village life to replace nomadic existence; second, it boosted population growth as a result of the huge increase in food supply; third, it reduced the time and energy necessary to produce food, creating surpluses that permitted the emergence of specialised tasks in the fields of politics, religion, technology and art.[95] Indeed, as Annette Jaimes points out, the much larger population estimate of 15 to 20 million north of Mexico itself implies a more advanced, sedentary agriculture, rather than nomadic hunting and gathering.[96]

The Europeans encountered Native American communities at very different stages of this agricultural revolution, a range of tribes or nations displaying a considerable cultural diversity. In the southwest region of North America, the Hohokam and Anasazi societies had been engaged in agriculture and village life for several thousand years before the arrival of the Spanish in the 1540s. By about 1200 CE, the 'Pueblo' people had developed villages with large terraced buildings containing many rooms. When the Spanish arrived, descendants of the Anasazi had constructed canals, check-dams, and hillside terraces for irrigating previously arid areas. On the northwest Pacific coast, tribes organised their communities around cedar wood and salmon and other spawning fish. Among the most impressive were the mound builders of the Ohio River Valley, who constructed gigantic geometric earthwork sculptures, shaped like humans, birds or serpents.[97]

By the time Christianity emerged, these Native American societies had reached a level of considerable complexity. Archaeologists have discovered a great variety of items in mound tombs, indicating that the mound builders participated in an advanced trading network linking villages across the continent.[98] The anthropologist H.J. Spinden reached a similar conclusion in 1929: 'about four-sevenths of the agricultural production of the United States [is] in economic plants domesticated by the American Indian and taken over by the white man'.[99] According to Jaimes, 'American Indians had perfected elaborate and sophisticated agricultural technologies throughout the hemisphere long before the arrival of the first European.'[100] Stiffarm and Lane also argue that 'the methods adopted in North America included planting rather than sowing seeds in the Old World fashion – a practice that allowed for seed selection and the perfection of specific plant strains – as well as crop rotation and fertilisation'.[101]

However, Nash claims that almost from the beginning of European settlement in Virginia, for example, the tribe led by Powhatan 'eagerly incorporated technological innovations and material objects of the newcomers into their culture, but they rejected or resisted the other aspects of European life' – their religious, social and political organisations, values and beliefs.[102] Archaeologists excavating a Mississippi Valley city known as Cahokia, which they estimated to have had a population of 30,000 to 40,000, found numerous ornaments, tools and artefacts including ceramics, finely sculptured stonework, embossed and engraved copper and mica sheets, indicating that it was a genuine urban centre with complex housing structures, markets and specialists in tool-making, hide-dressing, potting, jewellery, weaving and salt-making.[103] Moreover, 'towns of up to 10,000 were not especially uncommon in the great river basins areas east of the Mississippi. Dobyns estimated that 150 communities of 2000 or more people existed in the year 1500 in Florida alone.'[104] These discoveries would seem to put paid to the idea that the European settlers could not have employed natives as wage-labourers because of the low density of the population in North America – an argument that features prominently in Elliott's account of the differences between the Spanish and British American empires.[105]

'Rational' or 'Irrational' Genocide?

Even if we accept, for the sake of argument, that assimilation/acculturation wasn't possible, was it necessary to kill off 95 per cent of the Native Americans to wrest their land from them? In fact, there is a strong case for arguing that acculturation was possible, as demonstrated in Latin America, and that what prevented it in Anglo America was the racist, genocidal attitudes of the European settlers. As Robin Blackburn points out: 'The English perception of racial difference had a sharper edge to it than the Spanish or Portuguese, especially where people of colour were concerned.'[106] Mann devotes a chapter of The Dark Side of Democracy to genocidal 'democracies' in the New World. If we look at colonial societies in general, it has been the settler-colonial sub-group that perpetrated the greatest violence against natives. And within the general category of settler-colonies, there are four types of economy, involving an ascending scale of settler violence.

These genocidal, settler-colonial societies, established not only on the American continent but also in Australia and Africa, were based either on (1) trade, (2) plunder and tribute-taking, (3) the use of native labour (either dispersed or concentrated), or (4) the settlers' labour alone. Mann argues that two 'lesser forms of ethnic cleansing' were possible. The communities could have divided the land in order to live in adjacent though segregated territories. The colonists would no doubt have taken the most fertile land but native communities might nevertheless have survived. Alternatively, the settlers could have facilitated the assimilation of the natives into the stronger settler society, encouraging them to become traders or small farmers and/or employing the majority as labourers. However, the Anglo-American settlers did not use native labour but sought to displace them in order to take over their land. Politically, the colonists sought to impose direct rule on the Native Americans, ensuring their submission at first to the colonial government, then, after independence in 1775, to the new American government. As Mann puts it: 'the Europeans insisted on direct rule, involving the complete submission of native rulers and masses to their powers and laws ... There now resulted a clash of rival sovereignties over the same territory.'[107]

Why didn't the North American European colonists assimilate the Native Americans into settler society, as the Spanish colonists eventually did in Mexico and in Central and South America, or as the Portuguese did in Brazil? According to Nash, there were three main reasons for the decline of Native American society in the seventeenth century: one was unrelenting European immigration at a time when native ranks were being radically reduced by disease; a second factor was the inability of the very different Native American tribes and nations to unite in the face of the growing European threat; and thirdly, the inability or refusal of most European settlers to use native labour in their agricultural or infrastructural enterprises, in sharp contrast to Spanish (or Portuguese) colonial practice. In the Spanish colonies south of the Rio Grande, natives were more densely settled than in Anglo America and were organised as a subjugated labour force in the silver mines and in agriculture, for example, in Mexico and Peru. Because the natives supplied the bulk of the labour force, they had to be assimilated into the European culture and religion. Hundreds of missionaries were dispatched from Spain to convert them 'for the greater glory of the church'.[108] Elliott puts forward a demographic argument: 'After an uneasy period of cohabitation, the English settlers, faced with sparser indigenous populations which did not lend themselves so readily to mobilisation as a labour force, chose instead to adopt an exclusionary rather than an inclusive approach, along the lines already established in Ireland.'[109]

Few of the conditions prevailing in Spanish America were present in Anglo America. The English settlers brought no substantial military force to subdue the natives of Virginia or New England and force them into agricultural labour. Nor did the Anglican Church send clerics to convert them. In Virginia, the maize and fur trades were areas of economic life in which the natives initially served the Europeans. But by about 1616, once the settlers were self-sufficient in maize, and given the negligible importance of fur (contrary to the situation in New England), the only resource the Europeans required of the natives was their land. Since the natives now had nothing to contribute to their goals, the settlers regarded them simply as an obstacle to be pushed out of the way. As Nash puts it: 'In an almost complete reversal of Spanish Indian policy, the English in Virginia after 1622 worked to keep the two cultures apart.'[110] For him, the reasons are largely material differences in: the exploitable resources of the English and Spanish colonies – the vast reserves of gold and silver in Spanish America – and the density of native society in the two areas. However, Nash does mention differences in the social backgrounds of the two sets of colonists, and in their attitudes towards the indigenous people. And we have seen how more recent research has suggested the presence of a much larger northern native population than previously thought. Nash concludes that despite the native demographic collapse – some 75 per cent of natives died during the first century of contact – 'an impressive degree of acculturation and assimilation took place in the Spanish colonies'.[111] We shall question whether the explanation for the difference lies solely with economic factors.

There is a related school of thought among historians of slavery on the American continent, exemplified in the work of Frank Tannenbaum and those he influenced. He writes:

> The contrast ... between the Spanish and Portuguese slave systems on the one hand and that of the British and the United States was very marked, and not merely in their effect upon the slave, but even more significantly upon the place and moral status of the freed man. Under the influence of the law and religion, the social milieu in the Spanish and Portuguese colonies made easy room for the Negroes passing from slavery to freedom.[112]

In Latin America, slavery developed in a different legal and moral milieu, giving rise to a different set of moral and political perceptions and modes of action from those prevailing in Anglo America.[113]

Slavery was always brutal, but in the Spanish and Portuguese colonies the brutalities were probably less frequent than in Anglo America, and were punishable by law. Moreover, in Latin America, there were several roads to freedom, whereas in Anglo America manumission was practically impossible.[114] In addition, freedom, once achieved, allowed the former slave to enjoy legal equality.[115] Tannenbaum suggests an order of severity in which the British, Americans, Dutch and Danish were the harshest, the Spanish and Portuguese the mildest, with the French in between. Of these, the Dutch were the most severe, the Portuguese the least.[116]

Blackburn argues that there was an alternative to African slavery to meet the rapidly growing labour needs of farmers and planters producing goods such as tobacco, sugar or cotton in order to satisfy the ever expanding markets of Europe. 'Racial slavery was costly and inflexible, even in ways that could be measured by the market, let alone in more general human terms.'[117] Weren't contract or indentured labour or free wage-labour alternatives, from whichever source they came? Britain or France probably could not have spared large numbers of indentured labourers because of their own economic needs, which is why the number of indentures declined. But couldn't British or French planters or merchants have signed up labourers in Africa or Asia, offering them free return passage after, say, five years? It would probably have been hard for individual planters to devise an alternative system since this would have required an institutional, regulatory framework supervised by a public authority. But, as we saw earlier, 'this is in effect what Spanish colonial officialdom had done in the sixteenth century, devising ... circumstances in which free and semi-free waged labour was available to the owners of mining concessions.'[118] A similar picture applied in Brazil.

Moreover, the colonial system gave rise to extremely harsh forms of labour, such as in the navy, often involving the pressgang, which nonetheless relied on wage-labour. Again, the Portuguese and Spanish Atlantic islands of Madeira, the Azores and the Canaries developed an intensive form of agriculture, utilising highly productive forms of independent craft and free labour to produce wine and wheat.[119] Of course, transporting labourers from Africa or Asia would have been more expensive since they would not have consented to being tightly packed into ships as slaves were.[120] On the other hand, the mortality rate of the voyages would have been much lower and labour productivity would have been much higher. Many writers, from E. Genovese to, more recently, S. Engermann and K. Sokoloff have pointed to the low productivity of slave labour. While slavery enabled planters to take advantage of abundant natural resources and fertile soil, slaves were grudging workers. In addition, 'there was heavy mortality among the slaves, very low rates of fertility among the women, and a consequent need for ever greater supplies of new slaves from Africa'. African slavery was expensive for another reason. 'By comparison with Brazilian methods, the new plantation required a more intensive, and a more invigilated, work regime.'[121]

Furthermore, the slaves' poverty prevented them from becoming part of the commercial market, a crucial barrier to the economic development of the American south.[122] Indeed, it was for these reasons that the Civil War was fought. In addition, Blackburn argues that respect for the territorial rights of the Native Americans would have reduced the availability of land for indentured servants who had served their time, making them more amenable to waged employment. He quotes Las Casas who pointed out that 'trade was quite highly developed among the Indian nations and could have been extended to promote peaceful agreements on land use'.[123] Blackburn makes a strong case for his claim that 'there was an ideological and extra-economic component in the decision to opt for African slavery ... colonial settlement could have proceeded in a more humane fashion, as the more imaginative and generous-spirited members of the slave societies occasionally argued'.[124]

So why didn't the English colonials exploit native labour on their farms and plantations? Wouldn't they have been cheaper, as slaves or even as contract labourers? It is surely not far-fetched to apply Blackburn's argument about the alternatives to African slavery to the fate of the Native Americans. He argues, firstly, that the Caribbean and North American areas settled by the English and French were

> inhabited by tribes and confederations which practised shifting cultivation, hunting and gathering. Unlike the Aztec and Inca empires, the colonial incorporation of these peoples offered prospects of continuing resistance and

little gain ... Amerindian captives were difficult to capture and difficult to keep, and the men were unused to agricultural routines.[125]

Other scholars suggest additional reasons why Native Americans were not enslaved in large numbers in colonial Anglo-America: Indian men were proud and refused to work; agriculture was considered women's work.[126] The dwindling numbers of Native Americans has also been emphasised, although, as we saw, Kay has argued that between 1700 and 1840, their population between the Great Lakes and the Mississippi valley did recover. Moreover, many colonies did employ Native Americans as slaves, especially in the earlier period, although with limited success.[127]

Secondly, as we have seen, many Indian tribes had developed extensive systems of agricultural cultivation, putting them on a level similar to European systems. Thirdly, they certainly offered mass resistance to European settlers, given that their lands were being systematically stolen, their people ethnically cleansed and in some places, for example South Carolina, enslaved. The natives in Anglo America were never offered the option of wage-labour, as in Spanish or Portuguese America, or even contract labour. Had the Indians been presented with these opportunities, is it not possible that a degree of assimilation or acculturation would have taken place, with the people of Anglo America today consisting of a large number of mestizos, as in Mexico or South America? Because these alternatives were not offered, and as the market for plantation products grew, planters turned to Africa to fulfil their labour needs.

From a purely practical economic viewpoint, there would have been at least two good reasons for using native rather than African slave labour. Firstly, the European colonists undertook a huge and massively expensive operation when they began transporting slaves from West Africa. They had to pay the tribal chiefs, the ship owners carrying the slaves across the Atlantic, and the merchants supplying a minimum amount of food to keep them alive. Twelve million African slaves were forced on to ships moored on the African coast. Of these, a million and a half died during the voyage.[128] Secondly, African slave labour was forced and, therefore, grudging and unproductive. So, the question arises, was the enslavement of 12 million Africans the best option for the colonists? Would not it have been more rational to follow the Spanish and Portuguese example of using natives as free wage-labour? The Spanish used little African slave labour. Blackburn gives examples from Cuba and Mexico of the use of free labour and its higher productivity. Moreover, in the course of the eighteenth century, African slaves became more expensive. 'The rising price of slaves itself stimulated concern among planters and colonial officials, prompting them to look for ways to reduce dependence on the Atlantic traffic.'[129]

Did the toll of disease among Indians mean they were too fragile for their labour to be dependable? But mortality rates among African slaves were also high, despite their greater resistance to disease. In the Caribbean plantations, planters estimated the slaves' life expectancy to be no more than seven years.[130] Moreover, evidence suggests that in the eighteenth century the native population began to develop some immunity to European diseases. Hence it is difficult to argue that the Native American people could not have been a source of labour for the plantations and farms when the demand for labour began to grow substantially. It would surely have been cheaper to employ Indians than to import 12 million African slaves. The key question therefore remains unanswered. Why did the European settlers of Anglo America choose genocidal ethnic cleansing over wage-labour?

In the case of slavery, Eltis too believes it cannot be explained solely by economic factors. He argues that had the planters enslaved large numbers of their own people – convicts, victims of pressganging, and so on – instead of 'merely' imposing indentured labour on them, this would have been more profitable than buying and transporting African slaves. The reason they didn't was their inability to see English indentured servants as chattel slaves, in other words, as 'outsiders' whom they could legitimately enslave. Only in the nineteenth century did European planters and merchants widen their perception of which groups they could not ideologically see as slaves to encompass Africans, and indeed all humans.[131] Furthermore, if the difference in the experience of African slaves in Anglo and Latin America cannot be explained solely by economic factors, should this not also apply to the Native Americans? This runs counter to Nash's analysis, which adduces only economic factors to account for the natives' different experiences.

So, was the genocide of the Anglo-American natives 'rational' or 'irrational'? The conclusion would seem to be that it was both. It was 'rational' insofar as the main target of the early settlers was the natives' land. Their goal was to become farmers owning and cultivating their plot of land, thus escaping European political persecution and economic depredations (the enclosures). To this extent, their goal was material and utilitarian.

However, it was irrational insofar as they failed to offer the Native Americans an alternative, one that would arguably have served the economic interests of the Europeans themselves. As Stannard describes the Californian situation: 'The problem the whites were facing by this time, and that the new legislation was intended to address, was a shortage of Indian labour.' He argues that 'considering [the California] legislature's concern for cheap – indeed slave – labour, it would in retrospect seem mindless for the lawmakers simultaneously to encourage the destruction of that same Indian labour force. But that is precisely what happened.'[132] There would seem, moreover, to have been a sadistic element in the genocide. As we saw, the gold rush precipitated a genocidal massacre of natives by miners and ranchers who seemed to take pleasure in slaughtering them. The settlers' refusal to countenance the assimilation or acculturation of the Native Americans, as happened in most of Latin America, led them to commit two of the greatest crimes of human history – the enslavement of Africans, and the genocide of the Native Americans. In so doing, they deprived themselves of a potential asset – the labour of a people who could have made a significant contribution to the development of Anglo-American society, as they did in Latin America.

Social Class Character of the Anglo-American Colonists

I argued in Chapters 2 and 3 that the most rigorous concept for linking the historical and the psychological is that of 'social character' or 'character structure' or 'character orientation'. There is ample evidence that the difference between the treatment of the natives in Anglo America and Spanish America is not explicable solely in economic terms. We can thus infer that an important additional element was the difference in social character between the European settlers of Anglo -America – in particular, those groups that displayed marked brutality towards the Indians, such as the Puritans and the Scots-Irish – and the Spanish Crown bureaucrats and Catholic missionaries. From the evidence available, one could characterise the Crown bureaucrats as 'authoritarian-paternalistic'.

The early Anglo-American and later continental European colonists, were principally from European societies in which the bourgeoisie had failed to overthrow the old feudal-absolutist regimes – for example, Italy, Germany, and the Puritans in England before the Revolution – or to defeat colonial rule – for example Ireland and Poland. There were hardly any French settlers after the French Revolution of 1789. If the Anglo-American colonists had assimilated the Native Americans, there would have been less land for the Europeans. They would then perhaps have been forced to make greater efforts to carry out the bourgeois revolution in their European countries.

According to Marx's notion of the fetishism of commodities, social relations between producers assume the character of a relation between the products of their labour. The commodity is seen as a thing instead of the product of an exploitative system of production. From this it follows that the labour power of the labourer also becomes a thing. The greatest wave of colonial settlement of North America occurred as a result of the deepening crisis of European rural society that preceded industrialisation. Peasants who for centuries had enjoyed relative security in stable societies dominated by feudal lords suddenly found themselves threatened with loss of livelihood as feudalism crumbled before the creeping offensive of an urban capitalism demanding higher agricultural output to feed the new industrial workers. Peasants who had enjoyed traditional rights found that these were now being swept away, to be cast aside before the juggernaut of industrial capitalism. In the face of land enclosures and the rise of industrial production, peasants and artisans lost their independent craft and proprietorship status, swelling the ranks of the most alienated sections of society.

Many migrated to North America where they found the land occupied by another people whom they in turn treated as things to be disposed of as it suited them. To kill another human being is to transform them from an active subject into a passive object. The settlers thus projected their self-alienation on to the Native Americans. Van Every argues that removal of the natives represented a 'deplorable failure', not only for the natives, but for the wider interests of the United States. 'The opportunity for Indians to become useful and valued members of American society, an achievement many had seemed on the verge of attaining in 1825, had been heedlessly postponed for more than a century.'[133] In this sense, although the vast majority of settlers regarded the natives' removal as crucial for enabling them to colonise the land, from the broader perspective of American society as a whole, the holocaust of the Native Americans can be said to have been irrational.

Nevertheless, as noted above, the genocide was partly 'rational' and partly irrational. The search for and acquisition of land by the settlers was rational insofar as it served their economic and social interests. It was irrational, however, in that the genocide was not necessary for the fulfilment of their practical aims, and indeed could even be said to have been detrimental to the society as a whole. The explanation now required is, therefore, other than economic, but one that confronts the settlers' genocidal racism, an account that adduces ideological and psychological factors. Arguably, Indians could have been employed as wage-labourers on the plantations and farms, as they were on the Spanish ones, and it would have been cheaper than transporting 12 million Africans. One can only agree with Jaimes' judgement that the European settlers are 'marked forever with the indelible *wrongness* of having all along been some of history's most pathological thieves and murderers'.[134]

Robert Young, referring to Berkhofer's description in *White Man's Indian*, described this irrational element in the following terms:

> there is a continuous history of images of the American Indian from Columbus to the present which consists of extravagant representations which were patently projections of split off and disowned parts of the colonialists ... Columbus spoke of them ... as guileless and generous, but this didn't last, and by the sixteenth century they were routinely depicted as liars, deceivers and thieves 'as their master the divell teacheth to them'.[135]

Explaining this requires the re-introduction of the concept of social character. A useful approach will be to examine this psychological aspect in relation to three different colonising communities. The three I have chosen are the Spanish Crown bureaucrats, the New England Puritans, and Scots-Irish of North America.

The Spanish Crown and Church

King Ferdinand of Sicily and Aragon and Queen Isabella of Castile succeeded to the throne of Spain in 1469, creating for the first time a united Christian kingdom. To consolidate the Crown, however, they had to wage the War of Succession against the Portuguese, a four-and-a-half year battle against the rival claims of King Alfonso. Eventual success fortified the joint monarchs for the main task they needed to carry out in order to unify Spain – defeating the Muslim Arabs (Moors) who had controlled large areas of Spain since the mid eighth century. They achieved this in 1492 with the capture of Granada, after which the Moors were expelled as infidels.

The nobility had always used their power in Castile disruptively: indeed the name Castile originates from their myriad fortified castles. As true feudal lords, during the long wars against the Moors, the higher layers of the nobility, the *ricos hombres*, supplied the bulk of the sovereign's armies from retainers on their estates.[136] As Innes explains: 'these forces were led by the lesser nobility, the *hidalgos*, and by the knights, the *caballeros*, who constituted the cavalry ... The towns and their militia were primarily defensive.' Given the risks they took and the costs they bore, the nobility shared the spoils of war with the Crown. 'As a result, their estates became ever larger, and through the years all sections of the nobility grew in power and riches.' In classical feudal style, the nobility were a law unto themselves, exempt from taxation and from imprisonment for debt and torture, able even to renounce allegiance to the sovereign in order to serve his enemies. At the accession of Ferdinand and Isabella, 'the nobility were all-powerful, their estates larger and richer than ever before'.[137]

According to Elliott, the majority of Castilians wished to see an end to the anarchic feuding of the aristocracy. The monarchs set about forming alliances with those elements who most strongly resented the abuse of power by the aristocracy. In the Cortes of Castile, held in Madrigal in 1476, the Crown laid the foundations for an alliance with the municipalities which became a key weapon in its struggle to assert royal authority and curb noble power.[138] The monarchs expanded the *Santa Hermandad*, a kind of police force set up to maintain civil order. It was now transformed into a force restricting the abuses of civil law on the part of the nobility or their retainers. Also in 1476, the Crown asserted its control over the Order of Santiago, the most powerful of the three military-religious orders that possessed vast estates and revenues, an independent and rival power-base, a state within a state. In addition, in 1480 the Cortes of Toledo instituted the famous Act of Resumption by which the nobles were deprived of half the revenues they had usurped since 1464. But the Cortes' most important reform was the rehabilitation and strengthening of the old royal council of Castile. It became the central governing body, the lynchpin of the monarchs' governmental system. To prevent it falling under the control of the magnates, it was made up of one prelate, three *caballeros* (knights) and eight or nine *letrados* (jurists).[139]

Moreover, the Catholic monarchs preferred to appoint those from humble backgrounds to offices of state, not in order to encourage other social classes such as the gentry or the bourgeoisie, but to boost the power of the Crown. The issue of the power of the Cortes proved to be a thorny one. The monarchs were aware of the danger of allowing it to acquire too great an influence, on the other hand they were dependent on it financially. Hence they set about finding other sources of revenue, and their success enabled them to dispense with the Cortes between 1483 and 1497. Although they had to turn to the Cortes after 1497 because of the financial demands of the wars with Granada and Italy, it was not hard to bend it to their will.[140]

The Crown also had to assert its authority over the municipalities if it was to achieve supremacy over Castile. The walled cities which dotted the landscape enjoyed a large measure of independence due to the charters granted by successive kings. They exercised jurisdiction far into the surrounding countryside and had the right to form a general assembly, normally composed of heads of families, which chose the municipal officials. The Cortes of Toledo of 1480 instituted various measures aimed at strengthening royal control over the towns. However, there were limits to the power that the Crown was able to arrogate to itself and it had to remain satisfied with measures that might in time weaken seigniorial authority. But the monarchs did insist that the lords maintain high standards of justice and were ready to intervene when miscarriages of justice were alleged.[141]

Nevertheless, after many years of civil strife, it was necessary to reward supporters. Between 1465 and 1516, around 1,000 patents of nobility (*hidalguía*) were granted, largely for military achievements. Despite these grants of honour, the monarchs' basic policy was to oppose any extension of noble power. According to Kamen:

> the taming of the Castilian aristocracy was an outstanding achievement of the Catholic monarchs ... The great lords were taken into partnership with the crown and confirmed in their estates and private armies, but were given no extension of privileges. Instead, most of the major cities were taken back into royal control and new state officials were selected from lesser gentry rather than from among the magnates.[142]

Fighting the Moors

The years 1481–92 were taken up largely with the war against the Moors of Granada, which was to set the pattern for colonial conquest. In the early stages, the war was fought by local landlords and their peasant armies rather than the monarchy. Later, it came under the auspices of the monarchy with militia recruited from distant provinces, 'trained into the semblance of a regular (national) army'. In addition, 'volunteers flocked in from the rest of Europe, spurred by religious fervour and the romantic call of chivalry'.[143] The world into which the conquistadors were born was thus one of religious and ethnic intolerance, of crusading knights and armies, 'of war and devastation and change. The atmosphere in which they were brought up was entirely dominated by a sense of crusading fervour and of the invincibility of Spanish arms.'[144] The leading conquistadors themselves – Pizarro, Cortes, and others – came from the lesser nobility, the *hidalgos*. With the fall of Granada in 1492, a vacuum was created: 'no more infidels to slaughter, no more crusades to wage. The fighting machine of the *caballeros* had come to a halt.'[145]

In that same year Columbus undertook his first voyage, backed by the monarchs, no doubt the result of the confidence they derived from victory over the Moors. On his next voyage in 1493, there were a large number of miners, which suggests that the expedition's backers hoped to receive large quantities of gold. But most of 'the adventurers were soldiers of fortune, men whose interests were personal glory and profit'.[146] There were also some priests and a group of Indians brought to Spain after the first voyage, now converts returning as missionaries. The men who went out were thus adventurers rather than settlers, their leaders drawn from the *hidalgos*, with a background of inter-family conflict. The New World, far removed as it was from the interference of the state, provided full scope for their martial and feuding impulses.

The Colonists

By the time Cortes left Mexico and returned to Spain in 1540, control had passed into the hands of the Crown bureaucracy. We have mentioned the fear on the part of reformers such as Las Casas that the barbarities of the conquistadors was slowly eliminating the indigenous population, thus depriving the Spanish colonies of native labour. Forced labour was now prohibited and the death penalty introduced for the branding of slaves.[147] As for demographic changes, the Spanish population of Hispaniola was around 630 in 1495, perhaps a thousand by 1500. But the character of the colonists began to change. Most of the *hidalgo* gentlemen had returned to Castile, and 'those left behind, like those who could be attracted out, came largely from the lower rungs of Spanish life, some of them ... with clipped noses and ears, sure signs of convicted robbers in Castile as in Espaniola'.[148] As Kamen says:

> The pioneers in America were ... poorer Spaniards ... many of them soldiers and sailors unemployed after the wars in Granada and Italy ... others young and hardy men of limited means, including many hidalgos (like Cortes) and illiterate labourers who looked to America to better their fortunes ... Rural misery was an obvious reason for emigrating: thousands of peasants saw in America a hope of escape from feudal lords, heavy taxation and the harsh struggle for survival.[149]

According to Elliott, the Spanish colonists in America were based in the towns and bent on aping the lifestyle of the Spanish upper class, adopting their domestic and gastronomic standards. However, 'they were dependent for their subsistence on a countryside that was being turned over to the cultivation of European crops, and was worked with the labour of the conquered Indian population'.[150] Survival depended on the Spaniards' ability to exploit native labour in the fields and mines, but how could this be justified? The Crown insisted on its duty to Christianise the Indians, but its perceived obligations towards its pagan subjects conflicted with the economic demands of the settlers. Their ideas about the correct treatment of the natives derived from the *Reconquista* – the expulsion of the infidel Moors from Spain – whose rules of war allowed for enslavement of the vanquished population. Columbus did indeed send shiploads of natives to be sold as slaves, but, as we saw, there was opposition from the Church and the monarchy, and native enslavement was prohibited in 1500. And under the *encomienda* system, the *encomendero* 'accepted the obligation to protect a specified group of Indians and to instruct them in the ways of civilisation and Christianity'.[151]

The emergence of the united monarchy and a recently centralised government, together with the administrative needs of the new empire, resulted in considerable expansion of the state bureaucracy. Ferdinand and Isabella preferred *letrados* – officials trained in law – to *capa y espada* (cloak and sword) – military officials in charge of strategic towns.[152] This led to measures to improve their training. At their peak in the 1580s, the Castilian universities had an annual intake of about 20,000, the majority from the cities, and from the *hidalgo* class. Less than a third took a degree, but most of those who did went on to staff Spain's worldwide imperial bureaucracy.[153] Kamen argues that 'although the new breed of jurist administrators formed a "robe nobility" comparable to that of France, there were no visible status distinctions between them and the old nobility'.[154] The reason for this, he suggests, is that most *letrados* were already of noble background. Moreover, the *colegios mayores* (elite colleges of 20 to 30 students within the universities) also attracted aristocratic students, since these too were willing to embark on careers in the state bureaucracy. However, the growth of the administrative apparatus in the sixteenth century should not be exaggerated: there were perhaps 500 senior *letrados* in Castile under Philip II. With the addition of other *letrado* posts and the much larger number of *capa y espada* positions in Castile and America, the total would have been around 2,000.[155]

Spain and Her Rivals

It is important to stress the political differences between the Spanish monarchy and that of her rivals, particularly England. From the outset of the colonial period, the Spanish Crown adopted a more interventionist approach than did that of England. As Elliott notes: 'From the very beginnings of overseas discovery and settlement, the Spanish crown had shown a keen interest in obtaining detailed information about the character and extent of its newly acquired territories.'[156] Of prime relevance here was the discovery in Spanish America by the conquistadores of massive deposits of gold and silver.

> With much less immediate profit to be expected from overseas colonization, the British crown maintained a relatively low profile in the crucial opening stages of colonial development ... [displaying a] relative lack of concern ... over the character of the communities that its subjects were establishing on the farther shores of the Atlantic ... The Spanish crown, acutely aware of its own dependence on American silver and of the vulnerability of its silver resources to foreign attack, could not afford the luxury of so casual an approach to settlement in its overseas possessions.[157]

Power and Influence of the Church

In the words of Bartolomé Bennassar, 'daily life in sixteenth century Spain was saturated with religion'.[158] As in other Catholic absolute monarchies, an important legacy of classical feudalism was the continuing prestige and power of the Church as part of the ruling class. After all, 'it was in the name of the unity and purity of the Faith that the armies of the "Catholic King" were mobilised for two centuries'.[159] But the influence of Catholicism did not go unchallenged. Its centuries-long contact with Islam and Judaism continued even after the expulsion of the Jews in 1492 and the setting-up of the Inquisition between 1478 and 1483 to root out *conversos* and *moriscos* – Jews and Muslims who were ostensibly Christian converts but secretly maintained their former religion. Bennassar argues that this led to more dogmatic or assertive forms of religious expression than in other Western Christian societies, especially after the rise of the Protestant Reformation in central and northern Europe. The Church had retained immense political, economic and ideological power, rivalling the great seigniorial houses. Its wealth continued to grow throughout the sixteenth century, partly because of skilled management of its landed property but mainly thanks to donations into its coffers. On the other hand, the Inquisition testified to the inability of the Church to tolerate difference. In sum, like the state, the Church was two-faced, showing a benevolent, paternalist face to the Native Americans, and a brutal, sectarian face to heretics – *conversos*, dissidents and 'witches'. In the royal councils and as presidents of the *audencias* (judicial and administrative councils), 'prelates played political and administrative roles of the first order'.[160]

Although Golden Age Spain was 'saturated with religion', sexuality seems to have been allowed freer expression than in Protestant countries. As Bennassar says: 'I do not believe at all in that horror for the flesh that the Catholic, Mediterranean countries are supposed to have felt over the ages. Horror of the body is a northern product … of Puritanism and Jansenism.' Moreover, 'the court, the clergy, and the ruling classes were far from strict in the matter of sexual morality. It would be strange if the mass of the population were not susceptible to such examples and incitements.'[161] Saint-Saens agrees: 'the Spanish authorities were indeed aware of the strong tendency of Spaniards to indulge in sins of the flesh'. Sex was 'perceived by … males and females as an appetite that ought to be satisfied'.[162]

Psychology of Crown Bureaucracy and the Catholic Church

Establishing the social character of the Spanish Crown bureaucracy can only involve a rough approximation based on laws passed, edicts promulgated, and diaries and letters written. Here we shall attempt a broad delineation based on Fromm and Maccoby's character typology. As we saw in Chapter 3, social character is rooted in two factors, the mode of production, a point stressed by Fromm and Maccoby, but also the class struggle, which they don't mention. The process of assimilation and the mode of relatedness refer to the typical shared ways in which groups of human beings, firstly, acquire and assimilate objects, and secondly, relate to other people (and to themselves). The mode of assimilation is divided into the broad categories of the productive orientation and the four non-productive ones – exploitative, receptive, hoarding and marketing. The mode of relatedness to people, or the orientations in the process of socialisation, fall into four types: (1) symbiotic relatedness, (2) withdrawal-destructiveness, (3) narcissism, and (4) love. We might add a fifth type of particular relevance to the Spanish attitude to the Indians, namely paternalism. It would seem to be best described as a blend between symbiosis and love.[163] Thirdly, we need to look at the typical socio-political orientation(s) shared by members of a group.

We have suggested that the notion of 'state feudalism' is applicable to Golden Age Spain (see pp. 126–7 above). The ruling class consisted of the monarch and the leading Crown bureaucrats, officials and envoys, and also the principal churchmen. The historical records seem to indicate that, as regards the mode of assimilation, it wouldn't be far off the mark to analyse the Spanish Crown bureaucrats of the Golden Age as exploitative-productive. In terms of the positive aspects of the exploitative character, they were active, proud, and above all self-confident. This confidence flowed from their great success in defeating the Muslim forces of southern Spain in the *Reconquista* and in uniting the country, but also in subduing the nobility and creating a vast overseas empire. Anthony Pagden describes the image of sixteenth-century monarchy as 'the self-assured champion (and the exporter) of Christian cultural values, the secular arm of the papacy, and the sole guardian of political stability within Europe'.[164] On the negative side, however, the Spanish Crown bureaucrats were also exploitative, aggressive and arrogant.[165]

The productive element in their orientation refers to their ability to use their reason and imagination to create a new world. Their favourable response to Las Casas' campaign in defence of the Indians, their ability to see them as human beings and to offer protection against the abuses of the *conquistadores* and *encomenderos*, would testify to that. As for their mode of socialisation, the Spanish monarchy and bureaucracy, as also the Catholic missionaries, had, as already suggested, a social character we might describe as in part 'authoritarian-paternalistic'. This can be clearly seen in a letter written by Pedro de Gante, a Franciscan friar in Mexico City, to the Spanish Emperor Charles V in 1532. He describes the infirmary built by their monastery to look after the natives, admittedly with the ulterior motive of aiding their conversion, nevertheless 'a great comfort for the poor and needy'. Gante then requests the emperor to send funds for the infirmary, but also for a school, so that 'the natives will believe that your majesty loves them and considers them your children'. Now, it is inconceivable that the New England Puritan minister, Increase Mather, or his minister son, Cotton Mather, would have written to Charles II, King William and Queen Mary, or Queen Anne, suggesting they demonstrate their love for the natives. Indeed, in 1702, Cotton Mather wrote of a massacre of Pequot Indians, including women, children and old men: 'In a little more than one hour, five or six hundred of these barbarians were dismissed from a world that was burdened with them.'[166] As Hanke says,

> no European nation ... with the possible exception of Portugal, took her Christian duty toward native peoples so seriously as did Spain. Certainly England did not, for as one New England preacher said, 'the Puritan hoped to meet the Pequot Indians in heaven, but wished to keep apart from them on earth, nay, to exterminate them from the land'.[167]

People Versus Land

Pagden has analysed the different ideological approaches to the American empire on the part of British and Spanish rulers. A key difference between the

European conquerors and settlers was that the British (and French) colonies were 'overwhelmingly bases for trade and the production of agricultural produce. Spanish America, by contrast, had been the largely unintended consequence of the need, which by the late fifteenth century had become chronic, for gold and silver.'[168] Pagden stresses that the Spaniards were largely concerned with their rights over people – the Indians – whereas the British were more concerned with rights in things, in particular, land. According to the 'agriculturalist' argument, or 'res nullius', used by both Thomas More and John Locke, the Indians were hunter-gatherers and had failed to develop the land which Locke described as 'the vacant place of America'.[169] 'Few Englishmen believed that they had entered land belonging to anyone ... unless, of course, it was some other European power.'[170] The colonists therefore assumed they had the right to settle on the land and cultivate it, while those who had wasted it by leaving it idle had forfeited their right to it.

The Spanish, by contrast, did not use the 'res nullius' argument, partly because they realised that the lands they settled in were obviously occupied. Secondly, again, the Spanish Crown 'was as much concerned with its potential rights over the Indians themselves as with its rights over their property'. As Pagden says, the grants made by the Crown to the settlers – the *encomiendas* – were not 'entitlements to semi-independent occupation, as they were in Anglo America. They were titles to labour.'[171] The Native Americans were allocated to the landholder (*encomendero*) who was entitled to use their labour in return for a small wage and the duty to protect them and Christianise them. But their land largely remained Crown property. The Spanish Crown needed to reconcile its seizure of the lands and goods of the native population with its right to exercise sovereignty over them. The British and French argued that the Indians had voluntarily ceded or sold lands to the Europeans because they had seen the advantage of doing so. But it wasn't plausible to argue that the Native Americans in Spanish America had similarly surrendered their land and political autonomy.[172] So the notion of a 'just war' became important to the Spanish rulers, a concept whose spirit and language derived from the *Reconquista*.[173]

However, Pagden argues that as Spain went into decline in the late sixteenth century, 'the Spanish crown became more uneasy about the emphasis given to conquest in its claims to rights in America'. The important point here is that 'the triumphalism which underpinned the whole language of the just war ... began to wane as Spanish armies suffered defeat after defeat'.[174] This ties in with our argument that productiveness and destructiveness are related, respectively, to victory and defeat in class struggle. So long as the Spanish Crown was victorious, it was able to maintain a progressive and rational policy towards the natives. Once decline set in, however, it lost confidence in its right to colonial sovereignty over the Native American lands and people. But it was against another people that a lurch into destructiveness was now played out: the Moriscos – overtly Christian but secretly Muslim – who were expelled from Spain between 1608 and 1614. The decree of expulsion was approved by the king on 9 April 1609, a day which also saw the signing of the Twelve Years' Truce with the Dutch. 'By the skilful use of timing, the humiliation of peace with the Dutch would be overshadowed by the glory of removing the last trace of Moorish dominance from Spain, and 1609 would be ever memorable as a year not of defeat but of victory.'[175] Since the expulsion coincided with defeat at the hands of the Dutch rebels, it could thus plausibly be interpreted as a compensatory device, especially as it made no sense economically.

Honour and Faith

There appears to have been, in addition, a narcissistic element in the rulers' and bureaucrats' attitude to others and to themselves, as revealed in their preoccupation with honour and faith. As Marcelin Defourneaux describes Spanish society at the time: 'the qualities which animate all personal and social life are honour and faith'. This would seem also to have been an early example of Fromm's 'marketing' orientation, in this case religious faith serving to project to the outside world an image of moral rectitude. As Defourneaux writes:

> for many Spaniards, religion tended to a formalism which placed a special value on outward appearances and was quite different from the spiritual values which it sought to express ... When Philip IV required the nuns ... to do penance for the sins of his insatiable sensuality, the abbess ... reminded him in vain that penance requires first an effort from the sinner.[176]

Honour was a legacy of the medieval Christian tradition which held that 'the ideal of men of noble birth should be the doing of courageous and heroic deeds'. Moreover, Defourneaux argues that honour and faith were not simply attributes of the upper class but had percolated down to Spanish society as a whole. They were the two elements 'in the soul of Spain', as evidenced in the success over 50 years of the 'comedies of honour' by the playwrights Lope de Vega and Calderón. Faith and honour thus 'combined in a single entity: the honour of being a Christian ... affirmed in the doctrine of the "purity of blood"'.[177] Bennassar supports this conclusion: 'If there was one passion capable of defining the conduct of the Spanish people, it was the passion of honour.'[178] This is, arguably, an example of the manner in which ruling classes instil into society as a whole not only the predominant ideology but also the social character they require if their socio-economic and political domination is to be maintained.

Finally, what was the Spanish rulers' predominant socio-political orientation? Following Fromm and Maccoby's typology, the choice is between authoritarian, traditional, democratic, and revolutionary. Again, the historical evidence suggests that the predominant socio-political orientation of the members of the Crown bureaucracy was a blend between authoritarian and traditional, with possibly a 'dash' of the democratic. The authoritarian character, as defined earlier, is one whose 'sense of strength and identity is based on a symbiotic subordination to authorities, and at the same time, a symbiotic domination of those submitting to his authority'.[179] This was apparent in the role the Spanish rulers carved out for themselves as champions of Catholicism. Having driven out the Moors, and then subjected the Jews and the remaining Muslims to forced conversion (in 1492 and 1502 respectively), a new menace arose in Europe – the Protestant Reformation.

Against this, the Spanish rulers and bishops forged the weapon of the Inquisition, both to root out heretics and to assert their power in Europe. The traditional character, however, does not challenge the fixed social structure or the notion that those in power are there by right, yet neither do they 'believe that might makes right', nor does their 'identity rest on identifying with power'.[180]

In an important article Ruth El Saffar argues that under the Catholic monarchs Ferdinand and Isabella, a process of modernisation was set in train, one that witnessed urban development, the creation of schools, universities and the printing press, the professionalisation of the army and the discovery of the New World.[181] To achieve their goal, the monarchs needed to undermine alternative power bases in the society. These socio-economic and political changes were the conditions under which important psychological shifts took place, becoming the means by which a new form of identification was created: that of being an individual who had to break with the pre-modern bonds of village, home and family in favour of a new tie to the Crown. Part of that break involved men and boys severing themselves from the 'feminising forces' in their lives. 'The process of collective differentiation from the feminine unfolds over the course of the sixteenth century.'[182]

A new type of male thus emerged, whose character can be gleaned from the key literary works that El Saffar analyses. He is 'a lonely being, isolated, fearful, increasingly lettered and consequently alienated from the body and from women'. The process is one 'by which, over a century, the figures associated with the female/maternal/rural/oral world lose power'.[183] The torture and burning of witches that took place over a protracted period, continuing into the seventeenth century, must be seen as part of the struggle to repress and subordinate the mother and all that she embodied in the pre-modern world – tribal identity, ties to nature and the earth, the mysteries of life and death.[184] However, this drive to break with the maternal – an emotional condition of the rise of capitalism – was not completely successful. Cervantes' masterpiece *Don Quixote* reveals a dual process: both the dominant striving for male autonomy but also the desire for dependence on the maternal 'that was everyone's dark secret'. The required 'male' individual remained 'locked into an unconscious relationship with that which it is suppressing'.[185]

In an echo of Reich and Fromm, El Saffar also argues that the drama of the period tells us 'what the dominant class wants to perpetrate, and what it has to offer to those who accept its values'. The new man is to regard himself as a Spaniard rather than as a Jew, Catholic or Muslim.[186] According to El Saffar, the

> monarchical/ecclesiastical alliance plays a major role in the creation of the Oedipal structure that was being forged in the nuclear families and urban environment that began to emerge as central in the sixteenth century. The creation of paid armies, the colonisation of the New World and the economic allurements of the city pulled young men from their maternal/rural environments.

Class was a key factor here: 'Obviously all these forces come to bear differently on people depending on social class'. But whatever the class background, in the sixteenth century we see 'the massive removal of males at varying ages from home...'.[187]

How does this affect our analysis of the Crown and the Church and of their capacity to protect the Native Americans? The leading elements of these institutions were people whose confidence was at the highest possible level because of major historical victories. In the *Reconquista*, the Crown unified Spain, and subordinated the Jews and Muslim minorities to the Catholic Church. They then subsidised Columbus' voyage and the conquest of the New World. It seemed that nothing could stand in their way. Under such conditions of supremacy, arguably the Catholic friars and Crown bureaucrats could allow the 'feminine', maternal side of their psyche to live alongside the 'masculine' side. Offering protection to the Indians did not threaten their male individuality, and it was, crucially, the economically rational choice – one that enabled natives to become wage-labourers, and which the ruling class were able to make without lapsing into expressions of exaggerated maleness in order to cover up their feminine side.

Let the final word go to Lewis Hanke, who compared what he called the 'Spanish character' to a medal on one side of which is stamped the face of an imperialist conquistador and on the other that of a friar devoted to God: 'It is to Spain's everlasting credit that she allowed men to insist that all her actions in America be just, and that at times she listened to these voices.'[188]

The Puritans

The social character of the Puritans developed in response to two historically specific factors: first, the new productive forces they themselves were creating; and, second, the political and religious persecution they suffered in late feudal and early capitalist England, and also in New England. Puritanism began in sixteenth-century England as a tendency within the Established Church. It wasn't so much an expression of theological dissent as of a different idea of moral behaviour and of church discipline and civil government.[189] The cornerstone of Puritan ideology was the sanctity of labour. Labour was a social duty. 'The doctrine that labour was a duty to one's neighbour, to society, to the commonwealth, to mankind, came to be especially emphasised by the Puritan preachers.'[190] According to radical Puritan Robert Browne in 1588–9, an idle person ceased to be a member of the church of God. The Puritan's political radicalism grew directly out of his relationship to God: he was the elect, predestined to be God's chosen. One could not decide to carry out good works in order to be chosen, but they could be a sign of having been chosen, of being endowed with God's favour. 'As God's chosen people, the Puritans felt their triumph inevitable and their enemies to be God's enemies.' Expressing themselves in seventeenth-century biblical language, 'they were conscious of their mission as a historically progressive class engaged in a revolutionary struggle'.[191] As we know from the classic works of Tawney and Weber, the Puritan values of thrift, sobriety and hard work were the ideological expression of the drive to create a new economic system in the teeth of opposition from the existing power structure – the absolute monarchy and remnants of feudalism. These values survived the decline of Puritanism to be internalised in the eighteenth- and nineteenth-century bourgeois family, as an essential precondition for the rise of industrial capitalism.[192]

According to Hill, 'radical Puritanism appealed to the small men in town and country'. He qualifies this by conceding that 'Puritanism also, of course, appealed to a section of the gentry, who, as patrons and M.P.s were important in furthering the cause out of all proportion to their numbers.' But in general, the people who were drawn to Puritanism and supported their 'lecturers' (preachers) were 'the industrious sort of people ... yeomen, artisans and small and middling merchants'.[193] Lawrence Stone, too, maintains that it wasn't only the small or medium property owners but also sections of the gentry and even the landed nobility who were attracted to Puritanism.[194] Cromwell, for example, was himself a member of the prosperous East Anglian yeomanry. However, as Hill argues, 'though such men were potentially very important, and the Puritan gentry in the House of Commons were indispensable, still without the backing of large numbers of humbler men Puritanism could never have challenged the Crown and the bishops: the civil war could never have been fought and won'.[195]

Even in the seventeenth century it was recognised that 'Protestantism was peculiarly suited to a commercial and industrial community, and that popish religion created an unaptness for trade, hard work and accumulation'. Puritan asceticism carried an economic appeal to aspiring and industrious artisans and peasants in an age of incipient industrialisation. It 'appealed especially to those smaller employees and self-employed men, whether in town and country, for whom frugality and hard work might make all the difference between prosperity and failure to survive in the world of growing competition'.[196] These small entrepreneurs were developing new types of goods, new agricultural products and new methods of artisanal and agricultural production. Coupled with these innovations was the building of a radically new network of trade, extending the market so that it encompassed and unified the entire country, as well as spreading internationally.

Puritan Repression and Authoritarianism

The Puritans were highly repressed individuals who insisted on the sinfulness of sexual drives and, indeed, of any enjoyment or leisure, sublimating such drives into prayer and hard work. And many commentators, including Freud, have remarked on the 'anal' orientation of the Puritans – their obsessiveness and punctiliousness. Puritans were also perhaps the first historical example of the authoritarian personality, rigorously disciplined in work, prayer and everyday life. This repression and authoritarianism were necessary, or at least useful, psychic features accompanying the early process of accumulation. Consumption had to be subordinated to accumulation if the Puritans were to succeed in laying the basis for the new capitalist economy and overthrowing the political obstacle to it that the Crown represented.

The Puritans were also highly introverted, spending much time in anxious introspection as to whether or not they were members of God's elect. 'The

Puritan was constantly searching his soul, performing a moral and spiritual stock-taking to discover whether or not he was among the Elect of God.' Stone describes the Puritan personality as being based on 'the overpowering sense of sin and the preoccupation with individual salvation ... The interest in the self sprang from the urgent need to discipline the self – the "sphincter morality" as the Freudians describe it.'[197]

Puritan families brought their children up in a brutal manner. They believed in the idea of Original Sin, of the newborn child as an agent of the Devil.[198] The key objective of parental discipline was thus to break the child's will, rendering him or her impotent and submissive, repressing all feelings of love or sexuality.[199] The result was predictable.

> Deeply buried within their own psyches, rage and rebellion constantly erupted, placing constant pressures upon them which, more often than not, they resisted and rejected. Few passed through childhood without accumulating a deep and unfathomable reservoir of hostility toward their parents and toward the exercise of parental power and authority, feelings of rage that continued to shape their responses to themselves, to their God and to the world in which they lived.[200]

But to have acknowledged these feelings of rage and hostility would have been to unleash a wave of guilt that would have overwhelmed them. In their unconscious perception of themselves as impotent children facing the wrath of an almighty authority, they were inviting annihilation. Much safer, therefore, to repress these dangerous feelings, to turn them inwards against themselves, but also to project them outwards.

> How ... were their feelings of anger and the consequent aggressiveness manifested...? ... in three paramount ways. The first was the intense and sustained hostility which they felt towards themselves, evident ... in their efforts to mortify and subdue the body and the self ... The second consisted in their active rebellion against the will of God, and the constant fear which haunted so many that they might be rebellious even if they did not seem to be. And the third was evident in their behaviour toward other people and the outer world generally. Evangelicals often perceived the world as a dangerous and seductive place, and they often saw evidence of anger and hostility in other people which they denied within themselves.[201]

The Puritan view of the Native Americans

The Puritans developed a view of the Indians in particular as wild and destructive savages bent on destroying the civilised European colonists. Stannard, citing Greven's work, argues that the main targets of these projections were the Native Americans whose 'territory they were invading who became the unwilling victims of the Protestants' "unending ... warfare with the unregenerate world in which they lived"'.[202] Drinnon argues in similar vein that in regard to the

Puritans' attitudes to the Indians we are dealing with a clear case of projection in the psychoanalytical sense. By way of illustration, he cites a poem written in 1794 by Puritan pastor Timothy Dwight about the war with the Pequots (a native tribe attacked and massacred by the New England Puritans in 1637). According to Dwight, however: 'The Pequots resolved to attempt the destruction of the English, with the strength of their own tribes only.'[203]

Richard Slotkin also contends that 'the Puritans viewed the Indians as projections of the evil within themselves, as well as agents of an external malice'.[204] Or as Berkhofer describes it: 'the Puritans' image of the Indian was the projection of the fears and repressed desires in themselves upon the outsiders they encountered in America, and so the extermination of the Indian was part of the Puritan cleansing of sin from themselves'.[205] In King Philip's war (1675–8), the New England colonies were almost destroyed by a confederation of formerly friendly tribes led by Metacom of the Wampanoags (or 'King Philip' as the English had nicknamed him in friendship). Benjamin Tompson's two proto-epic poems on the war expressed 'the colonial sense of "victimisation" by a wrathful God and a wicked devil.'[206] Slotkin describes the poem as follows:

> the forces of disorder, greed, cruelty, lust, class conflict, and filial ingratitude destroy Tompson's arcadia ... it is Tompson's Indians who embody these forces. They are even accused of destroying the trees of the wilderness to make a fortress, thus victimising the woods along with the colonists. The Indians embody all evil in this poem. They are 'monsters shap'd and fac'd like men' and function as a scapegoat for Puritan self-doubts and feelings of guilt.[207]

'By conceiving of themselves as being purely victims of the Indians, rather than agents of their own troubles, the Puritans put the onus of their morally questionable acts on the Indians and justified their extermination of them.'[208] An interesting side-theme is shared by two of the key myths in Puritan literature – the 'myth of the hunter' and the 'myth of captivity' – 'the use of the wilderness as a metaphor for the human unconscious and of the beast as a symbol for the secret, darkened soul within each man'.[209]

Repression of the Puritans

At the beginning of the reign of James I, several hundred Puritan clergy of the Church of England presented him with a petition 'asking for a moderate liberty to accept or reject certain minor points of ritual such as the wearing of the surplice and the use of the sign of the cross in baptism, for the encouragement of preaching and of the stricter observance of Sunday and the non-observance of saints' days'.[210] In 1604, James presided in person over a conference at Hampton Court to discuss the petition. James expressed opposition to Puritanism, for reasons that were not theological (he was a Calvinist) but political: 'A Scottish Presbytery agreeth as well with monarchy as God and the Devil', and 'No Bishop, no King', summed up his attitude, no doubt realistically. As Morton says:

The Scottish Kirk, organised from the bottom through a series of representative bodies, rising to an Assembly composed of ministers and delegates from congregations, was indeed the logical embodiment of the democratic spirit inherent in Puritanism, and James was right in thinking that this was incompatible with royal absolutism.[211]

James carried out a purge in which 300 clergy who refused to conform were deprived of their livelihood. Depriving the church of a large proportion of the minority of its ministers 'who cared more for truth than for tithes' left it in the hands of the careerists and the small group of High Anglican supporters gathered around Archbishop Laud. Moreover, Laud attempted to dragoon the church into what looked to many people like Papistry, at a time when the latter was extremely unpopular. He imposed a fierce censorship of both press and pulpit which was underpinned by the Court of High Commission, an ecclesiastical version of the notorious Star Chamber court. The clergy resurrected its claim, lapsed since the Reformation, to regulate morality and conduct. Moreover, the use of parish churches as meeting places was forbidden, and a strict uniformity of ritual enforced.

The result of this repression was that between 1628 and 1640, some 20,000 Puritans emigrated to New England, fleeing a land that seemed to them to be returning inexorably to Catholicism. Many set up secret societies for private worship, groups that became centres of political dissent. Others maintained an outward conformity, waiting for change.[212] Slotkin sums up the situation:

> The Puritans' crisis of confidence in their prospects for communal success was partly the result of a series of historical defeats and partly the logical development of the Puritan conception of man's incapacity for virtuous heroism. After the initial successes of their colonies, and the triumph of Puritanism under Cromwell in England, the taste of victory began to sour. Cromwellian parliaments and administrators were as troublesome to New England's religious theory and polity as royal officials had been; and with the Restoration even the illusion of Puritan victory went glimmering. Within their own society, internal divisions, controversies, and heresies marred the peace and orthodoxy of the Bible commonwealth.[213]

Puritan Social Character

Stone suggests that sixteenth- and early seventeenth-century England was a society in which a majority of individuals found it hard to establish close emotional ties. The corollary was a high level of casual violence. He admits, though, that this is a comparative judgment based on the relative dominance of evidence from Puritans.[214] Historically, however, there was a progressive side to this. According to Fromm and Maccoby, the new merchant capitalist class (which would include the Puritans) that arose in Europe and North America in the seventeenth and eighteenth centuries was characterised by the 'hoarding-productive' attitude. This 'was adapted to the need for capital accumulation (rather than consumption), personal industriousness, the obsessional drive for work, and the absence of compassion'.[215] In sum, the Puritan mentality was a necessary precondition of the rise of capitalism. There is, however, an alternative, more positive view of the Puritan family and personality, developed by Edmund Morgan. He stresses the role of duty and discipline in Puritan life, their desire to create a visible kingdom of God on earth where external behaviour would follow God's laws.[216]

Can we reconcile these somewhat contradictory views, synthesising them into a coherent, if not necessarily consistent, character syndrome in which productiveness and destructiveness inhabit the same psyche? 'Hoarding-productiveness' as the dominant mode of assimilation combined with 'authoritarian-destructiveness' as the dominant mode of relatedness would seem to capture the Puritan social character most accurately.

In sum, the overriding feature of the Puritan psyche was an authoritarian social character, a product of the repression of the most important human drives and needs, in particular the need for close affective ties with the Other and for emotional and evaluative validation by other human beings. In addition, however, there was a well of simmering rage at the persecution, religious and political, that drove the Puritans out of England. At times of conflict with the Native Americans, this anger overwhelmed their normally calm exterior and rigid inner stability. Massacres and genocidal statements by Puritan preachers and politicians were, as we've seen, the ultimate expressions of this racism.

Finally, if we want to understand the psychological make-up or content of any social character, it is useful, as suggested in Chapter 4, to refer to the Freudian typology of the mind, with its division into ego, super-ego and id, together with Klein's notion of projective identification. The drive to destructiveness is arguably, at times, the result of repression by the super-ego of psychic forces located in the id, the repository of life-energy and life drives. In the case of the Puritans, destructiveness resulted from unconscious rage at the overpowering of the ego and the id by the super-ego. In Freudian terms, the Puritans were originally people with all-powerful super-egos, repressed ids, and weak and rigid egos, forming a social character they themselves developed unconsciously as an instrument necessary for the construction of a new capitalist world and a new colonial enterprise. Tragically, they failed to see that the Native Americans could have made a useful contribution to this new world. Moreover, when confronted by the natives' defence of their lands, the Puritan id became 'cancerous', transforming itself from a source of life-energy into a destructiveness that swamped the normally unyielding control-tower of the super-ego. This destructive rage was then projected on to the Native Americans, who were thus seen as presenting a mortal threat to the Puritans' enterprise.

The Scots-Irish

Of all the national and religious groups who migrated to North America from Europe, the Scots-Irish were among the most violent towards the Native Americans, and the most aggressive colonisers of their land. Kevin Kenny describes their political and military role: 'On both sides of the Atlantic, Ulster Presbyterians served as a military and cultural buffer between zones of perceived civility and barbarity, separating Anglicans from Catholics in Ireland and eastern elites from Indians in the American colonies.'[217] Most Scots-Irish emigrated from Ulster to North America in the first half of the eighteenth century. An interesting snapshot of their character is provided by Charles Oliver:

> The Scots-Irish came to prize aggressiveness and cunning, and they insisted on choosing their own leaders based on those traits. They developed a distrust of government, which seemed to exist only to burn their homes, seize their property, and kill their kin. And they reserved to themselves the right to judge the laws they lived under and determine whether they would obey them or not. They lived in rough, simple, ill-kept shacks. They saw no reason to build better homes when they were only going to get burned down eventually. They were at once fervently religious and intensely sensual.
>
> The Quakers in Pennsylvania and the Cavaliers in Virginia shared that assessment but at the same time thought these feisty people would form a perfect buffer between them and hostile Indians, so they invited the new immigrants to settle their frontiers. It was an invitation they would soon regret – before long the colonial governors were complaining that the Scots-Irish caused more trouble than the Indians, and that their presence inflamed the Indians even more. But it was too late. They kept coming, spilling down the Appalachian Mountains into the Carolinas, Georgia, and westward, into what would become Kentucky and Tennessee. By the time the great migration had ended, almost half a million of them had poured into the colonies.[218]

A letter written in 1729 by James Logan, Provincial Secretary of Pennsylvania, records that 'the Indians themselves are alarmed at the swarms of strangers and we are afraid of a breach between them, for the Irish are very rough towards them'.[219] An interesting account of the manners and customs of the Scots-Irish was provided by Rev. Edward Parker, a nineteenth-century Presbyterian pastor, in his book *History of Londonderry*: 'Their diversions and scenes of social intercourse were of a character not the most refined and cultured; displaying physical rather than intellectual and moral powers, such as boxing matches, wrestling, foot races and other athletic exercises.'[220] There were broadly three formative influences on the Scots-Irish: military, socio-economic, and religious.

Military

Large numbers of Scots from the Lowlands border area migrated to Ulster in the seventeenth century. They had grown accustomed to a way of life whose central feature was perpetual warfare. Their main enemies were the Celtic clansmen whom they came to regard as 'raiders, pillagers, cattle-thieves, and murderers'. They became hardened by an almost endless state of war, and 'had no scruples about making merciless reprisals'. The result, according to Ford, was that 'the Scots that flocked into Ulster carried with them prepossessions and antipathies implanted by centuries of conflict with predatory clansmen'.[221] Webb too notes that 'by the time of the great emigration to America – starting around the turn of the eighteenth century – the Scots-Irish had seen more than 700 years of almost continuous warfare along the border between Scotland and England'.[222] James Leyburn provides a similar picture of

> outward influences that worked upon the mind and spirit of the Scottish Lowlander: the comparative isolation from the great world, the backward agricultural methods, the centuries of conflict with the English, the particularism of a feudal system that undermined any tendency toward constitutional institutions, the niggardly soil, the meager life of the mind ... The Scot knew famine and plague, thin soil, insecurity of life and property, raids and aggression.[223]

The Scots developed a hardness 'which sometimes was not far removed from cruelty', a social character which made them amenable to the influence of Calvinism. The Scottish Kirk had removed from its members

> any assurance of eternal salvation by the work of the church ... A man's salvation depended upon himself: he must prove himself to be one of God's elect – a congenial doctrine to people who had always believed in self-reliance and a man's importance to himself ... God ... could be reached by any man, however humble, without the mediation of a priest ... God requires an individual to be a man in His presence, standing when he prays, not abjectly kneeling, stating his own case manfully, as he did to his human lord or laird.[224]

As a consequence, 'the Scot felt reasonably sure that he was among the elect, under God's special protection'.[225]

Ulster had witnessed the overcoming of feudalism with its reliance on traditional authority. The onset of capitalism was giving rise to new distinctions based on property and income. Many Scots immigrants rose up the social scale from the rung of lowly tenant farmers to that of independent farmers, small manufacturers and traders. By the time of the migration to America, many had become middle class and could afford the fare, with enough left over to buy land in the New World. But Ulster Presbyterianism remained rigidly Puritan: 'Church discipline, wherever the Presbyterian church existed in Ulster, was not for an instant relaxed: if anything, its intensity increased during the seventeenth century', with minute control over personal life, clearly exercised with the general approval of church members.[226]

The experience of the Scottish Ulstermen prepared them for life on the American frontier. In both places, they lived on land from which the native peoples had been forcibly ejected. The authorities declared the confiscation to be legal, but when the natives, whether Irish or Indian, refused to accept its legality, choosing to fight back rather than suffer expropriation, 'the settlers fought equally hard to retain the homes and farms they had made by their own labour'.[227] The hardness embedded in the Scottish Lowlanders' social character was intensified by their experience in Ulster. 'Conflict with the Irish, especially during and after the insurrection of 1641, toughened and hardened a character that had never been soft, with an added iron provided by steady church discipline.'[228]

In 1610, James I allocated the Ulster county of Coleraine (Londonderry) to the City of London for the purpose of colonisation.[229] In the subsequent decades, some 100,000 Scots settled in the province.[230] Their experience of Ulster seemed to replicate that of the Lowlands. English and Scottish settlement in Ulster did not remove the native Irish from the area, as had been intended, but 'assumed the character of an incursion of British landlordism among the Irish'. The effect was that the settlers lived 'surrounded by a hostile population, with almost daily risks from raiders and in almost constant alarm of a general rising'. The strength of the English military alert ruled out any serious prospect of an Irish uprising. But there appears to have been a constant struggle against marauding.[231]

In October 1641, however, shortly before the outbreak of the English Civil War, the native Irish did rise up in rebellion. There was a slaughter of Protestant settlers, with thousands killed.[232] Ford quotes a figure of 100,000 Scotch and 20,000 English settlers in Ulster in 1641.[233] During the Civil War, the Ulster Scot settlers steered a middle path between the royalists and the parliamentarians. In Strafford's time, they were pro-parliament and thus became the target of the royalists. However, when the Presbyterian leaders were ejected from the English House of Commons in 1648, the Ulster Scots denounced the Rump Parliament as sectarian. Indeed, the Belfast Presbytery reacted with indignation to the beheading of Charles I in 1647, eliciting the sharp retort of 'blockish Presbyters' from John Milton.[234] Charles Oliver sums it all up succinctly: 'All historians agree ... that their [Scots-Irish] culture is one shaped by war.'[235]

Socio-economic

During the 1650s, low rents and high wages in Ulster had attracted immigrants. By 1660, Scottish settlers numbered around 80,000, out of a population of between 217,000 and 260,000.[236] The period 1670–1700 witnessed a further influx of British settlers strongly influenced, as before, by economic conditions, both in Ulster and their country of origin. The early 1670s saw a 'dramatic worsening of the general situation',[237] especially between 1672–4, the years of the Dutch wars. The Bishop of Derry complained that his churches were in state of disrepair, a situation his parishioners were unable to remedy because of their extreme poverty. There was probably widespread famine in Ulster in the years 1674–5, but also in Scotland in 1673–4. However, in the late 1670s, improved conditions gave rise to a few years of sustained economic growth 'until confidence was shattered under James II' (1685–8).[238]

Ireland became the theatre of war in the conflict between the English Protestants King William and Queen Mary, and the deposed Catholic monarch James II. But the war merely intensified an ongoing economic crisis. Many settlers returned to Scotland, but the end of hostilities witnessed their return. They were joined by a new wave of immigrants attracted by cheap land and welcomed by landlords who, with rents heavily in arrears, were anxious to have them. Estimates of the number of settlers during the 1690s range from 50,000 to 80,000.[239] Famine in Scotland between 1695 and 1698 again stimulated increased emigration to Ulster.[240] After this, however, conditions in Scotland improved, while rents in Ulster rose, and the appeal of North America grew. The combined result of these three factors was that Scottish immigration to Ulster gradually petered out in the early eighteenth century. After a relatively prosperous few years, with bumper harvests in 1711–14, the situation deteriorated, and by the late 1720s 'a series of harvest failures heralded a period of austere conditions culminating in the famine of 1740-1'.[241]

According to Doyle, 'the main movement of Irish emigrants to America came in waves: in 1717/18–1720, 1725–1729, 1740–41, 1754–1755, 1766–1767 and 1770–1775. These movements were related to crises of living costs.'[242] As Kevin Kenny says, the majority of Ulster émigrés were tenant farmers rather than independent landowners. Their hope was that in America land would be both cheaper and more abundant.[243] Doyle argues that an additional factor in first encouraging Scottish emigration to Ulster, and then, starting around 1717, closing it off and re-directing discontented Scots-Irish to North America, was the different character of landlordism. For a century before 1717, Scottish landlords issued short leases to tenants, imposing swift, efficient patterns of production on them. The less efficient were forced off the land, while subdivision of land, especially subletting, was strongly discouraged.

In contrast, 'Ulster tenures were designed to attract and retain rural population, not discriminate between types of producers.'[244] Moreover, Scots landlords were 'hands-on', enabling them to be closely involved in 'discipline, innovation and output'. In contrast, Ulster landlords were usually of a different faith or ethnicity, generally living away from their estates, hence employing stewards and bailiffs to collect their rents. They discovered that only life tenures could entice Scots to immigrate and farm, and it was only with the political stability that emerged after the defeat of James II in 1690 (the Battle of the Boyne) that Ulster landlords began to edge towards a stricter Scottish or English pattern of landlordism. But by then tenant customs were strongly entrenched, including patterns of subletting that benefited intermediate farmers. Subletting also facilitated bonding between different layers of the Scots-Irish, bonding which intensified with the growing stress on kin duties. As Doyle explains: 'Futile, top-down attempts to change all this with the threat or possibility of hard times prompted the first real emigration to America, not of the capable and innovative but rather of tenants used to perhaps the most relaxed regimen in the British Isles, and fearing its loss.' Doyle emphasises that 'while inheriting the formative experiences and folk memories of the years 1610–1700, most Scots Irish emigrants came from a changing Ireland, that of the eighteenth century'.[245]

Religious

The final reason for Scots-Irish emigration to America was, as in the case of Puritans, the search for religious toleration. According to Kenny, this, alongside the need for land, was the reason their Scottish forefathers had left Scotland for Ulster over the three generations prior to the turn of the eighteenth century. The Scots-Irish were Protestants who dissented from the doctrines of the established Anglican Church: dissenters, had endured intense persecution, not only in Ireland, but in England and Scotland too, until the late seventeenth century. For example, under legislation introduced in 1703, office-holders in Ireland had to take communion according to the ritual of the Anglican Church, a law that excluded Presbyterians as well as Catholics. Dissenters' marriages were not recognised unless performed by an Anglican minister, and Presbyterians, like Catholics, were required to pay tithes to the established Church of Ireland. Not surprisingly, therefore, the Scots-Irish dissenters hoped that America would emerge as a haven of religious tolerance. As Kenny points out, from 1719, Presbyterians were allowed to conduct their own services without fear of prosecution,

> but they suffered daily reminders of their inferior status and lived in fear of renewed persecution. This climate of intolerance, on its own, would not have led to mass emigration. But when combined with crop failures, the renewal of leases at high rents ... and repeated crises in the linen industry, it helped trigger a wave of migration that reached periodic peaks over the rest of the century.[246]

The Social Character of the Scots-Irish

The social character of the Scots-Irish bears strong similarities to that of the Puritans. There was a strong current of self-hatred, especially among the 'evangelicals', preoccupied as they were with 'ways to abuse, to deny, and to annihilate their own enduring sense of self-worth, convinced that only by destroying the self could they conform absolutely and unquestioningly to the will of God'.[247] Charles Jeffry Smith, a young Presbyterian minister who travelled and preached throughout Virginia in the 1760s, wrote in his diary: 'I long to be wholly emptied of self and to have all my dependance upon Christ.'[248]

Coupled with self-hatred was a strong authoritarian streak of submission to the existing official authority, whether this be God, the state or the family. Regarding the latter, 'parental power was absolute ... and the crushing of the child's will by the exertion of systematic efforts on the part of parents was justified by the conviction that parental power and authority were beyond question ... Children should never feel that they could deflect or alter the will of a parent to suit their own wishes.'[249]

Like the Puritans, the Presbyterian Scots-Irish, especially the evangelical amongst them, had a tendency to see other people as 'dangerous and aggressive ... intent on doing harm to either their bodies or their souls', a view that in 'extreme instances could become a paranoid vision of the outer world'. Such a perception was undoubtedly 'rooted in the denial of anger and the projection of inadmissible feelings within the self upon other people'.[250] They had a black and white view of the world, a mentality by which they perceived themselves as embattled with everyone who did not share their values and beliefs. For the evangelicals among them, 'there were only two choices: to be a soldier for Christ, or an enemy of Christ, There could be no middle way.'[251] This hatred of the world was evident from the 'very violence of their language and the ferocity of their denunciations – both of individuals and of doctrines'. Such powerful expressions of hostility 'erupted from deep within these repressed individuals'.[252] As for child-rearing, we can adduce the following general principle: groups that have suffered political or religious persecution, or economic impoverishment and decline, react to these historical experiences with rage and hostility towards the world. This is particularly so if these experiences also leave them with a sense of powerlessness, as no doubt occurs with any defeat. Unable to win redress in the real, objective world, the anger and the attempt to compensate for powerlessness are played out within the family.

However, we have argued that social character is created through the unconscious collective labour of a class on the basis of two factors: firstly, the struggles of that class (for example, the defeats suffered by the Scots-Irish), and secondly, the way that labour is expressed in the group's relationship to the mode of production. Just as with the Puritans, the Scots-Irish played an important role in the agricultural and commercial development of American capitalism. Hence, as far as their mode of assimilation of the objective world goes, they developed a hoarding-productive orientation. As for their mode of relatedness, there can be little doubt that there was a strong element of destructiveness, ultimately expressed in the racial genocide of the Native Americans. Arguably, their destructiveness was even stronger than that of the Puritans, who collaborated with groups of Native Americans as well as exterminating them. And, of course, the Scots-Irish had suffered even greater hardships and worse defeats than the Puritans before migrating to America. So, like the Puritans, the Scots-Irish had developed strong, repressive super-egos, but, it seems, even more powerful destructive ids which they too projected on to the Native Americans.

To apply further the paradigm developed in Part One, it would seem that there arose among both the Puritans and Scots-Irish a predisposition for destructiveness. This had developed through the various historical experiences in which, as we have seen, they suffered severe economic and political setbacks, and were prone to more or less constant physical or military attacks by the English rulers. This predisposition was precipitated into actual violence as a result of the relentless, westward-colonising movement of the settlers, and the consequent attacks by Native Americans defending their land, which the Europeans believed to be rightfully theirs.

In conclusion, the actions of the European colonists in North America, in particular the extermination of the Native Americans, had a dual character – rational and irrational. Insofar as the settlers sought to colonise and develop the land, they acted rationally even if at times barbarically. But inasmuch as their genocide of the Indians was unnecessary and even harmful to their own material interests, it was irrational. To that extent, it admits of an explanation that is in part psychological.

CHAPTER SIX

The Armenian Genocide

In the month from the end of January to the 25th of February 1915, all the Armenian men in the Ottoman army were disarmed and cast into labour battalions ... The men were taken out under armed guard into secluded areas to be shot dead or bayoneted by Turkish soldiers, often assisted by gendarmes and the 'chetes' [auxiliary killing squads]. ... in city and town, village and hamlet, and in the Armenian sections of the major cities of Asia Minor and Anatolia, Armenians were rounded up, arrested, and either shot outright or put on deportation marches ... the able-bodied men were arrested in groups and taken out of the town or city and shot en masse. The women, children, infirm, and elderly were given short notice that they could gather some possessions and would be deported with the other Armenians of their city or town to what they were told was the 'interior'.[1]

The deportations and massacres spread across the length and breadth of Turkey. In the major western cities – Istanbul, Smyrna, Ankara and Tonya; in the east, large cities such as Yozgat, Kayseri and Sivas were also sites of massacres and deportation. Along the Black Sea coast, Armenians were taken out in boats and drowned, and the traditional eastern Armenian vilayets (counties) – containing hundreds of villages and dozens of cities, where the majority of the Ottoman Armenians had lived for centuries – were virtually cleared of their Armenian population. Balakian believes that further south, in the Syrian desert, more Armenians died than anywhere else. In the region of Deir el-Zor, the 'epicentre of death', Armenians died not only of massacre, starvation, and disease, but 'were stuffed into caves and asphyxiated by brush fires – primitive gas chambers'.[2]

At the time, scholars and journalists estimated that between 800,000 and 1 million Armenians died in 1915 alone. In the summer of 1916, there was a new wave of massacres in the Mesopotamian desert (northern Syria), where some 200,000 Armenians, survivors of the 'death marches', were murdered. Tens of thousands of women were abducted into harems or Muslim families, and a similar number of children were taken into families and converted to Islam. Cultural genocide thus accompanied physical genocide. After the war, fresh Armenian massacres were perpetrated in Marash in 1920 and in Smyrna in 1922. The death toll from 1915 to 1922 probably reached a million and a half.[3]

Historical Background

From the fourteenth to the end of the seventeenth century, the Ottoman Empire grew rapidly. At its height, in the seventeenth century, it was the greatest empire in the world, ruling territories from the Caucasus to North Africa, from the Middle East to southeast Europe – Greece, Bulgaria, the former Yugoslavia – even coming close to capturing Vienna in 1683. The eighteenth century, however, witnessed the slowing down of expansion, and in the nineteenth century decline set in. Greece achieved national liberation through its war of independence from 1821 to 1829. The Turco-Italian War of 1911–12 resulted in Turkey ceding Libya to Italy. Turkey also lost its Balkan territories – Serbia, Albania and Bulgaria – during the Balkan wars of 1912–13. From the early nineteenth century up to the Balkan wars, 'the Ottomans were deeply shaken by huge land losses', some 60 per cent of their territory.[4]

Turkey increasingly lagged behind in the economic, commercial and scientific fields, trailing Britain, the US and Germany who were blazing ahead in the race to industrialise. In 1853 Tsar Nicholas I described Ottoman Turkey as 'the sick man of Europe', a description that achieved wide currency. As a result of continuous war, many soldiers and civilians were killed, with a large percentage of the Muslim population living in the 'lost territories of the Balkans and the Caucasus ... forced to migrate to Anatolia'.[5] Two economic factors are important. First, the Ottoman empire came increasingly under the financial control of foreign powers; second, through the system of 'capitulations', its economic development, or lack of it, came to be dominated by minority non-Muslim communities: mainly Greeks and Armenians but also Jews.[6]

Firstly, economic subordination: the heavy financial toll exacted by the Crimean War drove the Ottoman regime (the Porte) to borrow overseas. International loans were indispensable since the lack of an indigenous modern capitalist class meant that the economy could not generate the capital necessary to finance the Tanzimat reforms. The British-administered Imperial Ottoman Bank was established in 1856, amalgamating with French interests in 1863. France became the Ottoman Empire's greatest creditor. In 1875, Turkey was declared bankrupt, and in 1877–8 lost a war against Russia. In 1881, the great powers set up the Ottoman Public Debt Administration to control Turkey's finances, run by representatives of Britain, France, Germany, Italy, Austria and Turkey itself, which ceded 12 to 15 per cent of its finances to that body.[7] This reassured investors, resulting in increased capital investment, particularly on the part of French and German interests. However, 'penetration and control at this level actually inhibited the ability of the Ottoman state to develop the economy, compromising Ottoman sovereignty particularly in the peripheral areas most susceptible to external penetration'.[8] Also, the intensification of European competition led to the division of the empire into zones of economic interest, as illustrated by the German Baghdad railway project.

Secondly, by the end of the eighteenth century, the non-Muslim minority groups – Greeks, Armenians, and to a lesser extent, Jews – had established a commanding lead in the empire's trade and finance:[9]

In addition to ... their higher level of education, their contacts with Europeans and with their own co-religionists in various European towns, and more generally by the energy and enterprise characteristic of minorities, the Rayahs [non-Muslim groups, better known as 'dhimmis'] were also aided by the diplomas of immunity they obtained as interpreters (berat) or servants (firman) in foreign embassies.[10]

Millets

Ottoman society had for centuries been divided into ethno-religious communities known as 'millets' – Muslim (for example, Kurds), Jewish, Greek Orthodox and Armenian. According to Hovannisian: 'The millet system allowed the Armenians to retain their cultural-religious identity in a plural society, but it rendered them powerless politically and militarily.'[11] The non-Muslim millets were subject to economic, social and legal discrimination, and had to pay taxes from which Muslims were exempt. In turn, non-Muslims did not have the obligation of military service which could last for many long years.

Nevertheless, a number of writers argue that, prior to the decline of the Ottoman Empire and the advent of modernity in the Tanzimat reform programme,

> Ottoman toleration of its non-Muslim communities compared favourably with the treatment by many European states of their religious minorities. This system of stability through institutionalised prejudice worked on condition that the dhimmis [non-Muslim minorities] continued to accept the hierarchical status quo and that the state continued to enforce it.[12]

Indeed, prior to the mid nineteenth century, Ottoman-Armenian relations were comparatively stable. 'Armenians, as non-Muslim monotheists ... like other Christian groups and Jews, occupied a position in the Islamic theocracy that, if definitively subordinated and even despised, was still legally assured.'[13]

Moreover, in the mid nineteenth century, these groups benefited from the Tanzimat reforms which guaranteed equality to minorities, removing the more obvious forms of discrimination, together with exemption from conscription, giving the rayahs a great competitive advantage.[14] A further complicating factor was the granting of 'capitulations' by the Porte to various European powers. These were legal and economic privileges conceded to citizens of Christian states or their Christian clients in the Ottoman Empire. These were granted 'by Ottoman rulers as a means of bestowing favour and consolidating alliances'.[15] According to Islam, law derives from religion, and only believers can enjoy legal rights or engage in legal activity. This meant that 'foreigners were judged and protected by their own laws ... and were exempt from all taxes except export and import duties, which had ceilings specified by capitulations'. The result was that foreign products flooded the Turkish market, creating a barrier to industrial development.[16] Capitulations became inhibitors of development, symbols of external domination and interference, 'compromising Ottoman sovereignty and helping to drive a wedge between Muslims and Christians'.[17]

Of course, internal factors also played a key role in the social and economic retardation of Ottoman society. The competition of foreign industrial goods precipitated the decline of the traditional handicrafts, and it was only in the

20 or 30 years before the First World War that significant industry developed. According to Issawi, this was despite the presence in Turkey of important preconditions for the rise of an industrial economy. It had quite a large, and not very poor population, representing a potential internal market. It was endowed with abundant supplies of raw materials: coal, iron, copper, lead and other materials, as well as agricultural raw materials: cotton, silk, wool, leather, tobacco, fruits and oilseed. The transport system was inadequate but the compensation for this was the concentration of the population along the coastal rims, since the main cities were situated on or close to the coast. Also, a large number of handicraftsmen provided a range of skills that could have been adapted for industrial work.

Though one can't ignore the Long Depression that lasted from 1873 to 1896 and which acted as a brake on development, the main barriers were social and political. First was the lack of a middle class possessing capital, the spirit of enterprise and managerial and technical skills. Could the non-Muslim communities have filled the breach? They were, indeed, behind the industrialisation that did take place, but were diverted from pursuing this further by two factors: feelings of insecurity, and the speedier rewards that beckoned from alternative outlets such as government loans, money-lending, trade, or the purchase of real estate in the growing towns. Moreover, the masses had a low educational level which, combined with aversion to industrial labour, made recruitment difficult. And there was tough opposition from the guilds. But even more serious was the existence of the commercial treaties – for example, the capitulations granting trading privileges to foreign powers – so that the government was unable to offer the fledgling national industry economic protection. This was aggravated by the internal duties on the sale and consumption of manufactured goods.

Perhaps the most important barrier was the government's lack of interest in economic development, and especially in industrialisation. This was partly due to the country's social structure and the fact that government policy was dominated by the military and bureaucratic elites rather than the small and mainly non-Turkish entrepreneurial middle class. An additional obstacle was the dominant belief that 'Turkey could not be industrialised', since the Muslims of Asia lacked the necessary 'spirit of application and hard work which had made possible Europe's factories'.[18] Arguably, however, perhaps the major factor in Turkey's slow economic progress was 'the unwieldiness and corruption of the bureaucracy, its ignorance of economic matters and its preoccupation with fiscal considerations to the exclusion of development policies'.[19] The deadweight of Ottoman bureaucracy was a modern example of the kind of society Marx described as Oriental Despotism. In this mode of production, newly emerging productive forces are unable to break through the thick crust of an ossified system of social relations.

Economic Structure

At the turn of the twentieth century, the vast majority of the Turkish population, Muslim and non-Muslim, lived and worked on the land. In the Anatolian countryside, in theory, 'the Sultan owned all the land ... and except with his consent, or that of his representative, no change of tenure was possible'.[20] In practice, the land was 'held' by feudal landlords and divided into holdings let out to peasant families on a long-term basis. These families were also under obligation to provide the landlords with soldiers in times of war.[21] A holding could be inherited by the landlord's son, or, on payment of a small sum, by certain close relatives. However, loyalty to the village was strong and it was unusual for land to pass into the hands of an outsider. As Lewis says: 'free movement was discouraged except to take up vacant holdings, and the laws generally worked to bind the peasants to the soil; *they reinforced established custom and insisted on its observance'*.[22] In the army, the peasants were 'poorly fed, rarely paid, and kept in active service beyond the legal period'.[23]

Issawi argues that agriculture was the sector of the Ottoman economy which changed least from 1800 to 1914. Yet significant shifts did occur, among them:

> the extension of cultivation, the marked expansion of cash crops, the increase in the proportion of marketed produce, the development of more capitalistic relations, and, towards the end of the period, the improvement of techniques and investment in irrigation schemes and agricultural machinery. Most of this change was the result of market forces operating through foreign individuals or agencies or through members of minorities, but in the second half of the period, the government played an increasingly important part.[24]

So economic backwardness can in part be ascribed to the empire's failure to give rise to a bourgeois class capable of overthrowing the traditional despotic regime and carrying through a bourgeois national revolution. Nor did the Sultans push through a revolution from above, as occurred in Germany or Japan. Their society stagnated and then decayed, preventing an enterprising class breaking through the frozen barriers from below. Moreover, Ottoman commerce, trade and finance were largely under the control of non-Muslim minorities, and also of foreign powers.

The 1915 genocide was not the first massacre of Armenians. The final quarter of the nineteenth century witnessed a 'new rash of disastrous Ottoman losses': following the 1877–8 defeat at the hands of the Russians, there occurred the Anglo-French displacement of the Turks from their overlordship of Egypt in 1879, and the Cretan insurrection and Greco-Turkish war which led to the Turkish evacuation of Crete in 1898.[25] As James Reid described it, 'the collapse of the Ottoman Empire deprived the ruling elite of any security it once had and created a condition of paranoia [in which individuals inclined in that direction already would be pushed to an extreme]'.[26] It was as a result of these losses that the first major massacres of Armenians took place in Anatolia in 1894–6. Indeed, one motive for the Armenian genocide was the drive to expropriate a Christian minority in order to transfer capital to a Muslim-Turkish bourgeoisie 'as an engine of Turkish nationalism and economic independence'.[27] The question remains, however, was it necessary to murder up to 1.5 million Armenians to achieve this transfer?

Despite the retarded development, by the eve of the First World War an embryonic Turkish bourgeoisie had emerged, its interests 'beginning to be recognised and promoted by the government'.[28] But its smallness is evident from the fact that in Istanbul in 1922, Muslims owned only 4 per cent of foreign trade enterprises, 3 per cent of transport agencies, 15 per cent of wholesale and 25 per cent of retail firms. In 1919, some 73 per cent of factories and workshops belonged to Greeks and 85 per cent of their employees were non-Muslims. By the same token, the reverse side of the rise of a bourgeoisie was the emergence of a small industrial working class. In 1913, in Istanbul and Anatolia, they numbered, according to one estimate, 298,000, according to another 200,000 to 250,000, out of a population of 15 million. These figures include 10,000 in government industries such as arsenals and textile factories, some 20,000 miners and 10,000 railwaymen, while other factories and larger workshops employed some 20,000. Most workers still worked in traditional handicrafts such as rugs, leather, shoes, metalwork and pottery.[29]

The 1908 Revolution

Military defeats and territorial losses convinced the Young Turks that drastic action was needed to save the empire. Their aim was to stop and, if possible, to reverse the collapse of the Ottoman Empire. To them, it felt like a matter of survival.[30] The Young Turk movement spearheaded the revolution of 1908 which introduced a bourgeois-democratic regime, reviving the discarded constitution of 1876, and clipping the wings of the Sultan. Bernard Lewis describes the reaction: 'the long night of Hamidian despotism was over. The constitution had once again been proclaimed and elections ordered. Turks and Armenians embraced each other in the streets; the age of freedom and brotherhood had come. The writings of that time reflect an almost delirious joy.'[31] Feroz Ahmad provides a similar account:

> The proclamation of the Constitution on 23/4 July 1908 was a success beyond all expectations of the Committee of Union and Progress (CUP). But as a result of the Sultan's sudden capitulation ... the government was completely demoralised and administration virtually came to a standstill ... the people, not knowing what freedom meant, thought that all the old institutions of law and order had come to an end. Having suffered injustices for so long, they decided to take matters into their own hands. The people of Trabzon demanded the dismissal of their *vali* [governor] or threatened to drive him out. Fearing the consequences if he refused, Memduh Pasa, the Minister of the Interior, accepted their demand ... In Bursa and Konya, Abdulhamid's agents were arrested and expelled and the *valis* were given a list of corrupt officials whose dismissals were demanded.[32]

Lewis summarises the key aspects of the Young Turk revolution: 'it was a patriotic movement of Muslim Turks, mostly soldiers, whose prime objective was to remove a fumbling and incompetent ruler and replace him by a government better able to defend the Empire against the dangers that threatened it'.[33]

Trotsky, too, emphasised the crucial role of the army officers in the revolution, given the small size and weakness of the working class. He pointed out that the most educated elements of the intelligentsia, such as teachers, engineers, and so on, had been unable to find scope for their talents in schools or factories in Ottoman society, and had therefore become army officers. Many had studied in Western Europe and become familiar with the regimes there. They returned home to be confronted by 'the ignorance and poverty of the Turkish soldier and the debased condition of the state. This has filled them with bitterness; and so the officer corps has become the focus of discontent and rebelliousness.'[34]

From the outset, the Young Turks were divided between two pre-existing tendencies: the liberals who favoured a measure of decentralisation and some autonomy for the religious and national minorities, and the nationalists who increasingly favoured more central authority and Turkish supremacy. Lewis describes the CUP as the instrument of the latter, 'the silent and self-effacing power behind the throne, later ... [the] unashamed contender for supreme authority'.[35] It seemed that liberal ideas and policies would prevail: the first two Grand Vezirs of the constitutional era were Said Pasa and Kamil Pasa, supported by Ottoman liberals and enjoying wide respect. However, it is hard to gauge the sincerity of the Young Turks in their proclamations of freedom and equality, especially after the new regime came under attack from internal and external sources. These attacks 'threw them into a mood of anger, bitterness and frustration'.[36] Externally, the new regime experienced what Lewis describes as 'aggression and betrayal' on the part of European and Balkan Christian powers. Austria took advantage of the Ottoman's protracted crisis to declare its annexation of Bosnia and Herzegovina; Bulgaria proclaimed its independence; Crete announced its union with Greece. All these events took place in October 1908.[37] Moreover, precedents had been set which encouraged Italy to attack the Ottoman province of Libya (Tripolitania) in September 1911, and which spurred the Balkan states to mount a combined attack on Turkey in October 1912.

Anger against the CUP and the constitutional revolution grew, partly because of the loss of territory and prestige, partly because of the cavalier approach of the Young Turks, remaining in the background, but manipulating government appointments from the shadows.[38] The internal crisis, which had been in part a direct result of the external crisis, culminated in April 1909 in an attempt to overthrow the regime by the forces of right-wing reaction – in particular, the Society of Muhammed, an advocate of militant pan-Islamism. The Society was opposed to 'the westernising reformism of both the CUP and the Liberal Union. Its propaganda was aimed at the religious and conservative elements in the Empire, and ... [it] was able to exercise considerable influence on the traditional deputies in the Chamber and the rank-and-file in the army'.[39] The rising took the form of a mutiny by the mainly Albanian soldiers of the First Army Corps based in Istanbul.[40] Ahmad emphasises the way in which religion played the role of vehicle of the counter-revolution: 'Islam had played a vital role in Ottoman society and ... used as a weapon against the Committee [the CUP], it provided the opposition with the largest audience.'[41] He also argues that the power of

THE ARMENIAN GENOCIDE   165

the CUP was always exaggerated, and was never great in Istanbul. It did enjoy considerable support when battling against the despotism of the Sultan and his bureaucracy, but with the destruction of their power, and only a few expectations satisfied, the disgruntled elements went into opposition. Once the principal aim of the CUP had been achieved, it fractured into numerous factions. In any case, 'those members dedicated to the ideal of reform and the creation of a modern state were always in a minority'. Moreover, there were many opportunists who had supported the CUP in the hope that their careers would benefit from the overthrow of the Sultan, but whose ambitions were frustrated by the CUP's refusal to take the reins of government. Also, the secularism of the Young Turks 'alarmed and alienated the religious elements'.[42]

The CUP was in complete disarray and the Liberals were able to replace it. But not for long. The CUP was still powerful in Macedonia, and the Third Army based there was loyal to the constitution. It left Salonika on 17 April and occupied Istanbul on the 23rd/24th. The National Assembly 'ratified the proclamation of the ... army, guaranteed the constitution and security in the country, and declared that the actions of the army were in conformity with the aspirations of the nation'. Five days later, the National Assembly voted to depose Abdul Hamid as Sultan, and to replace him with his brother. The counter-revolution, however brief, had exposed the CUP's inability to control the political situation and to maintain law and order. So, as Ahmad points out, 'the chaos that followed forced the army to intervene as the instrument of law and order, and not as the instrument of the CUP'.[43]

The failure of the attempted coup strengthened the power of the radical reformist group in the Chamber of Deputies and discredited the conservative, anti-reformist elements. The period between May and August 1909 was when most of the legislative work of the Chamber was done: firstly, to enshrine in the constitution the political changes that had taken place since the revolution of July 1908. Secondly, to modernise and centralise the Ottoman Empire and its administrative machinery. Thirdly, to legislate the 'capitulations' (foreign commercial privileges) out of existence.[44]

The first purpose was achieved through modifying a number of articles of the constitution: the result was that 'the sultan reigned but no longer ruled, his function restricted to confirming decisions already taken by the Cabinet or Parliament'.[45] The supreme authority was the Chamber of Deputies. The CUP were also determined to curb the powers of the Sublime Porte – the office of the Grand Vezir – which for two centuries had been the real seat of Ottoman government.[46] The discretionary authority of the Grand Vezir was now restricted, and ministers became responsible to the Chamber of Deputies. In the event of disagreement between the cabinet and the Chamber, the cabinet had either to submit or to resign. As Ahmad says: 'The last word was always with the Chamber.'[47]

Secondly, the Unionists (CUP) passed legislation aimed at centralising the government and unifying the empire through the 'Ottomanisation' of the disparate groups of which it consisted. Indeed, the Young Turks applied repressive and centralist policies not only to their Christian subjects such as the Armenians, but also to the non-Turkish Muslim peoples over whom they ruled. Towards Arabs, Albanians and other Muslims, they pursued a policy of Turkification, attempting to impose the Turkish language on them and rejecting demands for independence.[48] The CUP also passed a law authorising them to form special military units aimed at repressing Greek and Bulgarian bands in Rumelia and Armenian bands in eastern Turkey.

In this vein, the Chamber legislated to limit some of the freedom unleashed by the 1908 revolution, and, moreover, to prevent any recurrence of the counter-revolution recently suppressed. It also acted to restrict political freedom including the right to strike on the part of the growing labour movement.[49] The measures intended to centralise power were partially successful. But the rise of nationalism among the subject peoples stymied the attempt to Ottomanise the empire.

The third purpose of the CUP laws, bound up with the desire to create a modern state, was the abolition of the 'capitulations', 'long resented as a symbol of inferiority and subservience'.[50] But the foreign powers kept close watch over all new legislation and were able 'to frustrate the Porte's attempt to abrogate the capitulations' which remained in force until 1924 when they were abolished by the Treaty of Lausanne. But 'while they remained in force, the Ottoman Empire retained its status of a "semi-colony"'.[51] The dominance of the Unionists was not seriously challenged until 1911 when for the first time they faced an internal threat in the shape of a serious split in their ranks. At the start of 1911, there was growing dissatisfaction with the way the situation was developing, not least the manner in which opposition was restricted by martial law. A group called the 'New Party' was set up which offered major criticisms of the CUP's social and political policies, in particular the decline of democratic and constitutional procedures. In November, a new party was formed – the Liberal Union – which united all the groups, parties and personalities opposed to the CUP.[52]

In December, the CUP suffered defeat in a by-election in Istanbul. As Lewis says, 'public opinion in the capital had asserted itself in a striking form against the Unionist regime'. An additional voice, that of elder statesman Kamil Pasa, was raised against the CUP. Faced with this dual threat, the CUP took action. In January, they dissolved parliament and called a general election in which they shamelessly rigged the results, with only six opposition candidates out of a total of 275 securing election. In Lewis's words: 'the Unionists ... with an obedient parliament and a submissive Sultan ... seemed to be in full and undisputed control'.[53] But problems were mounting. The Libyan war against Italy was going badly and provincial revolts were developing. Having suppressed the Liberal parliamentary opposition by dissolving the old Chamber and packing the new one with its own supporters, 'the Committee inevitably called into being a new opposition, not democratic or parliamentary but military and conspiratorial – a ghost from its own past'. The Committee 'had gone to Istanbul and become the oppressors'.[54]

Once again young opposition officers in Rumelia took to the hills where they were welcomed by Albanian rebels. In May–June 1912, a group of 'Saviour Officers' was created in Istanbul, no doubt in response to the emergence of the rebel officers' group in Rumelia. Their aim was to remove an illegal government and parliament, to dismantle the power of the CUP, and to return to constitutional rule, initially by holding free elections. By the end of June, the Albanian rebellion was causing growing alarm, and criticism of the CUP government was mounting. The 'Saviour Officers' moved into action, issuing a manifesto to the press, and a declaration to the Sultan. These initiatives, backed up by ominous military movements, prompted the cabinet to resign. The new government under veteran politician Kamil Pasa continued to be preoccupied with the Italian war when a new blow struck on 2 October: an ultimatum from the Balkan states. Peace with Italy was hastily concluded; the Balkan war broke out the next day. 'The CUP, ousted but by no means destroyed, prepared for its return to power.'[55] The opportunity arose with the approach of the Balkan armies to the walls of Istanbul. Believing (wrongly) that the Liberal cabinet was about to cede Edirne, the CUP launched an assault on the Sublime Porte, assassinating the minister of war Nazim Pasa, and recapturing political control. The CUP prepared the ground in the army, the police and government offices for the assumption of total control, securing the appointment of Mahmud Sevket Pasa as Grand Vezir.[56] His assassination on 11 June provided the CUP with the excuse to assume total power, to crush the opposition and jettison the remaining shreds of freedom and democracy.[57] The rule of the Young Turks ended only with the defeat of the Ottoman Empire in 1918 'when the Committee of Union and Progress disbanded itself, its leaders fled abroad, and the liberal spokesmen emerged from exile, concealment or insignificance to quarrel for the privilege of presiding over the dissolution of the Ottoman Empire'.[58] Prior to that, however, they carried out the genocide of the Armenians.

Young Turk Achievements

The see-saw of fortunes between 1908 and 1914 fuelled the Young Turks' insecurity, their perception of themselves as failures and middle-class upstarts. But what were their achievements? The aim uniting all the different Young Turk committees and factions was the survival of the empire, their core belief that 'certain radical improvements in Ottoman state and society were needed to save them from inner decay and foreign attack'.[59] They did succeed in carrying out important reforms in law and administration, both provincial and municipal. The new system of government they created did provide the basis for the modern Turkish state that emerged from the ashes of the empire. In Istanbul, their programme of public works greatly improved the city's public amenities. In Lewis's words: 'The Young Turks may have failed to give Turkey constitutional government. They did, however, give Istanbul drains.'[60]

Moreover, in social life, the movement for Westernisation gathered pace. The old method of telling the time was replaced by the twenty-four-hour clock. The Westernisation of dress and manners accelerated. One symptom of this was the warning issued by the religious authorities to Muslim women not to wear European dress. But perhaps the Young Turks' greatest success was in the field of education, where they set up a new system of schools, training colleges and universities. As a result of this, the entry of women into both the educational institutions and the professions, previously the preserve of upper-class women, was greatly expanded. However, given what they'd set out to achieve – the salvation of the empire – the Young Turks' dream ended in failure, both in their own eyes and in the eyes of the world.

Peasantry

According to the Young Turk ideologue, Yusuf Akcura, the peasantry were the 'basic matter of the Turkish nation', and 'the group needing the greatest assistance, a view he combined with his ethnic-based Turkism and his pan-Turkist territorial irredentism'.[61] Indeed, 'in their first flush of glory and while they were at their most radical', the Young Turk leaders proposed 'measures intended to lighten the burden of the peasant', including land distribution, low interest loans, tithe reductions, and agricultural schools, promising 'to encourage the development of agriculture in every possible way. They considered it vital to save the peasant from the feudal lords.' Young Turk intellectuals stressed 'the importance of the small farmers' and encouraged cooperativisation.[62] The Young Turks' territorial ambitions and racial hatred developed into 'a related disdain for ... non-farming peoples'. Enver Pasha would later claim that the Young Turk army had drawn 'all its strength from the rural class', in contrast to the cities – Istanbul and Izmir – which contained non-Turkish majorities of Armenians, Greeks and Jews. This exemplifies Kiernan's view that two of the three key ideological features of genocide are racism and 'the romance of agrarianism'. The third feature, the cult of antiquity, is visible in the Young Turks' nostalgia for the glory days of the Ottoman Empire.[63]

However, the Young Turk leaders came up against a barrier: the intransigence of rural elites, 5 per cent of whom owned 65 per cent of the land. The Young Turks 'took the path of least resistance', bending to landlord power in the interests of their main goal, 'salvation of the empire', carrying out only modest reforms to modernise and commercialise agriculture. Kiernan concludes that 'under the Young Turks, most peasants suffered from increased forced labour and land expropriations, but the regime's ideological claim to foster the peasantry and cultivation is clear'.[64] Moreover, says Yilmaz, 'there was not much in the Unionist record that projected them as champions of either oppressed nations or the proletariat'.[65] The Young Turks in no way sympathised with the aspirations of the Ottoman national minorities – for example, the Armenians. As Ramsauer says, 'the Committee of Union and Progress was, paradoxically, inclined to side with the Sultan against any attempt to dismember the Ottoman patrimony'.[66] On the other hand, as Mann points out, 'until shortly before the genocide, [the Young Turks] were allied with the Armenians against the sultan'.[67] Nor were the Young Turks sympathetic to the aspirations for national independence of the principal Islamic but non-Turkish people – for example, the Arabs. Back in power after the coup of January 1913, 'the Unionists, while willing to make concessions, had no intention of granting complete autonomy as the Arabs hoped'.[68]

Politics of the CUP

The CUP had forerunners in the 1860s and 1870s – the Young Ottomans – who campaigned for constitutional government in order to curb the power of the Sultan and to satisfy the aspirations of the minorities for equal rights. Unlike the CUP, the Young Ottomans came from the ruling elite and were therefore in a position to assume power once they had forced the Sultan to concede the constitution. They did, after all, come from 'a ruling elite, prepared by education to command and to govern'.[69] In contrast, the Young Turks shared their social values but not their social background. As Ahmad explains:

> During the period of Abdulhamid's despotic rule, the base of the reform movement had become much broader. This was brought about by Abdulhamid's reforms. Whereas the Young Ottomans were members of and products of the ruling institution, the Young Turks belonged to the newly emerging professional classes: lecturers in the recently founded government colleges, lawyers trained in western law, journalists, minor clerks in the bureaucracy, and junior officers trained in the western-style war colleges. Most of them were half-educated and products of the state schools. The well-educated ones had no experience of administration and little idea about running a government.[70]

The CUP had no interest in fundamental social change. They were conservative in both outlook and policy. 'The importance of the 1908 *coup d'état* is not that it was revolutionary ... it was not. Its aim was to restore a constitution which had been granted thirty-two years earlier and thereby save the State.' In this respect the CUP was similar to the Young Ottomans – 'concerned only with the problem of how to save the Empire'.[71] *The Times* Istanbul correspondent wrote on 24 August 1908 that the Young Turk movement was essentially middle class.

> The high officials, generally ... were hostile to the movement ... The lower classes ... were, as a rule, indifferent. It was among the junior officers of the army and the navy, the middle and lower grades of the civil service, the professional classes and the 'ulema' (Muslim scholars of Islamic law), that the movement for reform carried all before it.[72]

Their opponents argued that they were too young and lacked experience in Ottoman administration. This marked them out from the Young Ottomans who, as members of the upper class, had held high office and whose complaint was merely that they were prevented from reaching the highest positions. As Mehmed Cavit, a leading Unionist, told the First Secretary of the British Embassy: 'the Young Turks were all young men who lacked experience in administrative work ... the respect which in all countries is conceded to age, is far greater here than elsewhere'.[73] In addition, the CUP lacked a centralised and nationally coordinated organisation. Its only real organisation was based in the Macedonian provinces with its headquarters in Salonika. Given all these factors – their conservatism, lack of confidence and organisation – the CUP 'was unable to assume power openly, and power was left formally in the hands of the government of Said Pasha'[74] – a traditional court politician, one of several liberal but patriotic establishment figures with whom the CUP collaborated. As Ahmad says, 'ever since 1908, the CUP had sought a Grand Vezir [first minister] such as Kamil who could give their movement respectability and legitimacy'.[75]

Refusal to grasp the reins of power was the trademark of the CUP from the revolution of 1908 until shortly before the outbreak of the First World War in 1914. When they mounted a coup against the Liberal government under Kamil Pasa in January 1913, during the first Balkan war, it was on patriotic grounds: it seemed the Liberals were about to cede the town of Edirne to the Bulgars. Even then, the CUP did not assume power themselves but installed a coalition government under Sevket Pasa, another liberal, non-Unionist politician.[76] The government faced huge problems: 'the Treasury was empty, the army demoralised and the Turks diplomatically isolated'. Kamil's answer to this mess had been peace at any price.[77] In March 1913, Edirne fell to a joint Serbo-Bulgar offensive, but the war continued, and the CUP-led army recaptured it in July.[78] The confidence of the Ottoman elite was severely dented by a succession of military defeats and territorial losses, both clear symptoms of imperial decline.

War and Genocide

A few weeks after the Ottoman Empire joined the First World War, minister of war Enver Pasha, a key member of the CUP triumvirate that now ruled the empire, headed a Turkish army in the invasion of Russia. The idea, inspired by the developing pan-Turkist ideal, was 'to unite all branches of our race'.[79] But in the ensuing Battle of Sarikamish that lasted from December 1914 to January 1915, they suffered yet another humiliating defeat.[80] This setback made a powerful impact on the Young Turks, unleashing a wave of paranoia in their collective psyche. Turkey's entry into the war in November 1914 and their extermination of the Armenians in 1915 and 1916 were linked in an

> evolving narrative of intertwining domestic and international events. From the Adana massacres of 1909 through the Balkan Wars of 1912–13 and then to World War One ... the Committee of Union and Progress was engaged in promoting a new Turkish nationalism, a growing and encompassing military culture, and a large, complex, and clandestine bureaucracy. All of these were crucial in the CUP's orchestration of the extermination of its Armenian population.[81]

Armenians and Kurds – Intercommunal Relations

One approach to the 1915 genocide is to highlight the role of the Kurdish militia in carrying out the CUP's orders, and to conclude that the Armenian-Kurdish dispute was an ethno-religious conflict in which the warring parties had been at each other's throats since time immemorial. Janet Klein has provided a useful counterweight to this view. In a recent essay, she argues that Kurdish violence towards the Armenians was neither the 'consequence of an inherent antagonism between Christian and Muslim communities who could not coexist on peaceful terms', nor the expression of hostility towards the Armenian revolutionary movement, nor simply the carrying out of government orders to massacre the Armenians.

The role of the Kurds in the genocide has to be seen in the context of the wider socio-economic and political changes at that time. 'The land, not only of Armenian but also of Kurdish peasants, was a target for appropriation by tribal chiefs and other notables, each seeking to expand his influence and wealth. Violence went hand in hand with the grab for land.' Discussing the massacres of Armenians between 1894 and 1896, Klein argues that the violence was 'linked to the transformation of the local power structure and changes in the nature of land tenure'.[82]

Moreover, the history of relations between the two communities is not just one of conflict, but also one of cooperation and mutual assistance. Klein argues that there is a history of positive Kurdish-Armenian relations in which 'tribal Kurds and settled Christians would help each other with food', and during the long winter months 'would spend their days and evenings together, singing and dancing'. There were many reports of mutual assistance in farming and in times of crisis. 'An Armenian village in the Bitlis district was reported by the British consul as having been saved from starvation by its Kurdish neighbours, who gave the villagers bread.' In the Sasun region, devastated by massacres in the 1890s, Kurds felt it was in their own interests to help the Armenians resettle by giving them cattle and seed.[83] Interestingly, the groups also joined forces to protest against bad government. 'In Erzerum, for example, Armenians and Muslims submitted a joint petition "asking for the dismissal of corrupt officials and asking for the retention of certain good officials".'[84]

Apart from its monumental criminality, the genocide of the Armenians was a self-destructive act, one of total irrationality, on a par, as we shall see, with the Nazi holocaust. The Young Turk regime deprived Turkey of a large section of its professional, administrative and commercial class. 'The Armenians were hard-working, capable and intelligent ... they became essential for the maintenance of the country.'[85] Moreover, resources needed for war – transport and military hardware – were diverted to the mass killing operation. As Staub says, 'Killing and removing Armenians resulted in a lack of support personnel that made the 1916 Russian invasion of Turkish Armenia easier.'[86] The very irrationality of the genocide means that explanations in terms solely of objective factors – historical, political, economic, social – are not enough: we need also, as in the other cases of genocide, to adduce psychological factors, albeit ones that are themselves explicable in terms of broad historical and socio-economic processes.

Psychological Consequences of Decline

James Reid poses the key question relevant to understanding the motivation of the perpetrators of genocide: 'Did the decline of the Ottoman Empire create conditions more conducive to increased aggressiveness inside the Empire? How did aggression function as a psychological determinant in the relationship between individuals and groups in the Ottoman Empire?'[87] Reid argues that in dealing with a period of deepening crisis, we need to adduce psychological as well as economic and social factors if we are to provide a complete explanation of its causes and effects:[88]

> In the case of the Ottoman Empire, it is especially crucial to note that political, societal and military disintegration provoked a collective state of mind and individual psychological orientations that engendered violent behaviour. The history of the nineteenth century shows an increasing trend towards widespread violence that stopped short of total annihilation in the wars of 1875–1878. As Ottoman society became pulverised through fissionary processes, its members resorted increasingly to violence and aggression as a solution.[89]

Reid undertakes three case-studies of the psychological crises that affected three leading Ottoman generals during the period 1875–8, which saw the outbreak of the Balkan revolts and the Russo-Turkish war. Their 'breakdowns' cannot be wholly explained by personal factors, since they shared a common 'psychocultural' mentality and, therefore, a potential for experiencing and reacting to historic moments in broadly similar fashion. All three experienced crucial military defeats and political setbacks for the empire as symbols denoting 'a collective psychological trauma attendant upon the Ottoman Empire's collapse in the Balkans'.[90] We shall look at two of Reid's case-studies here, after a word about family life. Raphaela Lewis describes the deep respect towards their elders inculcated in the young:

> Although all children were dearly loved, and in rich homes even spoiled and indulged, they were imbued from the earliest age with the greatest respect for older people, and in particular for members of their own families. This deference was shown to father, mother, elder brother and elder sister, and even an adult son would never sit, eat or smoke in the presence of his father without his permission. Want of respect, and disobedience to parents, were considered sins equal in gravity to idolatry, murder, false witness and desertion in the holy war, and this importance given to the inculcation of a proper attitude towards authority had a stabilising effect beyond the family, for a man's deference to his elders was readily translatable into loyalty towards an authoritative State.[91]

(1) Politician and General Suleyman Pasha's nervous breakdown in 1878: during the Russo-Turkish war of 1877–8, Suleyman commanded a force in Bulgaria, but intrigued against the Ottoman Commander-in-Chief, Mehmed Ali, in the hope of replacing him. Arriving at Yeni Zaghra, Bulgaria, he received a request for help from fellow-general Rauf, engaged in a fierce battle against Russian troops. Seeking to undermine Rauf and to put himself in a favourable light, Suleyman withheld his troops, allowing Rauf's force to be smashed. Suleyman then advanced and defeated a smaller Bulgarian force of three battalions, sending

a glowing report of his great victory to the Sultan and his war minister. According to British general Valentine Baker Pasha, every move Suleyman made had an ulterior motive, and was not undertaken to advance the Ottoman military cause. Following another intrigue, through which he lost 12,000 of his best troops, in October 1877 he was appointed general commander of the Ottoman army in Bulgaria. According to Reid, 'He proved himself an able politician, destroying his opponents, or leaving them isolated to be destroyed by the enemy. He survived, but in so doing, sacrificed parts of his army to attain prominence.'[92]

Suleyman began to show signs of mental disturbance. As the remnants of the defeated Ottoman army retreated from the Russian advance in 1877, 'he became obsessed with the delusion that one of his generals had come under attack'. Baker Pasha was sent with troops to rescue the general and his force, but on arrival discovered that ... the general and his troops were not under threat. As Reid describes it: 'his breakdown was preceded by a delusion that represented exactly what he had not done through much of the campaign. He had left units everywhere abandoned to their fates, and, when it was too late, he felt compelled to send assistance to a division that was not threatened in any way'. Stricken with guilt as he was, 'the defeats suffered by the Ottoman army had so unnerved Suleyman and preyed so strongly on his mind that he was projecting into the past what he should have done to avoid defeat'. Reid continues: 'This projection of an ideal self into the past where it did not exist amounted to what William James considered an insane delusion.' Suleyman's unconscious creation of a delusion of troops being in danger – a common occurrence in the past – in order to construct a different outcome was motivated by an urgent need 'to save the ideal self from a terrible admission of guilt'.[93]

One delusional symptom would not be sufficient evidence of a mental breakdown, but over the course of many weeks between December 1877 and January 1878, Suleyman displayed symptoms of wild confusion and mounting military incompetence and panic. His final plan, to stop the retreat of the Ottoman army to Filibe in order to attack a small Russian force at Ada Koy, gave rise to a suspicion that he was a traitor, since such a move would jeopardise the last surviving sizeable Ottoman army. Reid concludes: 'This chain of events suggested a personality in crisis ... Suleyman Pasha was experiencing a nervous breakdown that altered his ability to make decisions properly.'[94]

(2) Osman Pasha's sadistic treatment of soldiers in 1877: Osman's trademark became violence or the threat of it towards his troops, a symptom of a sadistic mental deformation. He could not rely on his soldiers' loyalty so he threatened them with death. Unsure of their commitment, he would drive them forward by firing on them from the rear. He also thought little of sending small groups against a more powerful enemy, fully aware that they would be killed or captured. Reid describes his attitude as a 'compulsion to reduce others to complete and helpless submission through aggression'. Osman may not have suffered from a chronic disorder or been in the throes of a mental breakdown, but 'when his crisis threshold was attained, he behaved in a sadistic manner as a response'.[95] Reid believes that officers like Osman tended to use sadistic measures against soldiers who they felt couldn't understand the 'metaphysics' of the aggressive

spirit, the 'élan' of military aggressiveness which carried men forward into battle, even against a storm of enemy fire.

Osman's sadism was embedded within his psyche in the manner of a social character – in Fromm's language, an enduring system of feelings, needs and drives that expresses itself in typical modes of behaviour that have been shaped by our historical experience and which we share with others occupying a similar position in the social structure. From this perspective, recourse to sadism was a typical mode of response to the crises and defeats inflicted on the declining Ottoman Empire by its enemies and rivals.

More generally, Ottoman psychological attitudes were formed in the cauldron of the empire's complex network of internal feuds and external conflicts. In the empire's matrix – its internal social organisation, its typical traditions, modes of thinking and behaving – local communities existed without a regulatory or legal system managing relations between them. Social relations between local groups were typically governed by custom. The nineteenth-century Tanzimat reforms – introduced under the influence of Britain, France and, later, Germany – attempted to create a new inter-group mutual accommodation through a general law replacing the the traditional practices. The new social ideal of assimilationism put pressure on all communities to abandon their particularist identity for a wider cultural identity. However, as Reid says, 'the effort to impose a new and alien law, elevating the status of non-Muslims, created more antagonisms, and left the old ones unresolved'.[96]

One traditional method of resolving inter-communal or inter-familial conflicts had been the *feud*. The feud 'comprised rivalries between or among noble families in all regions of the Ottoman Empire. These rivalries originated and continued for the sake of power, wealth, political and social status, and for the domination of one elite family over others.'[97] The *vendetta* differed from the feud in the nature of the offence for which revenge was sought. At the heart of the vendetta was the desire for blood revenge: murdering a member of one family required the wronged group to avenge the killing by murdering a member of the perpetrator family or community.

> Between the intense local and international conflicts fought on Ottoman soil in the nineteenth century, and the Tanzimat's efforts to abandon age-old institutions and practices, the Ottoman Empire plummeted to new depths of local conflict. The feud and the vendetta, which had been limited by custom, evolved into vigilantism where limits and controls were lacking.[98]

According to Reid, the vigilante carried the act of vengeance to new heights: 'Instead of one killing in response to a murder, large numbers of the enemy were killed, entire villages slaughtered or looted, or depredations far in excess of the original crime were perpetrated.'[99] Unable to rely on law or custom to protect him, the vigilante resorted to more extreme measures of self-protection, abandoning the restraints imposed by the traditional rules of the old social system.

However, the new reforms based on the ideals of assimilationism created confusion. When these new laws, replacing the old customs, were not accepted, communities felt the need to take self-protective measures. As a result, 'vigilantism increased in the course of the nineteenth century ... the cataclysmic nature of the empire's collapse, coupled with the inability of reform to succeed, served as the most important causes of vigilante behaviour'.[100] Nationalist wars aggravated conflicts among the empire's subjects, increasing the difficulties the reformed Ottoman army faced in controlling them. The state reacted by adopting its own version of vigilantism, settling bands of military colonists in widely dispersed regions to control the population. These Kurds, Circassians, Albanians, Laz, Bedouins, Turkmen and Zeibeks functioned as official or semi-official vigilantes, operating in the same manner as the vigilante communities they aspired to control. In wartime, they became a serious threat to the communities they encountered: 'government irregulars destroyed entire villages and killed substantial numbers of the population ... Vigilantism went far beyond the feud in such international conflicts, when bands of irregular soldiers formed from the military colonists were brought to serve the regular army in its campaigns.' During the crisis of the Ottoman Empire's collapse, 'the vigilante came to dominate the regulation of society at the local level in many areas, with dire consequences for public order'.[101]

By the end of the nineteenth century, the rise of the assimilationist ideal had transformed local feuds and vendettas into wars between large or medium-sized vigilante groups – for example, over the Macedonian question, over Kurdish attacks on Armenian enclaves in 1894–96, in the Young Turk revolution, and again in the First World War and the Greco-Turkish war.[102] Underlying most of these conflicts was the drive to assimilation, which took hold not only of the Ottoman elite that controlled the state, but of all the local communities. Instead of the ideal of a multi-ethnic, multi-cultural diversity replacing the old Ottoman Pan-Islamism, we see the emergence of Pan-Slavism, Pan-Turkism and, of course, a range of anti-imperial nationalisms. As Dadrian writes:

> The Ittihadist [CUP] programme of national renewal ... aimed at discarding as useless ... the traditional concept of multi-ethnic Ottomanism based on the premise of harmony among various nationalities. This concept was predicated upon the dual assumptions that the Turks would be first among the equals, thus maintaining their predominance, and that the other ethnic elements would ... integrate themselves in the Ottoman system, relinquishing most of their ethnic ties, with the temporary exception of their bonds to various religions.[103]

All these ideologies gave expression to irredentist and expansionist ambitions, seeking to liberate communities of fellow countrymen and women, including, for example, the promotion of Tsarist Russia's Pan-Slavism among the Ottoman Slavic peoples, of Greece's *Megale Idea*, and of Ottoman Pan-Islamism among the Muslims of the Caucasus, North Africa and the Turkic peoples of Central Asia. A byproduct of assimilationism was the concept of Total War, which advocated and sought to justify the 'eradication or deportation of an "enemy" population', or at least 'the total assimilation of conquered or subject peoples having different cultures from the ruling society'. The CUP were aggressively nationalist.[104]

This harks back to Mann's second thesis on the trumping of class by ethnicity, which now becomes the main kind of social stratification. This factor certainly seems to have been an important necessary condition of the Armenian genocide, but in itself – or even if taken together with the preconditions in Mann's other theses, particularly the transition from Plan A (repression) to Plan C (murderous cleansing), which then slides into a genocidal Plan D – it illuminates only the 'how' rather than the 'why'. It is not enough to explain the huge destructiveness involved in this and the other genocides.[105]

Psychological Aspects of Conflict

Reid argues that examining the psychological aspects of war is crucial in enabling us to understand the historical roots of crises. A large minority of soldiers and many civilians have become mentally ill as a result of their experience in war zones. According to Grinker and Spiegel,

> many soldiers under the influence of a new standard of conduct, the military superego, are enabled to release their aggressions successfully in the process of killing ... on returning from combat, they develop difficulties because renewal of inhibitions is not so easily effected. These men have no acceptable goal for their hostilities, no enemy to kill. They often fight among themselves for the sake of fighting, to relieve tensions ... Others displace their hostilities to officers, civilians, or the army in all sorts of rebellious expressions and behaviour ... Those superegos which in the past have been weak in dealing with aggressions refunction with difficulty, and the postcombat behaviour is likely to be hostile to the point of psychopathy.[106]

There is no suggestion that the Armenian genocide can be explained by reference to soldiers made mentally ill by their war experiences; rather, the psyches they brought to the war were already severely damaged by the crisis of Ottoman society.

As we have seen, the Ottoman Empire in the nineteenth century was a society increasingly prone to war, violence and chaos. This resulted in a heightened level of aggressiveness manifested by regular soldiers, and even more so by irregulars. The experience of a mounting level of violence – that is, of extreme trauma – may result in post-traumatic stress disorder (PTSD), one symptom of which is a 'diminished responsiveness to the external world, referred to as "psychic numbing" or "emotional anaesthesia". A person may complain of feeling [so] detached or estranged from other people ... that he or she has lost the ability ... to feel emotion[s] ... associated with intimacy, tenderness, and sexuality.'[107] Moreover, a society subject to increasing chaos, as was the Ottoman Empire, will produce aggressive personalities, whose psychological problems are aggravated as a consequence of war experiences. The decline and eventual collapse of the Ottoman Empire between 1683 and 1921 created increasing instability, and in the nineteenth century in particular 'Ottoman subjects were left with no alternative but to live in a highly aggression-oriented society'.[108] The common manner of dealing with such an environment was to become aggressive oneself, so that mental disorders in such a setting followed the 'drive-displacement model' more completely. In other words, the target of aggression became more widely diffused.[109] But both the wars and the damaged psyches of individuals were rooted in the crisis and gradual disintegration of Ottoman society, and the powerful perceived threat that this entailed.

As we saw in Chapter 2, several psychoanalysts, especially Anna Freud, have discussed the notion of 'identification with the aggressor' among the survivors of violence. Krystal argued that many victims of the Nazi's genocidal attack on Jews, Slavs and Gypsies identified with the aggressor in their subconscious. He also highlighted the repressed rage felt by many younger Holocaust survivors towards the parents who failed to protect them. 'Closely connected to the persistence of survivor guilt (derived from the rage) and pathological mourning is the unconscious identification with the aggressor on the part of the survivors ... some unconscious identification with the aggressor may have been indispensable to survival.'[110] This was illustrated in the case of Makrygiannes (1797–1864), a young Greek living under the Ottoman Empire, who was beaten by a friend's brother, then went to the church of his patron saint and prayed for good weapons. (This story echoes Anna Freud's theory of identification with the aggressor which we examined in Chapter 2.) This situation, in which trauma produces a compensatory drive in order to prevent the same thing happening again, was no doubt 'characteristic of a broad cross-section of the male population in the Ottoman Empire'.[111] So when the order came from the centre to exterminate the Armenians, it fell on fertile soil.

The groups displaying the highest levels of aggression, especially towards weaker and more vulnerable enemies, were the various irregular soldiers. This was perhaps related to the more urgent need they felt to defend home and family against an invading army. The waning of the traditional laws and customs in the nineteenth-century Ottoman Empire impelled the irregular soldiers to adopt the aggressive posture of the vigilante. As Reid says: 'Defence of one's honour – family, home and property – became a powerful motivation in the irregular soldier's aggressive tactics and strategy with regard to his neighbours.'[112] Another powerful incentive was the prospect of plunder, which drove irregulars to penetrate deep into enemy territory and sometimes to destroy entire villages. We are, after all, talking about a society in which there were multiple conflicts between the various communities. Moreover, the loss of external, central control was compounded by the declining ability of custom to regulate conflict.

In such a context, therefore, there was a premium on the maintenance of an aggressive stance towards one's neighbours. In an attempt to reassert some control, Ottoman governors began to establish military colonies of irregular soldiers. However, these state-sponsored militia would often become involved in local feuds, and heightened the level of violence through their possession of superior government-supplied firepower. In sum, 'in a society where threats of danger appeared on all sides, and the legal system retreated before these dangers, violent trauma was likely to promote a never-ending spiral of aggression'.[113] One is reminded here of de Zulueta's analysis of the relationship between trauma and violence (see Chapter 2, pp. 49–50). The result was a great rise in post-traumatic stress disorder, and the consequent increase and institutionalisation of vigilante behaviour.

Bands of irregulars appeared throughout the provinces during the nineteenth and early twentieth centuries, embodying the emergence of vigilantism and defined by aggression. Members of the bands internalised their loyalty exclusively to one another, so that the only meaningful external links were to their family, the band either replacing the family or else the latter becoming a kind of band within the band. Their experience of unrelenting violence led them to develop a key symptom of PTSD – 'diminished responsiveness to the external world', a feeling of 'detachment and estrangement from people and communities around them, who became the enemy'.[114] The evidence for this symptom of alienation and diminished responsiveness lay in the large numbers of raids, revolts and atrocities carried out by irregular troops during the many wars of the nineteenth century. State-sponsored 'military colonists such as Circassians, Albanians and others often lived as aliens among subject populations whom they despised, an attitude that was reciprocated'.[115] There were cases in which groups of colonists had themselves suffered violent uprooting from their homelands. As refugees from distant wars, they became Ottoman protégés and acquired the military postings that enabled them to assert a new power against local communities. For example, Circassians sought refuge from Russian attacks in the Caucasus, and were granted asylum by the Ottoman Empire. Moreover, Albanians, Kurds, Turkmen and others moved from one province of the empire to others. The increasing acts of violence against innocents were no doubt the product of great communal traumas experienced in the past by these groups. Valentine Baker Pasha, a British officer serving with the Ottoman army in the Russo-Turkish war of 1887–8, believed the irregulars committed atrocities because of the trauma they had experienced, which induced them to hanker after vengeance: 'These men ['armed villagers'...] had in many cases seen their wives and families shamefully maltreated by both Bulgarians and Cossacks, and it is not to be wondered at if, in some instances, they were guilty of retaliation.'[116] And clearly, 'The greater the trauma ... the more complete became the detachment from the world, and the worse the aggressive behaviour.'[117]

As the Ottoman state declined, becoming unable to govern its empire, it began to create conflicts between its various communities in order to divide and rule, and thus channel any rebellious energy into local conflicts. The strategy was fairly successful, although there were many uprisings against Ottoman authority throughout the nineteenth century. The rural police, called 'zaptiyes', were drafted in to help implement the state's divide and rule policy, and became notorious vigilantes of the time. When the government sent these police into a region, 'it actually created the vigilantism which plagued the empire, and increased the violence of the local conflicts to heights of greater intensity'.[118] The inter-communal violence of vigilantism, and the consequent high incidence of PTSD, would almost certainly have resulted in the creation of a new, *destructive* social character (see Chapter 3). In this way, the psychosocial groundwork for the genocide of the Armenians was laid down over the preceding decades, triggered by the massive trauma affecting both the ruling CUP elite and local vigilante brigand-communities.

The government had already created the Special Organisation – a quasi-military body led by army officers, consisting of 30,000 to 34,000 men, drawn from the ranks of the Turkish gendarmerie, Muslim bands including muhajirs (refugees), and tens of thousands of criminals specially released from prison for the purpose of liquidating the Armenians.[119] The CUP also set up a special administration to carry out the genocide. It consisted of 'three levels of bureaucrats who were given a supreme authority that superseded the traditional government structure in the provinces': these were 'Responsible Secretaries', 'Delegates' and 'General Inspectors'. These positions were mostly held by former army officers – loyal party members whose job was 'to maintain the chain of command in the provinces so that the orders for arrests, deportations and massacre were implemented strictly'. A German vice-consul attributed the harshness of the deportations to these party administrators 'who vetoed the governor-general's decree exempting the sick, families without men, and women living alone'.[120]

There were, then, three sets of perpetrators – firstly, the CUP leadership, together with the state bureaucracy they inherited and party bureaucracy they created; secondly, the Kurdish and Circassian tribesmen; and thirdly, the criminals who carried out the slaughter alongside the tribesmen. Most likely these groups arrived at their destructive social character via different routes. The CUP and the bureaucracies reached it as a result of the collapse of their grandiose fantasies following the demise of the empire (though in the case of the bureaucrats there was no doubt also a strong authoritarian factor); the tribesmen through the rise of vigilantism born of trauma, and the criminals no doubt from the trauma of poverty and childhood neglect. Perhaps then we need to posit two different sub-categories of the destructive character: the narcissistic kind, and the traumatic – both, as suggested in Chapter 4, rooted in Freud's id. Of course, to the Armenians at the receiving end, the source and type of the destructiveness visited upon them made no difference. But it is important to be clear about the difference, as this affects our analysis and our strategy for radical social transformation.

We have seen how destructiveness depends on the ability of the perpetrators to dehumanise their victims, to perceive them as non-human, as things. Reid gives an example of irregulars who, in one village, cut a five-month-old baby into pieces in front of its parents, as though it were an object. Such an act, exemplifying extreme detachment from humanity, harks back to the discussion of Marx's concept of commodification (see Chapter 4).[121]

Given the swing in the fortunes of the Ottoman ruling elite, from rulers of a multi-ethnic empire to a defeated class, we should not be surprised to find symptoms of narcissism and narcissistic rage, as described by Miller, Fromm and Kohut (see Chapters 2 and 3). However, these feelings would have been overlaid by the kind of rationalisation described by Mann: 'we were once a proud, imperial power, but we are now the exploited victim. Since you still falsely denounce us as an oppressor, we reject all your moral standards. We will revive our pride and our power within limits imposed only by our own moral standards.' Moreover, Mann continues, 'the Armenians had suffered terrible pogroms, but the very survival of Turkey as a state was now threatened, and some Armenians, in collusion with foreign powers, were helping to destroy it.'[122] Armenian contacts with the Russians were especially damaging: 'Now the Young Turk leaders feared collaboration with the foreign enemy not only from a few radical nationalists but also from respectable, conservative Armenian community leaders. If all Armenians were enemies, what then?'[123] This smacks of collective paranoia. The feeling that, not just a few, but all Armenians were bent on destroying Turkey clearly suggests a massive projection of hatred and destructiveness by the Young Turk leaders onto the Armenians.

Psycho-political analyst from Turkey, Murat Paker, has analysed Turkish political culture as it developed under the Ottoman Empire, in particular during its period of decline in the course of the nineteenth century. Among the psychological features he identifies at its heart are:

> a grandiose sense of self; a sense of supremacy rooted in the mission or destiny to rule the 'Seven Seas'; the myth or fantasy of invincibility; leadership of the Islamic world ... justice and religious liberty *granted* to non-Muslims as long as they are loyal, that is, obedient to the Ottoman authority ... absolute dominance of the Ottoman state – all land belongs to the Sultan, all residents are subjects; the west is the other with a high emotional investment, disdained for being infidel, but desired for conquest.[124]

Paker describes the collective symptoms that resulted from the profound and prolonged trauma of decline:

> shock, panic, and thoughts of life and death (survival anxiety); the loss of the sense of reality, caused by continuous trauma, difficulty in understanding the changing world system (capitalism) ... as a response to the diminishing power and humiliation of the empire ... as the losses piled up, there was a move towards Turkish nationalism from a broader Ottomanism and Islamism.[125]

As we reach the period of dominance of the bourgeois-nationalist party, the CUP, there are two fundamental 'others' as seen from the 'perspective of the dominant political culture':

(1) The West: its attitude to the West was ambivalent – it is both enemy and role model. It is hated for its disempowerment of the Ottoman state, and cannot be trusted. On the other hand, to be able to confront the west, it has to be imitated. To this end, westernisation begins in the 1830s. There seems also to be an element of identification with the aggressor here.

(2) Non-Muslim minorities: again, they have a twofold aspect. They are potential or real collaborators with the western enemies and therefore cannot be relied on since they are likely to backstab us. On the other hand, they are hard-working people.[126]

There is an uncanny similarity between the situations that triggered the genocide of the Armenians by the Turks and that of the Jews by the Nazis – in both cases, the decision was taken as a result of a military setback on the Russian front. In the Armenian case, as Ben Kiernan describes it, with the outbreak of First World War, Ottoman war minister Enver Pasha 'quickly invaded the

Caucasus, but met humiliating defeat at Russian hands in December 1914–January 1915'.[127]

There is some evidence that the genocide resulted from an order to exterminate the Armenians coming direct from the CUP leadership, and not from any gradual, piecemeal build-up of violence embedded in the war situation. According to Robert Fisk, there exists a copy of a cable dated 15 September 1915 sent by CUP interior minister Talaat Pasha to his prefect in Aleppo, containing the following instruction: 'the government ... has decided to destroy completely all the indicated persons living in Turkey ... Their existence must be terminated ... and no regard must be paid to either age or sex, or to any scruples of conscience.'[128] Officially, however, the Ottoman authorities ordered the wholesale deportation of the Armenian population, alleging treason and separatism, this supposed emergency wartime measure serving as a mask concealing their true intention.[129]

When Turkey entered the War in November 1914, a requisition order deprived the provincial Armenian population of most of their goods. A second order in April 1915 authorised the arrest of all Armenian political and community leaders, some 2,345, none of whom were charged with sabotage or espionage, but most of whom were executed. The final stage of reducing the Armenian population to helplessness was deportation: a memorandum dated 26 May 1915 authorised military commanders to deport clusters of the population suspected of espionage or treason, or for reasons of military necessity. The authorities could deport Armenians if they merely sensed danger from that quarter. 'This vague but sweeping authorisation resulted in the deportation of the bulk of Turkey's Armenian population.'[130]

It seems clear that the CUP leadership, followed arguably by the state bureaucracy, had built up over the years a predisposition to genocidal violence, an inner state resulting from the multiple defeats and setbacks experienced by the empire as it went into terminal decline – a condition, moreover, with which they identified psychologically. The empire's crisis was their crisis, its failure their failure. Following Fromm and Maccoby, we can seek to understand the CUP's social character according to two criteria – the mode of assimilation, that is, their general orientation to the outside world, and the mode of relatedness, or their orientation to other people. In the absence of empirical studies, this discussion inevitably remains somewhat speculative, but is worth undertaking given the evidence that does exist.

In 1896, Murad Bey, a Young Turk leader and ideologist, wrote that 'the population is young, vigorous, temperate, devout: their crime is blind obedience to the infamous authorities; but as diverse circumstances render this obedience sacred, this cannot be held against them too much.'[131] To apply Fromm's framework: members of the CUP and the middle class from whom they derived grew up with an authoritarian-productive social character. It was in part already authoritarian since there was a strong emphasis on obedience within Ottoman culture; but, in Staub's words, 'the removal of the sultan and other political changes and upheavals must have added to the many-faceted life problems and intensified the people's need for authority'.[132] It is a reasonable assumption that this would have included the middle class and the CUP.

Nevertheless, the CUP's mode of assimilation also contained a strong productive element in that they did strive to modernise both the economy and society, with some considerable success. Their mode of assimilation thus consisted of both positive and negative features within the exploitative and hoarding orientations: in the exploitative category, a positive ability to take initiatives blended with negative exploitative and, probably, egocentric and arrogant traits; within the hoarding category, they seemed to have been both practical and economical but also anxious and suspicious.[133] However, as the goal of saving the empire receded from their grasp, fading into the realm of the clouds, their anger and destructiveness grew apace. As their inner world became more and more threatening they dealt with it by developing a social character that combined two main features: a hoarding mode of assimilation as they struggled to hang on to the glories of the Ottoman past; and a mode of relatedness that became increasingly authoritarian and destructive, brimming over with narcissistic rage, the obverse of their grandiose sense of self.[134]

With the disasters on the Russian front between December 1914 and January 1915, the predisposition to genocidal violence was converted into precipitation.[135] Up to a million and a half Armenians died in what the Turkish court-martial in 1919 concluded had the characteristics of a 'final solution'.[136] Now, as suggested in Chapter 4, to grasp the psychological content of a social character, we need to refer, firstly, to Freud's typology – the division between ego, super-ego and id – and, secondly, to Klein's theory of projective identification. With destructive rage pouring out of the perpetrators' id, threatening to swamp their entire psyche, their super-ego would have struggled to do its job of containing such an outpouring. In the end, the only way of doing so was to project it on to the Armenians: they were then perceived as the danger, the source of the anger and hatred, of all that threatened the Ottoman state. They had to be exterminated.

CHAPTER SEVEN

The Nazi Holocaust

When the Auschwitz victims filed into the gas chamber, they discovered that the imitation showers did not work. Outside, a central switch was pulled to turn off the lights, and a Red Cross car drove up with the Zyklon. An SS man, wearing a gas mask fitted with a special filter, lifted the glass shutter over the lattice and emptied one can after another into the gas chamber ... As the first pellets sublimated on to the floor of the chamber, the victims began to scream. To escape from the rising gas, the stronger knocked down the weaker, stepping on prostrate victims in order to prolong their own lives by reaching gas-free layers of air. The agony lasted for about two minutes, and as the shrieking subsided, the dying people slumped over. Within fifteen minutes (sometimes five), everyone in the gas chamber was dead.[1]

Between 1939 and 1945, 6 million Jews, at least 250,000 Roma, and tens of thousands of homosexuals and the mentally ill were massacred in death camps in Germany and Nazi-occupied eastern Europe as part of a programme of industrial genocide. This Holocaust did not occur in an economically underdeveloped, poverty-stricken part of the world but in an advanced society that had produced some of modern Europe's finest artists and intellectuals. Why did it occur in the 1940s, during the Second World War, and not earlier? The Nazi Holocaust is the genocide about which more has been written than any other. Several key overlapping debates form an important part of the framework for understanding its nature and causes: debates over its uniqueness, the class basis of the Nazi movement, its affinity with modernity, the role of ideology and of the Great Depression. My task in this chapter is to uncover the links between the objective development of German industrial capitalism and the subjective ideas and feelings of fear, hatred and destructive rage of the Nazi perpetrators.

The Holocaust and Modernity

A key theme among both Marxists and liberals is the association between the Holocaust and modernity – the extent to which the Jewish genocide, with the complex rational-bureaucratic machinery required to implement it, can be best understood as an expression of modern, technological rationality, albeit one created to carry out an utterly irrational objective. Early on, Ian Kershaw argued that the Holocaust 'would not have been possible without the apathy ... which was the common response to the propaganda of hate'; 'dynamic hatred of the masses was unnecessary'; apathy 'sufficed to allow the increasingly criminal "dynamic" hatred of the Nazi regime the autonomy it needed to set in motion the holocaust ... The road to Auschwitz was built by hate, but paved with indifference.'[2]

Zygmunt Bauman's analysis of the Holocaust is similar. He argues that 'mass destruction was accompanied not by the uproar of emotions, but by the dead silence of unconcern'.[3] The reason is the physical and mental distance modern society creates 'between the purported victims and the rest of the population ... the capacity of that present-day industrial society to extend inter-human distance to a point where moral responsibility and moral inhibitions become inaudible'.[4] In Traverso's words, 'Auschwitz was the product of the fusion of racial biology and modern technology.'[5] Again, 'Auschwitz's modernity does not have to do only with the death factories but also with its cultural backdrop, shaped by a bureaucratic rationality that presupposes an administrative management free of any interference of an ethical nature.'[6] So, 'the authorities who managed the camps were in most cases bureaucrats, zealous and disciplined implementers of policy'.[7] They represented what Hannah Arendt called 'the banality of evil'.

The indifference of bystanders is an important facilitating factor. But there are three arguments against Bauman's thesis, and by implication that of Kershaw and Geras too. First, Bauman's 'moral atheism' won't wash. In post-war Western society, we have witnessed the growth of large-scale movements of solidarity with oppressed peoples on the other side of the globe: the Vietnam Solidarity Campaign and the Anti-Apartheid Movement are just two examples of vigorous campaigns which played an important role in forcing governments to change tack. If Bauman were right, these campaigns would have been impossible. Arguably, under Nazism, the indifference of the majority was in part due to the crushing of the left and of most resistance.

Second, as Mann argues, those who organised the Holocaust were not faceless, mindless bureaucrats simply carrying out orders, but ideological Nazis whose efficiency was grounded in a rigorous adherence to their vision of a 'cleansed' world and who were rewarded with a high-status career. Mann opposes Arendt's view that Eichmann morally 'never realised what he was doing'.[8] Eichmann 'himself often took initiatives ... This was not a rule-governed bureaucracy: it was fluid, allowing officials to innovate in radical directions.'[9] Mann describes an 'elite group carrying out a world-historical mission, ideological efficiency experts, not banal bureaucrats. They knew exactly what they were doing, to the last drop of blood.'[10]

This relates to our discussion in Chapter 1 about the diffusion of responsibility, a factor in the repression of conscience by perpetrators, itself an important precondition of genocide. The bureaucratic division of labour facilitates displacement of responsibility.[11] However, Waller points out that not all perpetrators displace *all* responsibility for their atrocities, otherwise they would only carry them out when ordered to do so. Many perpetrators strive dutifully to perform their tasks well, thereby retaining enough responsibility to be good, efficient functionaries, 'not simply mindless extensions of others higher in the organisational hierarchy'.[12] As Mann says, 'Eichmann's evil was neither unthinking nor banal, but innovative, ruthless, and ideological'.[13]

Third, Bauman's thesis doesn't explain the Nazis' destructive drive against the Jews. Why did they want to exterminate them in the first place? At this point, the ideological argument is brought in – biological racism. But as an explanation of Nazi hatred of the Jews this is questionable. Geras provides a clue as to the Nazis' choice of victim, arguing that it represents a fusion of old and new ideological forms: of traditional Christian anti-Semitism with its accusation of 'god-killers', and the modern eugenic notion of 'sub-human'. This lethal combination resulted in the relegation of Jews to the zone of moral exclusion. Geras highlights the difficulty of imagining that 'just *any* people could have been as murderously dealt with over a whole continent, or as readily abandoned to its torment, rather than this particular people, hated and vilified there for going-on two millennia'.[14] But, again, this doesn't explain the resurgence of fanatical anti-Semitism on the part of the Nazis in the 1920s and 1930s. Moreover, we should be careful not to ascribe such anti-Semitism to the German people as a whole. As Mommsen puts it, 'in contrast to the conduct of a large proportion of the German upper class, anti-Semitic feeling was less easily mobilised in the population as a whole'.[15]

Eugenics

Biological racism is a crucial link in the total chain of explanation, but not sufficient in itself to explain Nazi anti-Semitism. Eugenics was an influential anthropological current in the early decades of the twentieth century. But not everybody espoused it, and by 1916, the year of a famous debate involving Franz Boas, for many the 'Father of Modern Anthropology', there was opposition to it within scientific circles. Eugenics is not like physics or chemistry whose remit is the discovery of the laws of different aspects of the natural world. Eugenics is an applied science which 'advocates the use of practices aimed at improving the genetic composition of a population'. Sir Francis Galton, the scientist who coined the term 'eugenics' in 1883, defined it as 'the study of all agencies under human control which can improve or impair the racial quality of future generations'.[16] In other words, it assumes from the outset that there are healthy and less healthy, superior and inferior, human groups. It is based on a set of evaluative assumptions in a way that legitimate sciences are not, as Callinicos describes it, treating 'racism as a kind of brute datum that does not itself require explanation'.[17] However, given the dubious scientific and ethical basis of eugenics, it is legitimate to ask why an individual or group might adopt it, whether there are underlying non-intellectual reasons, in a way that doesn't apply to modern physics or chemistry. I will thus argue here that there were deep-lying psychological reasons why the Nazis adopted eugenics as a central plank of their ideology.

Gluckstein distinguishes between 'racism at the base of society' and 'ruling class racism', the former 'driven by fear, anger and frustration generated within society', the latter by the need 'to divide and weaken opposition forces'.[18] The Nazis straddled both ends: as representatives of the alienated, impoverished middle class, they shared their anger and fear; as upstarts catapulted to political power, it was in their interest to deflect anger away from their Big Business allies and onto the Jews. The second expression of Nazi anti-Semitism was the notion that the Jews perpetrated 'the stab in the back' of the 1917 Russian Revolution responsible for Germany's defeat in the First World War. Many historians point to this identification in the Nazi mind between the Jews and Bolshevism, often referred to as Judaeo-Bolshevism. As Gluckstein puts it: 'A delusion had burned into Hitler's mind – defeat in the 1914–18 war was caused by the revolution; the revolution caused by the Jews was to be avenged.'[19] Delusions are pathological. On the assumption, derived from psychoanalysis, that symptoms have meanings, originating in the life-experience of an individual or group, it makes sense to enquire as to the origins of Nazi anti-Semitism. Where did their pathological hatred of the Jews come from? Was it a symptom that afflicted the top Nazis alone or did it go deeper – acquired as a result of the historical experience of the class from which they largely derived – the German middle class?

Middle-Class Basis of the Nazi Party

To begin with, we must establish the class basis of the Nazi movement, an issue which has caused much debate in recent decades. There are two questions here. First, who joined the Nazi Party and who voted for them during the late 1920s and 1930s? Second, to which sections of German society did the Nazis address their appeal? In a study of the relations between the Nazi Party and Big Business, Arthur Schweitzer analysed the German class structure during Weimar, based on a study by Geiger, as being made up of three classes: the capitalist class, who, with their families, numbered 574,752 or 0.92 per cent of the population; the middle class, numbering 16,026,135 or 25.68 per cent of the population and the 'labour' class, numbering 45,809,732, or 73.4 per cent of the population. The German capitalist class and working class were very conscious of their socio-economic position, recognising themselves as 'opponents in a distinct class situation'. 'Each class had its own interpretation of its class interest and class mentality and was guided by different class ideologies.'[20]

The middle class was divided into three sections, the old, the new, and the 'quasi-proletarian'. They did not enjoy a common economic position. The first section, the 'old' or traditional middle class, included artisans, dealers in goods and services, and most of the peasantry, as well as small entrepreneurs who lived on their incomes as managers or owners of capital. Second, the 'new' middle class were made up of salaried employees, who were dependent on employers, together with the lower strata of professionals who sold their services on the market, gaining a measure of economic independence. Third, the group of small independents: small shopkeepers, plumbers or electricians designated as 'quasi-proletarians'. According to Geiger, the old middle class, including families, numbered 17.77 per cent of the population, the new middle class 17.95 per cent and the quasi-proletarian 12.65 per cent, making up in total 48.37 per cent.[21] How then do we explain the previously given figure for the total middle class of 25.68 per cent? The answer lies in the ideological attitudes of these groups, in particular of the new middle class and the 'quasi-proletarians' who refused to consider themselves working class. The figure of 25.68 per cent included only the old middle class – 17.77 per cent – plus middling professionals such as independent physicians.[22]

The problem facing the labour movement was that it was unable to organise all sections of the working class, objectively defined, since two groups of dependent employees (who sold their services for salaries) rejected the ideology of the labour movement: first, salaried employees in industry and government, and second, the marginal independents or quasi-proletarians who owned their own shops and maybe cultivated a small plot of land, or else sold their services to customers, for example, as plumbers.[23] 'These groups were economically dependent. Neither income nor standard of living distinguished them very much from German labourers. Yet they retained or acquired some form of middle-class outlook on life. Solidarity within labour was thus confined to the traditional groups of labour.'[24] Moreover, the three groups of the middle class developed different economic interests, depending on their position in the economy. Peasants favoured high prices for food and tariff protection for their products, whereas shopkeepers and salaried employees wanted low food prices. Debtors, urban and rural, demanded low rates of interest for loans but middle-class savers wanted high rates. Employees, such as civil servants and teachers, joined trade unions, which won them higher salaries, whereas peasants and artisans hated unions since they raised their unit cost of production. This broad diversity of interests meant that a common middle-class interest did not develop spontaneously.[25]

However, many studies conducted in the 1920s apparently showed that the three middle-class groups shared a common sense of status. Within the class structure dominated by capital and labour, the status feelings of the middle groups amounted to a distinct 'class' attitude. As Schweitzer says, 'the unity of sentiments and status was especially pronounced in relation to the labour class, from whom all segments of the middle class deliberately tried to distinguish themselves'.[26] In addition to an anti-labour stance, many of the old middle class running small urban or rural enterprises, including the peasantry, shared a 'pre-capitalist' attitude – for example, opposition to free trade, the open craft (unregulated by the guilds), and the capitalist market, deemed to be based on unfair competition.[27]

At first, pro-capitalist attitudes developed among salaried employees such as civil servants, and some quasi-proletarians, putting ideological distance between themselves and the working class. And to begin with, 'anti-capitalist' attitudes spread only among members of the socialist unions and small sections of the marginal independents.[28] But the immense misery created by the Great Depression caused a shift in the attitudes of the middle classes. The small peasants now hated the large landowners and farmers, and the big banks, all of whom were destroying their livelihood. Similarly, the small urban entrepreneur hated the large corporations, chain-stores and big banks which threatened to put them out of business. Jones sums it up:

> Within this intermediary stratum, there were profound sociological differences stemming from the impact of industrialisation and rationalisation on a social structure inherited from a pre-industrial past. That segment of the German

middle class which derived an income from its own independent economic activity found itself at a severe economic disadvantage and entered a period of social and economic decline.[29]

The artisan producers whose goods were retailed by small independent shopkeepers were gradually displaced by large-scale manufacturers whose products were sold by department stores.[30] 'By the end of the 1920s, the economic position of the independent middle class had deteriorated to such an extent that it was no longer possible to distinguish it from the proletariat on the basis of income as a criterion.' Simultaneously, from the 1880s onwards, there was the rapid rise 'of a class of clerical and technical employees whose services were required for the smooth, efficient operation of an advanced industrial economy'.[31]

Nazi Ideology

Already during the 1920s, the Nazis set about wooing the vast dispossessed and disaffected middle classes. They created an ideology that was both anti-working class and anti-Big Business, its political programme reflecting the interests of the small businessman, the small peasant farmer and independent artisan, and also some sections of the professional middle class. It rejected free trade and promised protection for small business and craft organisations, for example, with cheap credit. The Nazis presented a vision of an artisan economy rooted in the work of small peasant and independent craftsman, a society based on blood and soil. They created a link in the minds of the middle classes between depression and democracy, between misery and the Treaty of Versailles. At the same time, anti-Semitism became a central plank of their programme. The misuse of power by the large banks and monopoly firms was to be eliminated, but at the same time these enterprises were to be protected against their Jewish competitors.[32] Jews − only 1 per cent of the Weimar population − owned almost half of all private banks, whose number and importance declined after 1920, and less than 1 per cent of the more numerous and increasingly important credit banks.[33] The result of Nazi propaganda was that the bitterness and anger of the dispossessed middle classes, their sense of exclusion and inferiority, came to be expressed in terms of extreme nationalism and anti-Semitism. Their social resentment was transmuted into national resentment, their frustration and hatred directed not at their ruling class but at the foreign powers and the Jews.

Impact of the Great Depression

Up until 1929, however, the Nazi Party was small. In 1929, just before the Depression, its membership numbered 96,918. After the Crash, it grew in leaps and bounds, rising to 129,563 towards the end of 1930. And as the Depression tightened its grip, by 1933 it had soared to 849,009,[34] with its militias, the SA and the SS, able to deploy 400,000 men at the time of the July 1932 elections.[35] The upward swing in Hitler's electoral fortunes was even more dramatic. In the national elections of May 1928, the Nazis won 810,000 votes, 2.6 per cent of the poll. In the elections of September 1930, they took 6,409,000 votes, 18.3 per cent of the total, mainly at the expense of the liberal centre parties whose middle-class voters were deserting them. In the four elections between 1928 and November 1932, support for these centre parties virtually collapsed: they lost 80 per cent of their support, which declined from 25 per cent to 3 per cent of the national total, whereas the Nazi vote increased by 1,277 per cent.[36] So why, in a battery of successive elections, did the middle classes transfer their allegiance to the Nazis?

Following the Wall Street Crash of 1929, the three sections of the middle class all experienced a major threat to their existence, albeit in different ways. A credit crisis resulting in extreme deflation was followed by a flight of capital, a run on the banks and the failure of some. This monetary and banking crisis produced three effects: a drying-up of short-term credit for small businesses (the Central Bank mainly helping Big Business); extreme downward pressure on middle-class employment; and the freezing of interest rates at a high level. The Central Bank raised its discount rate from 7 per cent to 15 per cent.[37]

Moreover, a price differential between consumer and producer goods arose, the prices of farm products and some consumer goods falling sharply while the prices of producer goods were protected by Big Business cartels. The banks attempted to foreclose farms, provoking many farmers to violent resistance. The great increase in foreclosures was in fact a major reason for the peasant vote shifting from the liberal and two conservative parties to the Nazis.[38] The combined effect of price and income decline and credit crunch was especially felt by the urban middle class, most of whose savings had been destroyed in the hyperinflation of 1923. Shopkeepers were ineligible for unemployment relief as they were not insured. Successive governments did try to subsidise the peasants but the greatest share of subsidies went to owners of the large estates in East Prussia.[39]

Sudden misery changed the outlook of the middle classes. They felt a strong antagonism towards capitalism and democracy, blaming these for the depression and deflation. In Schweitzer's words: 'Economic suffering and protest against misery, reinforced by unchanged status preferences, produced ... a change in the ideology of the middle class.'[40] Pro-capitalist attitudes, especially among the dependent group, that is, salaried employees, rapidly disappeared as their economic situation deteriorated. They came to hate industrial capitalists who resorted to replacement of older with younger workers and of workers with machines. Anti-capitalist ideas developed first among white-collar workers and marginal independents, for example, small shopkeepers, plumbers, etc., then spread to the peasantry, and lastly to artisans and traders outraged at the competition of chain stores and department stores, whose mechanised methods enabled them to capture the markets of small firms.[41]

These sentiments became the core of a new, distinct middle-class ideology, one that was both anti-Big Business and anti-working class, indifferent to the democratic ideals of the Weimar republic, and strongly preferring a pre-industrial way of life.[42] Under the impact of the Great Depression, the middle class became radicalised. The traditional handicraft organisations drew up a programme for economic reform directed largely against Big Business. It contained ten points, beginning with proposals to increase the demand for artisan products, curb the power of large enterprises, and exclude trade unions from the sphere of small business. This was a plan for a new type of economy in which the major decisions would be taken by the guilds. Werner Sombart labelled it 'middle-class socialism'.

Unification and Nazification of the Middle Classes

Under the shadow of the Great Depression, the Nazis intensified their wooing of the increasingly united middle class. They aspired to lead them by articulating their anxiety and discontent, and to ascend to power on the wave of resentment. Nazi policy towards them falls into four categories: 1) glorification of romantic middle-class ideals; 2) political redirection of their anti-democratic attitudes; 3) identification with their economic programme; 4) fighting for leadership of their organisations.[43]

1. The Nazis captured the hearts and minds of ever-widening swathes of peasants and small businessmen through extolling the pre-capitalist ideology of the middle class. The peasants had clear aims: security of land tenure, protection against creditors, and the stability and continuity of the family farm. The Nazis elevated them into two ideals: the peasantry were the wealth-creating class of the new Germany. And they were to live the best possible lives on their farms and produce the healthiest children.[44] As Himmler put it: 'the yeoman of his own acre is the backbone of the German people's strength and character'.[45] Moreover, the peasants' land was to be inalienable. In Kiernan's words: 'imposing the Nazi ideal of rural life on Germany demanded ... the enforcement of peasant self-sufficiency and restrictions on personal and commercial rights'.[46] The result was that 'the vision of a society, built upon blood and soil, in which the peasants were to be honoured as the important social class, produced a great enthusiasm for the Nazis in all segments of the rural population'.[47]

Similar versions were offered to small businessmen and unemployed urban labourers. The urban middle class were encouraged by the model of an artisan economy in which there would be proper apprenticeships, trade organisations governed by an ethical code enforceable by special courts, and in which industrialism and ruthless competition would be banned. This model appeared to herald a new epoch.[48]

2. The Nazis became adept at exploiting the wounded pride and anger of the middle class. They steered their hatred of other groups into a more specific antagonism towards capital, labour and foreign powers. The labour movement was identified with communism, Germany's arch enemy, which had administered the 'stab in the back' of revolution that sent her to defeat in the First World War. Socialists, democrats and liberals were all labelled 'communists'. Middle-class anger towards the Treaty of Versailles of 1919, with its heavy reparations and territorial forfeits, was converted into profound hatred of the foreign powers that had imposed it, reducing Germany to a proletarian nation. The Nazis' master

trick was to portray the Weimar Republic as the instrument of the victorious powers. Nazi propaganda linked depression to democracy, economic misery to Versailles, depicting the democratic form of government as alien to the German national character. A new Reich would remove democracy and 'create national freedom and full employment for all'.[49]

3. The Nazis identified themselves with the economic grievances of the middle-class groups and set out a programme to meet their demands. They campaigned against the forced sale of land or farms by the banks. They set their face against the industrial monopolies or cartels that charged high prices for the equipment and other supplies needed by the small businessman and peasant. They launched attacks against the chain and department stores, and the consumer cooperatives that were undercutting the small merchants. They demanded that the large corporations pay higher salaries to their impoverished white-collar workers, and continue employing older salaried employees. In conclusion, 'almost all the economic complaints of the various segments of the middle class were thus accepted by the Nazis and incorporated into their programme for immediate action upon their coming to power'.[50]

However, the Nazis introduced a distinction between German and Jewish capital: the latter had to be eliminated or driven from Germany, while the former had to be accepted. Only two branches of German capitalism had abused their power – the banks, and the trusts and combines. This abuse had to cease, in order to protect the products and sales of the peasants and small businessmen, but the same German banks and cartels had to be protected from Jewish competitors. According to Schweitzer, 'anti-Semitism became accepted by various segments of the middle class as a policy of economic reform. Not capitalism itself, but only the association of some capitalists with Jewry should be terminated.'[51]

4. On the organisational level a process of interpenetration occurred. The Nazis built up organisations to further middle-class interests, and party members were instructed to enter existing middle-class organisations to fight for leadership and to spread Nazi ideas. In the course of the 1920s, the bourgeois liberal parties and pressure groups failed to unite and fight for the interests of the middle classes. Despair at their economic and social decline was aggravated by the deepening lack of adequate political representation. As Larry Jones says: 'The secession of the Westarp faction [from the conservative DNVP], the founding of two new parties, and the conspicuous failure of Germany's bourgeois politicians to consolidate these groups into some sort of united front or party only added to the desperation which Germany's middle-class voters already felt.'[52]

In sum, ideological penetration, a 'radical' economic programme, and decisive political leadership profoundly influenced the middle classes. There arose for the first time in decades a single ideology uniting the different sections. Gone were the organisational proliferation and economic conflicts of different middle-class groups. The Nazification of the middle class had been achieved, their traditional parties swept away, and the Nazis established as the leaders of a counter-revolutionary mass movement. 'As the social basis of the party, the various groups of the middle class saw in the Nazi Party a political instrument for realising their economic interests as well as their middle-class ideology.'[53]

Nazi Party: Social Background of Members and Leaders

An early study by Hans Gerth found similarly that the leadership and membership of the Nazi Party were heavily weighted towards the middle class.[54] However, some 'revisionist' historians and sociologists oppose the 'classical' theory of Nazism as a movement of the middle classes, arguing that support came from all sections of the population, especially unemployed and white-collar workers. Mann argues that Nazi support was broadly based, coming not just from the middle classes but from a wide cross-section of German society, both in terms of membership and electoral support: the Nazis were bent on appealing to all social classes. He has thus set his face against both Marxist and non-Marxist traditional analyses of fascism.[55] Starting with membership of the party before it took power in 1933, Mann adduces figures indicating that blue-collar workers made up between 28 and 52 per cent of members. According to one statistical table, the figure of 52 per cent is for the Western Ruhr region in 1925–6. According to the same table, during the years 1930–2 in Germany, the working class made up 36 per cent of the membership, while 'middle class' groups – self-defined, and variously described as 'petty-bourgeois', 'white-collar', 'public employees', 'professionals', and 'farmers' – made up 59 per cent.[56] Mann argues that on these figures workers are slightly under-represented in the party (that is, compared to their numbers in the population[57]– this is on a figure of workers forming 55 per cent of the German labour force in 1933). Again, Schweitzer quotes a figure of workers and their families, defined in objective socio-economic terms, forming 73.4 per cent of the population, but only 50.71 per cent if self-definition is the criterion, that is, if one removes from that figure white-collar, salaried employees in industry and government, and quasi-proletarians such as self-employed house-painters who regarded themselves as middle class.[58] Of course, as Kater reminds us, the increase in workers joining the Nazis in the Great Depression years between 1929 and 1933 must be understood as a product of mass unemployment. 'This disaster left hardly any group in Germany untouched except the beneficiaries of large capital and investment holdings.'[59]

Mann argues, further, that skilled workers were slightly over-represented in the party compared to unskilled, also that few agricultural workers joined the Nazis.[60] But they did better in small to medium-sized towns than in the bigger cities. Outside the big cities, working-class Nazi membership ranged from 40 to 55 per cent, but in the large cities from 30 to 40 per cent.[61] Again, the Nazis did worst in large, industrial firms since their workers overwhelmingly owed allegiance to the left-wing parties and unions. The Nazis did better in smaller workshops, the service sector and the public sector, which often took on military veterans who were Nazis.[62] However, the party had far fewer workers than the socialist SPD and the communist KPD, the latter in 1927 having 80 to 90 per cent of its members as workers or craftsmen and their wives, while in the SPD, workers and their wives made up 60 to 80 per cent of its inter-war membership.[63] Nevertheless, Mann concludes that 'the Nazis kept a substantial worker and white-collar presence at every leadership level except the very top. Though not a proletarian party, they remained broadly rooted.'[64]

The 'classic petty-bourgeoisie' – artisan masters, small businessmen, traders, traditionally regarded as the Nazis' main socio-political base – made up 31 per cent to 36 per cent of party membership, and were, therefore, slightly over-represented, with ratios of 1.20 to 1.30.[65] White-collar workers in the private sector were over-represented, though Mann seems, then, to contradict himself by saying that the 'classic petty-bourgeoisie' were neither under nor over-represented. Within this group, 'artisan masters' were under-represented, with ratios of 0.3 to 0.6.[66] However, if we take Schweitzer's figures, 'the classic petty-bourgeoisie' – that is, the old middle class and the quasi-proletarians – make up 30.42 per cent, then Mann's first claim is correct – they were slightly over-represented.

A more important objection may be made to Mann's claim that the Nazi Party was broad based. He makes clear in discussing the issues of social mobility and social marginality that artisans should be counted as workers,[67] whereas most analyses of the German class structure during the Weimar regime count them as 'old middle class', as Schweitzer does, following Geiger. Kater, too, divides the 'lower middle class' into six sub-groups: 1) master craftsmen, that is, independent, self-employed artisans; 2) independent professionals not academically trained; 3) lower and intermediate employees; 4) lower and intermediate civil servants; 5) self-employed merchants; and 6) self-employed farmers, vintners and fishermen.[68] Moreover, using a Marxist definition of class as a group's relationship to the means of production, artisans, as self-employed and independent, are not working class but middle class. The upshot of this is that if the old middle class, of which artisans and their families made up a large part, constituting 17.77 per cent of the population,[69] and we therefore transfer artisans to the middle-class group of members, then clearly that considerably reduces the percentage of workers in the Nazi Party.

What about the Nazi leadership? Did the party's functionaries and Gauleiters represent a broad cross-section of German society? Was there a similar proportion of workers, middle-class and 'elite' members as amongst the membership? The higher up the party hierarchy one ascends, the more pronounced its petty-bourgeois character becomes. As Kater writes: 'Although it would be incorrect to claim that the entire Nazi functionary corps was staffed by "typically frustrated, lower-middle class individuals" or by "marginal petty bourgeois" ... representatives of that class were in the absolute majority.'[70] Moreover, 'the leadership corps was stamped by the value system of the German lower middle class, and its political and administrative actions can be viewed as the product of lower middle-class mentality'.[71] (For 'mentality' one could read 'social character'.) Kater concedes that the relative proportion of elite elements was higher among the leaders than in the party as a whole or in the German population. Also, the proportion of elite members rose with rank. The middle-class character of the Nazi leadership also held at local level. 'The majority of the Nazi leadership of Hamburg in the years 1926–27 derived from the middle and lower middle classes and still lived by values and goals that had been formed in the pre-war era.'[72]

Voting Behaviour

Several sociological studies of Nazi electoral support established the preponderance of the various sections of the middle class. Pratt's study quoted by Lipset showed the huge rise in the Nazi vote between 1928 and the first of two elections in 1932.[73] According to Lipset:

> Pratt related the Nazi vote in July 1932 to the proportion of the population in the 'upper middle class' defined as 'proprietors of small and large establishments and executives' and to the proportion in the 'lower middle class' composed of 'civil servants and white-collar employees'. The Nazi vote correlated highly with the proportion in both middle-class groups in different-sized cities and in different areas of the country, but the correlations with the 'lower middle class' were not as consistently high as those with the 'upper middle class'.[74]

So, the upper middle class, mainly small businessmen, were more thoroughly pro-Nazi, indicating a strong correlation between self-employed economic status and Nazi voting.

A study by Loomis and Beegle found that a high correlation between Nazi vote and proprietorship held also for farm owners as well as owners of small businesses and industry in Schleswig-Holstein and Hanover, but not in Bavaria, a strongly Catholic area where the Nazis were weak.[75] Heberle's study of the elections under Weimar in Schleswig-Holstein found that 'the classes particularly susceptible to Nazism were neither the rural nobility and the big farmers nor the rural proletariat, but rather the small farm proprietors, very much the rural equivalent of the lower middle class or petty-bourgeoisie which formed the backbone of the NSDAP in the cities.'[76] However, recent research suggests that Nazi electoral support was broader than previously thought, supporting Mann's claim that 'workers were no less attracted to Nazism than were other classes'. Childers found that up to 1928, the Nazis were most successful in areas where the population included many artisans, small shopkeepers and civil servants. Thus, 'the original Nazi nucleus was among the "old" lower middle class – the classic petty-bourgeoisie plus lower civil servants – but not the "newer" middle class of white-collar workers and managers'.[77] However, after 1930, the rise in unemployment was staggering, officially reaching 5,772,984 at the end of 1932. In October 1932, it was probably 8,754,000 if one includes short-time working and hidden unemployment.[78] Support widened and the Nazis became a national 'catch-all party of protest',[79] 'a mile wide but an inch deep'.[80] There were, however, important sectoral variations: agricultural workers were the strongest Nazi supporters, despite there being few party members amongst them, followed by workers in construction, services and public employment.[81] But the Nazi vote was lower in industrial working–class areas, except for areas with government-owned factories. Childers also found a correlation between Nazi-voting and handicrafts and small-scale manufacturing, especially after 1932.[82] So, 'the core of proletarian fascism lay not in large-scale private manufacturing in big cities, but in the agricultural, service, and government sectors and in smaller plants scattered through smaller towns and the countryside. Fascist workers were plentiful, not at the heart of contemporary class struggle but at its margins.'[83] In sum, 'by 1930, the Nazis drew about 30 per cent, and by 1932 some 40 per cent, of their votes from workers'. And whereas 50 percent of workers voted socialist or communist, 30 percent voted Nazi, 10 percent for the Catholic parties and 10 percent for the bourgeois parties.[84]

Mann overstates his case here. Childers addresses the findings of research carried out by 'revisionists' arguing that Nazi support didn't come just from 'the classic petty-bourgeoisie' but was more socially diverse than traditionally thought:

> Michael Kater's recent study of the NSDAP's membership and my own analysis of voting in approximately 460 cities, towns, and rural counties spread across Germany conclude that the party's following was, indeed, far more socially diverse than traditionally depicted, but both also agree that the hard core of the party's very volatile constituency was recruited primarily from elements of the lower middle class.[85]

Nazi leaflets and speeches were opportunistically aimed at various class and interest groups, with policies geared to their various needs.[86] Mann states that there was always a strong nationalist message, and, as we have seen, a commitment to the economic and political programme of the middle-class groups, newly united in their fight against 'alien exploitation'.[87] Mann also claims that the Nazis made a strong pitch for working-class support, indeed that they spent twice as much organising effort on workers.[88] For example, they attacked the reactionary conservatism of Chancellor Von Papen, and of the DNVP, the main right-wing, bourgeois German People's Party. Moreover, in the days leading up to the November 1932 Reichstag elections, the Nazis supported the Berlin transport workers' strike. However, this strategy of projecting an image of classlessness, of being 'all things to all persons', backfired: in a reduced turnout (at 80.6 per cent, the lowest since 1928), the Nazis lost 2 million votes, their share declining from 37.4 per cent in the July elections to 33.1 per cent. Many previous Nazi voters stayed at home or returned to the DNVP. Rural voters – a pillar of Nazi support since 1928 – were shocked by the Nazis' support for the strike and stayed away. While the Nazis lost 2 million, the Communist Party vote rose to 16.9 per cent. Kershaw sums it up: 'the middle classes were beginning to desert the Nazis'.[89]

Finally, just because workers voted for the Nazis doesn't make their party a workers' party, any more than the fact that a third of the British working class has traditionally voted Tory makes the Tories a workers' party. The social identity of a party is determined not only, or rather not principally, by the class of its supporters but by the main thrust of its policies and its organisational orientation. Mann himself acknowledges this when he says 'though not a proletarian party, they remained broadly rooted'.[90] Kershaw echoes Schweitzer's analysis of the Nazi Party as a middle-class party: 'Though the NSDAP claimed to be above sectional interest, it was, in fact, as the crisis gripped ever more tightly, better than any other party in tapping a whole panoply of mainly middle-class interest-groups through the sub-organisations it set up.'[91]

Creation of German Capitalism – Revolution From Above

The Nazis' success in building a mass movement thus stemmed largely from their ability to articulate the anxieties and frustrations of the middle classes. These reached a climax with the Great Depression, but had been building up for decades. As Jones writes:

> In the period before World War One, the economy underwent a series of changes which resulted in a partial rationalisation of its productive and distributive processes. This process was accelerated during the course of World War One and reached its climax in the middle of the 1920s before the world economic crisis deprived German management of the capital it needed for the purposes of rationalisation. The impact of rationalisation on the different elements of German society was extremely uneven, and in the long run it generated an element of structural instability which played a crucial role in the rise of National Socialism in the period before 1931. The greatest instability occurred within the ranks of the German middle class.[92]

Much discussion has focused on whether blame rests with international capitalism, German society as a whole, or a specific group within it. Important to this debate is the manner in which Germany industrialised in the years following the Franco-Prussian war of 1871, a success which enabled the Iron Chancellor Bismarck to forge ahead with national unification. Speedy industrialisation was necessary if Germany was to catch up and compete with its leading rivals on the world scene – in particular, Britain and the US. Between 1871 and 1900, Germany caught up in key industries such as coal and iron and steel. In the latter industry, 'the period 1890–1910 is shown to have been that in which Germany took the lead in Europe ... Only the United States ... was ahead of her as an iron and steel producer'.[93] According to Henderson, 'the late date at which the great development of German industry took place enabled her manufacturers to profit by the experience, and mistakes, of their rivals in other countries'.[94] Henderson reminds us that the two key features of German industrialisation were the early growth of cartels and the unusually close links between industry and the banks.[95] Cartels, or federations of businesses, were more conducive to rapid industrialisation than small family firms. In two of the key industries – the chemical and the electrical – 'adequate capital to meet the heavy initial expenditure on experimental research could be raised more easily by big concerns than by small firms'.[96] In addition, the depression of 1873 gave a boost to the process of cartelisation as large units are better able to weather the storms of economic crisis. Their growth was also fostered by the protective tariffs of 1879.[97] In addition, involvement of the banks in the development of ever-larger units of production promoted increasing interpenetration of industrial and finance capital.

Failure of the 1848 Revolution

In contrast to its rivals, Germany never overthrew its monarchy and landed aristocracy. The German middle class was too weak and cowardly to carry out a bourgeois revolution, as its counterparts in Britain, France and the US had done. It had 'funked its historical task', squandering its opportunity to overturn the old order – the absolute monarchy and the Junkers' semi-feudal, landed nobility – in the revolution of 1848. Although it occupied centre stage, the middle class heard the stirring, the early muscle-flexing, of the youthful working class in the wings. Recoiling in fear, it threw in its lot with the old ruling class instead. Marx didn't mince his words: 'The German bourgeoisie had developed so slothfully, cravenly and slowly that at the moment when it menacingly faced feudalism and absolutism it saw itself faced by the proletariat and all factions of the burghers whose interests and ideas were akin to those of the proletariat.'[98] Nevertheless, despite the absence of a successful bourgeois revolution from below, capitalist industrialisation was carried out through a 'revolution from above', engineered by the new state bureaucracy dominated by the Junker-born Bismarck.

After 1871, industrialisation was forced through by Bismarck's 'enlightened despotism'. He dragged the Junkers into an alliance with the top layer of the middle-class capitalists. Over the next 30 years, the concentration of production and retailing in the hands of fewer and fewer giant monopoly firms developed apace. The majority of the middle class lost out, unable to compete with Big Business, squeezed by a pincer movement of the new capitalist ruling class and a powerful labour movement that had developed equally rapidly. The contrast with Britain and France is considerable. Neither in Britain, where capitalist industrialisation developed early, nor in France where it developed late, did it result in the early dispossession and impoverishment of the petty-bourgeoisie, as happened in Germany. This is important as there is arguably one element deriving from the German bourgeoisie's 'weakness' in 1848 that is relevant to an analysis of the Holocaust. This is that Germany's extremely rapid development in between 1871 and 1914 hit the petty-bourgeoisie much harder than in societies where industrial development took place more slowly. As Stedman-Jones observes, 'the more industrial capitalism developed, the stronger was the economic power of the *grande bourgeoisie* in relation to the masses of small producers and dealers from which it had sprung, and the greater the distance between their respective aims'.[99]

Decline of the German Petty-Bourgeoisie

Germany's race to catch up with its more advanced competitors entailed a more rapid process of economic concentration and cartelisation than in France or Britain. However, there has been debate among historians as to the effect of German industrialisation on small business – artisans and shopkeepers. According to Blackbourn, 'pessimists' argue that 'craftsmen were at a disadvantage in competing for capital and labour, while suffering from rapid changes in taste and demand prompted by the new industrial civilisation. Whole groups like potters, farriers and basket-makers were laid waste.'[100] Counter-arguments are that the pessimist case rests on a false view of a pre-industrial golden age for craftsmen, and that, on the contrary, industrialisation created new opportunities for small producers and retailers, widening the scope for auxiliary and service roles and increasing purchasing power.[101] However, according to Blackbourn, what both sides miss is the continuing 'differentiation and competition among craftsmen, and the importance of their de facto dependence on distributors'.[102] As capitalism developed, it often strengthened longstanding disparities of wealth and income between different crafts. Moreover, by 1895, more than a third of all master craftsmen were one-man businesses. Also, at the end of the century as at the beginning, half of all masters were rural. Blackbourn further suggests that hidden in the statistics of growing small businesses is a complex dual process of 'concentration on the one hand, and semi-proletarianisation on the other'.[103] A local survey in 1890 showed that 87 per cent of craftsmen in the clothing branches worked alone. In 1895, the figure was over 50 per cent for all trades.[104] Many craftsmen were squeezed out of production altogether, while dependence increased with the decline in the relative importance and autonomy of craft production within the capitalist economy as a whole. 'Petty commodity production had, by the end of the nineteenth century, become a marginal activity.'[105]

As for shopkeepers, here too statistics suggest a large number of independents concealed great discrepancies of wealth and income. A minority of businesses in central city areas and the wealthier suburbs resembled well-established enterprises in the market towns, their owners enjoying a standard of living which bordered on the bourgeois. For the majority of shopkeepers, however, by the end of the nineteenth century more than half of all retail outlets were one-man or one-woman concerns. Their shops 'were the overcrowded and proletarian equivalents of the impoverished tailor or shoemaker'.[106] Moreover, a shortage of capital led to all shopkeepers facing the danger of a loss of independence, and a slide into dependence on wholesalers and deliverers for credit. This threatened to transform the independent small shopkeeper into 'an agent of large-scale commercial capital'.[107] Thus, by the beginning of the twentieth century, the dangers facing shopkeepers derived not so much from the competition of department stores and consumer cooperatives but from the tendency towards incorporation by capital and the resulting semi-proletarianisation. Blackbourn concludes that 'the problems of shopkeepers and craftsmen converged as the pace of capitalist development quickened'.[108]

Clearly, the German petty-bourgeoisie did not disappear, otherwise the Nazis would not have had a social base. But reports by official and semi-official bodies in the second half of the nineteenth century describe a 'sense of declining social status and narrowing horizons ... a feeling among craftsmen ... and shopkeepers ... that they were becoming more marginal members of society'.[109] By the end of the century, the organisations of the petty-bourgeoisie were angry and frustrated: they felt undervalued.[110] 'Even butchers appear to have sensed a decline in social worth in the course of the century.'[111] In sum, as the wealthy capitalists and higher professionals drew socially closer to landowners and officials, so lower down the social ladder, the line between greater and lesser bourgeoisie became sharper.[112] It seems that fears of proletarianisation led many craftsmen and shopkeepers to exaggerate the remaining 'small differences' between themselves and the working class – home-owning, the absence of unemployment (though not under-employment), and external badges of respectability.[113]

What about the peasantry? According to Wehler, substantial legal reforms in the years 1807–21 'emancipated' them from feudal bondage in the three main areas of seigniorial rights: (a) in land tenure – ownership, labour services, taxes in kind; (b) in personal rights – serfdom tying the peasant to the land; and (c) in the arbitration of disputes – that is, judicial rights. In all three, the oppressive powers of the landowning nobility were removed. The impetus for these changes came from the state's need to raise revenue following the destruction of the Napoleonic Wars. It was hoped that by 'liberating' the peasantry, by opening up the land to private ownership and reorganising agriculture along competitive lines, efficiency would be boosted.[114] However, these reforms could not have been carried through without the consent of the Junkers landowners. They benefited by the removal of legal obligations towards the peasants and the improved efficiency deriving from wage labour, but above all by the increase in disposable land.[115] The Prussian state also aided its aristocratic supporters by granting subsidised credit and tax benefits, whereas peasants had to buy their freedom at a high price, either in cash or by ceding land. The new system of large-scale capitalist agriculture thus arose at the expense of the peasantry, especially in the east where the area occupied by the large estates increased by two-thirds between 1811 and 1890. It was these that were best able to benefit from the new rationalised methods of cultivation, both providing for a rapidly growing population and profiting from the lucrative export trade. The agrarian sector was an important contributor to the funding of Germany's early industrialisation, through the increased tax yields arising from the accumulation of private wealth derived from exports.

The transition from inherited feudal servitude to formal legal independence stimulated a huge increase in population, doubling from 25 million in 1840 to 52 million in 1895.[116] But because of the relative decline in opportunities in the traditional occupations, hundreds of thousands emigrated – 2 million between 1850 and 1870. Many more poured into the new urban industrial centres where they formed a reserve army of unskilled labour required by the factory system alongside its artisans. As Wehler says: 'Population growth, increased consumption, capital accumulation, urbanisation and internal migration were thus closely linked functionally with the agrarian revolution. For this reason, the success of this revolution was one of the essential preconditions of the German industrial revolution.'[117] The abolition of feudal ties only reached its climax after the 1848 revolution. Between 1811 and 1848, 70,000 Prussian peasants had won independence by ceding land and a further 170,000 by cash payments. But between 1850 and 1865, 640,000 bought their freedom. New state-owned banks gave the peasants mortgage aid, but also increased the wealth of the landowners by increasing the peasantry's mortgage redemption debts.[118] The nobility were thus transformed into a class of large capitalist landowners. The agrarian revolution provided the Junkers with an economic base enabling them to consolidate their social privileges and their political power, especially in the army and state bureaucracy.

The First World War and the Rise of the Nazis

Germany's rapid development brought it into intensifying conflict with its rivals, culminating in the First World War, an inter-imperialist struggle which Germany lost. In the ensuing Treaty of Versailles of 1919, the victorious allies imposed harsh reparations on Germany which hit the middle classes hard. Then, in the hyper-inflation of 1923, their savings were wiped out and Germany had to be rescued by American loans, an uneasy stability that was toppled by the Crash of 1929 and the subsequent Great Depression. German industry collapsed, with production nose-diving by 42 per cent, unemployment rocketing to 5.6 million – 30 per cent of the workforce and 43 per cent of metal workers.[119] These events were also unmitigated disasters for the urban and rural middle classes, with whole sections of small business wiped out; they were also catastrophic for the professional middle class.

Ruling class fear of the labour movement, and their memory of the revolution of 1919, induced them to do a deal with the Nazis, even though they didn't have a majority. In fact, as we saw, the Nazi vote declined in 1932. So, in January 1933, the big capitalists manoeuvred to get Hitler appointed chancellor, and in return for political power he agreed to drop the anti-Big Business measures of the Nazi programme. As Fromm puts it: 'Nazism resurrected the lower middle class psychologically while participating in the destruction of its old socio-economic position. It mobilised its emotional energies to become an important force in the struggle for the economic and political aims of German imperialism.'[120] The disastrous failure of the left to unite against Hitler abandoned Germany to the Nazis.

During the 1930s, the Nazis' rearmament programme eliminated unemployment but led inevitably to Act Two of the inter-imperialist drama of which the First World War had been Act One. German capitalism sought to take back land, markets and sources of raw materials lost to the other Western capitalist powers in the First World War and earlier. Through that decade, anti-Semitism grew rapidly as an instrument of Nazi policy. Jews were systematically deprived of civil rights as the hatred, anger and fear of the middle classes were directed by Nazi ideology away from Big Business onto the Jews. They were depicted simultaneously as sub-human and as the all-powerful force behind both international finance and Germany's other great enemy, Bolshevism.

Middle-Class Authoritarian Social Character

No analysis of the rise of Nazism and the Holocaust can be complete without an understanding of the psychological dimension of the crisis of Germany's middle classes. In this vein, Saul Friedlander argued that beyond the undeniable importance of anti-Semitic ideology and the dynamics of bureaucracy, there is also 'an independent psychological residue'.[121] As a result of their historical experience as a social class in the development of German capitalism, the middle classes developed within the family a typical social character which some psychoanalysts have described as an authoritarian personality.[122] As

Blackbourn notes in his analysis of the decline of the petty-bourgeoisie: 'the values of fairness, thrift and self-reliance were sufficiently at odds with prevailing conditions of production and distribution that they probably account for some of that commonly noted "overcompensation" in the domestic sphere, which took the form of moral rigidity and patriarchal authoritarianism.'[123] Kater adopts a similar position regarding the Nazi leaders:

> these largely lower-middle-class functionaries possessed what has been called the 'authoritarian personality'. Patriarchal and prudish at home ... these men took full advantage of their elevated position in the family unit, one that had been established long before World War I. It was predicated upon a value system that was antiquated, anti-emancipatory and anti-modernist.[124]

This social character has been described as the simultaneous presence of sadistic and masochistic drives. Sadism was the desire for power over others combined with the urge to destroy. Masochism was the need to dissolve oneself in a strong power while participating in its strength. The Nazi leaders sought power over the masses, while the latter were exhorted to see themselves as having power over other nations and 'races' and over the Jews. Adorno and Horkheimer argued something similar when they wrote: 'The reactionary ticket which includes anti-Semitism is suited to the destructive-conventional syndrome. It is not so much that such people react originally against the Jews as that their drive-structure has developed a tendency toward persecution which the ticket then furnishes with an adequate object.'[125] Another interesting suggestion is that anti-Semites detect in Jews 'what they secretly despise in themselves: their anti-Semitism is self-hate, the bad conscience of the parasite'.[126]

Nazism and Psychoanalysis

What is striking about Reich's analysis of the success of fascism is the brilliant manner in which his analysis locks together the economic and psychological crises of the German middle class. He articulates the classic Marxist-Trotskyist analysis of fascism as a middle-class movement which won support from that class because of its official stance against Big Business. From the outset, Reich displays a solid grasp of the historical and structural crisis of the German middle class.

> The rapid development of capitalist economy in the nineteenth century, the continuous and rapid mechanisation of production, the amalgamation of the various branches of production in monopolistic syndicates and trusts, form the basis of the progressive pauperisation of the lower middle class merchants and tradesmen. Not capable of competing with the cheaper and more economically operating large industries, the small enterprises go to ruin, never to recover ... As a consequence of his social situation, the lower middle class man could join forces neither with his social class nor ... with the industrial workers; not with his own class because competition is the rule there, not

with the industrial workers because it is precisely proletarianisation that he
fears most of all.[127]

However, Hitler did a deal with Big Business: in return for the chancellorship,
he dropped the anti-corporate programme through which the Nazis had won the
allegiance of the middle class. Yet, the middle class continued to support Hitler
even after he betrayed them. So what enabled him to retain their allegiance?
Reich points out that the Nazis were highly skilled in working on the emotions
of their supporters and avoiding relevant arguments as far as possible.[128] One
precondition of winning and retaining the mass support of the middle class was
that Hitler possessed an authoritarian character structure in tune with and indeed
echoing that of his followers.[129] However, our aim is to discover the roots of
the collective, not individual, paranoia which afflicted Hitler as a member of the
class primarily affected.

The heart of the middle or lower-middle-class character structure is the
ambivalent attitude towards authority: 'rebellion against it coupled with
acceptance and submission – (the) basic feature of every middle class (character)
structure from the age of puberty to full adulthood ... especially pronounced in
individuals stemming from materially restricted circumstances'.[130] Reich then
distinguishes between the mass psychology of 'the lower middle class' and that
of the working class.

> Always ready to accommodate himself to authority, the lower middle class
> man develops a cleavage between his economic situation and his ideology.
> He lives in materially restricted circumstances, but assumes gentlemanly
> postures ... It is its accommodating attitude that specifically distinguishes the
> structure of the lower middle class man from the (character) structure of the
> industrial worker.[131]

Reich noted: 'The social position of the middle class is determined by (1) its
position in the capitalist production process, (2) its position in the authoritarian
state apparatus, (3) its special family situation ... determined by its position in the
production process [which] is the key to an understanding of its ideology.'[132]
Moreover, 'in the figure of the father, the authoritarian state has its representative
in every family, so that the family becomes its most important instrument
of power ... He reproduces his subservient attitude towards authority in his
children ... It is in the lower middle classes that this structure is ... embedded ...
most deeply.'[133]

Fromm took up the analysis where Reich left off.[134] The middle classes feared
independence and had a deep-seated respect for authority. They loved the
strong and despised the weak. They suffered deep emotional deprivation in early
childhood, being forced to renounce instinctual urges at an early, pre-genital
stage, this renunciation occurring not in a loving way, but abruptly, and through
punishment. The result was repressed rage and destructiveness. At a time of
social breakdown, instead of rage being directed at the ruling class responsible
for the state of society, it was projected on to scapegoats.

THE NAZI HOLOCAUST 203

As we saw in Chapter 2, Kohut relates violence to narcissistic rage, which is at the origins of some of the most gruesome aspects of human destructiveness, often in the form of well-organised activities in which the 'perpetrators' destructiveness is alloyed with absolute conviction about their greatness and with their devotion to archaic omnipotent figures'.[135] Kohut also describes Hitler's psychosis after 'he emerged from a hypochondriacal phase with the fixed idea that the Jews had invaded the body of Germany and had to be eradicated'.[136] Kershaw reflects that Hitler's 'capacity for hatred was so profound that it must have reflected an immeasurable undercurrent of self-hatred concealed in the extreme narcissism that was its counterpoint must surely have had its roots in the subliminal influences of the young Adolf's family circumstances'.[137] Alice Miller has described Hitler's childhood as racked by regular, brutal beatings at the hands of a disciplinarian father. Bullock also points to the psycho-pathological needs that led to genocide.[138] But this leaves unanswered the key question: what social and economic forces allowed a psychopath like Hitler to reach a position of supreme power?

Prior to Germany's defeat in the First World War, the middle class individual still felt part of a stable social and cultural world in which she or he had a definite place. But with defeat and the collapse of the monarchy, followed by hyper-inflation, their security was swept away, intensifying these emotional features. Of course, had the workers' revolution of 1919 been successful instead of being finally defeated in 1923, it would have offered the middle classes an alternative to Nazism, one that would arguably have enabled them to develop a different, more independent, social character. In a fascinating essay, Loewenberg argues that the experience of young children in the First World War, with its terrible physical and emotional privations, with defeat and its aftermath, were the crucial factors that made that generation of the middle classes psychologically available for the Nazi appeal. 'The ... adults who became politically effective after 1929 and who filled the ranks of the SA and other paramilitary party organisations ... were the children socialised in the First World War.'[139]

An earlier article by American psychoanalyst Martin Wangh spelt this out: 'the economic and social stresses of 1930 to 1933 reawakened in the youth of this generation the anxiety previously experienced in the years 1917–1920. And once again, the lower middle class was particularly imperilled by declassement and unaccustomed poverty.'[140] Kattenacker puts an interesting but slightly different slant on it, showing how Nazism was the most extreme manifestation of the alienation of the German middle classes. 'National Socialism embodies a fundamentally new variant of the concept of "revolution", namely the delayed revolt of the lower middle-class masses against modernity and against the consequences of an unnatural and politically and socially unbearable industrialisation.'[141]

The psychoanalyst Henry Dicks studied a group of SS members and reached similar conclusions. These individuals from middle-class backgrounds grew up with paranoid, sadomasochistic personalities, deep rage and hatred rooted in early childhood experience which was projected outwards so that cowards became bullies, 'killers ... terrified of their victims – the projected part of themselves'.[142] Of course, not all members of the middle classes developed these inner traits to the same degree. Nazi killers revealed an extreme example of this general class psychology, an 'inner authority image of ruthless contempt for weakness and dependence', too terrifying to contemplate in oneself as it contravened the moral expectation of strength, manliness and obedience and therefore had to be projected outwards on to the scapegoat.[143] Dicks describes one SS killer as 'an individual whose need to belong had been perverted, while the resultant anti-parental hate had been displaced on to authority-approved targets'.[144] In general, the Nazi paranoid-aggressive was 'self-centred, hardened against guilt, hating both pitiless authority and helpless weaklings'.[145] As Norman Cohn argued: 'It is likely that when anti-Semites kill not simply Jewish men but also Jewish women and children, when they see the extermination of all Jews as an indispensable cleansing or disinfection of the earth, they are moved by terrors stemming from the earliest stages of infancy.'[146] This in no way goes against the description of the Nazi killing machine as a smooth, bureaucratic operation: 'Though this gigantic operation was carried out in a cold, matter-of-fact, bureaucratic spirit ... we must assume that the majority of SS and Nazi activists shared violent racist beliefs with their Fuhrer.'[147] Hence there is no contradiction between ascribing violent racism to SS murderers and the notion of a bureaucratic, assembly-line enterprise – the industrialisation of death – as described by Arendt in her report on the Eichmann trial in 1961.[148]

Psychological tests were carried out on Eichmann during his trial by psychiatrists I.S. Kulcsar and Shoshanna Kulcsar. A separate test was conducted by the Hungarian psychologist Lipot Szondi. They claim that Eichmann was not just the bureaucratic conformist depicted by Hannah Arendt. 'He was not simply taking orders. He was imaginative in carrying them out. He used the regime and its ideology to satisfy his own murderous desires.' The authors believe that Eichmann was not specifically anti-Semitic, but that he hated the entire human race, killing Poles, Russians, communists and Jews with equal relish.[149] Mann too takes issue with Arendt's claim that morally 'he never realised what he was doing ... Eichmann was very anti-Semitic'. Paraphrasing Losowick, Mann insists that 'Eichmann's evil was neither unthinking nor banal, but innovative, ruthless, and ideological.'[150]

Further evidence of middle-class pathology was provided by Klaus Theweleit, who developed a fascinating psychoanalysis of the writings of members of the Freikorps, the right-wing militia formed in the wake of Germany's defeat in the First World War.[151] They played a key role in suppressing the German workers' revolution of 1918–23. It was from the ranks of the Freikorps that many future Nazi leaders and cadres were recruited. The Freikorps were drawn almost exclusively from the Burgertum (middle class), as Mommsen attests in his book *From Weimar to Auschwitz*.[152] In an in-depth study of letters, novels and diaries written by Freikorps members, Theweleit discovers a key feature of their psyche: their hatred and fear of women, women's bodies and their sexuality. This dread emerges in earliest infancy, even before the onset of Freud's triangular Oedipal struggle around the age of three. Indeed, Theweleit rejects the Oedipus complex as a central factor in the analysis of the Nazi mentality: 'in and of themselves, the Oedipal categories of psychoanalysis don't seem capable of apprehending fascist phenomena'.[153]

At the outset of life, infants experience their bodies as part of the mother's – there is no sense of a separate body or ego with needs and desires focused on the outside world. The ego can only emerge as separate from the mother through the experience of a nourishing, enriching 'good object' in the form of her breast. In the absence of the 'good object', the infant's body will remain submerged in that of the mother, dissolved in her, so that, as Barbara Ehrenreich puts it in her Foreword to Theweleit's study: 'women's bodies are the holes, swamps, pits of muck that can engulf'.[154]

For the Freikorps, the women they encounter on the warfront and in their fantasies, apart from wives and mothers left at home, fall into two categories. First is the 'rifle woman', 'female communist' or working-class woman who fights alongside the men. 'The sexuality of the proletarian woman/gun slinging whore/communist is out to castrate and shred men to pieces ... her imaginary penis [her weapon] ... grants her the hideous power to do so.'[155] However, the Freikorps' fantasy of the 'rifle woman' takes on concrete reality in the camouflage of the 'Red' nurse, 'Red Army' women, or rather prostitutes, fighting for the workers' revolution, who also took on medical duties.[156]

The second category consists of 'White' nurses, upper-class women or idealised, heroic mother figures, 'clearly above any suspicion of whoring',[157] who carry out nursing duties for their menfolk.[158] But even the 'good mother' is a 'split figure. One side of her (their own mother) is loving and protective, especially of children against their fathers; the other side (mothers of comrades, etc.) is hard ... mothers-of-iron who don't bat an eyelid at the news of the death of (their) sons.'[159]

In the second volume of his study, Theweleit returns to this theme of the emergence of the 'I', the infant's separation from the mother's body, its differentiation of 'self' from 'other', 'developing a sense of having a body of its own, of having ceased to be the maternal body', discussed by both Klein and the Hungarian-American psychoanalyst Margaret Mahler.[160] For Mahler, the key factor in the growth of the idea of 'I' is the formation of the 'mental representations of the body as body image'. The infant develops perceptions of 'inner processes, for instance those linked with feeding, contact reception, complemented later by distance perception'.[161] However, the sensations experienced by the infant can also be unpleasurable, the interior becoming 'a site of ferocious emotional upheaval'. Klein described

> feelings of unpleasure across the body's periphery, lack of affection, etc., as obstacles to the formation of the internal 'good object', the child's introjection of the nourishing breast of the mother. What is introjected instead is the 'bad' half of the breast – the mother's absence, or what that absence palpably conveys of her antipathy to the child.

The problem is that the infant 'has no means of either integrating or discharging the affects it now experiences; thus the evil mother becomes lodged in the child's interior'.[162] The result of the internal dominance of the bad object, of the infant's perception of the mother as unloving and unreliable, is its withdrawal of libido from her, and from the rest of the world of objects. According to Mahler, 'the result is a narcissistic state, in which the ego becomes fragmented and the self-boundaries blurred, fused with the mother's'.[163]

This stress on the mother whose inadequate care makes her the object of hatred and fear may seem a little surprising, given our knowledge of the traditional, oppressive nature of patriarchal authority in German society, indeed in Western society generally, particularly its Protestant areas. As regards Nazi Germany, the regime continued to underwrite the time-honoured hierarchy: 'it lent support to the formal power of the father (demanding absolute obedience of children) and to the position of the mother as the great bearer of children'.[164] However, Theweleit follows Mahler and Klein in their stress on the importance of the mother. He refers to Mahler's notion of the 'psychotic' child, 'who live[s] in constant danger and fear of intrusive, unpleasurable, symbiotic states'.[165] These individuals have not yet experienced full birth or individuation and remain symbiotically attached to the mother's body. Theweleit argues that this 'psychotic' type was 'far more "normal" and more common than Oedipus' who 'seems likely to have been a highly unusual specimen'. Indeed, the position of the father as the agent of society 'bears no relation to the psychic need of the not-yet-fully-born-child, for whom the father is more or less non-existent. What this child seeks (its whole long life, if need be) is unification with maternal bodies, within which it can become "whole", born to completion.'[166] Martin Wangh locates in this process the aggression later re-directed against the outgroup: 'A defective individuation experience, and a consequently disturbed object-relationship, will manifest itself early by just such displacement of aggressive cathexes on to the stranger.'[167]

The Middle-Class Family

We need to understand the historical evolution of this 'psychotic' type within the middle-class family, itself the product of the changing class relations of German capitalism. In 1948, the American psychiatrist Bertram Schaffner carried out a detailed study of the political attitudes of Germans of different age-groups whose childhood had been spent under the Empire, the Weimar Republic and the Nazis. It concluded that 'the basic premises of German family life show no significant differences during these seventy-six years [i.e., 1870–1946]'.[168] A central finding was the 'zero-sum' relationship of power between the father and mother. Formal power and authority was concentrated in the hands of the father around whom family life revolved and who provided the model for his children to follow. He expected them to obey his instructions and his rules without question. The father thus imposed a military-style discipline, an approach he regarded as necessary to achieve the highest level of welfare. But he still expected to be treated with respect and gratitude by his children and, in his old age, to be looked after by them if necessary.[169]

In contrast, the mother would always be subservient to the father and, like the children, obey her husband's orders. Her place was in the home and the kitchen, her role summed by the three German Ks: *Kinder, Kuche, Kirche*, ('children, kitchen, church').[170] The wife was thus expected to subordinate her needs and her personality to those of her husband, her success as a wife judged by the extent to which she adjusted herself to the standards and demands of the man.[171]

Apart from the basic injustice of the power relationship, perhaps the most sinister aspect of this form of marriage was the degree to which the wife was expected to allow 'her emotional adjustment to her husband to take precedence over her relationship to her children. Thus, the authoritarian position of the father automatically weakens the ties between a mother and her children, and increases the dependence of both upon the central father-figure.'[172] One crucial result of this patriarchal power relationship was 'to make the status of the mother, in the eyes of the children, a variable and indefinite one ... It becomes hard for them to rely on her completely, and they may develop resentments because she has "betrayed" them to the father. Thus a woman's relationship to her children and her status within the home are variable and insecure.'[173] It seems, therefore, plausible to conclude that the German middle-class infant, in many if not most cases, experienced their mother as unreliable or even fickle. The result would have been a high level of anger towards her, a frightening experience for an infant totally dependent on its mother. The rage would have been repressed, and later in life projected on to outgroups. According to Waite, comparative studies have revealed that family life tended to be more authoritarian in Germany than in other countries.[174] Wangh argued, in addition, that 'in the lower middle class ... these authoritarian and patriarchal features were even more exaggerated'.[175]

Schaffner's analysis did not seek out differences in the degree of authoritarianism between the various classes of German society. However, Wangh's stress on the lower-middle-class family as the worst offender is correct for two reasons. First, the purpose of Schaffner's 1948 study was to eliminate Nazis and Nazi-minded individuals 'from all the functions under ICD [Information Control Division] control – newspapers, magazines, publishing houses, as well as radio, theatre, films and music'.[176] Clearly, at that time these occupations were largely closed to people of working-class background. Second, Fromm's attitude survey of German workers in the late 1920 found that a significant minority were non-authoritarian. It is likely, therefore, that Schaffner's interviewees were mostly of middle and upper-class background. And we analysed earlier the extent of middle-class disaffection and alienation stemming from their gradual exclusion and swamping by Big Business as a result of the manner in which industrial capitalism developed in Germany between 1871 and 1914. There is perhaps an uncanny parallel between their experience as a class of being 'swamped' and that of the middle-class infant being swamped and its ego boundaries dissolved. Now, if it is true that the German working-class family did operate on the basis of a lower level of authoritarianism, how can we account for this? Arguably, one factor would have been the strength of the German labour movement which had built up formidable organising powers since unification in 1871. This strength bred a degree of confidence which may well have been reflected in a greater level of freedom in family relationships, including a lower level of patriarchal authority. We are, therefore, talking about individuals with stronger Freudian egos and less oppressive super-egos. Of course, in the absence of further historical or psycho-historical evidence, such an observation remains speculative.

To return to Theweleit. In light of the depth of patriarchal authoritarianism among pre-war German middle and upper-class families, he is arguably wrong to play down Oedipal conflict and its stunting effect on emotional growth. The Jewish Hungarian-French psychoanalyst Bela Grunberger linked anti-Semitism to hatred of the father. As a religion, Judaism represents worship of the father, 'a severe, omnipresent, omniscient father, an implacable judge; in a word the super-ego'.[177] In Christianity, Christ, the son, is reunited with his mother, the virgin, while the father is banished to heaven, a fulfilment of every boy's secret and repressed Oedipal desire. This has aroused guilt in the Christian towards the Jew who remained faithful to the father. So, according to Grunberger, the Jew carried out the function of the father, installing within every man a judge to punish him for his Oedipal desires. This 'explains why he particularly has been chosen by the anti-Semite for the abreaction [expression and release of previously repressed emotion through reliving the experience that caused it] of his Oedipus conflict. The Jew represents the father...'.[178]

Now, this analysis suffers from gross psychologism, in turn due to its ahistorical character. It fails to explain why anti-Semitism was at a low level in certain periods but grew in extent and intensity at times of crisis and dislocation such as in Russia in the second half of the nineteenth century or Germany during the late 1920s and early 1930s. Here Wangh's paper offers a more historically-rooted and class-based perspective. The economic and social crisis sparked off by the 1929 Crash had a catastrophic impact on the middle classes, and caused severe psychological regression among the youth of that generation. Many, as noted above, had been young children during their fathers' absence in the First World War. At such times, when sons are alone with their mothers, the Oedipal conflict becomes sharper, with the intensification of their fear of paternal retribution. This castration anxiety was further increased by the famine of 1917, since prolonged hunger arouses oral regression and magnifies fantasies of physical destruction. Wangh argues further that the defeat of 1918 made the return of their fathers even more difficult to accept than if Germany had been victorious. How much harder is it to give back one's place next to the mother if the father doesn't seem to deserve this renunciation? Wangh concludes that 'defeat, starvation, revolution, inflation – all these served only to prove to the son of the lower middle class that his so emphatically autocratic father was incapable of protecting the family'.[179] Infants in whom such anger, anxiety and guilt are aroused have recourse to defensive measures. With famine, they are likely to hark back unconsciously to the early period when the relationship with the mother was largely conducted through the satisfaction of oral needs. But anger, whether directed against the mother for withholding food or the father for not protecting the family, will intensify guilt and the fear of retaliation, and lead to a further defence measure – projection. This enables the infant to protect the object of his/her aggression by displacing it on to a culturally available outsider – in this case, the Jew. According to Wangh,

> projection ... has the purpose of retaining the love object threatened by aggression born of frustration. It denies this aggression against its object. It claims to be good and demands: love me and hate the enemy; he is the

aggressive one. Two decades later, the sado-masochistic fantasies and the splitting bred by these circumstances found their way back to consciousness in the storm-troopers' wooing of the Fuhrer and in the refrain of the song: 'Jewish blood must squirt off the knife'.[180]

And, of course, middle-class Germans born earlier, in the 1890s or 1900s, surely also suffered emotionally through the impact on their parents of the marginalisation, declining status and impoverishment of the middle classes.

Ordinary Men?

According to Christopher Browning, there was nothing unusual about the men who made up the reserve police battalion drafted into Poland to assist with the Final Solution and who murdered some 38,000 Jews in 1942–3, deporting a further 45,000 to the Treblinka death camp.[181] These were not obviously men of a twisted mentality, sadistically inclined individuals whose 'natural' home was the SS, but ageing reserve policemen from Hamburg, one of the least Nazified cities in Germany, who mostly found their task distasteful, yet carried out the orders. The social composition of the battalion was 63 per cent working class, 35 per cent 'lower middle class', mostly white collar, with very few skilled workers. Some 25 per cent out of a sample of 174 were Nazi Party members in 1942, with only six who had joined before 1933. Those of 'lower middle class' background contained some 30 per cent of party members, only slightly higher than the 25 per cent of the working-class group who were party members.[182] These were, therefore, men with a social background and political culture who, on the face of it, 'would not seem to have been a very promising group from which to recruit mass murderers on behalf of the Nazi vision'.[183] What makes the events all the more horrific is that the men were given the opportunity by their commanding officer, just before the first massacre of 1,500 Jews at Jozefow, not to participate in the shootings.[184] Only 10 or 12 men out of roughly 500 laid down their rifles.[185] However, another group, after shooting for some time, approached their sergeant, telling him they could not continue, while others 'who did not request to be released from the firing squads sought other ways to evade'.[186]

We can compare the behaviour of the majority of Battalion 101 – conformity to peer pressure and fulfilment of expectations – with that of the German sailors and soldiers – workers in uniform – in November 1917, when they carried out acts of disobedience to authority:

in a desperate attempt to change the odds, [the German High Command] ordered to sea the very fleet which they had kept hidden from the risks of battle through most of the war. The mood among the rank-and-file was more bitter, if anything, than the year before. They knew that if they allowed the fleet to challenge the British fleet, they would face defeat and certain death. When sailors at Wilhelmshaven were ordered to move their ships at the end of October, they responded by putting out the boilers ... They were immediately arrested ... Five days later, thousands of sailors marched through Kiel to protest at the arrests. They were joined by the port's workers. Clashes with patrols loyal to the government left nine dead on the streets. But the patrols were met with counter-fire and forced to retreat from the town.[187]

How can one explain reserve Battalion 101's compliance with brutal mass murder? To begin with, one might perhaps expect a higher level of conformity and obedience on the part of policemen. But at a deeper level, perhaps the answer lies also in the massive political defeat that Hitler's assumption of power in 1933 represented for the German working class. At such historical moments, as suggested in Chapter 2, the victorious class is more able to impose its ideology and social character on members of the defeated class than before. So, arguably, we are discussing not simply the inevitable barbarisation of human beings in wartime, but the greater willingness of German workers to accept orders, even illegal ones, from their rulers. It is hardly surprising, therefore, that after 1933 their social character had retreated from its previous independence, coming gradually into line with the authoritarian-destructive character of their middle-class Nazi leaders. Clearly, as a consequence of the catastrophic defeat of 1933, workers lost confidence whereas the rulers gained confidence. We also saw in Chapter 2 how, according to Schneider, capitalism's class structure is reproduced within the mind of the individual. As regards the individual psyche following the catastrophe of 1933, the inner expression, or psychoana-lytical concomitant, of that defeat would have been a great strengthening of a repressive, punitive super-ego, a weakening of the id and an ego more tightly controlled by the official ruling ideology. Once again, in psychological as well as social and political terms, we see how the Final Solution was the 'punishment' for the defeat of 1933.

Intentionalists Versus Functionalists

Most historians are agreed that there was a close connection between Hitler's invasion of Russia in June 1941 (Operation Barbarossa) and the decision to exterminate European Jewry, as argued, for example, by Omer Bartov.[188] They are divided, however, over whether the Nazis had always intended to murder the Jews but lacked a suitable opportunity, or whether, on the contrary, the decision was taken under the pressure of events following the invasion. This is referred to as the debate between 'intentionalists' and 'functionalists', one that raged during the 1970s. The intentionalists argued that the Nazis had always intended to exterminate the Jews and were only awaiting the right opportunity. The functionalists argued that they arrived at the Final Solution in a pragmatic way, as a result of external events, or the outcome of changes in the Third Reich's power structures, specifically the rivalry between top Nazi officials competing with each other to be the best Jew-exterminators – what Hans Mommsen called 'the cumulative spiral of radicalisation'.[189] But, as Yehuda Bauer and others have argued, this is to deny the pivotal role played by Hitler in ordering the

Holocaust.[190] Moreover, as Mommsen himself points out, this rivalry was based on an assessment by lower-level bureaucrats as to what Hitler's wishes were.[191]

Expulsion Versus Ghettoisation

Browning notes that expulsion and ghettoisation were the twin pillars of early Nazi policy. 'The first is what the Germans sought to do in this period (1939–1941), and the second is what they actually did.'[192] After the invasion and occupation of Poland, the Nazis incorporated the territories of East Upper Silesia, Warthegau and West Prussia. Their first plan was to deport the millions of Poles and Jews living there and replace them with 'ethnically pure' Germans living further east and southeast. However, only 7 per cent of the population was German, 5 per cent was Jewish and the rest Polish. As two officials from the Office of Racial Policy (RPA), wrote, they needed to carry out a 'ruthless decimation of the Polish population and ... the expulsion of all Jews and persons of Polish-Jewish mixed blood'.[193] 'Ultimately perhaps 1 million Poles would remain and 5.6 million Poles, along with 530,000 Jews from the incorporated territories as well as the Jews of Germany, Austria and the Protectorate, would be sent east.'[194] Moreover, 'central Poland was to be a vast reservoir of cheap Polish labour – deprived of its present and potential leadership through extensive executions'.[195] By December 1939, three months after war broke out, 1 million Jews from western Poland and Germany had been expelled to central Poland, under the control of the General Government – an area of central and southern Poland under Nazi rule from 1939 to early 1945, designated as a separate administrative area of the Third Reich.

However, two problems arose. As Browning explains: 'Himmler's resettlement schemes threatened economic paralysis in both the incorporated territories and the General Government by removing indispensable workers from the former and overfilling the latter.'[196] Himmler's

> grandiose design for a sweeping racial reorganisation of eastern Europe was steadily whittled away. In the fall of 1939 he had envisaged the deportation of about one million people (including *all* Jews) from the incorporated territories into the General Government by the end of February 1940, and eventually the removal of all so-called racially undesirable elements from these lands.[197]

Between September 1939 and April 1941, total expulsions to the east numbered 503,000, of which 63,000 were Jews (roughly 12.5 per cent).[198]

The Madagascar Plan

As late as the summer of 1940, after the fall of France, Eichmann was instructed to work out a plan for the transfer of 4 million Jews to Madagascar, a French colony. It is clear that at this stage the Nazis were not thinking of exterminating the Jews. In Himmler's memorandum of May 1940, he wrote:

I hope completely to erase the concept of Jews through the possibility of a great emigration of all Jews to a colony in Africa or elsewhere ... However cruel and tragic each individual case may be, this method is still the mildest and best, if one rejects the Bolshevik method of physical extermination of a people out of inner conviction as un-German and impossible.[199]

The Governor-General of Nazi-occupied Poland, Hans Frank, continued to worry about the overcrowding that would result from the deportation of millions of poor Jews from Germany's eastern provinces. But like Himmler, he, too, could not yet envisage physical extermination: 'In the end, one cannot simply starve them to death.'[200]

However, by the end of 1940, expulsion fever among the Nazi leaders began to rise again. At a meeting on 17 December 1940, there was a discussion of a 'third short-range plan' to resettle ethnic Germans from the east. To make room, Reinhard Heydrich, head of the SS, planned to deport some 831,000 people in the coming year. In addition, the army wanted to relocate 200,000 to the General Government to create training areas. So, according to this plan, over a million people were to be resettled in the General Government. However, once again, as Browning puts it, 'the grandiose schemes of the Nazis reflected their ambitions more than their capacities'.[201] This time, the problem was not Frank but the decision, also taken that month by the Nazi leaders, to invade the Soviet Union the following spring. 'The transportation situation in the months before Barbarossa made realisation of the expulsions on the planned scale unattainable.'[202] After cancellation of the plan to expel the Jews to the General Government in the summer of 1940, and following the abandonment of the Madagascar Plan in the autumn due to fear of the British navy, the Nazis devised a third plan, expulsion to 'a territory yet to be determined'. In February 1941, Hitler told his close lieutenants that 'originally he had thought of breaking the power of the Jews in Germany, but now his goal had to be the exclusion of Jewish influence in the entire Axis sphere'.[203] This increased the number of Jews from the 4 million envisaged under the Madagascar Plan to 5.8 million if one adds in those living under the rule of Germany's allies in southeast Europe.[204]

Browning argues that 'the decision for Barbarossa did not alter the existing determination to create a Europe free of Jews, but expulsion and commensurate population decimation – not systematic extermination – remained the central vision. What did change was the destination of the expelled Jews.'[205] When Himmler addressed the Gauleiters in December 1940, he indicated that the new territory into which the Jews were to be expelled was not Poland. The General Government was to be a 'reservoir of labour' for Germany. This was on the eve of the finalisation of two crucial policies: the 'third short-range plan' for sending more than a million Poles from the incorporated territories into the General Government, and the decision to invade the Soviet Union. It was the latter that was to be 'the territory yet to be determined' for the expulsion of the Jews, but clearly this could not be openly discussed. It would achieve two objectives: break the 'demographic logjam' in the General Government, and create space for the expulsion of the Jews. So, in 1941, in the immediate aftermath of the invasion of Russia, the plan was to deport all Jews to Siberia, where, together with millions of unwanted Soviet citizens, most would have little chance of survival. Götz Aly, too, argues that 'a clear distinction must be drawn between this [third expulsion plan] and the later form of assembly-line extermination'.[206]

Ghettoisation

The second solution, closely linked to the first, was concentration or ghettoisation. This arose out of several factors: the Nazis' need to deal with the problems caused by the uprooting and concentration of the Jews; the need to exploit Jewish labour; the wish to plunder Jewish property; and the need to accommodate German officials and businessmen, military personnel and ethnic Germans in those cities where the Jews had been concentrated. However, there was disagreement among the local German authorities regarding ghetto policy, especially given the lack of clear guidelines from above. At the heart of these disputes was a split between 'attritionists' and 'productionists'. The former viewed the 'dying out' of the Jewish population as their goal, seeing the ghettos as vast concentration camps facilitating the extraction of wealth through deliberate starvation. The latter saw their task as minimising the burden of the Jews on the Reich by maximising their economic potential – exploiting their labour to benefit the German war economy.

In September 1939 Eichmann was thinking about 'an area as large as possible in Poland to be carved off for the erection of an autonomous Jewish state in the form of a protectorate'.[207] The idea was that of 'a *Judenstaat* or *Reichs-Getto*, first east of Cracow, and then around Lublin'.[208] Also in that month, Heydrich gave 'directives for the ... concentration of Jews in ghettos, the establishment of Councils of Jewish Elders, and the deportation of all Jews to the General Government area'.[209] However, in the spring of 1940, the attitude towards Jewish labour changed due to a labour shortage in German industry. Deportation of Reich Jews to the east was again postponed and the idea of the Lublin reservation given up. Emigration from the Third Reich was still pursued in theory but was increasingly restricted, first by limited avenues of exit and secondly by the prohibition against male Jews of military age leaving. All Jews (males 15 to 55 years old and females 15 to 50) were ordered to register for labour. In May and June 1940, Jews were conscripted into industry, including the armaments sector.[210] As Aly says: 'In the autumn of 1939, Hitler, Himmler and Heydrich had wanted to create a "Jewish reservation of Lublin" on Poland's eastern border. They then filed away the plans and abandoned the project since it proved incompatible with other military and economic goals.'[211] The result was a 'considerable cutback in SS plans for the massive transfers of population, including a near total postponement of deportations aimed at making even the incorporated territories "judenfrei".'[212]

The ghettoisation of the Polish Jews took place roughly in three waves: Lodz together with the Warthegau and the bordering western areas of the Warsaw

district in the spring of 1940; Warsaw and the rest of its district in the autumn of
1940; and the districts of Cracow and Radom, and the city (but not the district)
of Lublin in the spring of 1941. The objectives in each case were different: Lodz
and Warsaw were 'concentration points' for Jews of the surrounding regions;
Cracow, Radom and Lublin did the reverse, expelling Jews to the surrounding
areas. The rationalisation in each case also differed: in Lodz, ghettoisation was
said to be the most effective method of depriving the Jews of their property
prior to deportation; in Cracow, Radom and Lublin, the shortage of housing –
aggravated but not caused by the growing military presence in the spring of 1941
– was invoked as the main reason. And in Warsaw, the need to avoid epidemics
by sealing off the Jews provided the impetus. Browning concludes that the
'ghettoisation of the Polish Jews occurred at different times, in different ways,
and for different reasons', but the underlying reason permeating the different
situations was that Jews and Germans could not and should not live together.[213]
In January 1941, Hitler approved a plan to make Germany free of Jews by
the end of 1942.[214] Then, in September 1941, Eichmann ordered his first mass
deportation of thousands of Jews from Germany and the Protectorate to the
Lodz ghetto in Poland.[215] Later, they were moved on to Auschwitz.

Moderate Functionalism or Synthesis?

Browning offers a middle position between the opposing arguments, one he
describes as 'moderate functionalism', according to which 'Hitler had not decided
on the Final Solution as the culmination of any long-held or premeditated plan,
but ... he had indeed made a series of key decisions in 1941 that ordained the
mass murder of European Jews.'[216] He sums up the situation as follows:

> Did Hitler and his closest associates, such as Heinrich Himmler, arrive at a
> fundamental decision for the systematic mass murder of all European Jews
> in the German sphere already in the early months, perhaps even in January,
> of 1941? I would argue otherwise. The decision for Barbarossa did not alter
> the existing determination to create a Europe free of Jews, but expulsion
> and commensurate population decimation – not systematic extermination –
> remained the central vision. What did change, clearly, was the destination of
> the expelled Jews.'[217]

The resolution of the conflict between the intentionalist and functionalist
positions lies perhaps in a synthesis – one that shows how the external expression
of the Nazis' 'genocidal attitude' towards the Jews shifted in the context of
changing circumstances. The more interesting debate today is that conducted
within the 'functionalist' camp between those who argue that the Nazis arrived
at the Final Solution as a result of their euphoria following the early victories
in the Russian campaign (in the two months or so after the invasion in June
1941[218]), as against those who believe that the decision was taken as a result of
growing setbacks on the Russian front.

Bolshevism and Jewry

In Nazi ideology, as we have seen, there was a complete identification of Bolshevism with Jewry. Hence, once Operation Barbarossa was under way, Nazi death squads ('Einsatzgruppen') were dispatched to murder Jews and 'Bolsheviks' alike. In July 1941, Heydrich issued orders for the execution of all Communist Party functionaries and of 'all Jews in state and party positions'.[219] During the first eight weeks, the death squads, together with sections of the army, murdered over 80,000 Jews and Soviet prisoners, mainly men. In the first six to seven months, the death squads murdered some 500,000 Jews and Soviet prisoners. In mid-August, the order was issued to murder *all* Soviet Jews, including women and children. Arguably, a crucial factor behind this shift from mass murder to genocide was the dogged resistance of the Red Army slowing down the thrust of the German armies into the Soviet Union. This represented a setback for Hitler and his generals. Having been confident that the Red Army would be defeated in less than ten weeks, their perception became deranged. 'Beginning in late July, as a result of the failure to win a quick victory over the Red Army, German obsession with security increased.'[220] Again, 'in the eyes of German officials, especially outside the civil administration, the economic usefulness of Jews as forced labourers was far outweighed by their being perceived as a threat to security'.[221] Even so, this shift did not yet amount to a decision to exterminate all of European Jewry. During the month of September, the German army scored a tremendous victory in the Ukrainian campaign, one that Hitler had demanded of reluctant generals who had argued for a direct march on Moscow. On 25 September, the Germans won a spectacular victory in the capture of Kiev. On 7 October, they completed the double encirclement of Vyazma and Bryansk.[222] However, even on 6 October, one day before victory was complete, 'Hitler apparently still had reservations concerning the deportation of Jews [from the Reich], noting that "only the great shortage of transport" prevented them from commencing at once.'[223]

Failure of Barbarossa

The evidence seems to establish that Hitler and the Nazi elite decided to proceed with the Final Solution some time in the autumn of 1941 – between the end of October and early December. According to Browning, it was in October, according to Kershaw and Mayer, it was in November. Exactly when makes a difference, as by the end of October the German military situation had begun to deteriorate. 'Germany's string of military successes finally came to an extraordinarily abrupt end in late October. The bad weather, terrible roads, shortage of supplies, exhaustion of German troops and stubborn retreat of the remnants of the Red Army all combined to bring the Wehrmacht to a halt. There was no open road to Moscow.'[224] According to Browning, on 17 October Heydrich 'articulated the policy that no Jews should be allowed to escape "the direct reach of the measures for a basic solution to the Jewish question *to be enacted after the war*'". However, by the last week of October, the final step of deciding on the physical destruction of the Jews by gassing 'had been taken, planning was underway, and implementation ... scheduled for a time period characterised as both "the next spring" and "after the war"'.[225]

It seems reasonable to infer that Hitler and the top Nazis reached this decision as a result of their military reversals in Russia, in particular, the failure to capture Moscow. There were, in addition, threatening signals emanating from the rapprochement between Britain, the US and Russia, for which Hitler also blamed the Jews.[226] Of course, the Nazis had talked about 'getting rid of the Jews' before this date, but at the level of rhetoric or fantasy. Only during the final two months of 1941, with the defeat of the attack on Moscow, did the Final Solution of mass extermination by gassing in death camps take shape as a concrete, practical aim, a decision formalised at the Wannsee Conference in January 1942. We can thus see the unfolding of a spiral of cumulative destructiveness, an intensification of racist hatred as it expresses itself in ever more violent anti-Semitism – from expulsion and resettlement to ghettoisation to mass extermination. But none of these stages flowed inevitably from the previous one. Each phase is both contained in but separable from the earlier one. As Mommsen says: 'it is crucial to distinguish between the partial destruction of the Jews of eastern Europe, based on the Commissar Order, and the systematic policy of the Final Solution, in spite of the fact that the latter developed from the former'.[227] External factors drove the Nazis to an escalation of barbarism, to ever more brutal expressions of their hatred and fear of the Jews, looming defeat on the Russian front being the final trigger.

Arno Mayer puts clearly the argument that while the slowdowns in the blitzkrieg between late July and late October 1941 unsettled the Nazis and intensified the anti-Jewish furore of the assault squads, it was the desperate but unsuccessful race to Moscow in November–December 1941 that precipitated the rush to the 'Final Solution'. 'The gradual miscarriage of Barbarossa shook the hitherto unshakeable defiance and presumption of the Nazi fundamentalists and their accomplices, with the result that they turned to venting their rage on the Jew.'[228] The decision to murder the Jews was taken as the shadow of defeat began to creep over the Nazi project. Philippe Burrin also takes the view that the decision to exterminate European Jewry 'had arisen from a murderous rage increasingly exacerbated by the ordeal of the failure of [Hitler's] campaign in Russia and, through it, the failure of his entire venture'. Burrin, however, believes the date of the decision to have been mid-September, arguing that Hitler knew by August that a definitive victory over the Soviet Union before winter set in was unlikely and that the war would therefore extend into the following year. In such a frame of mind, given the Nazi fantasy of the omnipotence of the Jews, the major obstacle they represented to Nazi victory and the fulfilment of Nazi goals, they had to be physically liquidated. He describes their extermination as 'an act of vengeance'.[229] Mommsen, too, believes that 'the victories of the Red Army and the looming prospect of defeat began to destroy the Nazi dream-world of cynical power politics and the megalomaniac schemes for the future'.[230]

Aly, as we saw, also distinguishes between mass deportation and industrial genocide. He stresses the shock the Nazi leadership received as they realised the extent to which they had underestimated the strength of the Soviet army.

'How deep the shock went can be judged only if one is aware of how heavily the German leadership had wagered on the risky card of speedy victory. As the military castles in the air dissolved into nothing during August, so did those of the ethnic resettlement policy-makers.'[231] Aly, too, believes that the final leap to mass extermination resulted from a material factor – 'the cumulative failure of all the deportation projects, which was in turn connected with a self-created, cumulative strait-jacket' (the compulsion to get rid of the Jews).[232] Aly points to a second military problem preoccupying the Nazi leaders in addition to the debacle on the eastern front, namely the attacks by the Royal Air Force. Targeting German cities in the northwest, these bombardments 'led to massive "setbacks in mood", regularly documented by the SD [the security service], which crystallised around the lack of medical care for the wounded'.[233] These raids ratcheted up Nazi rage against the Jews.[234]

In sum, the Final Solution was precipitated by two factors, one material, the other psychological, both activated by the stalling, and ultimately the failure, of the Barbarossa offensive: first, the Nazis' inability to carry out their resettlement plans due to their failure to defeat the Soviet army, and second, the murderous rage towards the Jews that swept over them stemming from that frustration. In the end, of course, both factors were rooted in their pathological hatred and fear of the Jews.

Nazi Irrationalism

Nothing illustrates better the deranged nature of Nazism than this decision to commit untold resources to the murder of millions of non-combatants at a time when military defeat was looming. As Mommsen puts it: 'The fact that the Final Solution tied down large quantities of materials, including vital transport capacity, and critically diminished the labour force that was so desperately needed, ought to have suggested the need for a modification of the deportation and murder programme.'[235] Raul Hilberg also stressed the profound economic irrationality of the Holocaust. The leading German industrialist Krupp had tried to persuade Himmler not to deport the Jewish industrial workforce. 'In the General Government of Poland, 300,000 workers out of 1 million were Jews; in the textile sector, restructured in order to produce German shoes and uniforms for Germany, 22,000 out of 27,700 were Jews. The decision to eliminate the ghettoes in the spring of 1942 had catastrophic economic consequences.'[236] According to Hilberg, 'in the preliminary phase [isolation and expropriation of the Jews], financial gains, public or private, far outweighed expenses, but ... in the killing phase, receipts no longer balanced losses'.[237] As Callinicos notes:

> the Holocaust destroyed scarce skilled workers and diverted rolling stock from military purposes. Individual capitalist firms such as I.G. Farben undoubtedly profited from the extermination of the Jews, but, however instrumentally rational the bureaucratic organisation of the Holocaust may have become, this crime was dictated by considerations neither of profitability nor of military strategy.[238]

Indeed, the greater the defeats suffered by the German army after 1942, the more frenetic did the Nazis' attempts to round up and exterminate the Jews become. Both Hilberg and Bauman refer to the economic and military irrationality of the deportation of the Romanian and Hungarian Jews in the spring of 1944.[239]

It could, therefore, be argued that the debate between intentionalists and functionalists is not the right one, or rather is not a debate between two rigidly definable positions. Did the Nazis always intend to murder the Jews? It all depends on one's definition of 'intention'. If one means a concrete, worked-out plan of action, then the answer is 'no'. But if the question is whether they harboured feelings of hatred accompanied by genocidal fantasies towards the Jews, even years before the decision to exterminate them, then the answer is 'yes'. But as any self-respecting psychotherapist will attest, there is a world of difference between a fantasy of murder and acting it out. If there weren't, every adult member of society would be up on a murder charge at some point in their lives!

The problem with Browning's argument that it was the Nazis' euphoria over the initial successes on the Russian front that drove them to undertake the Final Solution is that it implies an 'intentionalist' position: it suggests that the Nazis had always consciously intended to murder the Jews and were only waiting for the right moment. Moreover, it contradicts Browning's own professed view of 'moderate functionalism'.[240] Furthermore, if euphoria were the trigger, the Nazis had already chalked up lightning victories in their earlier campaigns in Poland and France – but neither of those successes drove them in the direction of the Final Solution. The evidence suggests only that those earlier victories encouraged them to pursue their expulsion and resettlement programmes more vigorously. As Browning says: 'In September 1939, in the flush of victory over Poland, Hitler approved the plan for the demographic reorganisation of Eastern Europe, including the Lublin reservation. In May and June 1940, with the astonishing victory over France, he approved Himmler's memorandum on the eastern populations and the Madagascar Plan.'[241]

One could argue, however, that those victories didn't carry the same weight as did the early successes against the Soviet army, given that, for the Nazis, Jewry and Bolshevism were identical, and that it was to the east that Hitler looked for the great expansion of German territory – 'lebensraum'. On Browning's logic, once the early victories were dramatically overturned by the Soviet counter-offensive, the Nazis should at that point have halted their programme of mass extermination of the Jews. There was at least one precedent for stopping or delaying action plans. As Browning himself documents, in December 1940/January 1941, Heydrich had devised a 'third short-range plan' for the deportation of more than a million Poles from the incorporated territories together with Jews from Vienna and Danzig. But this plan was aborted on 15 March 1941 as the preparations for the invasion of Russia monopolised all rail transportation.[242]

Mommsen initially seems to fall on the side of the 'moderate' functionalist argument. He doesn't deny the importance of subjective factors. Indeed, he asserts that 'the real problem in providing a historical explanation of the Holocaust lies in understanding the overall political and psychological structure that gave rise to it'.[243] Moreover, Hitler's 'immediate and instinctive perception of impending dangers was rooted in a deep psychological insecurity, masked by a mixture of megalomania, joviality, harshness, determination'.[244] He acknowledges that Hitler's anti-Semitism was 'nothing short of paranoid'[245] and that, finally, Hitler and his subordinates attempted to enter a state of denial over the Holocaust, even as it was being implemented. 'This collective repression of disagreeable facts and criminal actions is an inevitable adjunct of any kind of political irrationalism.'[246] And as the war ground towards its end, 'the criminal and destructive energies that lay at the root of Hitler's personality ultimately prevailed over tactical and political considerations'.[247]

However, Mommsen doesn't attempt to relate the internal to the external factors – the events and institutional changes that, for him, constitute the real explanation of the Holocaust. 'A desire to enhance their own prestige and to extend their own authority was an important motive for many national socialists, especially the Gauleiter; their rival attempts to declare their districts "Jew-free" play a conspicuous role in the genesis of the Holocaust.'[248] Mommsen here adduces economic interests as a factor: both in the case of the Gauleiter and in that of the Reich Security Head Office (RHSA), who wanted to establish an SS economic empire and believed they could profit from the anti-Jewish Aryanisation measures. Industrial and banking interests, and the commercial middle class, also sought to benefit at the expense of their Jewish rivals. However, while such economic interests may provide some explanation of anti-Jewish legislation, they are hardly sufficient to explain genocide. On the contrary, many of these industrial and banking circles sought to benefit from Jewish forced labour in the concentration camps.[249]

Another mechanism adduced by Mommsen in helping to explain the radicalisation of the persecution of the Jews was the 'Judenferate' (Jewish affairs sections) set up in each government department after 1933. 'These sections felt the need to justify their existence by introducing cumulative anti-Jewish legislation.'[250] Again, Mommsen argues that

> ideological factors – the effects of anti-Semitic propaganda and the authoritarian element in traditional German political culture – are not sufficient in themselves to explain how the Holocaust became reality. The political and bureaucratic mechanisms that permitted the idea of mass extermination to be realised could also have occurred under different social conditions. The ultimately atavistic structure of the national socialist regime, coupled with the effective power of newly established bureaucracies, proved to be the decisive factor in the selection of negative 'elements of *Weltanschauung*' [worldview] and in the overwhelming loss of reality that was epitomised by Hitler's mentality.[251]

However, it is hard to see how these bureaucratic and regime structures can explain 'Hitler's mentality', or the Nazis' extreme hatred and fear of the Jews. They are, at best, precipitating factors, necessary conditions. But for an overall, viable explanation, we need predisposing as well as precipitating factors, a bundle of conditions both necessary and sufficient. Finally, Mommsen argues that the Holocaust was ... founded upon improvised measures that were rooted in earlier stages of planning and also escalated them. Once it had been set in motion, the extermination of those people who were deemed unfit for work developed a dynamic of its own. The bureaucratic machinery developed by Eichmann and Heydrich functioned more or less automatically.[252]

This is functionalism gone mad, a view of human action as almost entirely determined by external structures from which agency and motive, conscious or unconscious, have been eliminated.

The adoption of the Final Solution reflected Nazism's delusional notion of the Jews as the all-powerful masters of the world, a belief that was pathological in virtually a clinical sense. Hitler ceaselessly returned to the theme of the Jews being responsible for unleashing Second World War onto the people of Europe, just as they had the First. Kershaw describes how Hitler's address to his party leaders on 12 December 1941 made clear his belief that

> The Jews ... had caused the war. They would now have to pay for it by forfeiting their own lives ... 'if the international Jewish financiers in and outside Europe should succeed in plunging the nations once more into a world war, then the result will not be the Bolshevising of the earth, and the victory of Jewry, but the annihilation of the Jewish race in Europe.' This was no inauguration of the extermination programme. But it reflected a genocidal mentality, a certainty in Hitler's mind that Jews would carry the blame for another war ... and that as a consequence they would *somehow* perish.[253]

Kershaw again: 'However logical the path to genocide might have been, given the course of Nazi persecution of the Jews, the pathology of demonic anti-Semitism that lay at its roots defies rationality.'[254] If the war on Russia was suddenly, and totally unexpectedly, turning against Germany, who else but the Jews were to blame? In Hitler's mind, 'the war could never be won unless the Jews were to be destroyed'.[255]

The image of the Jews as omnipotent can thus be interpreted as a projection of the Nazis' fantasy wish which, in turn, expressed their own narcissistic rage at their secret fear of helplessness. Psychoanalyst Kohut refers to Hitler's 'grandiose fantasy [which] contains elements of a magical-sadistic control over the world ... he has large populations under his (magical) control whom he influences as if they were inanimate pieces of machinery'.[256] This 'severe, chronic narcissistic rage can ... continue throughout a lifetime in the individual ... and the same holds true for certain of the most destructive propensities of the group ... Hitler's followers with their vengeful destructiveness constitute a historical example in the realm of group psychology.'[257] Theweleit argues in a similar vein that

> the German psyche is ... imprinted with the *loss of war* ... The Great War touched the masculinity of several German male generations in its most sensitive area: in the conviction that German men were born to be warriors and victors. It deprived them of the victory they considered their 'birthright' and subjected them, as Germans, to a narcissistic wound of the first order.[258]

So, while the decision to exterminate the Jews was sparked by the first portent of defeat on the Russian front, in the end it was rooted in the pathology of Nazism whose seeds were planted several decades earlier: in the objective historical defeats of the German middle classes. These were in turn translated into their subjective family and childhood experiences.

Postscript

Could the Holocaust have occurred elsewhere than in Germany? As we have seen, there needed to have been two sets of preconditions that together amounted to necessary and sufficient conditions: 1) the necessary predisposing conditions – an authoritarian or other predisposing social character, and 2) the necessary precipitating conditions – for example, social collapse (as in Germany with defeat in the First World War, the hyperinflation of 1923, the Great Depression, the rise of Nazism and the failure of the left to unite and fight). Several countries in Europe and North America arguably fulfilled the first but not the second condition: an authoritarian social character existed among certain middle-class groups and in the US among certain communities that established themselves following the 1775–83 War of Independence.[259] It seems there may be a link between an authoritarian social character and the failure of some middle classes to carry out the bourgeois revolution, followed by their subordination instead to the old, semi-feudal, landed aristocracy, enabling the latter to instil its traditional authoritarian-military character into the middle class itself – as, for example, in Poland, Italy and Japan. So, the Holocaust could have occurred in the latter countries but was unlikely to have occurred, for example, in Britain or France, which did witness successful bourgeois revolutions after which the urban and rural middle classes enjoyed a long period of economic success. Not impossible but unlikely. More psychohistorical research is needed to develop our understanding of that link.

CHAPTER EIGHT

The Rwandan Genocide

Following the militias' example, Hutus young and old rose to the task. Neighbours hacked neighbours to death in their homes, and colleagues hacked colleagues to death in their workplaces. Doctors killed their patients, and schoolteachers killed their pupils. Within days, the Tutsi population of many villages were all but eliminated, and in Kigali prisoners were released in work gangs to collect the corpses that lined the roadsides.[1]

The Rwandan genocide of 1994, in which between 800,000 and 1 million Tutsi civilians were slaughtered by their Hutu compatriots, resembles the other genocides considered here in one important respect but differs in two others. It resembles the others in that it was part of a plan to exterminate an entire 'ethnic' group. The massacre of the Tutsis was exterminatory genocide in a sense in which, for example, the slaughter of over 8,000 Bosnian Muslim men in Srebrenica in 1995 was not. In Bosnia, women and girls, around 16,000, were escorted to Tuzla by Bosnian Serbs.[2] In Rwanda, women and children were all killed in an attempt to destroy any possibility of Tutsi survival.

However, the Rwandan genocide differs from the others, firstly, in that it was carried out for the most part by ordinary people – peasant farmers mainly – rather than by a specialised military force. According to one statistic, the number of perpetrators was between 175,000 and 210,000, almost 7 per cent of the Hutu population and 15 per cent of active male Hutus.[3] In 1998, 4,500 children aged between 14 and 18 and 1,200 women were imprisoned in Rwanda for participation in genocide.[4] As the final report of the Kigali conference noted: 'The massive participation of the population in the Rwandan genocide is virtually without historical precedent.'[5] The genocide of the Native Americans was also partly carried out by ordinary people – the settlers – but large numbers were murdered by the military. And, of course, the settlers weren't exactly 'ordinary' in that they were aggressive colonists armed to the teeth.

Secondly, in the case of Rwanda, the victims were not a traditionally downtrodden group but one that had been privileged even before European colonialism imposed its rule on the country – first the Germans in 1897, followed by the Belgians in 1916. There was a long history of Tutsi collaboration in Hutu oppression predating the colonial era.

Pre-Colonial Period

Nineteenth-century European explorers of Rwanda and Burundi discovered a society divided into three groups, each with its own characteristic physical appearance and economic role: the Twa (1 per cent of the population) were pygmoids who were hunter-gatherers or else were servants of the elite and the king; the Hutu, who constituted the vast majority and had a traditional Bantu appearance, were peasants who cultivated the soil; and the Tutsi, some 15 per cent of the population, who differed sharply from the others in physical appearance, being tall and thin and displaying sharp, angular facial features and who were cattle-herders. This suggests the possibility that the groups had different geographical origins. However, these physical and economic differences were overridden by what the groups had in common – language, religion and territory – bolstered by living together as neighbours and through much intermarriage.[6] Moreover, the sometimes claimed identification of Hutus with farming and Tutsis with herding is questionable. In the past, Tutsis had worked the land and Hutus had tended cattle. These were not roles fulfilled by these groups from time immemorial, as though biologically determined, but historical artefacts, political constructions created by state power. In fact, the modern division of labour was a socio-economic feature that predated colonialism. In this context, we need to understand the nature of the two identities. Since they shared a common community, were part of the same cultural group, what is the basis of their socio-political differentiation? Mamdani suggests there are three kinds of identity – market-based, cultural and political. The difference between Hutus and Tutsis can surely best be conceived as one of political identity, a distinction created and sustained, at first, by the pre-colonial state, but taken over and strengthened by colonialism.[7]

The pre-colonial state of Rwanda seems to have emerged from the amalgamation of several independent chiefdoms into a single, unified kingdom, under the leadership of a royal clan.[8] In pre-colonial Rwanda, as the early Europeans found it in the second half of the nineteenth century, kingship was at the 'apex of a complex pyramid of political, cultural and economic relationships'.[9] Under the king were three types of chiefs: one dealing with the allocation of landholdings, another responsible for recruiting men, in particular for the army, and the third in charge of grazing land. The majority of chiefs were Tutsis.[10] It has been said that the pre-colonial Rwandan state had a distinctive ideological characteristic – it combined Hutu 'supernatural' power with Tutu military power.[11] Going back two centuries or so prior to colonisation, there was already a process of social and political polarisation between the Hutus and Tutsis. Three institutional and social changes help us to understand how this developed.[12] First, important advisors of the king, absorbed into the court from leading Hutu lineages, and known as ritualists (abiiru), saw their authority weaken by the end of the nineteenth century. Secondly, important changes occurred in the distinctive patron–client relationship, eliminating reciprocity in exchanges between a Hutu client, individual or lineage, and their Tutsi landowning patron. This exposed the Hutus to harsher forms of exploitation, enabling the Tutsi landowners to arbitrarily confiscate cattle, and remove their Hutu clients' landowning rights, subjecting them to intensifying discipline and reducing them to serf-like status.

While the decline of the Hutu ritualists and the strengthening of the Tutsi patrons at the expense of their Hutu clients deepened the polarisation, certain counter-tendencies mitigated it. Although in earlier times only Tutsis were recruited for military service, by the end of the nineteenth century every Rwandan male was affiliated to the army. To the limited extent that the state was able to mould Rwandans into a single people, the army became the melting-pot for this. War became a social cement, in which the three groups, though unequal, were united as 'Baryarwanda' facing a common enemy. In addition, the state operated through two parallel hierarchies, that of the smallest administrative unit headed by the hill and army chiefs, and that of the district level headed by the cattle and land chiefs. While these existed, Hutu peasants were able to play off one set of officials against another. In the pre-colonial period, there were also many Hutus and Twas at the lower administrative levels, a factor that changed radically under colonialism. Overall, however, the changes in the pre-colonial period resulted in the 'centralisation of state power and a reorganisation of society along hierarchically exploitative lines'.[13]

Colonialism

Rwanda was governed by Germany from around 1897 until 1916, when Belgian forces took over and imposed their rule until independence in 1962. German rule was indirect, giving considerable leeway to the existing monarchy, allowing it to pursue its policies of centralisation, annexation of the Hutu principalities and growth in the power of Tutsi chiefs. Belgian policy, after a few indecisive years, was to have a far more transformative effect on the social fabric, though its main thrust was to deepen and solidify tendencies already laid down by pre-colonial and German rule. The most important element was the strengthening of the power and status of Tutsi chiefs and the parallel downgrading of the Hutu ones, many of whom were replaced by Tutsis. According to Prunier, towards the end of Belgian rule, in 1959, 43 chiefs out of 45 were Tutsi, as well as 549 out of 559 sub-chiefs.[14]

The principal period of far-reaching Belgian impact was between 1926 and 1931, when the 'Voisin' reforms were carried out, named after governor Charles Voisin. Under the traditional system, there were three types of chief on any hill – of whom one, Chief of the Land, was often a Hutu. In 1929, these three roles were fused into one, virtually always allocated to a Tutsi. Hence the Hutu peasants, who, as we saw, had previously been able to play one chief off against another, found themselves controlled by a single chiefly authority, and one whose support by the colonial regime had become far more rigorous than the vague backing the traditional chiefs had received from the royal court.

Moreover, the Belgians introduced, or spread and reshaped, the hated ubuletwa or forced-labour system. This was justified by the alleged need to 'rationalise' taxes and the 'public interest work' carried out by the indigenous population. The function of ubuletwa was also changed: where previously the royal chief had dealt with entire lineages on a hill, that is, a collective, the colonial administration now regarded it as an individual duty. Every individual, including children, had to perform the corvée. Moreover, Tutsi chiefs felt emboldened by official Belgian backing to shift traditional land rights in their favour. One example was ubukonde – the granting of land held by a clan to clients for agricultural purposes. Belgian legislation enabled Tutsi chiefs to take over Hutu landholdings in the northwest and southwest. In addition to legislation, there was the creeping privatisation, as the Belgian regime encouraged Western capitalist firms to penetrate the ancient economic fabric, a policy that allowed Tutsis close to the citadel of power to benefit. Finally, there was the transformation of *ubuhake* contracts from a complex institution that often provided support to clients from patrons – for example, a patron ceding the use of a cow to a client – to one involving arbitrary forms of exploitation including 'possible confiscation of any personal cattle at the pleasure of the patron'. It was deeply resented by Hutus who were aware of the Belgian authorities' sponsorship of *ubuhake* and regarded it as a foreign imposition.

The Belgian reforms effected a radical transformation of Rwandan society, a strengthening of the grip of the colonial regime in pursuit of its economic and political interests. One important result of this, starting in 1927, was a widespread movement of conversion to Catholicism, especially among the privileged Tutsis who saw it as a means of consolidating their position as lieutenants of colonialism. As Prunier describes it: 'A necessary prerequisite for membership of the elite of the new Rwanda the Belgians were creating was to become a Christian.'[15] The Church was happy to fulfil this role of hosting the rich and powerful, having previously acted as a sort of European *ubuhake* or patron supporting the poor, downtrodden clients – *abagaragu* – who looked up to the missionaries for protection.[16]

Before 1927, the Church did not have deep roots in Rwandan society, but by 1932, at the end of the period of reforms, it had become a major institution in the colonial structure, counting hundreds of thousands of converts, including the king. The Church performed its traditional role of ideological prop to the colonial regime, impacting on many aspects of society. It imposed on African life a strong moralistic ethic, condemning adultery and polygamy as sinful, and extolling capitalist, indeed, traditionally 'Protestant', virtues such as thrift and hard work. The Church also monopolised the education system. Since it was fee-paying, its coverage of the population was limited, so that illiteracy remained high. The Church ensured that the Tutsis, as the 'natural-born' elite, had priority, as a means of perpetuating clerical control over future chiefs.

An important cultural effect of Belgian colonialism was the disappearance of the *kubandwa* cult. Apart from war, the other pre-colonial 'social cement' was religion, in particular, *kubandwa*. This term is the passive form of the verb 'to grab' or 'put pressure on'. 'So the faithful, the *imandwa*, were literally "the ones who are grabbed". They were grabbed by *Ryangombe*, the Lord of the Spirits.'[17] *Kubandwa* fostered social cohesion because it was home-grown and trans-ethnic, recruiting adherents from all three sections of society. In contrast, Christianity, though also trans-ethnic, was clearly Tutsi-dominated and foreign.[18] In sum, Catholicism spread a blanket of conservatism over Rwandan society, providing most Tutsis with a career-ladder while inculcating obedience and conformity into poor Tutsis and the Hutu majority. However, the conversion process didn't happen overnight. The royal court and the majority of chiefs resisted until 1930, prompting the colonial state to use strong-arm methods when persuasion failed. Chiefs who refused to convert were branded 'sorcerers, diviners and superstitious and were deposed'.[19] In 1930, when *Mwami* (king) Musinga refused to convert, the Belgians regarded this as a threat to their colonial rule and deposed him, sending him into exile in Congo.

Another crucial ideological factor in consolidating Belgian rule was the racialisation of the Tutsi/Hutu divide. Whereas before colonialism, Tutsis had power and privilege, and occupied the apex of the status hierarchy, they were nevertheless regarded as being of the same racial stock, the differences between them being social and political. Colonialism introduced the notion of race, defined both biologically and historically. Late nineteenth-century race theory created, in Mamdani's words, a 'marker dividing humanity into a few superhuman and the rest less than human, the former civilised, the latter putty for a civilisational project'.[20] We have seen in earlier chapters how this bipolar division of humanity provided the rationale for the destruction of entire peoples.

The European powers that colonised Africa created the myth that ruling native groups were of foreign origin and therefore superior to the mass of 'ordinary' local natives, and that this superiority was due to racial difference. The Tutsis were said to be Hamites, descendants of Noah's son Ham, who thus emanated originally from the Middle East. They were black, but otherwise of Caucasian stock, whereas the Hutu were 'constructed as indigenous Bantu'.[21] This is known as the Hamitic hypothesis.[22] 'In colonial Rwanda, there were no ethnic groups, only races.'[23] In 1960, the Public Relations Office in Belgium spoke of the inhabitants of Rwanda as belonging to 'two main racial groups: the Tutsi feudal stock-breeders, comprising 14 per cent of the population and the Hutu farmers, amounting to 85 per cent'.[24] Indeed, after the 1933 census, colonial legislation imposed a new layer of legal identity on the pre-existing political identities of 'Hutu' and 'Tutsi'. This meant that even poor Tutsis were privileged, exempt from the onerous duty of forced labour. As Mamdani says: 'to be a Tutsi was to have a privileged relationship to power, to be treated preferentially, whether as part of power, in proximity to power or simply to be identified with power'.[25]

In sum, the Belgian reforms of 1926–31 created a centralised colonial state – efficient and Catholic, but also brutal. Between 1920 and 1940, the burden of taxation and forced labour weighing down on the native population became increasingly onerous. Men were constantly mobilised to build permanent structures, to dig anti-erosion terraces, or to grow crops such as coffee for export, or maniocs and sweet potatoes as a back-up food supply. 'These various activities could swallow up to 50–60 per cent of a man's time. Those who did not comply were abused and brutally beaten.'[26]

It is true that the Belgians issued decrees stating that in any conflict between farmers and herders, the state would support the former, that is, the Hutu cultivators as opposed to the Tutsi pastoralists. A subsequent decree compelled the *mwami* to double the size of the arable land available to Hutu families. However, in spite of reforms apparently favouring Hutu agriculture against Tutsi cattle-rearing, 'the Hutu peasantry experienced Belgian rule as harsher than any previous regime in living memory'.[27] There were two reasons. Firstly, the reorganisation of state, especially local administration, resulted, as we have seen, in the creation of a single hierarchy of local chiefs, the vast majority of whom were Tutsis. Secondly, the Belgian authorities took over the institution of 'customary law' but gave it a far more despotic interpretation: any use of force by an existing authority was regarded as 'customary' and therefore legitimate.

Nevertheless, a Hutu 'counter-elite' did develop out of three sources: firstly, the pre-colonial elite in the northern non-Rwandan principalities forcibly incorporated into the Rwandan state and subordinated into a Hutu status by the alliance of the German authorities and the Rwandan *mwami*. Secondly, the labour market in adjacent Congo and Uganda provided escape-routes for Hutu peasants fleeing from the servitude imposed by the Tutsi-Belgian association. Many of the migrants returning to Rwanda became leaders of the protest movement that arose in the first post-war decade.[28] Thirdly, schooling was provided by an alliance of missionaries and the colonial state, allowing a small number of Hutus into education. However, it reproduced the social and political divisions between Tutsis and Hutus through a two-tier system, Tutsi students benefiting from a 'civilised' French education with Hutu children restricted to an inferior 'nativised' Kiswahili schooling.

As Mamdani points out, it was a taste of reform, not its absence, that convinced most Hutus that nothing short of radical social and political change would end their subordination. Despite a small increase in access to education, Hutu graduates entering the job market in the mid 1950s discovered that jobs in the civil service and private sector remained a Tutsi preserve. They turned to the Church as the sole institutional outlet that would grant them opportunities, not just to work but also to articulate their main grievance: 'the institutionalised exclusion of Hutus from a Belgian-supported Tutsi monopoly over all avenues of social advancement'.[29] This was an important factor in the 1959 upheaval.

The Social Revolution of 1959: The Hutu Republic

Reforms were attempted in the post-war period but they were insubstantial and did nothing to alter the overwhelming balance of power and privilege in favour of the Tutsis. In 1956, the final opportunity for reform from above was squandered when the *mwami* supported a Tutsi move to defeat a proposal to provide separate representation for Hutus on the Conseil Superieur, the highest advisory body of the state. Moreover, the 1956 elections set out a two-tier system of elections: an all-male universal suffrage at the lowest administrative level, and indirect elections to the higher councils through electoral colleges, whose members were nominated by the chiefs. The result was predictable: a victory for the Hutu majority at the lower levels combined with a consolidation of Tutsi power at the top. It is true that in 1949 *ubuletwa* (forced labour) was abolished and in 1954 *ubuhake* (client-patron) ties were dissolved. However, given the absence of a land reform redistributing pasture land owned by Tutsis, Hutu owners of cattle remained dependent on their patrons for access to grazing land. In general, the failure of the state to introduce serious reforms over the decade of the 1950s 'convinced the Hutu political elite that nothing short of political power would crack the Tutsi hold on social, economic, and cultural resources'.[30]

Hutus were becoming increasingly restive, anxious to achieve social justice and equality, their resentment and aspirations fanned by the anti-colonialism and pan-Africanism sweeping across Africa in the 1950s and early 1960s. There were two approaches to the issue of independence. Indeed, the UN decolonisation mission of 1957 was greeted by two rival documents. One, *Mise au Point*, called for a rapid transfer of power to the king and his High Council (the Conseil Superieur), arguing that this would end racial tensions between blacks and whites. This document enshrined the Tutsi elite programme, a demand for independence first, with the retention of traditional prerogatives. The second, the *Bahutu Manifesto*, called for a double liberation of the 'Hutu from both the "Hamites" [i.e., foreign-Tutsi] and "Bazungu" (whites) colonisation'.[31] The demand of the Hutu counter-elite was thus democracy before independence, stressing that they represented the interests of the indigenous majority. So, two opposed brands of nationalism were pitted against each other: a Hutu-initiated popular nationalism from below and a Tutsi-sponsored nationalism from above.

The tendency one can informally describe as 'Hutu power' thus emerged in the late 1950s (in contrast to the formal Hutu Power of the civil war of the early 1990s) as the objective of the Hutu nationalists. Its ideological basis was the carrying out of the 'Hutu Revolution', the belief that the Rwandan nation is Hutu and that power in an independent Rwanda must therefore also be Hutu. The Tutsi may live in Rwanda, but as an alien minority, 'at suffrance of the Hutu nation'.[32] At the same time, between 1959 and 1964, two tendencies emerged on both sides of the Hutu-Tutsi political divide: accommodationists and exclusionists, the former believing in the possibility of the two groups living together in a single community, the latter, containing the adherents of both Hutu power and Tutsi power, arguing the opposite. The year 1959 was ushered in with a sharp split between Hutu and Tutsi political leaders. The Hutu leader Kayibanda adopted an exclusionist position, calling for Hutu power and the removal of the Tutsi from political life. Facing a loss of political power, the Tutsi elite went into exile to prepare for an armed return to power.

Prunier describes the tension prevailing in late 1959, a powder-keg which any spark could have ignited. The one that did eventually cause it to explode was an attack on a Hutu sub-chief and activist of the PARMEHUTU (Party of the Movement and Emancipation of the Hutus) by young members of the Tutsi UNAR (Rwandese National Union). Created in August 1959, the UNAR was a conservative Tutsi party which supported the monarchy, but was hostile to Belgium and committed to immediate independence. The (false) news of Hutu sub-chief's death spread like wildfire, prompting Hutu activists to mobilise and attack Tutsi chiefs and UNAR members. Poor Tutsis were forced to align themselves with the rich Tutsis on the basis of 'racial' superiority, because the Hutus, sharing this perception, targeted them together with the chiefs.

The Belgian authorities felt betrayed by their Tutsi protégés' demand for independence and began to replace most of the Tutsi chiefs with Hutu ones. Some 300 Hutu chiefs and sub-chiefs replaced the Tutsi incumbents who had fled, or been deposed or killed, in a fast-developing 'peasant revolt'.[33] The new chiefs promptly embarked on the persecution of the Tutsis on the hills they controlled, triggering a mass exodus which drove some 300,000 abroad by late 1963. Despite the general insecurity, the Belgians organised communal elections in 1960, in which the overwhelming victor, with 70.4 per cent of the votes, was the PARMEHUTU centre-north Hutu party on a 70 per cent turn out. The offices of the chief were abolished and new authorities created – bourgmestres – or burgomasters, on the Belgian model. They ruled 229 communes, out of which only 19 were Tutsi and 160 PARMEHUTU. The new Hutu burgomasters had learned from their Tutsi predecessors: they recreated the old 'feudal' client-patron ties, replacing Tutsi patrons with equally oppressive Hutu ones. In short, what has come to be portrayed as a 'social revolution' was, according to Prunier, an 'ethnic transfer of power'.

> Under the banner of 'democratic majority rule' on the one side, and 'immediate independence' on the other, it was a fight between two competing elites, the newly developed Hutu counter-elite produced by the church and the older neo-traditionalist Tutsi elite which the colonial authorities had promoted since the 1920s.[34]

However, Mamdani disputes Prunier's dismissal of the social revolution of 1959, arguing that, despite its limitations, it counted real achievements. The Hutu leaders made three claims about the 1959 revolution: first, that the shift in power from Tutsi to Hutu was a national achievement, transferring power from the alien Tutsis to the indigenous Hutus; second, that it was a victory for democracy, embodying a shift from minority to majority rule, but also creating new democratic institutions at both local and national levels; and third, that the revolution had carried out important reforms, such as abolishing *uburetwa* (forced labour) in 1959, as well as appropriating *igikinki*, land allocated by the king to the Tutsi elite as pasturage, and re-distributing it to landless Hutu peasants.[35]

The UN Trusteeship Commission was unhappy with these developments, influenced as it was by the Third World members of the UN. The latter, on colonial questions, were under the sway of the Eastern Communist bloc which in turn supported the Tutsi UNAR party since it seemed to them the one most opposed to Belgian, and therefore Western, capitalist interests.[36] The UN tried to persuade the Belgians to broker a reconciliation between Tutsis and Hutus, but this failed. So in January 1961, to prevent further UN interference, Kayibanda, the PARMEHUTU leader, summoned 3,125 burgomasters and municipal councillors to an emergency meeting at which they declared Rwandan independence. There was further violence, resulting in some 150 Tutsis being killed, and 3,000 houses burnt down, with new waves of refugees fleeing to Uganda. In September 1961, legislative elections were held, as a result of which PARMEHUTU received 78 per cent of the vote and UNAR 17 per cent.[37]

Beginning in late 1960, commando groups of Tutsi exiles, called *inyenzi* (cockroaches) by the Hutu, began carrying out cross-border raids from Uganda. The Tutsi exiles were organising for a military revival. However, they were riven by personal animosities, political differences, and by disagreements over tactics and over their attitude to the new Hutu regime. In May 1962, one group of exiles decided to support the new government, while another opted for military confrontation launched from different countries of exile. There were different outcomes depending on the country. With Burundi hosting some 50,000 exiles, it soon became the main base for surprise attacks on the Rwandan

Hutu government. Another, somewhat desperate, offensive was undertaken in December 1963, but being badly planned and lacking proper equipment it was beaten back by the government, who in turn launched a brutal wave of repression in which some 10,000 Tutsis were murdered. The truth was that the Tutsi exiles had become increasingly remote from the reality of Rwandan society, so that by 1964, as Prunier puts it, 'exile politics was dead'.[38]

The main result of the *inyenzi* attacks was to strengthen the position of President Kayibanda. Indeed, he adopted the same style of leadership as the former *mwami* – remote and authoritarian. From the time of the Tutsi *inyenzi* attacks of 1963–4, the Hutu Republic distinguished clearly between external and internal Tutsis. The former were regarded as a political diaspora bent on overthrowing the Hutu state, and were therefore treated as dangerous outsiders. The latter were tolerated as 'semi-citizens' with civic but not political rights, that is, they enjoyed rights within civil society but were barred from playing any role in Rwanda's political institutions. Underpinning this division was an inversion of the former colonial ideology: in pre-independence Rwanda, Tutsi domination had been seen as 'grandiose and powerful'; under the post-1959 dispensation, the Tutsis remained 'foreign invaders' whose rule had been harsh and tyrannical, while the Hutus had been the 'indigenous peasants' enslaved by them. But now the Hutus were Rwanda's only rightful inhabitants, the silent majority whose rule represented the sole democratic legitimacy.

There was a symmetry between the old and the new versions of the ideology. According to the 'neo-traditionalist' version that prevailed from 1931 to 1959, the poor (*petits*) Tutsi shared in the sense of racial superiority, of belonging to an 'ethnic aristocracy' despite their poverty, whereas after 1959, the poor Hutu acquired that sense of pride and privilege simply because it was 'their' Hutu government that ruled. In both cases, the respective elites encouraged their people to participate in the delusion. The thread linking the two versions was the Catholic Church: at first it had upheld Tutsi rule, but after 1959 transferred its allegiance to the Hutus. However, as late as 1973, seminaries remained havens of Tutsi supremacy and, with the educational system still largely under Church control, the Tutsi domination of education remained intact. Indeed, many Hutus left the seminaries to join an under-staffed state administration.[39]

Ironically, the Kayibanda regime had come in for criticism over its failure to do more to advance the educational and employment opportunities of Hutus. Many Hutu school leavers, lacking the resources to attend college or even secondary school, wandered the streets in search of work. Even graduates were unable to find employment. This created a pool of disaffected youth nursing a keen sense of grievance, and available for manipulation by unscrupulous politicians.

In education, the criticism focused on the government failure to remedy the under-representation of Hutus – while Hutus were a majority in the schools, university students in the middle and late 1960s were 90 per cent Tutsi, despite official government policy restricting them to 10 per cent of enrolment. So, given Belgian discrimination in favour of Tutsis, in education they occupied far more than their allotted share. The result of the youth agitation was the law of August 1966 which established state control of education. In February 1973, Hutu students, frustrated at the lack of opportunities arising out of their revolution, expelled Tutsi professors and priests from the colleges and seminaries. Other Tutsi priests fled. By now, the Hutu clergy had refused to remain marginalised in their own church.[40] Nevertheless: 'While Hutu came to occupy the top echelons of the Church hierarchy, its middle level continued to include a substantial number of Tutsi.' Indeed, although the Church had become Hutu-dominated, it remained more open, and 'a measure of institutional inequality existed among the clergy; in the 1980s, three of the eight bishops were Tutsi'.[41]

When it came to employment, the government was deemed to have performed even worse. Since independence, Rwanda had followed a policy of ethnic quotas. As in education, Tutsis, forming 15 per cent of the population, were not supposed to take up more than 9 per cent of civil service posts, or other employment opportunities. Given the absence of any policy governing fair Hutu representation in employment, even a small increase in Hutu school or college enrolment resulted in a swelling of the ranks of unemployed school leavers or graduates. It was this discontented, alienated group that sparked the crisis that led to the coup of 1973. However, this event occurred in a wider context: the massacre of some 200,000 young Hutus by the largely Tutsi army in neighbouring Burundi in May–June 1972.[42]

In response to the violence in Burundi, the Kayibanda regime felt Tutsi over-representation was an issue it could exploit to boost its popularity. Vigilante committees were organised between October 1972 and February 1973 to scrutinise schools, the university, the civil service and even private businesses to cleanse these institutions of Tutsis wherever they were found to be exceeding their quota. But the tactic backfired, one reason being the tension between northern and southern Hutu politicians which led to the respective vigilante groups operating in different ways. For example, in the hills, peasants embarked on personal score-settling with authority figures, irrespective of their ethnic status.

As the turmoil deepened, wider issues came to the fore. The government seemed paralysed, and their stagnation brought to the surface hitherto buried conflicts within both the state and society – the former expressing itself as a fight between the northern and southern Hutu elites, the latter as one between rich and poor. The people were broadening the attack on the Tutsis into an attack on the rich. General Habyarimana's coup was welcomed on all sides, particularly among the urban population: students, business people, state officials, Hutus and Tutsis. 'Thus was born the Second Republic, which immediately declared itself the custodian of the revolution and the protector of all its children, Hutu as well as Tutsi.'[43]

The Second Republic

The new regime claimed to be completing the 'national revolution' of 1959 through a 'moral revolution'. A key ideological change was the re-definition of the Tutsi political identity from a race to an ethnic group. This meant that they were no longer foreigners but a group indigenous to Rwanda with the right to stay. The practical consequence of this was the lifting of the barrier confining them to the civic sphere and their admittance into the political sphere, albeit within limits proportionate to their minority status. However, given their history as a privileged minority, the Tutsis faced discrimination in the civic arena too, their participation in both civic and political life thus subject to state regulation. The new regime attempted to construct a balance between two hitherto opposed objectives: reconciliation with the Tutsis and justice for the Hutus, especially those in the under-privileged north, a redress to be achieved through a redistribution of opportunities within Tutsi-dominated institutions – the Church, education and employment.[44]

Throughout Habyarimana's rule, Tutsis remained politically marginalised: there was not one Tutsi burgomaster or prefect, with only one Tutsi officer in the army, two Tutsi members of parliament out of 70, and only one Tutsi minister in a cabinet of 25 to 30 members. In general, the Tutsis, fearing official discrimination in the public sector, preferred to work in the private sector. We can see how significant the Second Republic was if we consider that between 1973 and the Rwandan Patriotic Front (RPF) invasion of 1990, there was no political violence against the Tutsis. They were excluded from institutional life, but, insofar as they accepted that, were left in peace and able to prosper. They enjoyed civil and political rights but had to abandon all thought of participation in power, including local power and the army, which had to remain the preserve of the Hutus as the statutorily defined majority.

However, as under the First Republic, it seems that the quota system had its limitations, and there is no consensus as to the rigour of its enforcement. On the one hand, it seems that the proportion of Tutsis in public and private sector employment greatly exceeded the quotas; on the other, members of the predominantly Tutsi business community complained in 1977 that the regime accorded too much weight to regional and ethnic criteria at the expense of merit. But Habyarimana insisted on retaining quotas. The year 1980 witnessed a plot against the regime led by the violently anti-Tutsi former security chief Lizinde, unhappy at the policy of reconciliation with the Tutsis. Habyarimana used the coup as an opportunity to liquidate the southern opposition while continuing to seek reconciliation between Hutu and Tutsi.

Habyarimana was able to establish stability in Rwanda, though at a price: a year after seizing power, he banned all political parties, but in 1974 created his own, the MRND (*Mouvement Révolutionnaire National pour le Développement*). This was a totalitarian organisation, the tightest in the non-communist world, which all citizens were compelled to join, and from which all political appointments were made. Prunier describes it as 'benevolent despotism'. However, on the other side of this 'benevolence' were elements of a police state: 'the party was everywhere, every hill had its cell, and party faithfuls, hoping for promotion … willingly spied on anybody they were told to spy on and a few others as well'.[45]

Poverty and Progress

A major reason put forward by Habyarimana to justify his benevolent despotism was the extent to which Rwanda, throughout its early post-independence years, remained racked by poverty. There was a shortage of arable land but an annual population increase of 3.7 per cent. In 1962, there were only two countries with a lower *per capita* income than Rwanda. However, development did take place, and by 1987, there were 18, and with a *per capita* income of US$ 300, Rwanda was comparable with China (US$ 310).[46] At the heart of this progress was the dramatic increase in agricultural production during the first two decades of independence. Between the early 1960s and the early 1980s, Rwanda was one of three sub-Saharan countries to raise its per capita food production. By the mid 1980s, the population was five times the average of the colonial period – over 8 million compared to between 1 and 2 million. But it was better nourished and had been famine-free for 30 years. The main reason for this was the expansion of the crop area. One result of the 1959 revolution had been the abolition of the 'customary' control by Tutsi chiefs over extensive land areas, especially the *igikinki* areas assigned by the king to these chiefs as pasture for cattle. This in turn facilitated two developments: first, large numbers of landless peasants were brought in from the hills to settle in the drier areas; second, fertile but swampy land was drained and made cultivable.[47] Other effects of Rwanda's development were that while primary activities (subsistence agriculture) accounted for 80 per cent of GNP in 1962, this had fallen to 48 per cent by 1986, whereas secondary activities rose from 8 per cent to 21 per cent, and services from 12 per cent to 31 per cent. The proportion of children at school rose 49.5 per cent in 1978 to 61.8 per cent in 1986, despite the rapid population increase. This was a remarkable achievement, especially in the light of the 17 years of famine between 1900 and 1950.[48]

However, towards the late 1980s, economic progress went into reverse. Around 1986, the world prices of Rwanda's two main exports, coffee and tin, collapsed, severely affecting the country's political stability. And in 1989, the state budget was reduced by 40 per cent, intensifying discontent amongst a peasantry already weighed down with heavy taxes and increasing bouts of 'voluntary' *umuganda* ('cooperative, communal labour') which seemed in reality like forced labour.[49] Intended for public projects such as planting forests, constructing terraces to combat erosion, and bridge-building, such 'corvée' was especially galling when performed on lands owned by regime henchmen. The peasants were also concerned about the availability of land dwindling through overpopulation, and causing a steady decrease in a food supply increasingly dependent on the weather. As regards food production, the World Bank was now describing Rwanda as one of the three worst performing sub-Saharan countries. The scandal surrounding the World Bank-funded Gebeka project epitomised the regime's growing crisis. Gishwati forest, one of Rwanda's last major forests, was logged to create fields for cattle-grazing. Although both the land and the funds were public, profits from the scheme were pocketed by powerful regime figures and World Bank expatriates who had invested in the development. It was a major blow to the ideals of the 1959 revolution, in particular the promise to Hutu farmers to make land and cattle available. This economic unravelling led in 1990 to the imposition by the IMF of their notorious Structural Adjustment Programme which, in turn, caused a sharp devaluation of the Rwandan currency.[50]

Mamdani argues, however, that the crisis that gripped Rwanda in the 1990s was political rather than economic. The demands of the Hutu-led movement for independence focused on representation and justice. But they were also the basis of the post-independence critique of Rwandan society. As often occurred in post-revolutionary states, there was a growing disjuncture between ideals and reality. Mamdani distinguishes between an internal and an external critique of the independent Republic: the former emerged from within the regime, whereas the latter emanated from the ranks of Tutsi exiles, mainly in Ugunda.[51]

The internal critique, he argues, had three sources – the ruling party, a 'mushrooming' of civil society organisations, and various political parties. It came in two phases, beginning with student protests during the First Republic focused around the criticism that the revolution had been confined to the political sphere, leaving Tutsi privilege largely in place and failing to address Hutu social and economic grievances. Following the 1973 coup, this critique led to further coup attempts by members of Habyarimana's government, who alleged that the redefinition of the Tutsis as an ethnicity rather than a race and the attempt to integrate them meant the regime was pro-Tutsi.

Whereas the first phase of criticism concentrated on representation for Hutus and was anti-Tutsi in character, the second centred on the issue of justice. Here, the grievance was that the beneficiaries of the revolution were a small Hutu elite. The first phase had united the Hutus in opposition to the Tutsis, demanding the right to appropriate their political privileges and economic benefits. The second dissolved the earlier Hutu unity, pitting underprivileged northerners against privileged southerners, poor against rich, in a class movement aimed at a redistribution of wealth and power between different sections of Hutus.

The Tutsi Diaspora

Some half a million Tutis refugees lived outside Rwanda in the region of the Great Lakes. UNHCR figures of those living in exile are: Burundi (266,000), Uganda (82,000), Tanzania (22,000) and Zaire (13,000).[52] However, the actual figures of Tutsi refugees in Uganda were estimated in 1990 at 200,000 though only 82,000 had registered as refugees.[53] These left post-revolutionary Rwanda in three waves to escape government-inspired massacres. Rough figures of Tutsis murdered are 1,000 in 1959–61, 20,000 in 1963–4, 2,000 to 10,000 in 1990–3, and on a smaller scale in 1973.[54]

For Mamdani, the greatest failure of the Second Republic was its inability to re-integrate the Tutsi diaspora. This was largely because doing so would have been to acknowledge that Rwanda was not just the state of the Hutus, and that the Tutsis were as integral to the Rwandan political community as the Hutus. Habyarimana may have brought the internal Tutsis in from the cold of their identity as 'racial outsiders', and provided them with a new 'ethnic home' by re-identifying them as an indigenous ethnicity, but he could not, or would not, extend the same benefit to the Tutsi diaspora. These remained 'ethnic strangers', without an ethnic home, comparable to the Jews of pre-war Europe. Of course, the comparison is limited, as the Jews had been merchant wanderers for nearly 2,000 years, whereas the Tutsis had been exiles only since 1959.

Prelude to Civil War

The invasion of Rwanda by the RPF in October 1990 was, arguably, as much the product of regional developments, specifically the Ugandan context, as of internal Rwandan events. At the heart of the crisis was the definition of citizenship that was the legacy of the post-colonial era. The concept of 'ethnic indigeneity' became central to this definition, and in Uganda this led to the expulsion of those ethnic groups deemed non-indigenous – the Ugandan Asians in 1972, for example, and the Banyarwanda (those who come from Rwanda) in 1982–3.[55] The Tutsi exiles of 1959 allied themselves to the Ugandans, becoming the spearhead of the joint National Resistance Army (NRA) that overthrew Milton Obote's repressive regime in 1986. The political refugees went on to challenge the system by which each group had its own separate 'customary laws' that defined it as an ethnicity, enforced by its own Native Authority administering its own 'home area'. The idea was to legally de-racialise 'the native', sub-dividing the broad categories of 'race' and 'native' into separate ethnicised groups.[56]

However, for the Tutsi exiles, the limits of the Habyarimana reform drove them to seek a new legal basis for permanent residence within Uganda. Initially, they achieved this through a campaign that succeeded in persuading the Museveni government to change the legal basis of citizenship from two generations to ten years of residence. However, Museveni responded to his first major political crisis by moving to reverse this reform. Threatened with being recast as exiles, the Tutsi guerrilla fighters in the NRA risked being caught in 'the closing scissors of a postcolonial citizenship crisis in Rwanda and Uganda'.[57] The RPF invasion of October 1990 thus also needs to be understood as 'an armed repatriation of Banyarwanda refugees from Uganda to Rwanda'.[58]

Three factors encouraged the leaders of the Tutsi exile community in Uganda, organised by the RPF, to accelerate their plans to invade Rwanda. First, Habyarimana's Hutu regime was in the throes of a deep crisis. Second, it was planning to allow sections of the Tutsi Ugandan exiles to return. This was bad news for the Tutsi militants bent on invasion since it threatened to undermine their support among the refugees if the latter discovered there was a chance of repatriation without conflict. Third, a movement among Rwandan Hutu intellectuals was calling for the democratisation of the regime, and Habyarimana was on the point of introducing a multi-party system. This threatened to deprive the RPF of a key propaganda point – that it was fighting a despotic single-party Hutu regime. Quite possibly, Habyarimana's decision to allow many Tutsi exiles to return from Uganda was influenced by the knowledge that they had created a significant armed force.

Civil War – Hutu Power

A key political feature of the early 1990s was the transformation of 'Hutu Power' from fringe to mainstream ideology. It enables us to trace the descent of Rwanda from the hope of colonial independence to the hell of civil war and genocide. The slogan of the 1959 revolution and the First Republic under Kayibanda was 'Hutu Nation'. The Second Republic under Habyarimana promised reconciliation between Hutus and Tutsis. The 1990 invasion raised the spectre, frightening to the majority of Hutus, of a return to Tutsi power. Foreign Minister Bizimungu accused the RPF invaders of wanting to bring back 'forced labour and feudal servitude'. And the more successful the RPF were on the battlefield, the more this fear took hold of ordinary Hutus. The increasing appeal of Hutu Power propaganda was the direct consequence of the fear that a new RPF regime would indeed appropriate Hutu peasant lands and return them to the Tutsis expropriated after 1959. The fear intensified as the RPF army drew closer. Did peasants flee from their land as the RPF approached because of government exhortation? It seems they did so both because of their fear of the RPF and because the government advised them to. Speaking about the Rwanda of the late 1980s, the Newburys remarked on 'the extraordinary degree to which the revolution of a generation before seemed almost to have been removed from the collective historical consciousness'.[59]

Moreover, the more credible Hutu Power propagandists sounded to the Hutu masses, the more they turned the Tutsi minority into a hostage population. The converse applied too: Hutus in RPF-held territory became hostages. While there is no evidence that the RPF perpetrated mass killings of Hutu civilians, they did carry out widespread displacement of Hutu peasants, resorting to pillage and forced labour. It seems that the object was to pressure the government to make concessions, while the Hutus attempted to achieve a similar goal through massacres of Tutsi civilians, the first since 1964. Some 3,000 were murdered in four massacres between 1990 and 1993, the first two as a response to RPF attacks, the third carried out by death squads directed by the security service, and the fourth in the wake of a signing of a power-sharing protocol at the Arusha conference in January 1993, aimed at those who supported the call to share power. Each pogrom was timed to follow either a turning-point in the civil war or the accompanying negotiations.[60] Behind the pogroms were, arguably, not central government itself, but Hutu Power elements within government with links to local officials around the country. 'While initiated from the centre, every massacre was executed locally.'[61] It seems also that there was an effort to use the 'customary' as opposed to the 'civic' power of the state, the former referring to the obligations of those *indigenous* to the land as opposed to the rights of those *resident* on the land. The 'customary' rules included obligations on the community, so that local officials were instructed to kill Tutsis as part of their communal work obligations (*umuganda*). This 'customary' ideology was the one most suited to the genocidal aims of the Hutu Power extremists. 'With clearing the land of those branded alien considered a "customary" obligation, the genocide would ultimately be branded a community project.'[62] As we have seen, the RPF invasion of Rwanda turned Hutu Power from a marginal tendency into a key political player. As the prospect of defeat loomed ever larger, Hutu Power entered its most serious crisis. Its response was to spawn the genocidal tendency.

Genocide

In the space of 13 weeks, beginning on 7 April 1994, around 800,000 Tutsis were slaughtered by their Hutu compatriots – a rate of at least 300 murders an hour. Seventy-five per cent of Tutsis living in Rwanda were exterminated, the largest genocide since the Nazi Holocaust, and the fastest. Possibly, also, the most complete of all time, with the exception of the Native Americans. The crucial context for the genocide – without which, arguably, it would not have occurred, and without which it cannot be understood – was the civil war. There are two factors here, first, the economic crisis which began before the war but which the latter greatly exacerbated, and second, the impact of the Hutu army's defeat at the hands of the RPF.

Rwanda's economic reversal after 1985 manifested itself firstly in a shortage of land: an increasing population was looking for cultivable land from a static pool. A USAID study of population growth and agricultural change in the country found that average farm holdings had shrunk by 12 per cent from 1984 to 1989.[63] Another study discovered that 57 per cent of rural households were already farming less than one hectare of land in 1984, while 25 per cent of these had less than half a hectare. Moreover, these shrinking plots of land had to feed an average family of five, at a time when food production, after 1985, went into decline. The problem was aggravated even further by the prevailing inheritance practice which required the family farm to be sub-divided among all the sons, thus fragmenting as well as diminishing the plot. The conclusion of the USAID report is that 'disputes over land are reported to have been a major motivation for Rwandans to denounce neighbours during the ethnic conflicts of 1994'.[64]

The Rwandan army expanded from 5,000 to more than 30,000 in the course of the years of civil war. In 1991, the Hutu government launched a programme to create local self-defence groups. However, by February 1993, the RPF had doubled the size of its captured territory, so the programme was extended from border communes to interior communes. In 1994, these local self-defence units, created in every village and commune, made up the core element of the apparatus of destruction that carried out the genocide. Four issues made up the explosive material that filled the powder-keg of genocide: the problem of day-to-day survival, the defeat of the Rwandan army, the volatility of the unemployed youth, and a new influx of Hutu refugees from Burundi.

The first issue meant that when the RPF attacked the most fertile farming areas in January and February 1993, the amount of produce reaching the markets fell by 15 per cent.[65] The second generated fear of a restoration of Tutsi power, and of what it would mean, as RPF military victories were followed by another group of peasants and civilians being 'flushed out of the "liberated" areas'. Hutu refugee camps mushroomed around the capital city, the numbers rising from 80,000 in late 1990 to 950,000 after the RPF offensive in February 1993. Around 350,000 were 'redisplaced', some for the fourth time.[66] The third issue resulted in unemployed youth being organised into armed militias, first by the ruling party – the Interahamwe – in 1992, followed by the extremist Hutu Power tendency CDR (Coalition pour la Défense de la République). Fourth, in October 1993 a wave of Hutu refugees fled to Rwanda from Burundi, escaping a slaughter carried out by the Tutsi-dominated army. There had been a massacre in 1972 of some 200,000 Hutus, and now, after the murder of the Hutu president, 200,000 Hutus fled. The impact of this was, in Mamdani's words, that 'power-sharing was just another name for political suicide. History had ruled out political coexistence between Hutu and Tutsi.'[67] The spark that ignited the powder-keg was the shooting-down of the plane carrying President Habyarimana on 6 April 1994. To this day, the identity of the perpetrators has remained a mystery, but suspicion has fallen on elements within the Hutu Power movement, MRND extremists seeking an excuse to launch a genocidal assault on the Tutsi population.

The Killers

Who were the killers? According to Mann, there were five levels of perpetrators of the 1994 genocide, in a descending order of authority and responsibility:

1. The Hutu MRND little house clan that seized power on 7 April 1994;
2. Other Hutu Power political factions that entered the post-coup regime;
3. Cooperating Hutu officials and army and police officers;
4. Cooperating Hutu local social elites;
5. Hutu paramilitaries;
6. A large number of ordinary Hutus.[68]

One institution that Mann omits is the Church. Mamdani describes it as one of the two prime movers, the other being the army. Of these two leading forces, one was located in society, the other in the state. Without these two, he argues, there would have been no genocide.[69] Rather than a sanctuary, a place of healing, the Church became 'a battleground for settling scores' and a mortuary.[70] Some 105 priests and 120 nuns, a quarter of the clergy, were murdered. But clergy were not only victims, some of them were also killers – around 12, according to the UN Centre for Human Rights. One Catholic father sheltered 8,000 refugees but provided the militia with the names of those who had expressed support for the RPF. And according to Mamdani, 'most major massacres of the genocide took place in churches'.[71] Indeed, the Church was not the only 'life-nurturing' institution whose members participated in the genocide: schools and hospitals also witnessed horrific murders:

> a huge number of the most qualified and experienced doctors ... men as well as women – including surgeons, physicians, paediatricians, gynaecologists, anaesthetists, public health specialists and hospital administrators – participated in the murder of Tutsi colleagues, patients, the wounded and terrified refugees who had sought shelter in their hospitals, as well as their neighbours and strangers.[72]

According to Prunier, there were differences between the capital and the provincial 'prefectures': in Kigali, the executions were organised centrally and proceeded rapidly. They began in the evening of 6 April, carried out by the Presidential Guard, some 1,500 strong, just hours after the downing of the president's plane. Within 36 hours, they had eliminated 'priority targets' – political opponents, including Hutu politicians, journalists and civil rights activists. They had also summoned help early on from the two militias or paramilitaries – the Interahamwe and Impuzamugambi. According to Prunier, they had been 'waiting for such a moment from the date of their conception'.[73] The genocide was carried out by an efficient centrally run killing machine. The killers received their orders from civil servants – prefects and burgomasters, and also councillors, at both central and local government levels. Having received orders from Kigali, they transmitted them on to the local Gendarmerie and Interahamwe, mobilising the peasants to participate in the killings and calling in the Forces Armées Rwandaises (FAR) army if Tutsi resistance became too strong.[74] This ties in with Mann's list of perpetrator categories cited above.

The militia, numbering some 50,000, roughly equal to the regular army, tended to recruit members from the 'lower class', though young middle-class people were also attracted to the camaraderie, material benefits and what they saw as a political ideal. But the later recruits, especially those who joined in the heat of battle, were raw, ill-disciplined youths, drunk for much of the time. Towards the end of the civil war, these paramilitaries descended into armed banditry as the administrative structure that had sustained and controlled them disintegrated. The speed and proficiency of the killings testified to the quality of the local administration. As Prunier argues: 'If the local administration had not carried out orders from the capital so blindly, many lives would have been saved.'[75] The vast majority 'carried out their murderous duties with attitudes varying from careerist eagerness to sullen obedience'.[76] Of course, their obedience was reinforced by the fact that they were members of the Hutu MRND(D) party: 'Habyarimana's single party later revamped by the addition of a second "democratic" D.'[77] We mentioned earlier Prunier's comparison of the Rwandan tradition of obedience and conformity to that of Prussia, 'with its ultimate perversion into the disciplined obedience to Nazi orders'.[78] As one perpetrator, Alphonse, told the French journalist Jean Hatzfeld: 'I do not believe our hearts detested the Tutsis. But it was inevitable to think so, since the decision was made by the organisers to kill them all.'[79]

However, Mamdani argues that none of the instruments used to perpetrate genocide were created for that end, but 'were turned to that purpose in the face of defeat in the civil war'.[80] The Presidential Guard had been created in 1992 to wage war, not genocide. The administrative ten-cell groups were meant to be civil defence units. The youth wings of the political parties were intended to promote participation in the process of political competition. And the structure of local administration was built as an aide to the process of colonial government. None of these institutions were intended as instruments of genocide, yet they became just that in the wake of impending defeat in the civil war.

The RPF invasion of 1990 created a dual fear and, therefore, a dual motivation among the future 'genocidaires' (genocidal killers): the Hutu middle class feared for the loss of their socio-economic and political power – the enormous gains of the 1959 revolution which had ushered in the 30-year period of Hutu power.

But the main agents of the genocide were ordinary peasants. The level of compulsion propelling them varied from one place to another, but in certain areas the government account of a 'spontaneous movement of the population to "kill the enemy Tutsi" is true'.[81] On the one hand, these actions were the result of years of indoctrination in the ideology of the 'democratic majority', and of demonisation of Tutsi 'feudal' oppressors. On the other, the prospect of defeat in the civil war greatly magnified the Hutu fear of the restoration of Tutsi power – that it would usher in a new period of servitude, a return to the dark pre-independence days when the Tutsi had acted as the willing instruments of harsh colonial powers.

Of course, people either killed or were themselves killed. One such 'victim-killer' pleaded compulsion, admitting that their victims were innocent, but in the same breath adjusted his plea to the dominant ideology, 'mythifying them as aggressive enemies'. 'Such "victim-killers" were often disgusted and horrified at what they were doing which is partly why large groups of Hutu peasants started to flee their Hills even before the arrival of the RPF troops.'[82] Mamdani argues that at the heart of the Hutu-Tutsi bipolar world lay the struggles of their respective middle classes: both were the beneficiaries of any victory and the victims of any defeat. As we saw, the three major landmarks of post-colonial Rwandan history testify to this: 1959 in Rwanda which witnessed the birth of Hutu Power; 1972, when the Tutsi army killed around 200,000 Burundi Hutus, mainly school pupils; and 1993, again in Burundi, when members of the Tutsi army murdered the Hutu president Ndadaye, impelling 200,000 panic-stricken Hutus to flee to Rwanda.

Irrationality of Genocide

The Rwandan genocide differs from the others considered in this book insofar as the Hutu population had a realistic grievance against the Tutsis, which helps to explain why unprecedentedly large numbers of ordinary Hutus became perpetrators. As one perpetrator told Hatzfeld: 'Others amused themselves by torturing Tutsis, who had made them sweat day after day.'[83] But there were also horrific examples of intra-familial murder – Hutu parents killing their own children because their spouse was a Tutsi, or children of Hutu fathers killing their Tutsi mothers – that surely cannot be explained in terms of ordinary, everyday anger or fear but testify to a deep-seated collective frenzy of irrational hatred way beyond what might be explained by realistic grievances. Moreover, the official Hutu government army, the FAR, had a military force three times the size of the invading Tutsi-dominated RPF.[84] Nevertheless, the invaders were able to defeat the defenders, albeit over a period of nearly four years.

Arguably, a factor in that defeat was that, at the very time when the civil war was approaching its endgame, the Hutu regime embarked on the genocide, thereby diverting sizeable central and local bureaucratic and military resources towards the goal of physically exterminating the Tutsis. The sequence of events that unleashed the violence was thus similar to that which had prefigured other genocides, particularly those of the Armenians and the Jews, namely, the spectre of defeat. It was the prospect of defeat that transformed potential into actual perpetrators. In all three cases, the growing military setbacks seemed to breathe new life into the regime as it turned its ire away from the external enemy and on to the internal one, even though, of course, this made defeat even more likely. The genocide was also irrational in that, even in long-distant colonial times, not every Tutsi had been an oppressor – there had also been poor Tutsis who, objectively defined, belonged to the same social class as most Hutus. As Prunier asserts: 'In the countryside, in contrast to the city, there was no difference of economic level between Tutsi and Hutu.'[85] Moreover, the very idea that one might be able to protect oneself, one's family and social group by killing every member of a former oppressive group, with no repercussions of memory or revenge, smacks of severe pathology. It served to guarantee that the RPF would not cease fighting until the Hutu regime had been dismantled. Not that this was inevitable: Hutus had been in power for 30 years and their fear of powerlessness in the face of a Tutsi army was also unrealistic. Finally, the genocide was irrational in that it involved the destruction of leading professionals, as it did with the Armenians and the Jews. Most personnel in foreign embassies, local NGOs and international agencies were Tutsis. Any attempt to rebuild Rwanda after the economic crisis and civil war would have relied heavily on their contribution. Their loss made reconstruction much harder, for all the Rwandan people. Clearly, the murder of the Tutsi professionals was also fired by a significant element of social envy.[86]

In sum, the Rwandan genocide embodied a basic irrationality resembling the Young Turk decision to exterminate the Armenians and the Nazi decision to liquidate the Jews. As in the latter cases, and as in the genocide of the Native Americans, it was a project carried out against the objective interests of the perpetrators. As with those genocides, there was an element of collective pathology that cannot simply be explained in terms of socio-economic and political factors, or of past history, but requires, in addition, a psychological analysis. Prunier makes a similar point in referring to the 'irrational fear' the RPF inspired with

> its supposedly devil-like fighters and tales of massive killings everywhere; the interim [that is, Hutu] government viewed the RPF more as if they were the Four Horsemen of the Apocalypse than a human enemy ... it seems there was also a strong element of psychological projection: 'They can only do to us what we did to their kith and kin.'[87]

However, given the history of Tutsi collaboration with colonialism, it was perhaps less strong than in the case of the Ottomans' projection on to the Armenians or the Nazis' on to the Jews.

Peter Uvin has analysed the ways in which prejudice was institutionalised in Rwandan society. Despite everything that Tutsis and Hutus had in common, the notion persisted that Tutsis were an alien group, 'with an inherent potential for evil'.[88] As we have seen, they suffered discrimination in education and in public sector jobs, though probably not by as much as official quotas stipulated. Uvin argues that basic psycho-cultural images of the two groups became the 'building blocks' of society. The 'Hutu Manifesto', written in 1955 by future president Kayibanda, stated that 'the problem is basically that of the monopoly of one race, the Tutsi ... which condemns the desperate Hutu to be forever subaltern workers'. For their part, the Tutsi notables wrote that 'there could never be fraternity between Hutu and Tutsi, for the Tutsi had conquered the Hutu and the latter shall always be their slaves'.[89] By the time of independence in 1962, these images had become so frozen in the minds of both groups that 'a century of myths and their associated practice had created the ideology that was to underlie the post-independence instability'.[90] The Hutu rulers deliberately fostered anti-Tutsi racism as a strategy of self-legitimation, keeping it alive 'through a systematic public structure of discrimination and education'.[91] At the other end, 'racist prejudice was a means for small people, squeezed from all sides, to make sense of their predicament, to explain their misery and humiliation through projection and scapegoating'.[92]

In terms of the psychological aspects then, there clearly prevailed in Rwanda the same authoritarian–destructive social character that played such a crucial role in the genocides we have already examined. Prunier writes of the deadweight of Rwandan cultural traditions that demanded obedience to authority as the primary rule; a compulsion to obey summed up in the saying 'an order is as heavy as a stone'. This politico-cultural tradition of 'systematic, centralised and unconditional obedience to authority' stretches back beyond German and Belgian rule to the Banyiginya kingdom, though it was reinforced by the experience of colonial rule. And after independence, a strong, centralised state continued to dominate the lives of ordinary Rwandans. Prunier compares the culture of conformity and obedience dominant among ordinary Rwandans to that which prevailed in Prussia, the authoritarian tradition of the Prussian state and 'its ultimate perversion into the disciplined obedience to Nazi orders'.[93] It is, of course, a key factor in the development of what Fromm and Reich describe as the authoritarian social character. Mamdani makes a similar point: 'they killed in response to orders from above because most believed in the moral rightness of obeying one's government, particularly in a war situation'.[94]

In addition, most Rwandans were illiterate, making it even more likely that, given their authoritarian tradition, they were inclined to believe what their rulers told them.[95] A Kigali lawyer interviewed by Philip Gourevitch made the same point:

Conformity is very deep, very developed here. In Rwandan history, everyone obeys authority. People revere power, and there isn't enough education. You take a poor, ignorant population, and give them arms, and say 'It's yours. Kill.' They'll obey. The peasants, who were paid or forced to kill, were looking up to people of higher socio-economic standing to see how to behave.[96]

And in the words of anthropologist Jean-Jacques Maquet, describing 'the leadership style of the old kings':

The role of the ruler was a mixture of protection and paternalistic profit ... The subject was supposed to fit within this form of leadership. He was supposed to adopt a dependent attitude ... dependence is inferiority extended to all spheres of life. *When a ruler gives an order, he must be obeyed, not because his order falls within the sphere over which he has authority, but simply because he is the ruler.*[97]

There was thus an inner compulsion to submit both to the political authority of the state and the social authority of the group. As Prunier also puts it, 'mass killers tend to be men of the herd and Rwanda was no exception'.[98]

There can be little doubt that this one-way authoritarian relationship between state and citizen percolated down into family relations. Swedish psychoanalyst Tomas Bohm paid two visits to Rwanda where he interviewed perpetrators of the genocide. In his analysis of prejudice, he makes use of Klein's concepts of the paranoid-schizoid and depressive positions (see Chapter 2). Prejudice, he argues, is the offspring of the former, and is unconscious – no different from unconscious beliefs in general except that it is more rigid. The paranoid-schizoid position is characterised by an 'omnipotent simplification', a certainty about right and wrong, with no need, therefore, for a 'mental transitional area' where uncertainties are worked through. The depressive position, on the other hand, carries a 'tolerance for uncertainty and complexity', in which we are not 'subjected to regressive pulls from our inner selves or from large group regression around us'.[99]

But the starting point of prejudice, its emotional basis, is hatred that comes from within. This is created either by frustration, presumably in early infancy by parental failure to satisfy the child's basic needs, or by identification with 'hating care-givers', or 'from a surrounding group regression'.[100] While the perpetrators' feelings of destructive hatred towards the Tutsis were no doubt rooted in the historical reality of the latter's role in subjugating ordinary Hutus, they do not seem to have had much foundation in the experience of individual Hutus. As Hatzfeld described it: 'None of them [Hutus] had ever quarrelled with his Tutsi neighbours over land, crops, damage or women.'[101] And as one interviewee admitted: 'You will never see the source of a genocide ... we were taught to obey absolutely, raised in hatred, stuffed with slogans ... We had lived with Tutsi friends without noticing it, and we became contaminated by ethnic racism without noticing it.'[102]

This point is important and seems to confirm what was suggested in the previous paragraph about the family. The issue here is the manner in which the adults' exposure to social conflict, their being ground down by poverty, their experience of current or memory of past oppression under colonialism and its Tutsi lieutenants, and their consequent feelings of helplessness, all helped to shape their social character and what they then transmitted to their children. For there is no way adults can harbour feelings of hatred, anger and dread towards the outside world while developing loving, nurturing and respectful relationships with their children.

These historical, material factors were no doubt central in creating a social character at the heart of which were obedience and conformity, and fear and hatred of the outside world. Arguably, the 1959 revolution, in which the Hutus overthrew the Belgian colonial power and its Tutsi 'policemen', should have helped to transform or at least modify that social character, at least among the more combative and therefore confident sections of the Hutu population. However, the lack of far-reaching change benefiting all Hutus, their resentment at the Tutsis' continuing privileges, and their consequent feelings of impotence, presumably entailed their retention of aspects of the historically prior social character. Moreover, the economic crisis of the second half of the 1980s would have stoked up fears of a return to pre-independence poverty. That anxiety and the fear generated by the RPF invasion of 1990 – together with the spectre of defeat and of renewed subjugation at the hands of their erstwhile oppressors – pushed them over the edge into wholesale destructiveness. It was the only way they felt, unconsciously, that they could overcome what must have become feelings of dread, if not terror, and the accompanying helplessness.

This is why Bohm's phrase 'hating care-givers' is so crucial here. I examined these psycho-social processes in the discussion of attachment theory in Chapter 2: The children of angry, hating and fearful parents are likely to develop destructive social characters, with a predisposition for a lurch into violence, collective or individual, when external political, economic or military crises – for example, the shooting down of President Habyarimana's plane – act as precipitants. As de Zulueta observes: violence is 'a by-product of psychological trauma and its effects on children, infants and adults'.[103] Moreover, such traumas become fixed in the mind of a group across time. As Volkan put it: 'the group draws the mental representation of a traumatic event into *its very identity*. It passes the mental representation of the event – along with associated shared feelings of hurt and shame, and defences against the perceived shared conflicts they initiate – from generation to generation.'[104]

A predisposition to destructiveness, and the prevalence of violent feelings, is revealed among the killers interviewed by Jean Hatzfeld. One perpetrator, Alphonse, remarks: 'Man can get used to killing, if he kills on and on. He can even become a beast without noticing it. Some threatened one another when they had no more Tutsis under the machete. In their faces, you could see the need to kill.'[105] The Hutus' predisposition to destructiveness, expressed in deep-lying prejudice, was precipitated into genocide by the civil war that raised the fear of a return to subjugation, and by the need to obey authority. But fear of the Tutsis was also stoked up by the Hutu rulers. As another perpetrator, Pancrace, told Hatzfeld: 'The radio was yammering at us since 1992 to kill all the Tutsi; there was anger after the president's death and a fear of falling under the rule of the *inkotanyi* [tough RPF fighters]. But I do not see any hatred in all that.'[106]

Another factor, as we have seen from the analyses of the other genocides, is narcissistic rage. In the case of Rwanda, Hatzfeld says:

> the most impressive facet of the men's personalities … would be their egocentrism, equally overpowering in all of them, at times … unbelievable. When they talk about the genocide, they are not describing an event in which they were … peripheral figures; they place themselves at the centre of a swirl of activity involving victims, survivors, officials, priests … while they minimise their participation and shift the blame on to others … at the same

time they focus only on themselves in the story ... the killers worry only about their own fates and ... feel no compassion for anyone but themselves ... their own suffering ... The monstrous nature of the extermination haunts the survivors and even tortures them with guilt, whereas it exculpates and reassures the killers, perhaps protecting them from madness.[107]

Alice Miller has described the sudden loss of control which can lead to an intense narcissistic rage, and de Zulueta has analysed such rage as a deeply held need for revenge – 'for undoing a hurt by whatever means, and a deep unrelenting compulsion in the pursuit of those aims'.[108] These seem accurate descriptions of the frenzied attack by the Hutus on all Tutsis and on anyone who defended them or expressed misgivings about murdering them.

The final issue is that of commodification. As we saw in Chapter 4, with the advent of capitalist society, ushered in by European colonialism,[109] social relationships gradually assumed the form of relations between things. And 'when human beings are oppressed by social and psychological conditions that make them feel powerless, alienated from any sense of their own capacity or effectiveness ... they are driven to seek that ultimate badge of supreme power over other human beings – killing them, reducing them to objects' (See my Chapter 4). The Hutus called the Tutsis *inyenzi*, cockroaches, human objects to be crushed underfoot. As another killer, Pio, told Hatzfeld: 'We no longer saw a human being when we turned up a Tutsi in the swamps. I mean a person like us, sharing similar thoughts and feelings.'[110]

In the absence of further empirical evidence, it is difficult to draw definitive conclusions about the features making up a dominant Hutu social character or range of characters. In particular, it is difficult to assess what was, or is, the dominant Hutu 'mode of assimilation', their manner of relating to the world of things, including nature, and their 'mode of relatedness', of relating to others. In Chapter 3, following Fromm and Maccoby, we emphasised that a group's social character is also shaped by its relationship to the mode of production. The Hutu population, as we have seen, were mostly farmers. As one killer, Fulgence, told Hatzfeld: 'Agriculture is our real profession, not killing.'[111] Therefore, they could not have been wholly destructive but must also have had a productive element in their social character. Arguably one can ascribe to them two positive or productive features of the hoarding orientation – practical and economical – together with one negative or non-productive feature of the receptive orientation – submissiveness.[112] As for their mode of relatedness, this does seem to have included two non-productive elements – narcissism and destructiveness. This is not surprising in a population racked by poverty and uncertainty, with a history of exploitation and oppression by colonial powers aided by an indigenous 'comprador' class. As with the other three perpetrator groups discussed here, history – the social pressures they encountered, together with the mode of their response – shaped the Hutu social character, including their transition from pain to violence. As for their mode of socio-political relatedness, this was clearly authoritarian.[113] Perhaps the most accurate description of the predominant Hutu social character, one that united the Hutu Power elite with the ordinary peasant farmers, and taking into account the great number of ordinary Hutu perpetrators, would be receptive-productive/hoarding-authoritarian-destructive.

Finally, again, if we want to understand the psychological make-up or content of any social character, it is useful, as I suggested in Chapter 4, to refer to the Freudian typology of the mind, that is, his division between ego, super-ego and id, and also to Klein's notion of projective identification. The drive to destructiveness is arguably, as previously suggested, located in the id, which is also the repository of life-energy and life-drives. The destructive id is the 'cancer-cell' version of the 'normal-cell' life-drive. Taking the Freudian typology as our model, destructiveness implies the overpowering of the ego and super-ego by the cancerous id: the Hutus were, arguably, people with powerful and rigid super-egos, unstable ids, and weak egos. However, in the orgy of killing, the super-ego transmitted the order to kill Tutsis, prompting the id to jettison its 'normal' everyday life drive and morph into its destructive self. There would seem, therefore, to be some difference between the Hutu leaders who initiated the genocide (categories 1–4 above, p. 238), and the ordinary Hutu peasants who obeyed their orders. Destructive fear of and hatred towards the Tutsis was likely to have been stronger among the Hutu leaders, whereas ordinary Hutus and Tutsis, living side-by-side, seemed to get on with one another for much of the time. In their case, powerful super-egos were perhaps more important than destructive ids in impelling them to carry out the genocide.

Summary and Conclusion

In this book, I have tried to establish five principal points: first, that there is such a phenomenon as human nature, a cluster of needs, drives and capacities that is present in all human beings in all societies either actually or potentially. Its main constituent is human self-creativity through the labour process – a collective activity that has resulted historically in a succession of different modes of production. Moreover, human beings are inherently social beings, though this potentiality is often distorted or obscured by the workings of a particular society, and specifically of its class character. Human nature, in other words, never appears in a pure form, since it is filtered through successive social structures that shape its manifestations.

Second, the concept of social character is the crucial link mediating between the external society and the individual, bridging the gap between structure and agency, allowing us to see human beings as both determined by and determining social structures. Character is the human equivalent of an animal's instincts and is the means by which human energy is organised in pursuit of specific goals. It is the manner in which such energy is shaped by the adaptation of human needs and capacities to the mode of existence or workings of a given society. In Fromm's words, it is 'the essential nucleus shared by members of a group which has developed as a result of the basic experiences and mode of life common to that group'.[1] In other words, it is the cluster of more or less fixed features shared by members of a group, generally a social class, that drives them to orient their psychic energy in a manner conducive to the fulfilment of their goals (see Chapter 3).

Social character is the product of two factors: the mode of production, mostly of a class in the Marxist sense, but also of a community such as a settler-colonial society; and the struggles in which that class or community has been engaged. However, social character is not fixed but is reshaped historically through the actions of human beings as they transform nature, society and themselves. Social character may be said to be the counterpart in the emotional sphere of ideology in the intellectual domain. Moreover, different groups and the individuals within them generally embody more than one kind of character. The 'building blocks' of the notion of social character are the psychoanalytical concepts developed by Freud (ego, id, super-ego, unconscious repression) and by Klein together with the object-relations theorists (humans as object-seeking, good and bad objects, projective identification). The concept of social character is also a useful tool facilitating the integration of psychoanalysis into Marxism.

Third, human destructiveness in its collective form results from two sets of factors – predisposing and precipitating elements. The first refers to social character as it has developed through the responses of the members of a society, more specifically its rival social classes, to long-term socio-economic and natural processes, the ways in which they have harnessed their energy, consciously or unconsciously, to the needs and interests of these different class forces. The second refers to the impact of external events – economic crises or other profound social changes – on the members of a society, again in terms of its social classes, and the ways in which they respond and deal with such events as influenced by their social character. Genocide can thus be understood as the 'irrational' destructiveness of social classes or communities that have suffered major historical defeats or other forms of extreme stress. As I stated at the end of Chapter 4, 'the resulting denial of the satisfaction of their human needs, the ensuing feelings of isolation and powerlessness, have propelled them in the direction of projecting on to outgroups the impotent rage, hatred and destructiveness engendered by these defeats'.

Fourth, those social classes or communities responsible for the irrational form of genocide discussed here – the English Puritans, the Scots-Irish, the Young Turks, the Nazis – were largely 'aspiring' middle class in origin. We can also include the Hutu Power leaders, although clearly their followers – the poor Hutu peasant farmers – could hardly be described as 'aspiring'.

Fifth, genocide, the extreme manifestation of human destructiveness expressed in the intention or wish to exterminate an entire people, is a modern phenomenon rooted in the social, economic and psychological nature of capitalism. As noted in the Introduction, it is the product of a 'society based on individual greed and competitiveness, political domination, the alienation of human labour and the commodification of human beings and their relationships'.

There is evidence that our psychosexual life and the family contexts and personal ties through which it is expressed are shaped by the commodity relations of capitalist society. It therefore makes sense to posit a link between unconscious repression and the production of commodities. If so, isn't repression historically amenable to human, political action, contrary to what Freud argued? And can it not be seen, therefore, to be a phenomenon whose manifestations, like the state, could progressively wither away or at least be mitigated under socialism? In 1929, M.D. Eder developed a vision of a rational society in which the super-ego is done away with by the ego which originally brought it forth. He saw in the 'disappearance of control by the super-ego and its replacement by control by the ego a more hopeful line of advance for the individual and even for the whole race'.[2]

Let me conclude with the following quotation from Trotsky who, sympathetic to the new science of psychoanalysis, argued for the possibility of uniting Marxist and Freudian visions:

> The nature of man himself is hidden in the deepest and darkest corner of the unconscious ... The human race will not have ceased to crawl on all fours before God, kings and capital, in order later to submit humbly before the dark laws of heredity and a blind sexual selection! ... Man will make it his purpose to master his own feelings, to raise his instincts to the heights of consciousness, to make them transparent, to extend the wires of his will into hidden recesses, and thereby to raise himself to a new plane ... Social construction and psycho-physical education will become two aspects of one and the same process. All the arts – literature, drama, painting, music and architecture – will lend this process beautiful form... The average human type will rise to the heights of an Aristotle, a Goethe or a Marx. And above this ridge, new peaks will rise.[3]

Notes

Introduction

1. Michael Mann, *The Dark Side of Democracy: Explaining Ethnic Cleansing*, Cambridge University Press, 2005, p. 2.
2. Raphael Lemkin, 'Genocide', in A.L. Hinton (ed.), *Genocide: An Anthropological Reader*, Blackwell Publishers Ltd., 2002, p. 27.
3. Leo Kuper, 'Genocide: Its Political Use in the Twentieth Century', in Hinton (ed.), *Genocide*, p. 55.
4. David Stannard, *American Holocaust*, Oxford University Press, 1992, p. 279.
5. Martin Shaw, *What Is Genocide?*, Polity Press, 2007, pp. 33–4.
6. Dori Laub, *Can Psychoanalysis Enhance Historical Understanding of Genocide?*, Genocide Studies Program, Yale University, 2002, pp. 5–6.
7. Georg Lukács, *History and Class Consciousness*, Merlin Press Ltd., London, 1971, p. 28.
8. Sigmund Freud, *Mass Psychology and the Analysis of the 'I'*, Penguin Books, London, 2004, p. 54.
9. Jacqueline Rose, 'Introduction' to Sigmund Freud, *Mass Psychology and Other Writings*, Penguin Books, 2004, pp. 8–9, reprinted in Jacqueline Rose, *The Last Resistance*, Verso, 2007, Chapter 3, p. 63.
10. Mark Levene, *Genocide in the Age of the Nation State, Volume I: The Meaning of Genocide*, I.B. Tauris & Co. Ltd., 2008, p. 205.
11. Ramsey MacMullen, *Feelings in History*, Claremont, 2003, p. 135, quoted in Ben Kiernan, *Blood and Soil: A World History of Genocide and Extermination from Sparta to Darfur*, Yale University Press, 2007, p. 23.
12. Karl Marx and F. Engels, *The German Ideology*, Lawrence and Wishart, 1965, p. 93.
13. Ernest Jones, *The Life and Work of Sigmund Freud*, Penguin Books, 1962, p. 217.
14. Letter to Mehring, 14 July 1893, in Karl Marx and F. Engels, *Selected Correspondence*, Foreign Languages Publishing House, 1953, p. 541, quoted in John Strachey, 'Introduction' to Reuben Osborn, *Marxism and Psychoanalysis*, Barrie & Rockcliff, 1965, p. viii.
15. Issac Deutscher, *The Prophet Unarmed: Trotsky, Volume 2, 1921–1929*, Oxford University Press, 1959, p. 178.
16. Ibid., p. 179.
17. Leon Trotsky, *Literature and Revolution*, University of Michigan Press, 1966, p. 220.
18. Leon Trotsky, *Culture and Socialism*, 1926, quoted in Deutscher, *The Prophet Unarmed*, p. 180.
19. Erich Fromm, *The Crisis of Psychoanalysis*, Jonathan Cape, 1971, p. 14.
20. Otto Fenichel, in Russell Jacoby, *Social Amnesia: A Critique of Contemporary Psychology*, Transaction Publishers, 1997, p. 91. See endnote 52, p. 173.
21. Ibid., pp. 91–2.
22. Stephen Frosh, *The Politics of Psychoanalysis: An Introduction to Freudian and Post-Freudian Theory*, Macmillan, 1987, p. 14.
23. Joel Kovel, 'The Marxist View of Man and Psychoanalysis', in *The Radical Spirit*, Free Association Books, 1988, p. 179.

24. Rose, *The Last Resistance*, p. 35.

25. Laub, *Can Psychoanalysis...*, p. 9.

26. Walter Benjamin, 'The Storyteller: Reflections on the Works of Nikolai Leskov', in *Illuminations: Essays and Reflections*, trans. H. Zohn, ed. H. Arendt, Schocken, 1969, p. 84, quoted in Laub, *Can Psychoanalysis...*, p. 7.

27. Lukács, *History and Class Consciousness*, p. 28.

28. Oliver James, *The Selfish Capitalist: Origins of Affluenza*, Vermilion, 2008, Chapter 2. Erich Fromm, *The Sane Society*, Routledge & Kegan Paul, 1956.

29. Tim Kasser and Richard Ryan, 'A Dark Side of the American Dream: Correlates of Financial Success as a Central Life Aspiration', *Journal of Personality and Social Psychology*, Vol. 65, pp. 410–22, quoted in James, *Affluenza*, pp. 56–63.

30. Wilhelm Reich, 'Dialectical Materialism and Psychoanalysis' (1929), *Studies on the Left*, Vol. 6, No. 4, 1966, p. 41.

31. John Rickert, 'The Fromm-Marcuse Debate Revisited', *Theory and Society*, Vol. 15, 1986, p. 387.

32. Karl Korsch, *Marxism and Philosophy*, Monthly Review Press, 1970, p. 9, quoted by Rickert in ibid., p. 352; also Richard Lichtman, *The Production of Desire*, Free Press, 1982, p. 10.

33. Lichtman, *The Production of Desire*, p. 3.

34. Ibid.

35. Ibid., p. 10.

36. Reich, 'Dialectical Materialism and Psychoanalysis', pp. 36–7.

37. Lichtman, *The Production of Desire*, p. 11.

38. Jacoby, *Social Amnesia*, p. 75.

39. Lichtman, *The Production of Desire*, p. 11.

40. Max Horkheimer, 'Authority and the Family', in *Critical Theory: Selected Essays* (1968), Continuum, 2002, quoted in Jacoby, *Social Amnesia*, p. 87.

41. Lichtman, *The Production of Desire*, p. 199.

42. Osborn, *Marxism and Psychoanalysis*; Reimut Reiche, *Sexuality and the Class Struggle*, New Left Books, 1970; Michael Schneider, *Neurosis and Civilization: A Marxist/Freudian Synthesis*, Seabury Press, 1975; Joel Kovel, *The Age of Desire: Case Studies of a Radical Psychoanalyst*, Pantheon Books, 1981; Lichtman, *The Production of Desire*; Eugene Victor Wolfenstein, *Psychoanalytic-Marxism Groundwork*, Free Association Books, The Guilford Press, 1993.

43. Andrew Samuels, *The Political Psyche*, Routledge, 1993.

44. Mann, *The Dark Side*, Chapters 1 and 2.

45. E.R. Service, *The Hunters*, Prentice-Hall, 1966; D. Pilbeam, *The Evolution of Man*, Thames and Hudson, 1970, both quoted in Erich Fromm, *The Anatomy of Human Destructiveness*, Jonathan Cape, 1974, p. 147.

46. Lawrence Keeley, *War Before Civilisation: The Myth of the Peaceful Savage*, Oxford University Press, 1996, p. 39.

47. Mann, *The Dark Side*, p. 17.

Chapter 1

1. Michael Mann, *The Dark Side of Democracy: Explaining Ethnic Cleansing*, Cambridge University Press, 2005, pp. 3–10.

2. Ibid., p. 5.

3. Ibid., p. 7.

4. Israel W. Charny, *Genocide: The Human Cancer* (1982), Hearst Books, 1986, p. 144, quoted in Mann, *The Dark Side*, p. 9.
5. Mann, *The Dark Side*, p. 9.
6. Wilfred Bion, *Experiences in Groups and Other Papers*, Tavistock Publications, 1961, p. 132.
7. Ibid., p. 102.
8. Erich Fromm, *The Sane Society*, Routledge & Kegan Paul, 1956, p. 6.
9. Sigmund Freud, *Civilisation and Its Discontents* (1929), trans. J. Riviere, Hogarth Press, 1953, pp. 141–2, quoted in Fromm, *Sane Society*, p. 20.
10. Michael Schneider, *Neurosis and Civilisation*, Seabury Press, 1975, p. 161.
11. Jean Hatzfeld, *Machete Season*, Farrar, Straus & Giroux, 2005, p. 106.
12. Martin Shaw, *What Is Genocide?*, Polity Press, 2007, Chapters 1 and 2.
13. Ibid., Chapter 5.
14. Ibid., p. 66.
15. Ibid., p. 67.
16. Ibid., p. 70.
17. Ibid., p. 71.
18. Ibid., pp. 73–4.
19. Ibid., p. 64.
20. Ibid., p. 92.
21. Anthony Giddens, *The Constitution of Society: Outline of the Theory of Structuration*, Polity, 1984, p. 376, quoted in ibid., p. 95.
22. Shaw, *What Is Genocide?*, p. 96.
23. Gerard Prunier, *Rwanda: History of a Genocide*, Hearst & Co., 1995, p. 237.
24. Ben Kiernan, *Blood and Soil: A World History of Genocide and Extermination from Sparta to Darfur*, Yale University Press, 2007, p. 32.
25. Ibid., p. 23.
26. Mark Levene, *Genocide in the Age of the Nation State, Vol. 1, The Meaning of Genocide*, I.B. Taurus, 2005, pp. 205–6.
27. Ibid., p. 107.
28. Ibid., p. 116.
29. Ibid., p. 114.
30. Ibid., p. 205.
31. Ibid., p. 142.
32. Ibid., p. 130.
33. T. Adorno, E. Frenkel-Brunswik, D.J. Levinson, R.N. Sanford, *The Authoritarian Personality*, Harper & Row, 1950.
34. Bob Altemeyer, *The Authoritarians*, Lulu, 2006, p. 8.
35. Ibid., p. 15.
36. Ibid., p. 15.
37. Ibid., p. 17.
38. Ibid., p. 22.
39. Ibid., p. 24.
40. Ibid., p. 26.
41. Ibid., pp. 9–14.
42. Ibid., Chapter 3.
43. Ibid., p. 52.
44. Ibid., pp. 53, 60.
45. Ibid., pp. 92–5.
46. Ibid., p. 53.
47. Ibid., p. 103.

48. James Waller, *Becoming Evil: How Ordinary Men Commit Genocide and Mass Killing*, Oxford University Press, 2007.

49. Fromm, *The Sane Society*, p. 14.

50. Kant's *Critique of Practical Reason* (1788), quoted in Alex Callinicos, *The Resources of Critique*, Polity Press, 2006, p. 234.

51. Douglas M. Kelly, *22 Cells in Nuremberg*, W.H. Allen, 1947, p. 194.

52. Christopher Browning, *The Origins of the Final Solution: The Evolution of Nazi Jewish Policy, September 1939–March 1942*, University of Nebraska Press, 2004, p. 391.

53. Hannah Arendt, *The Origins of Totalitarianism*, George Allen & Unwin, London, 1958, Part One. Enzo Traverso, *The Jews and Germany: From the 'Judeo-German Symbiosis' to the Memory of Auschwitz*, University of Nebraska Press, 1995, Chapter 5.

54. Waller, *Becoming Evil*, p. 139.

55. Ibid., pp. 173–4.

56. Ibid., p. 178.

57. Ibid., p. 179.

58. Ibid., p. 180.

59. Ibid., p. 183.

60. Ibid., p. 200.

61. Ibid., p. 207.

62. Ibid., pp. 217–8.

63. Ibid., p. 231.

64. Ibid., p. 235.

65. Ibid., pp. 242, 244.

66. Ibid., p. 245.

67. Ibid., p. 251.

68. Ibid., p. 255.

69. Ibid., pp. 255–7.

70. Ibid., p. 259.

71. Ibid., p. 148.

72. Ibid., p. 154.

73. Ervin Staub, *The Roots of Evil: The Origins of Genocide and Other Group Violence*, Cambridge University Press, 1989.

74. Erich Fromm, *The Anatomy of Human Destructiveness*, Jonathan Cape, 1974, p. 35.

75. Stanley Milgram, 'Behavioural Study of Obedience', *Journal of Abnormal and Social Psychology*, Vol. 67, 1963, pp. 371–8, quoted in Fromm, *The Anatomy*, pp. 47–52.

76. Fromm, *The Anatomy*, p. 50.

77. Ibid., pp. 51–2.

78. Philip Zimbardo, 'Pathology of Imprisonment', *Trans-Action*, Vol. 9 (1972), pp. 4–8, quoted in ibid., pp. 53–7.

79. Fromm, *The Anatomy*, p. 58.

80. Ibid., pp. 66–8.

81. Ibid., p. 219.

82. Ibid.

83. Vamik Volkan, *The Need to Have Enemies and Allies: From Clinical Practice to International Relations*, Jason Aronson, 1994, p. xxv, quoted in Peter Uvin, 'Prejudice, Crisis and Genocide in Rwanda', in *African Studies Review*, Vol. 40, No. 2, 1997, p. 105.

84. Richard Lichtman, *The Production of Desire: The Integration of Psychoanalysis into Marxist Theory*, The Free Press, 1982, p. 67.

85. Lloyd D. Easton and Kurt H. Guddat (eds), *Writings of the Young Marx on Philosophy and Society*, Doubleday Anchor Press, 1967, pp. 420, 421, 461, quoted in ibid., p. 83.
86. Karl Marx, *Early Writings*, ed. T. Bottomore, McGraw Hill, 1964, p. 128, quoted in Lichtman, *The Production of Desire*, p. 75.
87. Lichtman, *The Production of Desire*, p. 83.
88. Karl Marx, *Capital*, Vol. 1, Foreign Publishing House, 1962, p. 177.
89. Lichtman, *The Production of Desire*, p. 69.
90. Karl Marx, *The Eighteenth Brumaire of Louis Bonaparte* (1851), in K. Marx and F. Engels, *Selected Works*, Vol. 1, Foreign Languages Publishing House, 1962, p. 247.
91. Karl Marx, *Sixth Thesis on Feuerbach* (1845), in K. Marx and F. Engels, *Selected Works*, Vol. 2, Foreign Languages Publishing House, 1961, p. 404.
92. Marx, *Early Writings*, p. 43, quoted in Lichtman, *The Production of Desire*, p. 63.
93. Norman Geras, *Marx and Human Nature: Refutation of a Legend*, Verso, 1983, p. 24.
94. Alex Callinicos, *Making History*, Polity Press, 1989, p. 26.
95. Karl Marx, Introduction to *Grundrisse* (1857), Penguin, 1973, p. 92, quoted in Geras, *Marx and Human Nature*, p. 112. (See Lichtman's critique of this distinction in *The Production of Desire*, p. 87.)
96. Marx, *Capital*, Vol. 1, Foreign Publishing House, 1961, p. 609, quoted in Geras, *Marx and Human Nature*, pp. 79–80.
97. Geras, *Marx and Human Nature*, p. 19.
98. Callinicos, *Making History*, p. 26.
99. Christian Keysers and Valeria Gazzola, 'Expanding the Mirror: Vicarious Activity for Actions, Emotions and Sensations', *Science Direct, Current Opinion in Neurobiology*, Vol. 19, Nos. 1–6, 2009, p. 1, available online at www.sciencedirect.com.
100. Mann, *The Dark Side*, p. 34.
101. See Benedict Anderson, *Imagined Communities*, Verso, 1983.
102. M.J. Meggitt, *Desert People*, University of Chicago Press, 1960, quoted in E.R. Service, *The Hunters*, Prentice-Hall, 1966, quoted in Fromm, *The Anatomy*, p. 146.
103. Service, *The Hunters*, quoted in Fromm, *The Anatomy*, p. 147.
104. D. Pilbeam, *The Evolution of Man*, Thames & Hudson, 1970, quoted in Fromm, *The Anatomy*, p. 147.
105. Kiernan, *Blood and Soil*, p. 1.
106. Lawrence Keeley, *War Before Civilisation: The Myth of the Peaceful Savage*, Oxford University Press, 1996, p. 39.
107. David Konstan, '*Anger, Hatred, and Genocide in Ancient Greece*', *Common Knowledge*, Vol. 13, No. 1, Project Muse: Scholarly Journals Online, 2007, Duke University Press, p. 182.
108. Ibid., p. 186.
109. Ibid., p. 187.
110. Fromm, *The Anatomy*; see also my Chapter 4, pp. 94–5, 101.
111. G.E.M. de Sainte Croix, *The Class Struggle in the Ancient Greek World*, Duckworth, 1981, p. 332.
112. Konstan, 'Anger, Hatred', p. 186.
113. Ben Kiernan, 'The First Genocide: Carthage, 146 BC', *Diogenes*, Vol. 51, No. 3, 2004, p. 28.
114. Kiernan, *Blood and Soil*, p. 51.
115. Kiernan, 'The First Genocide: Carthage, 146 BC', *Diogenes*, Vol. 51, No. 3, 2004, p. 29. Kiernan, *Blood and Soil*, p. 53.

116. Kiernan, *Blood and Soil*, pp. 53, 58.
117. Neil Faulkner, 'Crusade and Jihad in the Medieval Middle East', *International Socialism Journal*, Vol. 109, 2006, p. 129.
118. Hans Eberhard Mayer, *The Crusades*, Oxford University Press, 1992, pp. 40–1.
119. Faulkner, 'Crusade and Jihad', p. 129.
120. Ibid.
121. Ibid., p. 131.
122. John Docker, *The Origins of Violence: Religion, History and Genocide*, Pluto Press, 2008, p. 59.

Chapter 2

1. A useful introduction to Freud is Richard Wollheim's *Freud*, in the Modern Masters series edited by Frank Kermode, Fontana Press, 1973. See also Sigmund Freud, *Three Essays on Sexuality* (1905), Pelican Freud Library, Vol. 7, 1977; Sigmund Freud, *An Outline of Psychoanalysis* (1940), trans. and ed. James Strachey, Hogarth Press, 1940, Chapter 2; Stephen Frosh, *Psychoanalysis and Politics*, Macmillan, 1987; and Erich Fromm, *The Crisis of Psychoanalysis*, Jonathan Cape, 1971, Chapter 8, esp. pp. 135–7.
2. Sigmund Freud, *Beyond the Pleasure Principle* (1920), Pelican Freud Library, Vol. 11, 1987, p. 326; *The Ego and the Id* (1923), ibid., pp. 380–8; and *An Outline of Psychoanalysis*, Chapter 2.
3. Sigmund Freud, *Civilisation and Its Discontents* (1929), in *The Standard Edition of the Complete Psychological Works of Sigmund Freud*, Vol. 21, Hogarth Press, 2001, p. 122.
4. Freud, *Beyond the Pleasure Principle*, pp. 293–4; Stephen Frosh, *Psychoanalysis Outside the Clinic*, Palgrave-Macmillan, 2010, p. 86.
5. Freud, *The Ego and the Id*, pp. 367–80; *Civilisation and Its Discontents*, pp. 112, 97, 113.
6. Freud, *The Ego and the Id*, pp. 377–8.
7. Freud, *Three Essays on Sexuality*, pp. 116–9.
8. Freud, *Civilisation, and Its Discontents*, p. 113.
9. Erich Fromm, *Freud's Model of Man and Its Social Determinants*, Jonathan Cape, 1971, Chapter 2, p. 43.
10. Jacqueline Rose, 'Introduction' to the new edition of Sigmund Freud, *Mass Psychology and the Analysis of the 'I'* (1921), Penguin Books, 2004, pp. vii to xiv, reprinted in *The Last Resistance*, Verso, 2007, pp. 62–8.
11. Freud, *Mass Psychology*, pp. 17–18.
12. Ibid., p. 54.
13. Ibid., p. 55.
14. Ibid., pp. 57–63.
15. Rose, *The Last Resistance*, p. 67; Freud, *Mass Psychology*, p. 91.
16. Paul Roazen, *Freud: Political and Social Thought,* Hogarth Press, 1969, p. 218.
17. Michael Schneider, *Neurosis and Civilisation*, Seabury Press, 1975, p. 70.
18. Ibid.
19. Ibid., pp. 70–1.
20. Ibid., p. 71.
21. Georg Lukács, *Geschichte und Klassenbewusstsein*, Berlin, 1932, p. 110, quoted in ibid., p. 72. (English edition: *History and Class Consciousness*, Merlin Press, 1971, p. 90.)

22. Wilhelm Reich, *Character Analysis*, Pocket Books, 1972, pp. 240–8, quoted in Schneider, *Neurosis*, pp. 73–5.

23. Schneider, *Neurosis*, p. 75.

24. Bronislaw Malinowski, *Sex and Repression in Savage Society*, Routledge & Kegan Paul, 1927, p. 14.

25. Richard Lichtman, *The Production of Desire: The Integration of Psychoanalysis into Marxist Theory*, The Free Press, 1982, p. 70.

26. Ibid., p. 188.

27. Ibid., p. 186.

28. Ibid., p. 110.

29. Ibid., p.110.

30. Ibid., p. 186.

31. Ibid., p. 199.

32. Ibid., p. 254.

33. Margaret Mead, *Coming of Age in Samoa* (1928), Penguin Books, 1977; *Sex and Temperament in Three Primitive Societies* (1935), Harper Collins, 2002.

34. Malinowski, *Sex and Repression*, p. 9.

35. Ibid., p. 39.

36. Lukács, *History and Class Consciousness*, p. 100, quoted in Schneider, *Neurosis*, p. 86.

37. See W.R.D. Fairbairn, *Psychoanalytic Studies of the Personality* (1952), Brunner-Routledge, 1994. For a useful introduction to object-relations theory, see Frosh, *The Politics of Psychoanalysis*, pp. 94–111.

38. See Juliet Mitchell (ed.), *The Selected Melanie Klein*, The Free Press, 1987, esp. Chapters 6–10. For a useful introduction to Melanie Klein, see Frosh, *Politics of Psychoanalysis*, pp. 112–29. For Klein's acceptance of the death instinct, see R.D. Hinshelwood, *A Dictionary of Kleinian Thought*, Free Association Books, 1991, pp. 367–8.

39. Michael Rustin, 'A Socialist Consideration of Kleinian Psychoanalysis', *New Left Review*, Vol. 131, January–February 1982, pp. 81 and 96.

40. Frosh, *Psychoanalysis Outside the Clinic*, p. 133.

41. Robert M. Young, *Whatever Happened to Human Nature?*, 1996, available at http://human-nature.com/human/preface.html.

42. Judith Butler, *Giving an Account of Oneself*, Fordham University Press, 2005, p. 75.

43. Frosh, *Psychoanalysis Outside the Clinic*, p. 149.

44. Ibid., p. 149.

45. Theodor Adorno et al., *The Authoritarian Personality*, Harper & Row, 1950.

46. Fred I. Greenstein, 'Personality and Political Socialisation: The Theories of Authoritarian and Democratic Character', *Annals of the American Academy of Political and Social Science*, September 1965, p. 86.

47. Stephen Frosh, *Hate and the Jewish Science: Anti-Semitism, Nazism and Psychoanalysis*, Palgrave-Macmillan, 2009, p. 182.

48. Else Frenkel-Brunswik, 'Further Explorations by a Contributor to 'The Authoritarian Personality', in *Studies in the Scope and Method of The Authoritarian Personality* (SSMAP), Free Press, 1954, pp. 236–7, quoted in Greenstein, 'Personality and Political Socialisation', p. 90.

49. Ibid.

50. Adorno et al, *Authoritarian Personality*, pp. 482–3, quoted in Greenstein, 'Personality and Political Socialisation', p. 90.

51. Greenstein, 'Personality and Political Socialisation', p. 91.

52. Adorno et al., *Authoritarian Personality*, p. 206.

53. Ibid., pp. 185–207; Theodor Adorno, *Stichworte*, Frankfurt, 1969, quoted in Russell Jacoby, *Social Amnesia*, Transaction Publishers, 1997, p. 87.

54. See John Bowlby's seminal *Child Care and the Growth of Love*, Pelican Books, 1953.

55. de Zulueta, Felicity, *From Pain to Violence*, John Wiley & Sons, 2006, pp. 123–5, 136.

56. de Zulueta, *From Pain to Violence*, p. 136.

57. Routledge, 1988, pp. 26–7, quoted in ibid., p. 61.

58. de Zulueta, *From Pain to Violence*, p. 61.

59. Ibid., p. 72.

60. Ibid., p. 75.

61. Ibid., p. 77.

62. Ibid., p. 79.

63. Ibid., p. 5.

64. Ibid., p. 7.

65. Anna Freud, *The Ego and the Mechanisms of Defence* (1936), Karnac Books, London, 1993.

66. Ibid., p. 110.

67. Ibid., p. 116.

68. Ibid.

69. Ibid., p. 118–9.

70. Ibid., p. 120.

71. Heinz Kohut, *The Analysis of the Self*, University of Chicago, 1971, pp. 82–6. See also Preface and Chapter 1.

72. Alice Miller, *The Drama of Being a Child*, Virago, 1987, p. 49.

73. Erich Fromm and Michael Maccoby, *Social Character in a Mexican Village*, Prentice-Hall, 1970, p. 75.

74. Sigmund Freud, *Totem and Taboo*, in *The Standard Edition of the Complete Psychological Works of Sigmund Freud*, Vol. 13, p. 89, quoted in ibid., p. 75.

75. Fromm and Maccoby, *Social Character*, p. 75.

76. ChangingMinds.org.

77. Miller, *The Drama*, p. 52.

78. Stephen Frosh, *Identity Crisis: Modernity, Psychoanalysis and the Self*, Macmillan, London, 1991, p. 70.

79. Heinz Kohut, *The Restoration of the Self*, University of Chicago, 1977, p. 5.

80. A. Miller, 'Depression and Grandiosity as Related Forms of Narcissistic Disturbances', in A. Morrison (ed.), *Essential Papers on Narcissism*, New York University Press, 1979, quoted in Frosh, *Identity Crisis*, p. 75.

81. Miller, *The Drama*, p. 48.

82. de Zulueta, *From Pain to Violence*, p. 134.

83. Heinz Kohut, *Self Psychology and the Humanities: Reflections on a New Psychoanalytical Approach*, co-editor C.B. Strozier, Norton, 1985, p. 141, quoted in ibid., p. 134.

84. de Zulueta, *From Pain to Violence*, p. 147.

85. Ernest Wolf, *Treating the Self: Elements of Clinical Self Psychology*, Guilford, 1988, p. 80, quoted in ibid., p. 134.

86. Ervin Staub, 'A Conception of the Determinants and Development of Altruism and Aggression: Motives of the Self and the Environment', in C. Zahn-Waxler, E.M. Cummings and R. Ianotti (eds), *Social and Biological Origins of Altruism and Aggression*, Cambridge, 1984, pp. 135–63, quoted in de Zulueta, *From Pain to Violence*, p. 152.

87. de Zulueta, Felicity, *From Pain to Violence*, p. 98.

88. Ibid., p. 148.

89. Ibid., p. 149.
90. Ibid., p. 223.
91. Reich, *Character Analysis*, p. 290, quoted in Paul Robinson, *The Freudian Left*, Cornell University Press, 1990, p. 35.
92. Herbert Marcuse, *Eros and Civilisation*, Routledge & Kegan Paul, 1956, p. 35.
93. Russell Jacoby, *The Repression of Psychoanalysis*, University of Chicago Press, 1983, p. 70.
94. Otto Fenichel, 'A Critique of the Death Instinct', in *Collected Papers*, Norton, 1953, quoted in Marcuse, *Eros and Civilisation*, p. 28.
95. Freud, *The Ego and the Id*, p. 396, quoted in Marcuse, *Eros and Civilisation*, p. 83.
96. Marcuse, *Eros and Civilisation*, p. 83. See also Paul Robinson's useful summary in *The Freudian Left*, pp. 211–14.
97. Robinson, *The Freudian Left*, p. 212. See also Jeffrey Weeks' discussion in *Sexuality and Its Discontents*, Routledge & Kegan Paul, 1985, Chapter 7. I shall return to it in Chapter 3.
98. W.R.D. Fairbairn, 'The Repression and the Return of Bad Objects' (1943), in *Psychoanalytic Studies of the Personality*, pp. 78–9.
99. Paul Robinson, 'Cleaning Up Freud', review of Erich Fromm's *The Anatomy of Human Destructiveness*, Partisan Review, Vol. 41, 1974.
100. Otto Fenichel, *The Psychoanalytic Theory of Neurosis*, W.W. Norton, 1945, pp. 59–61.
101. Erich Fromm, *The Anatomy of Human Destructiveness*, Jonathan Cape, 1974, pp. 477–8.
102. Ibid., p. 167; Lawrence Keeley, *War Before Civilisation: The Myth of the Peaceful Savage*, Oxford University Press, 1996, p. 39.
103. Reich, *Character Analysis*, p. 257.
104. Eugene Wolfenstein, *Psychoanalytic Marxism*, Free Association Books, 1993, pp. 73–4; Fromm, *The Anatomy*, p. 254.
105. Fromm, *The Anatomy*, pp. 67–8, 270.
106. Ibid., p. 271.
107. Ibid., p. 272.
108. Ibid., p. 274–6.
109. Ibid., p. 271.
110. Slavoj Žižek, *Violence: Six Sideways Reflections*, Profile Books, 2008. See also J. Baggini, 'The Book of the Week: *Violence* by Slavoj Žižek', *Times Higher Education*, 14 February 2008.
111. Žižek, *Violence*, p. 50. See also Frosh, *Psychoanalysis Outside the Clinic*, p. 151.
112. Žižek, *Violence*, p. 51.
113. Ibid., p. 52.
114. Ibid.
115. Alex Callinicos, *Against Postmodernism*, Polity Press, 1989, p. 73.
116. Alex Callinicos, *Resources of Critique*, Polity Press, 2006, p. 115.
117. Karl Marx, *Theses on Feuerbach* (1845), in K. Marx and F. Engels, *Selected Works*, Vol. 2, Foreign Languages Publishing House, 1962, pp. 403–5.
118. K. Marx and F. Engels, *The German Ideology* (1845), Lawrence & Wishart, 1965, p. 42.
119. Slavoj Žižek, 'Neighbours and Other Monsters', in Slavoj Žižek, Eric Santner and Kenneth Reinhard, *The Neighbour: Three Inquiries in Political Theology*, University of Chicago Press, 2005, p. 140.
120. Žižek, *Violence*, p. 48.
121. Žižek, 'Neighbours and Other Monsters', p. 143.

122. Ibid., pp. 143–4.
123. Slavoj Žižek, *The Sublime Object of Ideology*, Verso, 1989, p. 148.
124. Anika Lemaire, *Jacques Lacan*, Routledge & Kegan Paul, 1977, p. 181.
125. Bice Benvenuto and Roger Kennedy, *The Works of Jacques Lacan: An Introduction*, Free Association Books, 1986, pp. 170–2, 179.
126. Ibid., p. 171.
127. Žižek, *Violence*, p. 115.
128. Stephen Frosh, private communication to the author.
129. Benvenuto and Kennedy, *Works of Jacques Lacan*, ibid., p. 152.
130. Callinicos, *Resources of Critique*, pp. 114–15.
131. Benvenuto and Kennedy, *Works of Jacques Lacan*, p. 166.
132. Žižek, *Violence*, p. 11.
133. Frosh, *Psychoanalysis Outside the Clinic*, p. 179.
134. Butler, *Giving an Account*, p. 77.
135. Ibid.
136. Ibid., p. 75.
137. Ibid.
138. Ibid.
139. Ibid., p. 87.
140. Frosh, *Psychoanalysis Outside the Clinic*, p. 146.
141. Butler, *Giving an Account*, pp. 78–9.
142. Ibid., p. 83.
143. Ibid., p. 84.
144. Ibid., p. 101.
145. Judith Butler, *Frames of War: When Is Life Grievable?*, Verso, 2009, pp. 176–7.
146. Ibid., p. 176.
147. Butler, *Giving an Account*, pp. 70–1.
148. Ibid., p. 84.
149. Sigmund Freud, 'Why War?', in *The Standard Edition of the Complete Works of Sigmund Freud*, Vol. 22, Hogarth Press, 2001; Fromm, *The Anatomy*, p. 210. See also Jacqueline Rose's essay 'Why War?', in *Why War? Psychoanalysis, Politics, and the Return to Melanie Klein*, Blackwell, 1993, pp. 15–40.
150. Fromm, *The Anatomy*, pp. 210–16.
151. de Zulueta, *From Pain to Violence*, p. 5.

Chapter 3

1. See Thomas Meisenhelder, 'From Character to Habitus in Sociology', *Social Science Journal*, Vol. 43, 2006, p. 55.
2. See, for example, Margaret Archer, *Culture and Agency: The Place of Culture in Social Theory*, Cambridge, 1986.
3. John Rickert, 'The Fromm-Marcuse Debate Revisited', *Theory and Society*, Vol. 15, 1986, p. 387.
4. Sigmund Freud, 'Character and Anal Eroticism', in *Collected Papers 2*, Hogarth Press, 1953, pp. 45–50, quoted in Rickert, 'The Fromm-Marcuse Debate', pp. 352–3.
5. Wilhelm Reich, *Character Analysis*, third edition, New York, 1961, Preface to the First Edition, p. xxvii.
6. Bertell Ollman, *Social and Sexual Revolution: Essays on Marx and Reich*, Pluto, 1979, p. 165.

7. Ibid., p. 164.

8. Ibid.

9. Ibid., pp. 165–6.

10. Ibid., pp. 166, 184.

11. Wilhelm Reich, *The Mass Psychology of Fascism* (1933), Farrar, Straus & Giroux, 1970.

12. Ibid., p. 30.

13. Reimut Reiche, *Sexuality and Class Struggle*, trans. David Fernbach, New Left Books, 1968, p. 46.

14. Jeffrey Weeks, *Sexuality and Its Discontents*, Routledge & Kegan Paul, 1985, p. 169.

15. Erich Fromm, 'Freud's Model of Man and Its Social Determinants', in *The Crisis of Psychoanalysis*, Jonathan Cape, 1971, pp. 53–4.

16. Erich Fromm, 'Marx's Contribution to the Knowledge of Man', in *The Crisis of Psychoanalysis*, pp. 70–1.

17. George Orwell, *The Road to Wigan Pier* (1937) Penguin, 1984, p. 141, quoted in Slavoj Žižek, *Violence: Six Sideways Reflections*, Profile Books, 2008, p. 140.

18. Žižek, *Violence*, p. 141.

19. Erich Fromm, *The Anatomy of Human Destructiveness*, Jonathan Cape, 1974, pp. 226–7.

20. Erich Fromm, *Man For Himself*, Routledge & Kegan Paul, 1949, p. 58.

21. Erich Fromm, *Fear of Freedom*, Routledge & Kegan Paul, 1942, p. 239.

22. Ibid., p. 243.

23. Fromm, *Anatomy*, p. 252.

24. Ibid., p. 253.

25. Erich Fromm and Michael Maccoby, *Social Character in a Mexican Village*, Prentice-Hall, 1970, p. 16.

26. Fromm, *Fear of Freedom*, p. 242.

27. Ibid., p. 240.

28. Ibid., p. 246.

29. Fromm and Maccoby, *Social Character*, p. 11.

30. Fromm, *Fear of Freedom*, p. 252.

31. Fromm and Maccoby, *Social Character*, p. 1.

32. Ibid., p. 17.

33. Karl Marx, *Theses on Feuerbach*, in K. Marx and F. Engels, *Selected Works*, Vol. 2, Foreign Languages Publishing House, 1962, pp. 403–5. See also Chris Harman, 'Base and Superstructure', *International Socialism Journal*, Vol. 2, No. 32, 1986, pp. 3–44; Franz Jakubowski, *Ideology and Superstructure in Historical Materialism*, Pluto Press, 1990.

34. Fromm, *Man For Himself*, Routledge & Kegan Paul, 1949, pp. 62–82.

35. Ibid., p. 68.

36. Ibid., p. 70.

37. Ibid., p. 72.

38. Ibid., p. 73.

39. Fromm, *Anatomy*, pp. 288–9.

40. Ibid., p. 290.

41. Ibid., p. 292.

42. Ibid., p. 332.

43. Ibid., quoting H. von Hentig, *Der Nekrotope Mensch* (1964).

44. Ibid., p. 348.

45. Ibid., Chapter 13, quoted in Klaus Theweleit, *Male Fantasies*, Vol. 2, Minneapolis: University of Minnesota Press, 1977, pp. 19, 438.

46. Elias Canetti, *Crowds and Power*, trans. Carol Stewart, Penguin, 1973, p. 266, quoted in Theweleit, *Male Fantasies*, p. 19.

47. Theweleit, *Male Fantasies*, p. 19.

48. Ibid., p. 438.

49. Ibid.

50. Rainer Funk, 'Foreword' to Erich Fromm, *Beyond the Chains of Illusion: My Encounter with Marx and Freud* (1962), Continuum, 2006, p. ix.

51. Rainer Funk, 'Erich Fromm and the Intersubjective Tradition', presented at the XVI Forum of the International Federation of Psychoanalytic Societies, Athens, October 2010, published in *Fromm Forum*, Tuebingen, 2011, pp. 60–4.

52. Erich Fromm, *Beyond Freud: From Individual to Social Psychoanalysis*, American Mental Health Foundation, Inc., 1992, p. 58, quoted in ibid., p. 4.

53. Rainer Funk, 'Violence in Our Time – Psychology and Religion', *Fromm Forum*, Vol. 9, 2005, p. 3.

54. Fromm and Maccoby, *Social Character*, p. 68.

55. Ibid., p. 74.

56. Ibid.

57. Ibid., p. 76.

58. Anna Freud, *The Ego and the Mechanisms of Defence*, Karnac Books, 1993, Chapter 9.

59. Fromm and Maccoby, *Social Character*, p. 80.

60. Ibid., pp. 81–2.

61. Ibid.

62. Erich Fromm, *The Dogma of Christ*, New York, 1963, Chapter 5.

63. Fromm, *Man For Himself*, p. 78.

64. Ibid., p. 80.

65. Karl Marx, *Capital*, Vol. 1, Foreign Languages Publishing House, Moscow, 1961, Chapter 24, section 3, p. 595.

66. Fromm, *Man For Himself*, p. 81.

67. Erich Fromm, *The Sane Society*, Routledge & Kegan Paul, 1956, p. 110.

68. Fromm, *Man For Himself*, p. 82.

69. Fromm and Maccoby, *Social Character*, p. 7.

70. Ibid., pp. 26–9.

71. Ibid., p. 110.

72. Ibid., p. 106.

73. Ibid., pp. 79, 117.

74. Ibid., p. 121.

75. Ibid., pp. 122–3.

76. Ibid., p. 124.

77. Ibid., p. 189.

78. Ibid., p. 197.

79. Fromm, Erich, *German Workers 1929 – A Survey – Its Methods and Results*. The study, undertaken under the auspices of the International Institute for Social Research – i.e., the Frankfurt School relocated to the US – was published in 1984 under the title *The Working Class in Weimar Germany: A Psychological and Sociological Study*, edited by Wolfgang Bonss, Berg Publishers, 1984. Robert McKenzie, *Angels in Marble*, Heinemann, 1968; J.H. Goldthorpe et al., *The Affluent Worker in the Class Structure*, 3 vols., Cambridge University Press, 1969; Robert Altemeyer, *The Authoritarians*, Lulu, 2006.

80. Christopher Hill, *Society and Puritanism in Pre-Revolutionary England*, Secker & Warburg, 1964; E.P. Thompson, *The Making of the English Working Class*, Gollancz, 1963.

81. Molière, *The Miser*, Nick Hern Books, 2004.

82. See Marshall Berman's *All That Is Solid Melts Into Air: The Experience Of Modernity*, Verso, 1983.

83. Stephen Frosh, *Identity Crisis: Modernity, Psychoanalysis and the Self*, Macmillan, 1991, pp. 7–8.

84. Ibid., pp. 43–4.

85. Ibid., p. 44.

86. Christopher Lasch, *The Culture of Narcissism: American Life in an Age of Diminishing Expectations*, W.W. Norton, 1979.

87. Frosh, *Identity Crisis*, p. 101.

88. Ibid., p. 103.

89. Erik Erikson, *Childhood and Society* (1950), W.W. Norton, 1963, pp. 224.

90. Ibid., p. 228.

91. Ibid., p. 234.

92. Ibid.

93. Quoted in Frosh, *Identity Crisis*, p. 74.

94. Frosh, *Identity Crisis*, p. 64.

95. Sigmund Freud, *On Narcissism: An Introduction* (1914), The Pelican Freud Library, Vol. 11, 1984.

96. Joel Kovel, *The Radical Spirit*, Free Association Books, pp. 188, 197.

97. Oliver James, *The Selfish Capitalist: The Origins of Affluenza*, Vermilion, Ebury Publishing, 2008, pp. 57–8.

98. Paul Babiak and Robert D. Hare, *Snakes in Suits: When Psychopaths go to Work*, Harper, 2007, p. 131.

99. Karl Marx, *The Eighteenth Brumaire of Louis Bonaparte*, in K. Marx and F. Engels: *Selected Works*, Vol. 1, Foreign Languages Publishing House, 1962, p. 247.

100. Fromm and Maccoby, *Social Character*, pp. 17–18.

101. Russell Jacoby, *Social Amnesia*, Transaction, 1997, pp. 81–2.

102. Thompson, *The Making of the English Working Class*, pp. 354–5.

103. Fromm, *Fear of Freedom*, p. 80, quoted in ibid., p. 357.

104. Fromm, *Fear of Freedom*, p. 183.

105. Ibid., p. 183.

106. Fromm, Erich *The Working Class in Weimar Germany*, op. cit. The study, undertaken under the auspices of the International Institute for Social Research – i.e., the Frankfurt School relocated to the US – was published in 1984 under the title *The Working Class in Weimar Germany: A Psychological and Sociological Study*, edited by Wolfgang Bonss, Berg Publishers, 1984.

107. Thompson, *The Making of the English Working Class*, p. 382.

108. Kovel, *Radical Spirit*, p. 174; see also the interview with Kovel by Sebastian Gardner and Richard Kuper, *Interlink Magazine*, No. 12, May–June 1989, pp. 20–2.

109. Richard Lichtman, *The Production of Desire: The Integration of Psychoanalysis into Marxism*, The Free Press, 1982, p. 252.

110. Ibid., p. 229.

111. Michael Maccoby, 'Social Character vs. The Productive Ideal: The Contribution and Contradiction in Fromm's View of Man', *Praxis International*, Vol. 2, No. 1, 1982.

112. Paul Robinson, 'Cleaning Up Freud', *Partisan Review*, Vol. 41, 1974.

113. Lucien Goldman, 'Is There a Marxist Sociology?', introduced and translated by Ian Birchall, *International Socialism Journal*, Autumn 1968, p. 20.

114. Rickert, 'The Fromm-Marcuse Debate'; Eugene Wolfenstein, *Psychoanalytic Marxism: Groundwork*, Free Association Books, 1993, pp. 70–5.

115. Herbert Marcuse, *Eros and Civilisation*, Routledge & Kegan Paul, 1956, p. 243.
116. Marcuse, 'Epilogue: Critique of Neo-Freudian Revisionism', in ibid., pp. 258–9. Marcuse's reply to Fromm appeared as an article 'The Social Implications of Freudian Revisionism' in *Dissent*, II, Summer 1955.
117. Rickert, 'The Fromm-Marcuse Debate', p. 358.
118. Fromm, *Fear of Freedom*, pp. 249–50, quoted in ibid., p. 358.
119. Rickert, 'The Fromm-Marcuse Debate', pp. 358–9.
120. Ibid., p. 359.
121. Erich Fromm, *The Revolution of Hope* (1968), Lantern, 2011, pp. 143, 157, quoted in Herbert Marcuse, 'A Reply to Erich Fromm', *Dissent*, Vol. 3, No. 1, 1956, p. 81, quoted in Jacoby, *Social Amnesia*, p. 14.
122. Jacoby, *Social Amnesia*, p. 15.
123. Erich Fromm, 'The Humanistic Implications of Instinctivistic "Radicalism"', *Dissent*, Vol. 2, No. 4, 1955, pp. 348–9. A further exchange between Marcuse and Fromm took place in the same journal: Marcuse's 'A Reply to Erich Fromm' and Fromm's 'A Counter-Rebuttal', *Dissent*, Vol. 3, No. 1, 1956.
124. Fromm, *Sane Society*, pp. 283–6.
125. Wolfenstein, *Psychoanalytic Marxism*, pp. 67–73.

Chapter 4

1. Michael Schneider, *Neurosis and Civilisation: A Marxist/Freudian Synthesis*, Seabury Press, 1975, p. 140. Foucault challenged both Weber and Freud on this, but lack of space prevents me from taking up this argument.
2. Ibid., p. 142.
3. Eugene Wolfenstein, *Psychoanalytic Marxism: Groundwork*, Free Association Books, 1993, p. 292; Schneider, *Neurosis and Civilisation*, p. 122.
4. Schneider, *Neurosis and Civilisation*, p. 142.
5. Ibid., p. 144.
6. Barry Richards, *Schizoid States and the Market in Capitalism and Infancy: Essays on Psychoanalysis and Politics*, Free Association Books, 1984, p. 147.
7. Lichtman, *Production of Desire*, p. 247.
8. Schneider, *Neurosis and Civilisation*, pp. 122–3.
9. Ibid., p. 123.
10. Ibid., p. 162.
11. Ibid.
12. Sigmund Freud, *The Ego and the Id* (1923), Freud Pelican Library, Vol. 11, 1984, pp. 384–5.
13. Erich Fromm and Michael Maccoby, *Social Character in a Mexican Village*, Prentice-Hall, 1970, p. 74.
14. Schneider, *Neurosis and Civilisation*, p. 118, quoted in Wolfenstein, *Psychoanalytic Marxism*, p. 112.
15. Karl Marx, *Capital*, Vol. 1, Foreign Languages Publishing House, 1961, p. 42, quoted in Paul Sweezy, *The Theory of Capitalist Development* (1942), Monthly Review Press, 1964, p. 24.
16. Marx, *Capital*, Vol. 1, p. 88.
17. Ibid., p. 71.
18. Ibid., p. 72.
19. Ibid.
20. Ibid., p. 82; Sweezy, *Capitalist Development*, p. 35.

21. Marx, *Capital*, Vol. 1, p. 88.
22. Ibid., p. 92.
23. Sweezy, *Capitalist Development*, p. 36.
24. Schneider, *Neurosis and Civilisation*, p. 122.
25. Ibid.
26. Wolfenstein, *Psychoanalytic Marxism*, p. 292.
27. Ibid., p. 296.
28. Ibid., p. 301.
29. Ibid., p. 299.
30. Marx, *Capital*, Vol. 1, p. 176, quoted in Wolfenstein, *Psychoanalytic Marxism*, p. 299.
31. Erich Fromm, *The Sane Society*, Routledge & Kegan Paul, 1956, p. 117.
32. Wolfenstein, *Psychoanalytic Marxism*, p. 302.
33. Ibid.
34. Ibid., p. 303.
35. Ibid.
36. Ibid., p. 304–5.
37. Erich Fromm, *The Fear of Freedom*, Routledge & Kegan Paul, 1942, p. 122.
38. Ibid., pp. 123–4.
39. George Orwell, *The Road to Wigan Pier*, Victor Gollancz, 1937, p. 49.
40. Erich Fromm, *The Anatomy of Human Destructiveness*, Jonathan Cape, p. 225.
41. Ibid., p. 226.
42. Joel Kovel, *The Age of Desire*, Pantheon Books, 1981, p. 70.
43. Ibid., p. 69.
44. Ibid., p. 70.
45. Ibid., p. 72.
46. Ibid., p. 74.
47. Ibid., p. 72.
48. Fromm, *The Anatomy*, p. 227 n. Marx, *Capital*, Vol. 1, p. 609, n. 2. See also my Chapter 1.
49. Fromm, *The Anatomy*, p. 230.
50. Antonio Gramsci, 'The Intellectuals', in *Selections from the Prison Notebooks*, ed. and trans. Quinton Hoare and Geoffrey Nowell-Smith, Lawrence and Wishart, 1971, p. 9.
51. Karl Marx, *Preface to the Critique of Political Economy*, in K. Marx and F. Engels, *Selected Works*, Vol. 1, Foreign Languages Publishing House, 1962, p. 363.
52. Fromm, *The Anatomy*, p. 231.
53. Ibid., p. 233.
54. Ibid.
55. Simon Baron-Cohen, *Zero Degrees of Empathy: A New Theory of Human Cruelty*, Allen Lane, 2011.
56. Ibid., p. 5.
57. Ibid., p. 62.
58. Lichtman, *Production of Desire*, p. 226.
59. Ibid., p. 235.
60. D.W. Winnicott, 'Aggression in Relation to Emotional Development', in *Through Pediatrics to Psychoanalysis*, Basic Books, 1975, quoted in Anthony Storr, *Human Destructiveness*, Penguin, 1991, p. 21.
61. Storr, *Human Destructiveness*, p. 21.
62. Ibid., p. 22.
63. Kate Soper, *What Is Nature?*, Blackwell, 1995, p. 144.

64. Fromm, *The Anatomy*, p. 265.
65. Ibid., p. 262.
66. Storr, *Human Destructiveness*, p. 48.
67. Ibid., p. 62.
68. Sigmund Freud, *The Interpretation of Dreams*, First Part, Standard Edition of the Complete Psychological Works, Vol. IV (1900), Vintage, 2001, p. 264.
69. Lichtman, *Production of Desire*, p. 204.
70. John F. Walzer, 'A Period of Ambivalence', in Lloyd de Mause (ed.), *The History of Childhood*, Souvenir Press, 1976, p. 374.
71. Lawrence Stone, *The Family, Sex and Marriage in England 1500–1800*, Penguin, 1977, p. 80.
72. Oliver James, *Britain On the Couch*, Vermilion, 2010; Fromm, *The Sane Society*, ibid.
73. Fromm, *The Fear of Freedom*, p. 154.

Chapter 5

1. David Stannard, *American Holocaust: The Conquest of the New World*, Oxford University Press, 1992.
2. Ibid., pp. 11, 267, 268.
3. Henry F. Dobyns, 'Estimating Aboriginal American Population: An Appraisal of Techniques with a New Hemispheric Estimate', *Current Anthropology*, No. 7, 1966, pp. 395–416, quoted in M. Annette Jaimes (ed.), *The State of Native America: Genocide, Colonization, and Resistance*, South End Press, 1992, p. 26.
4. Kirkpatrick Sayle, *Christopher Columbus and the Conquest of Paradise*, Tauris Parke Paperbacks, 2006, p. 316, quoted in Jaimes, *State of Native America*, p. 27.
5. John E. Kicza, 'First Contacts', in Philip J. Deloria and Neal Salisbury (eds), *A Companion to American History*, Blackwell, 2004; Peter C. Mancall, 'Native Americans and Europeans in English America, 1500–1700', in Nicholas Canny (ed.), *The Oxford History of the British Empire: The Origins of Empire*, Oxford University Press, 1998.
6. Gary B. Nash, *Red, White and Black: The Peoples of Early North America*, Prentice Hall, 1974, p. 127.
7. R.W. Smith, 'State Power and Genocidal Intent', in *Proceedings of the International Conference 1997*, p. 229, quoted in Michael Mann, *The Dark Side of Democracy: Explaining Ethnic Cleansing*, Cambridge University Press, 2005, p. 71.
8. Howard Zinn, *A People's History of the United States*, Harper, 2001, p. 126.
9. I am grateful to Professor Kevin Kenny for drawing my attention to this body of work.
10. Patrick Spero, 'The Landscape of Life on the Mid-Atlantic Frontier' (review of Kevin Kenny's *Peaceable Kingdom Lost* and David L. Preston's *The Texture of Contact: European and Indian Settler Communities on the Frontiers of Iroquoia, 1667–1783*), *American History*, Vol. 39, No. 1, March 2011, p. 31.
11. Richard White, *The Middle Ground: Indians, Empires, and Republics in the Great Lakes Region, 1650–1815*, Cambridge University Press, 1991.
12. Spero, 'The Landscape of Life', p. 31.
13. Nash, *Red, White and Black*, p. 30.
14. Ibid., p. 318.
15. Ibid.

16. Ward Churchill, *A Little Matter of Genocide: Holocaust and Denial in the Americas 1492 to the Present*, City Lights Books, 1997, p. 154.
17. Ibid., p. 156.
18. Jeanne Kay, 'The Fur Trade and Native American Population Growth', *Ethnohistory*, Vol. 31, No. 4, 1984, p. 281.
19. Ibid., p. 280.
20. Henry Dobyns, *Their Numbers Become Thinned: Native American Population Dynamics in Eastern North America*, University of Tennessee Press, 1983, p. 24, quoted in Jaimes, *State of Native America*, p. 31.
21. Charles Gibson, *Spain in America*, HarperCollins, 1966, pp. 63, 116–17.
22. Mann, *Dark Side of Democracy*, p. 84.
23. Nash, *Red, White and Black*, p. 143.
24. Ibid., p. 119.
25. Mann, *Dark Side of Democracy*, p. 84; Nash, *Red, White and Black*, pp. 100–1.
26. Mann, *Dark Side of Democracy*, p. 86.
27. Ibid.
28. Kevin Kenny, *Peaceable Kingdom Lost*, Oxford University Press, 2009, p. 71.
29. Robert F. Berkhofer Jnr., *The White Man's Indian: Images of the American Indian from Columbus to the Present*, Alfred Knopf, 1978, p. 13.
30. Mann, *Dark Side of Democracy*, p.85.
31. Dale Van Every, *Disinherited: The Lost Birthright of the American Indians*, William Morrow & Co., 1966, p. 11.
32. Ibid., pp. 11–12.
33. Ibid., pp. 132, 258; Zinn, *People's History*, pp. 146–8; Mann, *Dark Side of Democracy*, p. 93.
34. Van Every, *Disinherited*, pp. 262–3.
35. Mann, *Dark Side of Democracy* , pp. 89–90.
36. Ibid., p. 90.
37. Ibid. See also Stannard, *American Holocaust*, pp. 141–6.
38. Stannard, *American Holocaust*, p. 142.
39. Mann, *Dark Side of Democracy*, p. 91.
40. All quotations in this paragraph are from Mann, *Dark Side of Democracy*, p. 92.
41. F. Prucha, 'Andrew Jackson's Indian Policy: A Reassessment', in A.L. Hurtado and P. Iverson (eds), *Major Problems in American Indian History*, Wadworth, 1994, p. 212, quoted in ibid., p. 93.
42. Mann, *Dark Side of Democracy*, p. 93; See also Robert V. Remini, *The Revolutionary Age of Andrew Jackson*, Harper & Row, 1985, Chapter 7.
43. Remini, *The Revolutionary Age of Andrew Jackson*, p. 110.
44. Ibid., p. 114.
45. Stannard, *American Holocaust*, pp. 118–19.
46. Ibid., p. 95.
47. Stannard, *American Holocaust*, pp. 74–5.
48. Ibid., p. 75.
49. Ibid., pp. 82–3.
50. Ibid., p. 85.
51. Ibid., p. 87.
52. Ibid., p. 88.
53. Ibid.
54. Hilberg, Raul, *The Destruction of the European Jews*, Chicago, 1961, p. 596.
55. Stannard, *American Holocaust*, p. 90.
56. Ibid., p. 91.

57. Bartolomé de Las Casas, *The Devastation of the Indies: A Brief Account*, trans. Herma Briffault, Baltimore, 1992, pp. 27, 30–3, quoted in Ben Kiernan, *Blood and Soil: A World History of Genocide and Extermination from Sparta to Darfur*, Yale University Press, 2007, p. 77.

58. Kiernan, *Blood and Soil*, p. 77.

59. Ibid., p. 82.

60. Stannard, *American Holocaust*, p. 73.

61. Edward H. Spicer, 'Political Incorporation and Cultural Change in New Spain: A Study in Spanish-Indian Relations', in H. Peckham and C. Gibson (eds), *Attitudes of Colonial Powers Toward the American Indian*, University of Utah Press, 1969, p. 110.

62. Lewis Hanke, 'Indians and Spaniards in the New World: A Personal View', in Peckham and Gibson, *Attitudes*, p. 4.

63. Ibid., p. 12.

64. Ibid., p. 16.

65. Spicer, 'Political Incorporation', p. 107.

66. J.H. Elliott, *Imperial Spain: 1469–1716*, Penguin, 2002, p. 70.

67. Henry Kamen, *Spain 1469–1714: A Society of Conflict*, Longman, 2005, p. 94.

68. Ibid. See also Robin Blackburn, *The Making of New World Slavery: From the Baroque to the Modern, 1492–1800*, Verso, 1997, p. 134.

69. Elliott, *Imperial Spain*, p. 75.

70. J.H. Elliott, *Empires of the Atlantic World: Britain and Spain in America 1492–1830*, Yale, 2006, p. 122.

71. Ibid., p. 127. Spicer, 'Political Incorporation', p. 112.

72. Magnus Morner, *Race Mixture in the History of Latin America*, Little Brown, 1967, p. 41.

73. Spicer, 'Political Incorporation', pp. 109.

74. Ibid., p. 112.

75. Ibid., pp. 122–3.

76. Ibid., p. 124.

77. Ibid., p. 126.

78. Ibid., p. 127.

79. Ibid., p. 129.

80. Charles Thomson, *An Enquiry into the Causes of the Alienation of the Delaware and Shawanese Indians from the British Interest* (1759), quoted in Kenny, *Peaceable Kingdom*, p. 102.

81. Nash, *Red, White and Black*, pp. 294–5.

82. Ibid., p. 295.

83. Ibid.

84. Ibid., pp. 295–6.

85. James Lockhart, 'Social Organisation and Social Change in Colonial Spanish America', in L. Bethell (ed.), *The Cambridge History of Latin America, Vol. 2: Colonial Latin America*, Cambridge University Press, 1984, p. 316.

86. Ernesto Laclau, 'Feudalism and Capitalism in Latin America', *New Left Review*, May–June 1971, p. 37.

87. Lewis Hanke, *The Spanish Struggle for Justice in the Conquest of America*, Southern Methodist University Press, 2002, p. 1.

88. Ibid., p. 173.

89. Stannard, *American Holocaust*, p. 32.

90. Zinn, *People's History*, pp. 18–19.

91. Ibid., p. 22.

92.   Stannard, *American Holocaust*, p. 103.
93.   Churchill, *A Little Matter of Genocide*, p. 148.
94.   Nash, *Red, White and Black*, p. 92.
95.   Ibid., pp. 10–11.
96.   Jaimes, 'Introduction: Sand Creek the Morning After', in *State of Native America*, p. 29.
97.   Nash, *Red, White and Black*, pp. 11–13.
98.   Ibid., p. 13.
99.   J.H. Spinden, *Population of Ancient America,* Anthropological Report, Smithsonian Institute, Washington DC, 1929, quoted in Leonore A. Stiffarm with Phil Lane Jnr., 'The Demography of Native North America', in Jaimes, *State of Native America*, p. 30.
100. M. Annette Jaimes, 'The Stone Age Revisited: An Indigenist View of Primitivism, Industrialism and the Labor Process', *New Studies on the Left*, Vol. XIV, No. 3, 1990–1, pp. 57–70.
101. Stiffarm and Jaimes, 'The Demography of Native North America', p. 30.
102. Nash, *Red, White and Black*, p. 74.
103. Ibid., p. 14; Stannard, *American Holocaust*, p. 32.
104. Stiffarm and Jaimes, 'The Demography of Native North America', p. 29.
105. Elliott, *Empires of the Atlantic World*, pp. 102–3.
106. Blackburn, *The Making of New World Slavery*, p. 236.
107. Mann, *Dark Side of Democracy*, p. 73.
108. Nash, *Red, White and Black*, pp. 75–6.
109. J.H. Elliott, 'Contrasting Empires', *History Today Magazine*, August 2006.
110. Nash, *Red, White and Black*, p. 76.
111. Ibid.
112. Frank Tannenbaum, *Slave and Citizen: The Negro in the Americas*, Random House, 1946, pp. 88–9.
113. Ibid., p. 42.
114. Ibid., pp. 66ff.
115. Ibid., p. 93.
116. Ibid., p. 65, footnote.
117. Blackburn, *The Making of New World Slavery*, p. 352.
118. Ibid., p. 353.
119. Ibid., pp. 354, 362.
120. Ibid., pp. 355–6.
121. Ibid., p. 260.
122. Ibid., p. 363.
123. Ibid., p. 356.
124. Ibid., p. 353.
125. Ibid., p. 311.
126. I am grateful to Professor Kevin Kenny for these points.
127. Nash, *Red, White and Black*, p. 118.
128. Blackburn, *The Making of New World Slavery*, p. 3.
129. Ibid., p. 388.
130. Ibid., p. 339.
131. Eltis, 'Europeans and the Rise and Fall of African Slavery in the Americas', pp. 1422–3.
132. Stannard, *American Holocaust*, p. 144.
133. Van Every, *Disinherited*, p. 253.
134. Jaimes, 'Introduction', *State of Native America*, p. 30.

135. Robert Berkhofer, *The White Man's Indian: Images of the American Indian from Columbus to the Present*, Alfred Knopf, 1978, pp. 6, 19, quoted in Robert M. Young, 'Psychoanalysis and the Other: Psychopathology and Racism', conference paper, Oxford, May 1993, p. 2; available at www.human-nature.com/rmyoung/papers. See also Young's chapter 'Projective Space: The Racial Other', in *Mental Space*, Process Press, 1994.

136. Hammond Innes, *The Conquistadors*, Book Club Associates, 1972, p. 18.

137. Ibid.

138. Elliott, *Imperial Spain*, p. 86.

139. Ibid., p. 90.

140. Ibid., pp. 92–4.

141. Ibid., p. 96.

142. Henry Kamen, *Empire: How Spain Became a World Power, 1492–1763*, Harper, 2003, p. 24.

143. Innes, *The Conquistadors*, p. 22.

144. Ibid., p. 24.

145. Ibid., p. 25.

146. Ibid., p. 28.

147. Ibid., p. 318.

148. Kirkpatrick Sale, *Christopher Columbus and the Conquest of Paradise*, Taurus Parke, 2006, p. 156.

149. Kamen, *Empire*, p. 96.

150. Elliott, *Imperial Spain*, p. 68.

151. Ibid., p. 70.

152. Kamen, *Spain 1469–1714*, pp. 26, 29, 82, 105, 114.

153. Ibid., pp. 152–3.

154. Ibid., p. 154.

155. Ibid., p. 155.

156. Elliott, *Empires of the Atlantic World*, p. 34.

157. Ibid., pp. 27–8.

158. Bartolomé Bennassar, *The Spanish Character: Attitudes and Mentalities From the Sixteenth to the Nineteenth Century*, University of California Press, 1979, p. 70.

159. Ibid., p. 69.

160. Ibid., p. 80.

161. Ibid., pp. 201–2.

162. Alain Saint-Saens (ed.), *Sex and Love in Golden Age Spain. Part 1: The Demand for Pleasure*, University Press of the South, 1999, pp. 19, 20.

163. Erich Fromm and Michael Maccoby, *Social Character in a Mexican Village*, Prentice-Hall, 1970, Chapter 4.

164. Anthony Pagden, *Spanish Imperialism and the Political Imagination: Studies in European and Spanish-American Social and Political Theory*, Yale University Press, 1990, p. 2.

165. Fromm and Maccoby, *Social Character*, p. 79.

166. Stannard, *American Holocaust*, p. 114.

167. Theodore Parker, *Collected Works*, X: 121, London, 1863–5, quoted in Hanke, *Spanish Struggle*, p. 175.

168. Anthony Pagden, *Lords Of All the World*, Yale University Press, 1995, p. 66.

169. Locke quoted in ibid., pp. 77–8.

170. Ibid., p. 93.

171. Ibid., p. 91.

172. Ibid., p. 92.

173. Ibid., pp. 92, 99.

174. Ibid., p. 101.

175. Elliott, *Imperial Spain*, p. 305.
176. Marcellin Defourneaux, *Daily Life in Spain in the Golden Age*, Praeger, 1971, pp. 29, 31.
177. Ibid., pp. 32, 35–6.
178. Bennassar, *Spanish Character*, p. 213.
179. Fromm and Maccoby, *Social Character*, p. 80.
180. Ibid., p. 81.
181. Ruth El Saffar, in Herman Vidal (ed.), *Cultural and Historical Grounding for Hispanic and Luso-Brazilian Feminist Literary Criticism*, University of Minnesota Press, 1989.
182. Ibid., p. 166.
183. Ibid., p. 168.
184. Ibid., p. 169.
185. Ibid., p. 176–7.
186. Ibid., p. 177.
187. Ibid., p. 181.
188. Hanke, *Spanish Struggle*, p. 178.
189. A.L. Morton, *A People's History of England* (1938), Lawrence & Wishart, 1965, p. 219.
190. Christopher Hill, *Society and Puritanism in Pre-Revolutionary England*, Secker & Warburg, 1964, pp. 129–30.
191. Morton, *People's History*, p. 220.
192. Lawrence Stone, *Family, Sex and Marriage in England 1500–1800*, Penguin, 1977, p. 176; Max Weber, *The Protestant Ethic and the Spirit of Capitalism*, Unwin University Books, 1930; R.H. Tawney, *Religion and the Rise of Capitalism*, John Murray, 1926.
193. Hill, *Society and Puritanism*, pp. 130, 135, 133.
194. Lawrence Stone, 'Puritanism', in *The Past and the Present Revisited*, Routledge & Kegan Paul, 1987, p. 212.
195. Hill, *Society and Puritanism*, p. 135.
196. Ibid., pp. 131, 134.
197. Stone, *Family, Sex and Marriage*, pp. 152, 154.
198. Ibid., p. 177.
199. Philip Greven, *The Protestant Temperament: Patterns of Child-Rearing, Religious Experience and the Self in Early America*, Alfred Knopf, 1977, pp. 32–43.
200. Ibid., p. 110.
201. Ibid.
202. Ibid., p. 121, quoted in Stannard, *American Holocaust*, p. 232.
203. Richard Drinnon, *Facing West: The Metaphysics of Indian-Hating and Empire-Building*, University of Oklahoma Press, 1997, pp. 66–8.
204. Richard Slotkin, *Regeneration Through Violence: The Mythology of the American Frontier 1600 to 1860*, University of Oklahoma Press, 1973, p. 178.
205. Berkhofer, *The White Man's Indian*, p. 83.
206. Slotkin, *Regeneration*, p. 88.
207. Ibid., p. 89.
208. Ibid., p. 514.
209. Ibid., p. 156.
210. Morton, *People's History*, p. 221.
211. Ibid., p. 222.
212. Ibid., pp. 222–3.
213. Slotkin, *Regeneration*, pp. 91–2.
214. Stone, *Family, Sex and Marriage*, p. 80.
215. Fromm and Maccoby, *Social Character*, p. 233.

216. Edmund S. Morgan, *The Puritan Family: Religion and Domestic Relations in Seventeenth-Century New England* (1942), Harper, 1966.
217. Kenny, *Peaceable Kingdom Lost*, p. 3.
218. Charles Oliver, 'They Shaped America But Did They Make it More Free?', Reason.com, July 2005, available at http://reason.com/archives/2005/07/01/the-fighting-scots-irish; review of James Webb, *Born Fighting: How the Scots-Irish Shaped America*, Broadway Books, 2005.
219. Quoted in Henry Jones Ford, *The Scotch-Irish in America* (1915), Adamant Media Corporation, 2006, p. 291.
220. Quoted in ibid., p. 243.
221. Ibid., pp. 90–1.
222. Quoted in Oliver, 'They Shaped America'.
223. James Leyburn, *The Scotch-Irish: A Social History*, University of North Carolina Press, 1962, pp. 67–8.
224. Ibid., p. 70.
225. Ibid., p. 75.
226. Ibid., pp. 141–3.
227. Ibid., p. 148.
228. Ibid., p. 153.
229. Ford, *The Scotch-Irish*, p. 32.
230. Ibid., p. 127.
231. Ibid., pp. 124–5.
232. Ibid., pp. 143–4.
233. Ibid., p. 127.
234. Ibid., pp. 147–8.
235. Oliver, 'They Shaped America'.
236. W. McAfee and V. Morgan, 'Population in Ulster, 1660–1760', in Peter Roebuck (ed.), *Plantation to Partition*, Blackstaff Press, 1981, p. 47.
237. Ibid., p. 53.
238. Ibid., pp. 53–4.
239. Ibid., pp. 57–8.
240. David Noel Doyle, 'Scots Irish or Scotch-Irish', in J.J. Lee and M. R. Casey (eds), *Making the Irish American: History and Heritage of the Irish in the US*, New York University Press, 2006, p. 158; McAfee and Morgan, 'Population in Ulster', p. 58.
241. McAfee and Morgan, 'Population in Ulster', p. 59.
242. Doyle, 'Scots Irish or Scotch-Irish', p. 161.
243. Kenny, *Peaceable Kingdom Lost*, p. 27.
244. Doyle, 'Scots-Irish or Scotch-Irish', p. 160.
245. Ibid.
246. Kenny, *Peaceable Kingdom Lost*, p. 27.
247. Greven, *Protestant Temperament*, p. 13.
248. Ibid., p. 81.
249. Ibid., p. 99.
250. Ibid., p. 110.
251. Ibid., p. 116.
252. Ibid., p. 121.

Chapter 6

1. Peter Balakian, *The Burning Tigris: The Armenian Genocide and America's Response*, Perennial, HarperCollins, 2003, pp. 178, 175.
2. Robert Fisk, *The Hidden Holocaust*, Panoptic, 1992, quoted in ibid., p. 176.

3. Balakian, *Burning Tigris*, pp. 178–80.

4. Murat Paker, 'Turkish-Armenian Conflict in the Context of the Dominant Political Culture in Turkey: A Psycho-Political Enquiry', 2010 (manuscript sent to the author), p. 3.

5. Ibid.

6. Charles Issawi, *The Economic History of Turkey: 1800 to 1914*, University of Chicago, 1980, p. 54.

7. Ibid., quoted in Ervin Staub, *The Roots of Evil: The Origins of Genocide and Other Group Violence*, Cambridge University Press, 1989, p. 173 footnote; Bernard Lewis, *The Emergence of Modern Turkey*, Oxford University Press, 2002, pp. 120, 159, 172; Donald Bloxham, *The Great Game of Genocide: Imperialism, Nationalism and the Destruction of the Ottoman Armenians*, Oxford University Press, 2005, p. 36.

8. Bloxham, *The Great Game*, p. 36.

9. Issawi, *Economic History*, p. 54.

10. Ibid.

11. Richard Hovannisian, 'Etiology and Sequelae of the Armenian Genocide', in George J. Andreopoulos (ed.), *Genocide: Conceptual and Historical Dimensions*, University of Pennsylvania Press, 1994, p. 118, quoted in Ben Kiernan, *Blood and Soil: A World History of Genocide and Extermination from Sparta to Darfur*, Yale University Press, 2007, pp. 396–7.

12. Bloxham, *The Great Game*, p. 15.

13. Ibid.

14. Issawi, *Economic History*, p. 55.

15. Bloxham, *The Great Game*, p. 11.

16. E.G. Mears, *Modern Turkey: An Economico-Political Interpretation 1908–1924*, Macmillan, 2004, Chapter 19, quoted in Staub, *The Roots of Evil*, p. 173.

17. Bloxham, *The Great Game*, p. 12.

18. Armin Vambery, quoted in Issawi, *Economic History*, pp. 272–3.

19. Ibid., p. 273.

20. Raphaela Lewis, *Everyday Life in Ottoman Turkey*, Dorset Press, 1971, p. 164.

21. Ibid., p. 165, quoted in Staub, *The Roots of Evil*, p. 175.

22. Lewis, *Everyday Life*, p. 165, emphasis added.

23. Staub, *Roots of Evil*, p. 175.

24. Issawi, *Economic History*, p. 199.

25. Kiernan, *Blood and Soil*, p. 397.

26. James Reid, 'Philosophy of State-Subject Relations, Ottoman Concepts of Tyranny, and the Demonisation of Subjects: Conservative Ottomanism as a Source of Genocidal Behaviour, 1821–1918', in Levon Chorbajian and George Shiranian (eds), *Studies in Comparative Genocide*, Palgrave Macmillan, 1999, p. 78, quoted in Kiernan, *Blood and Soil*, p. 397.

27. Bloxham, *The Great Game*, p. 14.

28. Issawi, *Economic History*, p. 15.

29. Ibid., pp. 11, 15.

30. Paker, 'Turkish-Armenian Conflict', p. 4.

31. Lewis, *Emergence of Modern Turkey*, p. 210.

32. Feroz Ahmad, *The Young Turks: The Committee of Union and Progress in Turkish Politics, 1908–14*, Hurst Co., 1969, p. 13.

33. Lewis, *Emergence of Modern Turkey*, p. 212.

34. Leon Trotsky, *The Balkan Wars 1912–13*, Pathfinder, 1981, p. 4.

35. Lewis, *Emergence of Modern Turkey*, p. 213.

36. Ibid., p. 214.

37. Ahmad, *Young Turks*, p. 22.
38. Lewis, *Emergence of Modern Turkey*, pp. 214–5.
39. Ahmad, *Young Turks*, p. 36.
40. Lewis, *Emergence of Modern Turkey*, p. 215.
41. Ahmad, *Young Turks*, p. 38.
42. Ibid., p. 37.
43. Ibid., p. 40.
44. Ibid., pp. 51–2.
45. Ibid., pp. 52–3.
46. Lewis, *Emergence of Modern Turkey*, p. 98.
47. Ahmad, *Young Turks*, pp. 53–4.
48. Lewis, *Emergence of Modern Turkey*, p. 219.
49. Ahmad, *Young Turks*, p. 55.
50. Lewis, *Emergence of Modern Turkey*, p. 254.
51. Ahmad, *Young Turks*, p. 57.
52. Lewis, *Emergence of Modern Turkey*, pp. 220–1.
53. Ibid., p. 222.
54. Ibid., pp. 222–3.
55. Ibid., p. 224.
56. Ibid., p. 225.
57. Ahmad, *Young Turks*, p. 118; Lewis, *Emergence of Modern Turkey*, p. 225.
58. Lewis, *Emergence of Modern Turkey*, p. 227.
59. Ibid.
60. Ibid., p. 228.
61. Kiernan, *Blood and Soil*, p. 405.
62. Feroz Ahmad, 'The Agrarian Policy of the Young Turks, 1908–1918', in *Economie et Societes Dans l'Empire Ottoman*, Colloques Internationaux, 601, Paris 1983, pp. 287–88, quoted in Kiernan, *Blood and Soil*, pp. 405–6.
63. Kiernan, *Blood and Soil*, p. 405.
64. Ahmad, *Young Turks*, pp. 279, 282–3, 286–7; Kiernan, *Blood and Soil*, p. 406.
65. Suhnaz Yilmaz, 'In Pursuit of Elusive Glory: Enver Pasha's Role in the Pan-Islamic and Basmachi Movements', in Baki Tezcan and Karl K. Barbir (eds), *Identity and Identity Formation in the Ottoman World: A Volume of Essays in Honor of Norman Itzkowitz*, University of Wisconsin Press, 2007, p. 189.
66. E.E. Ramsauer, *The Young Turks: Prelude to the Revolution of 1908*, Princeton, 1957, p. 31.
67. Michael Mann, *The Dark Side of Democracy: Explaining Ethnic Cleansing*, Cambridge University Press, 2005, p. 111.
68. Ahmad, *Young Turks*, p. 122.
69. Ibid., p. 15.
70. Ibid.
71. Ibid., p. 14.
72. Quoted in ibid., p. 16.
73. Quoted in ibid., p. 17.
74. Ibid., p. 17.
75. Ibid., p. 119.
76. Ibid., pp. 109, 111.
77. Ibid., p. 111.
78. Ibid., p. 108.
79. Jacob Landau, *Pan-Turkism: From Irredentism to Cooperation*, Bloomington Indiana University Press, 1996, p. 53, quoted in Balakian, *Burning Tigris*, p. 171.

80. Balakian, *Burning Tigris*, p. 178.
81. Ibid., p. 175.
82. Janet Klein, 'Conflict and Collaboration: Re-Thinking Kurdish-Armenian Relations in the Hamidian Period, 1876–1909', in Tezcan and Barbir, *Identity and Identity Formation in the Ottoman World*, pp. 155, 158.
83. Ibid., p. 156–7.
84. Ibid., p. 157.
85. Staub, *Roots of Evil*, p. 177.
86. Ibid., p. 184.
87. James Reid, *Crisis of the Ottoman Empire: Prelude to Collapse 1839–1878*, BL Franz Steiner Verlag, 2000, p. 386.
88. James Reid, 'Social and Psychological Factors in the Collapse of the Ottoman Era, circa 1780–1918', *Journal of Modern Hellenism*, No. 10, 1993, p. 156.
89. Reid, *Crisis of the Ottoman Empire*, p. 457.
90. Ibid., p. 479.
91. Raphaela Lewis, *Everyday Life* ibid., p. 95.
92. Ibid., Appendix 2, p. 481.
93. Ibid., pp. 481–2.
94. Ibid., p. 483.
95. Ibid., p. 485.
96. Reid, 'Social and Psychological Factors', pp. 118–9.
97. Ibid., p. 119.
98. Ibid.
99. Ibid.
100. Ibid., p. 120.
101. Ibid.
102. Ibid., p. 122.
103. Vahakn Dadrian, *The History of the Armenian Genocide: Ethnic Conflict from the Balkans to Anatolia to the Caucasus*, Berghahn Books, 1995, p. 195.
104. Reid, 'Social and Psychological Factors', p. 122.
105. Mann, *The Dark Side*, p. 139.
106. Roy R. Grinker and John P. Spiegel, *Men Under Stress*, Blakiston, 1945, p. 362, quoted in Reid, 'Social and Psychological Factors', p. 125.
107. *The Diagnostic and Statistical Manual of Mental* Disorders, third edition, Washington DC, 1987, p. 248, quoted in Reid, 'Social and Psychological Factors', p. 126.
108. Reid, 'Social and Psychological Factors', p. 127.
109. Ibid., pp. 126–7.
110. Henry Krystal, 'Clinical Observations on the Survivor Syndrome', in Krystal (ed.), *Massive Psychic Trauma*, International Universities Press, 1968, pp. 343–6, quoted in Reid, 'Social and Psychological Factors', p. 127.
111. Reid, 'Social and Psychological Factors', pp. 127–8.
112. Ibid., p. 128.
113. Ibid., pp. 128–9.
114. Ibid., p. 130.
115. Ibid., pp. 130–1.
116. Lieut.-General Valentine Baker Pasha, *War in Bulgaria: A Narrative of Personal Experience*, London, 1879, p. 96, quoted in Reid, 'Social and Psychological Factors', p. 142.
117. Reid, 'Social and Psychological Factors', p. 131.
118. Ibid., p. 133.

119. Dadrian, *History of the Armenian Genocide*, p. 197; Balakian, *Burning Tigris*, pp. 182-3; Bloxham, *The Great Game*, p. 70.
120. Balakian, *Burning Tigris*, pp. 185–6.
121. Reid, 'Social and Psychological Factors', p. 140.
122. Mann, *The Dark Side*, p. 133.
123. Ibid.; Dadrian, *History of the Armenian Genocide*, pp. 254–7.
124. Paker, 'Turkish-Armenian Conflict', p. 3.
125. Ibid., p. 4.
126. Ibid.
127. Kiernan, *Blood and Soil*, p. 407; see also Balakian, *Burning Tigris*, pp. 171, 178.
128. Robert Fisk, *The Great War for Civilisation*, Fourth Estate, 2005, p. 390.
129. Dadrian, *History of the Armenian Genocide*, p. 219.
130. Ibid., pp. 220–2.
131. Quoted in Ramsauer, *The Young Turks*, p. 42, quoted in Staub, *Roots of Evil*, p. 176.
132. Staub, *Roots of Evil*, p. 176; Erich Fromm and Michael Maccoby, *Social Character in a Mexican Village*, Prentice-Hall, 1970, pp. 16–23, 84–5; see also my Chapter 3, section on the destructive character, pp. 109–16.
133. See Fromm and Maccoby, *Social Character*, p. 79.
134. Ibid., pp. 68–85; Paker, 'Turkish-Armenian Conflict', p. 3; see also my Chapter 3.
135. Balakian, *Burning Tigris*, pp. 171, 178, quoted in Kiernan, *Blood and Soil*, p. 407.
136. Jay Winter, 'Introduction' to *America and the Armenian Genocide of 1915*, Cambridge University Press, 2003, I, 19; Takvimi vekayi 3540, 8, quoted in Vahakn Dadrian, 'The Determinants of the Armenian Genocide', Working paper GS 02, Genocide Studies Program, Yale Center for International and Area Studies, New Haven, 1998, 7–8, quoted in Kiernan, *Blood and Soil*, p. 415.

Chapter 7

1. Raul Hilberg, *The Destruction of the European Jews*, Holmes & Meier, 1985, pp. 248–9.
2. Ian Kershaw, *Popular Opinion and Political Dissent in the Third Reich*, Oxford University Press, 1983, pp. 274, 277, quoted in Norman Geras, *The Contract of Mutual Indifference*, Verso, 1998, p. 18.
3. Zygmunt Bauman, *Modernity and the Holocaust*, Polity Press, 1989, p. 74, quoted in Geras, *The Contract*, p. 18.
4. Bauman, *Modernity and the Holocaust*, p. 192, quoted in Geras, *The Contract*, p. 18.
5. Enzo Traverso, *Understanding the Nazi Genocide*, Pluto Press, 1999, p. 17.
6. Ibid., p. 16.
7. Ibid.
8. Michael Mann, *The Dark Side of Democracy: Explaining Ethnic Cleansing*, Cambridge University Press, 2005, p. 244.
9. Yaacov Lozowick, *Hitler's Bureaucrats: The Nazi Security Police and the Banality of Evil*, Continuum, 2000, quoted in Mann, *The Dark Side*, p. 245.
10. Lozowick, *Hitler's Bureaucrats*, p. 8, quoted in Mann, *The Dark Side*, p. 245.
11. James Waller, *Becoming Evil: How Ordinary Men Commit Genocide and Mass Killing*, Oxford University Press, 2007, p. 250.
12. Ibid.
13. Mann, *The Dark Side*, p. 245.

14. Norman Geras, 'Marxists Before the Holocaust', in Gilbert Achar (ed.), *The Legacy of Ernest Mandel*, Verso, 1999, p. 200.
15. Hans Mommsen, *From Weimar to Auschwitz*, Polity, 1991, p. 241.
16. The quotations are from the Wikipedia entry for Eugenics.
17. Alex Callinicos, 'Plumbing the Depths: Marxism and the Holocaust', *Yale Journal of Criticism*, Vol. 14, No. 2, 2001, p. 404.
18. Donny Gluckstein, *The Nazis, Capitalism and the Working Class*, Bookmarks, 1999, pp. 175–6.
19. Ibid., p. 179.
20. Arthur Schweitzer, *Big Business in the Third Reich*, Indiana University Press, second edition, 1977, p. 62.
21. Ibid., p. 65.
22. Ibid., p. 61.
23. Ibid., p. 63.
24. Ibid., p. 64.
25. Ibid., p. 66.
26. Ibid., p. 68.
27. Ibid.
28. Ibid.
29. Larry Eugene Jones, '"The Dying Middle": Weimar Germany and the Fragmentation of Bourgeois Politics', *Central European History*, Vol. 5, 1972, pp. 24–5, quoted in Mommsen, *From Weimar to Auschwitz*, pp. 21, 285.
30. Jones, '"The Dying Middle"', p. 25.
31. Ibid.
32. Schweitzer, *Big Business*, pp. 85–6.
33. Donald L. Niewyk, *The Jews in Weimar Germany*, Transaction Publishers, 2001, p. 14.
34. Michael Kater, *The Nazi Party: A Social Profile of Members and Leaders, 1919–1945*, Blackwell, 1983, p. 263, quoted in Gluckstein, *The Nazis*, p. 90.
35. Alan Bullock, *Hitler: A Study in Tyranny*, Penguin, 1962, p. 218, quoted in Gluckstein, *The Nazis*, p. 68.
36. S.M. Lipset, *Political Man* (1959), William Heinemann, 1960, pp. 140–1.
37. Schweitzer, *Big Business*, p. 72.
38. Lipset, *Political Man*, p. 143.
39. Schweitzer, *Big Business*, p. 74.
40. Ibid., p. 75.
41. Ibid.
42. Ibid., p. 76.
43. Ibid., p. 82.
44. Ibid.
45. Quoted in Ben Kiernan, *Blood and Soil: A World History of Genocide and Extermination from Sparta to Darfur*, Yale University Press, 2007, p. 428.
46. Ibid., p. 427.
47. Schweitzer, *Big Business*, p. 82.
48. Ibid., p. 83.
49. Ibid., p. 85.
50. Ibid., p. 86.
51. Ibid.
52. Jones, '"The Dying Middle"', p. 53.
53. Schweitzer, *Big Business*, p. 88.

54. Hans Gerth, 'The Nazi Party: Its Leadership and Composition', *American Journal of Sociology*, Vol. XLV, 1940, pp. 100–13.
55. Michael Mann, *Fascists*, Cambridge University Press, 2004.
56. Ibid., Table 4.1, p. 378.
57. Ibid., p. 157.
58. Schweitzer, *Big Business*, pp. 62, 65.
59. Kater, *Nazi Party*, p. 52.
60. Mann, *Fascists*, p. 157.
61. Ibid., p. 158.
62. Ibid.
63. Ibid., pp. 159–60.
64. Ibid., p. 160.
65. Ibid., p. 161.
66. Cf. W. Brustein, *The Logic of Evil: The Social Origins of the Nazi Party, 1925–1933*, Yale University Press, 1996, fig. 3.6, quoted in Mann, *Fascists*, p. 161.
67. Mann, *Fascists*, p. 169.
68. Kater, *Nazi Party*, p. 5.
69. Schweitzer, *Big Business*, p. 65.
70. Kater, *Nazi Party*, p. 229.
71. Ibid.
72. Former Gauleiter Albert Krebs, quoted in Kater, *Nazi Party*, pp. 173–4.
73. Samuel Pratt, *The Social Basis of Nazism and Communism in Urban Germany* (MA thesis, Department of Sociology, Michigan State University, 1948), quoted in Lipset, *Political Man*, p. 141.
74. Lipset, *Fascism*, p. 147.
75. Charles P. Loomis and J. Allen Beegle, 'The Spread of German Nazism in Rural Areas', *American Sociological Review*, Vol. 11, 1946, pp. 730, 729, quoted in Lipset, *Fascism*, pp. 146–7.
76. Rudolf Heberle, *From Democracy to Nazism*, Louisiana State University Press, 1945, p. 112, quoted in Lipset, *Fascism*, p. 147.
77. Thomas Childers, 'Who, Indeed, Did Vote For Hitler?', *Central European History*, Vol. 17, No. 1, 1984, p. 53, quoted in Mann, *Fascists*, p. 190.
78. Ian Kershaw, *Hitler 1889–1936: Hubris*, Penguin, 1998, p. 404.
79. Childers, 'Who, Indeed, Did Vote For Hitler?', p. 53, quoted in Mann, *Fascists*, pp. 190.
80. Thomas Childers, *The Nazi Voter*, University of North Carolina Press, 1983, pp. 268–9, quoted in Mann, *Fascists*, p. 190.
81. Mann, *Fascists*, p. 190.
82. Childers, *Nazi Voter*, p. 255, quoted in Mann, *Fascists*, p. 190.
83. Ibid., p. 191.
84. Mann, *Fascists*, p. 190.
85. Childers, *Nazi Voter*, pp. 49–50.
86. Thomas Childers, 'The Social Language of Politics in Germany: The Sociology of Political Discourse in the Weimar Republic', *American Historical Review*, Vol. 95, 1990, quoted in Mann, *Fascists*, p. 177.
87. Mann, *Fascists*, pp. 178, 181.
88. J. Brown, 'The Berlin NSDAP in the Kampfzeit', *German History*, Vol. 7, 1989, quoted in Mann, *Fascists*, p. 181.
89. Kershaw, *Hitler 1889–1936*, pp. 389–91.
90. Mann, *Fascists*, p. 160.
91. Kershaw, *Hitler 1889–1936*, pp. 332–3.

92. Jones, "'The Dying Middle'", pp. 23–4, quoted in Mommsen, *From Weimar to Auschwitz*, pp. 21, 285.
93. J.H. Clapham, *Economic Development of France and Germany 1815–1914*, Cambridge University Press, 1966, p. 285.
94. W.O. Henderson, 'Germany's Economic Development, 1871–1914', Part 2 of Chapter II of E.J. Passant, *A Short History of Germany 1815–1945*, Cambridge University Press, 1962, p. 104.
95. Ibid., p. 110.
96. Ibid., pp. 110–11.
97. Ibid.
98. Karl Marx, 'The Bourgeoisie and the Counter-Revolution', Second Article, December 1848, in K. Marx and F. Engels, *Selected Works*, Vol. 1, Foreign Languages Publishing House, 1962, pp. 68–9.
99. Gareth Stedman-Jones, 'Society and Politics at the Beginning of the World Economy', *Cambridge Journal of Economics*, Vol. 1, 1977, p. 87.
100. David Blackbourn, 'Between Resignation and Volatility', in Geoffrey Crossick and Heinz-Gerhard Haupt (eds), *Shopkeepers and Master Artisans in Nineteenth-Century Europe*, Methuen, 1984, p. 37.
101. Ibid., p. 38.
102. Ibid., p. 39.
103. Ibid.
104. Ibid., p. 40.
105. Ibid.
106. Ibid., p. 42.
107. Ibid., p. 43.
108. Ibid.
109. Ibid., p. 45.
110. Ibid., p. 52.
111. Ibid., p. 46.
112. Ibid.
113. Ibid., p. 48.
114. Hans-Ulrich Wehler, *The German Empire: 1871–1918*, Berg, 1985, pp. 10–11.
115. Ibid., p. 11.
116. Ibid., p. 35.
117. Ibid., p. 13.
118. Ibid.
119. Schweitzer, ibid, p. 71; Gluckstein, ibid, p. 40.
120. Erich Fromm, *The Fear of Freedom*, Routledge & Kegan Paul, 1942, p. 191.
121. Martin Broszat and Saul Friedlander, 'A Controversy About the Historicisation of National Socialism', *Yad Vashem Studies*, Vol. 19, 1988, pp. 28–9, quoted in Geras, *Contract*, p. 160.
122. Wilhelm Reich, *The Mass Psychology of Fascism* (1933), Farrar, Straus & Giroux, 1970; Fromm, *The Fear of Freedom,* 1942.
123. Blackbourn, 'Between Resignation and Volatility', p. 49.
124. Kater, *Nazi Party*, p. 189.
125. Theodor Adorno and Max Horkheimer, 'Elements of Anti-Semitism', in *Dialectic of Enlightenment*, Stanford University Press, 2002.
126. Ibid., p. 144.
127. Reich, *Mass Psychology*, pp. 44–6.
128. Ibid., p. 34.
129. Ibid., p. 35.

130. Ibid., p. 37.
131. Ibid., p. 47.
132. Ibid., p. 44.
133. Ibid., pp. 53, 55. See Paul Robinson, *The Freudian Left*, Cornell University Press, 1969, pp. 48–9, for an interesting critique of Reich.
134. Fromm, *Fear of Freedom*, especially Chapter 5, 'The Psychology of Nazism'.
135. Heinz Kohut, *Self Psychology and the Humanities: Reflections on a New Psychoanalytical Approach*, Norton, 1985, p. 141, quoted in Felicity de Zulueta, *From Pain to Violence: The Traumatic Roots of Destructiveness*, John Wiley & Sons, 2006, p. 134.
136. Heinz Kohut, *The Analysis of the Self*, University of Chicago Press, 1971, p. 256.
137. Kershaw, *Hitler 1889–1936*, p. 13.
138. Alan Bullock, *Hitler and Stalin: Parallel Lives*, Harper Collins, 1991.
139. Peter Loewenberg, 'The Psychohistorical Origins of the Nazi Youth Cohort', *American Historical Review*, Vol. 76, 1971, p. 1458.
140. Martin Wangh, 'National Socialism and Genocide of the Jews: A Psycho-Analytic Study of a Historical Event', *International Journal of Psychoanalysis*, Vol. 45, 1964, p. 392.
141. L. Kattenacker, 'Social and Psychological Aspects of the Fuhrer's Rule', in W.H. Koch (ed.), *Aspects of the Third Reich*, Macmillan, 1985, pp. 131–2.
142. Henry V. Dicks, *Licensed Mass Murder: A Socio-Psychological Study of Some SS Killers*, Chatto/Heinemann, 1972, p. 265.
143. Ibid.
144. Ibid., p. 108.
145. Ibid., p. 249.
146. Norman Cohn, *Warrant for Genocide*, Penguin, 1970, p. 293.
147. Dicks, *Licensed Mass Murder*, p. 57.
148. Hannah Arendt, *Eichmann in Jerusalem: A Report on the Banality of Evil*, Viking Press, 1963.
149. I.S. Kulcsar, Shoshanna Kulcsar and Lipot Szondi, 'Adolf Eichmann and the Third Reich', in R. Slovenko (ed.), *Crime, Law and Corrections*, Charles C. Thomas, 1966.
150. Mann, *The Dark Side*, p. 245.
151. Klaus Theweleit, *Male Fantasies*, 2 vols., University of Minnesota Press, 1987/1989.
152. Mommsen, *From Weimar to Auschwitz*, p. 13.
153. Klaus, *Male Fantasies*, Vol. 1, p. 227.
154. Barbara Ehrenreich, Foreword to Theweleit, *Male Fantasies*, Vol. 1, p. xiii.
155. Theweleit, *Male Fantasies*, Vol. 1, p. 76.
156. Ibid., Vol. 1, p. 81.
157. Ibid., Vol. 1, p. 91.
158. Ibid., Vol. 2, p. 92.
159. Ibid., Vol. 1, p. 103.
160. Ibid., Vol. 2, p. 216.
161. Ibid.
162. Melanie Klein, 'Some Theoretical Conclusions Regarding the Emotional Life of the Infant' and 'The Psycho-Analytic Play Technique: Its History and Significance', in *Envy and Gratitude and other Works*, Delta, 1975, quoted in ibid., Vol. 2, pp. 216–7.
163. Margaret Mahler, *On Human Symbiosis and the Vicissitudes of Individuation, Vol. I, Infantile Psychosis*, International Universities Press, 1970, p. 109, quoted in Theweleit, *Male Fantasies*, Vol. 2, p. 217, Vol. 1, pp. 206–7.
164. Theweleit, *Male Fantasies*, Vol. 2, p. 252.

165. Ibid., Vol. 2, p. 211.
166. Ibid., Vol. 2, p. 213.
167. Wangh, 'National Socialism and the Genocide of the Jews', p. 387.
168. Bertram Schaffner, *Father Land: A Study of Authoritarianism in the German Family*, Columbia University Press, 1948, p. 13, quoted in Robert Waite, *The Psychopathic God: Adolf Hitler*, Basic Books, 1977, p. 296.
169. Schaffner, *Father Land*, Chapter 4.
170. Quoted in ibid., p. 38.
171. Ibid., p. 35.
172. Ibid.
173. Ibid.
174. Waite, *Psychopathic God*, p. 296.
175. Wangh, 'National Socialism and the Genocide of the Jews', p. 388.
176. Schaffner, *Father Land*, p. 6.
177. Bela Grunberger, 'The Anti-Semite and the Oedipal Conflict', *International Journal of Psychoanalysis*, Vol. 45, 1964, p. 383.
178. Ibid.
179. Wangh, 'National Socialism and the Genocide of the Jews', p. 392.
180. Ibid.
181. Christopher Browning, *Ordinary Men: Reserve Police Battalion 101 and the Final Solution in Poland*, HarperCollins, 1992, Tables 1 and 2, pp. 225–6.
182. Ibid., p. 48.
183. Ibid.
184. Ibid., p. 2.
185. Ibid., pp. 6, 57.
186. Ibid., pp. 62–3.
187. Chris Harman, *The Lost Revolution: Germany 1918 to 1923*, Bookmarks, 1982, pp. 40–1.
188. Omer Bartov, 'Operation Barbarossa and the Origins of the Final Solution', in David Cesarani (ed.), *The Final Solution: Origins and Implementation*, Routledge, 1994.
189. Mommsen, *From Weimar to Auschwitz*, p. 175, quoted in Callinicos, 'Plumbing the Depths', p. 399.
190. Yehuda Bauer, *Rethinking the Holocaust*, Yale University Press, 2000, p. 5.
191. Mommsen, *From Weimar to Auschwitz*, p. 175.
192. Christopher Browning, *The Origins of the Final Solution: The Evolution of Nazi Jewish Policy, September 1939–March 1942*, University of Nebraska and Yad Vashem, 2004, p. 36.
193. Ibid., p. 44.
194. Ibid., p. 45.
195. Ibid., p. 106.
196. Ibid., p. 56.
197. Ibid., pp. 67–8.
198. Ibid., p. 109.
199. Quoted in ibid., pp. 69–70.
200. Quoted in ibid., p. 71.
201. Ibid., p. 99.
202. Ibid., p. 100.
203. Ibid., p. 101.
204. Ibid., p. 103.
205. Ibid., p. 102.

206. Aly Götz, *Final Solution: Nazi Population Policy and the Murder of the European Jews*, Arnold 1999, pp. 176–7.
207. Arendt, *Eichmann in Jerusalem*, p. 69.
208. Browning, *The Origins of the Final Solution*, p. 37.
209. Arendt, *Eichmann*, p. 69.
210. Browning, *Origins of the Final Solution*, p. 176.
211. Aly, *Final Solution*, p. 2.
212. Ibid., p. 54.
213. Browning, *Origins of the Final Solution*, p. 137.
214. R. Breitman, 'Himmler: The Architect of Genocide', in Cesarani (ed.), *The Final Solution*, p. 80.
215. Arendt, *Eichmann in Jerusalem*, p. 88.
216. Christopher Browning, 'Beyond "Intentionalism" and "Functionalism": The Decision for the Final Solution Reconsidered', in *The Path to Genocide*, Cambridge University Press, 1992, p. 88.
217. Browning, *Origins of the Final Solution*, p. 102.
218. Christopher Browning, 'Hitler and the Euphoria of Victory: The Path to the Final Solution', in Cesarani (ed.), *The Final Solution*; and Browning, *Origins of the Final Solution*, Chapter 8.
219. C. Streit, *Wehrmacht, Einsatzgruppen and Anti-Bolshevism*, in Cesarani, D. (ed.), ibid., p. 105.
220. Jurgen Matthäus, 'Operation Barbarossa and the Onset of the Holocaust, June–December 1941', Chapter 7 of Browning, *Origins of the Final Solution*, p. 278.
221. Ibid., p. 297.
222. Browning, *Path to Genocide*, p. 119.
223. Ibid., p. 120.
224. Browning, *Origins of the Final Solution*, p. 427.
225. Ibid., p. 373. Emphasis in first quotation added.
226. David Cesarani, 'Introduction' to Cesarani (ed.), *The Final Solution*.
227. Mommsen, *From Weimar to Auschwitz*, p. 236.
228. Arno Mayer, *Why Did The Heavens Not Darken?*, Random House, 1988, p. 235.
229. Philippe Burrin, *Hitler and the Jews: The Genesis of the Holocaust*, Edward Arnold, 1994, pp. 146–7.
230. Mommsen, *From Weimar to Auschwitz*, p. 226.
231. Aly, *Final Solution*, p. 201.
232. Ibid., p. 256.
233. Ibid., p. 203.
234. See also Jorg Friedrich, *The Fire: The Bombing of Germany 1940–1945,* Columbia University Press, 2006.
235. Mommsen, *From Weimar to Auschwitz*, p. 239.
236. Traverso, *Understanding the Nazi Genocide*, p. 58.
237. Raul Hilberg, *The Destruction of the European Jews*, Vol. 3, New York, Holmes & Meier, 1985, p. 1006, quoted in Callinicos, 'Plumbing the Depths', pp. 385–414.
238. Callinicos, 'Plumbing the Depths', p. 403.
239. Traverso, *Understanding the Nazi Genocide*, pp. 58–9, Bauman, *Modernity and the Holocaust*, p. 106.
240. Browning, *Path to Genocide*, p. 91.
241. Browning, *Path to Genocide*, p. 121.
242. Ibid., p. 95.
243. Mommsen, *From Weimar to Auschwitz*, p. 224.
244. Ibid., p. 232.

245. Ibid., p. 234.

246. Ibid., p. 238.

247. Ibid., pp. 238–9.

248. Ibid., p. 240.

249. Ibid.

250. Ibid.

251. Ibid., pp. 252–3.

252. Ibid., p. 250.

253. Ian Kershaw, *Fateful Choices: Ten Decisions That Changed the World 1940–1941*, Penguin, 2007, pp. 433–4.

254. Ibid., p. 433.

255. Ibid., p. 434.

256. Kohut, *The Analysis of the Self*, p. 150.

257. Heinz Kohut, *The Restoration of the Self*, University of Chicago, 1977, p. 129.

258. Theweleit, *Male Fantasies*, Vol. 2, p. 357.

259. See Philip Greven, *The Protestant Temperament: Patterns of Child-Rearing, Religious Experience, and the Self in Early America*, Alfred Knopf, 1977, especially Parts 1 and 2.

Chapter 8

1. Philip Gourevitch, *We Wish to Inform You That Tomorrow We Will Be Killed With Our Families* (1998), Picador, 2000, p. 115.

2. Jean Hatzfeld, *Machete Season: The Killers in Rwanda Speak*, Picador, Farrar, Straus and Giroux, 2005, p. 106 (French edition: *Saison de Machettes*, Editions du Seuil, 2003).

3. S. Straus, *The Order of Genocide: Race, Power and War in Rwanda*, Ph.D dissertation, University of California, Berkeley, 2004, quoted in Michael Mann, *The Dark Side of Democracy*, Cambridge University Press, 2005, p. 463.

4. Human Rights Watch, 1999; OAU, and 2003. World Reports: Burundi, Rwanda, Sudan. Organisation of African Unity, IPEP Report, 2000, paras. 16.35 and 16.69, quoted in Mann, *The Dark Side*, p. 463.

5. International Conference on Genocide, Impunity and Accountability, Kigali, 1–5 November 1995, quoted in Mahmood Mamdani, *When Victims Become Killers: Colonialism, Nativism, and the Genocide in Rwanda*, Princeton University Press, 2001, p. 199.

6. Mamdani, *When Victims Become Killers*, Chapter 2, 'The Origins of Hutu and Tutsi'; Mann, *The Dark Side*, p. 431.

7. Mamdani, *When Victims Become Killers*, esp. pp. 73–5.

8. Ibid., p. 62.

9. Gerard Prunier, *The Rwanda Crisis: History of a Genocide*, Hurst & Co., 1995, p. 11.

10. Ibid., p. 12.

11. Mamdani, *When Victims Become Killers*, p. 62.

12. Ibid., p. 63.

13. Ibid.

14. Prunier, *Rwanda Crisis*, p. 27.

15. Ibid., p. 31.

16. Ibid., p. 15.

17. Ibid., p. 20.

18. Ibid., pp. 33–4.
19. Report Administration Coloniale Ruanda-Urundi, 1927, p. 38, quoted in ibid., p. 92.
20. Mamdani, *When Victims Become Killers*, p. 77.
21. Ibid., p. 99.
22. Ibid., p. 80.
23. Ibid., p. 99.
24. The Belgian Congo and Ruanda-Urandi Information and Public Relations Office, *Ruanda Urundi*, 60, No. 4, quoted in ibid., p. 99.
25. Mamdani, *When Victims Become Killers*, p. 101.
26. Prunier, *Rwanda Crisis*, p. 35.
27. Mamdani, *When Victims Become Killers*, p. 94.
28. C. Newbury, *The Cohesion of Oppression: Clientship and Ethnicity in Rwanda, 1860-1960*, Columbia University Press, 1989, p. 178, quoted in ibid., p. 111.
29. Mamdani, *When Victims Become Killers*, p. 114.
30. Ibid., p. 116.
31. Quoted in ibid., p. 116.
32. Ibid., p. 126.
33. Ibid., p. 124.
34. Prunier, *Rwanda Crisis*, p. 50.
35. Mamdani, *When Victims Become Killers*, pp. 133–4.
36. Prunier, *Rwanda Crisis*, p. 52.
37. Ibid., p. 53. Rwanda became formally independent in July 1962.
38. Ibid., pp. 56–7.
39. Ian Linden, *Church and Revolution in Rwanda*, Manchester University Press, 1977, p. 372.
40. Ibid., p. 373.
41. Mamdani, *When Victims Become Killers*, p. 232; Prunier, *Rwanda Crisis*, p. 75.
42. Mamdani, *When Victims Become Killers*, p. 215; Prunier, *Rwanda Crisis*, p. 60.
43. Mamdani, *When Victims Become Killers*, pp. 137–8.
44. Ibid., pp. 136, 138, 139.
45. Prunier, *Rwanda Crisis*, pp. 76–7.
46. Ibid., p. 78.
47. Mamdani, *When Victims Become Killers*, pp. 145–6.
48. Prunier, *Rwanda Crisis*, pp. 78–9; Mamdani, *When Victims Become Killers*, pp. 144–5.
49. Prunier, *Rwanda Crisis*, p. 87.
50. Ibid., p. 88.
51. Mamdani, *When Victims Become Killers*, p. 149.
52. Ibid., p. 161.
53. Ibid., p. 164.
54. Figures in Mann, *The Dark Side*, p. 430.
55. Mamdani, *When Victims Become Killers*, p. 160.
56. Ibid., p. 37.
57. Ibid., p. 38.
58. Ibid., p. 160.
59. C. Newbury and D. Newbury, 'Identity, Genocide and Reconstruction in Rwanda', paper presented at European Parliament conference, 1995, quoted in Mamdani, *When Victims Become Killers*, pp. 187–8.
60. Mamdani, *When Victims become Killers*, p. 192.
61. Ibid., p. 193.

62. Ibid., p. 194.
63. D.C. Clay, 'Fighting an Uphill Battle: Demographic Pressure, the Structure of Land Holding and Land Degradation in Rwanda', Department of Agricultural Economics, Michigan State University, 1993, quoted in Scott Grosse, 'More People, More Trouble: Population Growth and Agricultural Change in Rwanda', Deptartment of Population Planning and International Health, School of Public Health, University of Michigan, Ann Arbor, 1994, quoted in Mamdani, *When Victims Become Killers*, p. 197.
64. Grosse, 'More People', quoted in Mamdani, *When Victims Become Killers*, p. 197.
65. Mamdani, *When Victims Become Killers*, p. 204.
66. Ibid.
67. Ibid, p. 216.
68. Mann, *The Dark Side*, p. 449.
69. Mamdani, *When Victims Become Killers*, p. 233.
70. Ibid., p. 232.
71. Ibid., p. 227.
72. Ibid.
73. Prunier, *Rwanda Crisis*, p. 243.
74. Ibid., p. 244.
75. Ibid.
76. Ibid., p. 246.
77. Ibid., p. 409.
78. Ibid., p. 245.
79. Hatzfeld, *Machete Season*, pp. 220–1.
80. Mamdani, *When Victims Become Killers*, p. 217.
81. Prunier, *Rwanda Crisis*, p. 247.
82. Ibid., pp. 247–8.
83. Hatzfeld, *Machete Season*, p. 51.
84. Rene Lemarchand, 'Rwanda: The Rationality of Genocide', *Issue: A Journal of Opinion*, Vol. 23, No. 2, 1995, p. 8.
85. Prunier, *Rwanda Crisis*, p. 249.
86. Ibid., p. 232.
87. Ibid., p. 295.
88. Peter Uvin, 'Prejudice, Crisis and Genocide in Rwanda', *African Studies Review*, Vol. 40, No. 2, 1997, p. 102.
89. Ibid., p. 103.
90. Ibid., p. 104.
91. Ibid., p. 112.
92. Ibid.
93. Prunier, *Rwanda Crisis*, p. 245.
94. Mamdani, *When Victims Become Killers*, p. 206.
95. Prunier, *Rwanda Crisis*, pp. 141–2.
96. Quoted in Gourevitch, *We Wish to Inform You*, p. 23.
97. J-J. Maquet, *Le Système des Relations Sociales dans le Rwanda Ancien*, Tervuren: MRCB, 1954, pp. 186–7, quoted in Prunier, *Rwanda Crisis*, p. 57.
98. Prunier, *Rwanda Crisis*, p. 248.
99. Tomas Bohm, 'Psychoanalytic Aspects of Perpetrators of Genocide', *Scandinavian Psychoanalytic Review*, Vol. 29, 2006, p. 23.
100. Ibid.
101. Hatzfeld, *Machete Season*, p. 45.

102. Ibid., pp. 173–5.
103. Felicity de Zulueta, *From Pain to Violence: The Traumatic Roots of Destructiveness*, John Wiley & Sons, 2006, p. 5.
104. Vamik Volkan, *The Need to Have Enemies and Allies: From Clinical Practice to International Relations*, Jason Aronson, 1994, p. xxv, quoted in Uvin, *Prejudice*, p. 105.
105. Hatzfeld, *Machete Season*, p. 49.
106. Ibid., p. 219.
107. Ibid., pp. 240–2.
108. de Zulueta, *From Pain to Violence*, p. 134.
109. Prunier, *Rwanda Crisis*, p. 28.
110. Hatzfeld, *Machete Season*, p. 47.
111. Ibid., p. 62.
112. Erich Fromm and Michael Maccoby, *Social Character in a Mexican Village*, Prentice-Hall, 1970, p. 79.
113. Ibid., p. 85.

Summary and Conclusion

1. Erich Fromm, *Fear of Freedom*, Routledge & Kegan Paul, 1942, p. 239.
2. M.D. Eder, 'On the Economics and the Future of the Super-Ego', *International Journal of Psychoanalysis*, Vol. 10, 1929, pp. 249–55, quoted by R. Reiche, *Sexuality and Class Struggle*, trans. D. Fernbach, New Left Books, 1968, pp. 130–1.
3. Leon Trotsky, *Literature and Revolution* (1924), University of Michigan Press, 1960, pp. 255–6.

Bibliography

Adorno, Theodor W. (2005) *Critical Models: Interventions and Catchwords* (New York: Columbia University Press).

Adorno, Theodor W. and Horkheimer, Max (2002 [1947]) 'Elements of Anti-Semitism', in *Dialectic of Enlightenment* (Stanford: Stanford University Press).

Adorno, Theodor W., Frenkel-Brunswik, E., Levinson, D.J., Sanford, R.N. (1950) *The Authoritarian Personality* (New York: Harper & Row).

Ahmad, Feroz (1969) *The Young Turks: The Committee of Union and Progress in Turkish Politics, 1908–14* (London: Hurst Co.).

Ahmad, F. (1983) 'The Agrarian Policy of the Young Turks, 1908–1918', in *Economie et Societes Dans l'Empire Ottoman, Colloques Internationaux du CNRS* (Paris: Centre National de la Recherche Scientifique).

Altemayer, Bob (2006) *The Authoritarians*, available at http://home.cc.umanitoba.ca/~altemey.

Aly, Gotz (1999 [1995]) *Final Solution: Nazi Population Policy and the Murder of the European Jews* (London: Arnold).

American Psychiatric Association (1987 [1952]) *The Diagnostic and Statistical Manual of Mental Disorders*, third edition, Washington DC.

Anderson, Benedict (1983) *Imagined Communities* (London: Verso).

Archer, Margaret (1986) *Culture and Agency: The Place of Culture in Social Theory* (Cambridge: Cambridge University Press).

Arendt, Hannah (1958) *The Origins of Totalitarianism* (London: George Allen & Unwin).

Arendt, Hannah (1963) *Eichmann in Jerusalem: A Report on the Banality of Evil* (New York: Viking Press).

Babiak, Paul and Robert D. Hare, *Snakes in Suits: When Psychopaths go to Work*, Harper, 2007.

Baggini, J. (2008) 'Book of the Week: *Violence* by Slavoj Žižek', *Times Higher Education*, 14 February.

Baker Pasha, Valentine, Lieut.-General (1879) *War in Bulgaria: A Narrative of Personal Experience* (London: Sampson Low, Marston, Searle and Rivington).

Balakian, Peter (2003) *The Burning Tigris: The Armenian Genocide and America's Response* (New York: HarperCollins).

Baron-Cohen, Simon (2011) *Zero Degrees of Empathy: A New Theory of Human Cruelty* (London: Allen Lane).

Bartov, Omer (1994) 'Operation Barbarossa and the Origins of the Final Solution', in *The Final Solution: Origins and Implementation*, edited by D. Cesarani (London: Routledge).

Bauer, Yehuda (2000) *Rethinking the Holocaust* (New Haven: Yale University Press).

Bauman, Zygmunt (1989) *Modernity and the Holocaust* (Cambridge: Polity Press).

Benjamin, Walter (1969) 'The Storyteller: Reflections on the Works of Nikolai Leskov', in *Illuminations: Essays and Reflections*, translated by H. Zorn, edited by H. Arendt (New York: Schocken).

Bennassar, Bartolome (1979) *The Spanish Character: Attitudes and Mentalities From the Sixteenth to the Nineteenth Century* (Berkeley: University of California Press).

Benvenuto, Bice and Kennedy, Roger (1986) *The Works of Jacques Lacan: An Introduction* (London: Free Association Books).

Berkhofer, Robert F. Jnr. (1978) *The White Man's Indian: Images of the American Indian From Columbus to the Present* (New York: Alfred Knopf).

Berman, Marshall (1983) *All That Is Solid Melts Into Air: The Experience Of Modernity* (London: Verso).

Bion, Wilfred (1961) *Experiences in Groups and Other Papers* (London: Tavistock Publications).

Blackbourn, David (1984) 'Between Resignation and Volatility', in *Shopkeepers and Master Artisans in Nineteenth-Century Europe*, edited by Geoffrey Crossick and Heinz-Gerhard Haupt (London: Methuen).

Blackburn, Robin (1997) *The Making of New World Slavery: From the Baroque to the Modern 1492–1800* (London: Verso).

Bloxham, Donald (2005) *The Great Game of Genocide: Imperialism, Nationalism and the Destruction of the Ottoman Armenians* (Oxford: Oxford University Press).

Bohm, Tomas (2006) 'Psychoanalytic Aspects of Perpetrators of Genocide', *Scandinavian Psychoanalytic Review*, 29.

Bottomore, T. (ed.) (1964) *Marx: Early Writings* (New York: McGraw Hill).

Bowlby, John (1953) *Child Care and the Growth of Love* (London: Pelican Book).

Bowlby, John (1988) *A Secure Base: Clinical Applications of Attachment Theory* (London: Routledge).

Breitman, R. (1994) 'Himmler, the Architect of Genocide', in *The Final Solution: Origins and Implementation*, edited by D. Cesarani (London: Routledge).

Broszat, Martin and Friedlander, Saul (1988) 'A Controversy About the Historicisation of National Socialism', *Yad Vashem Studies*, 19.

Brown, J. (1989) 'The Berlin NSDAP (The National Socialist German Workers Party) in the Kampfzeit', *German History*, 7.

Browning, Christopher (1992) *Ordinary Men: Reserve Police Battalion 101 and the Final Solution in Poland* (New York: HarperCollins).

Browning, Christopher (1992) 'Beyond "Intentionalism" and "Functionalism": The Decision for the Final Solution Reconsidered', in *The Path to Genocide* (Cambridge: Cambridge University Press).

Browning, Christopher (1992) *The Path to Genocide: Essays on Launching the Final Solution* (Cambridge: Cambridge University Press).

Browning, Christopher (1994) 'Hitler and the Euphoria of Victory: The Path to the Final Solution', in *The Final Solution: Origins and Implementation*, edited by D. Cesarani (London: Routledge).

Browning, Christopher (2004) *The Origins of the Final Solution: The Evolution of Nazi Jewish Policy, September 1939–March 1942* (Lincoln: University of Nebraska Press and Yad Vashem, Jerusalem).

Brustein, W. (1996) *The Logic of Evil: The Social Origins of the Nazi Party, 1925–1933* (New Haven: Yale University Press).

Bullock, Alan (1962) *A Study in Tyranny* (London: Penguin Books).

Burrin, Philippe (1994 [1989]) *Hitler and the Jews: The Genesis of the Holocaust* (London: Arnold).

Butler, Judith (2005) *Giving an Account of Oneself* (New York: Fordham University Press).

Butler, Judith (2009) *Frames of War: When Is Life Grievable?* (London: Verso).

Callinicos, Alex (1989) *Against Postmodernism* (Cambridge: Polity Press).

Callinicos, Alex (1989) *Making History* (Cambridge: Polity Press).

Callinicos, Alex (2001) 'Plumbing the Depth: Marxism and the Holocaust', *Yale Journal of Criticism*, 14.2.

Callinicos, Alex (2006) *The Resources of Critique* (Cambridge: Polity Press).

Cesarani, David (ed.) (1994) *The Final Solution: Origins and Implementation* (London: Routledge).

Charny, Israel W. (1982) *Genocide: The Human Cancer* (New York: Hearst Books).

Childers, Thomas (1983) *The Nazi Voter: The Social Foundations of Fascism in Germany, 1919–1933* (Chapel Hill: University of North Carolina Press).

Childers, Thomas (1984) 'Who, Indeed, Did Vote For Hitler?', *Central European History*, 17. 1.

Childers, Thomas (1990) 'The Social Language of Politics in Germany: The Sociology of Political Discourse in the Weimar Republic', *American Historical Review*, 95.

Churchill, Ward (1997) *A Little Matter of Genocide: Holocaust and Denial in the Americas 1492 to the Present* (San Francisco: City Lights Books).

Clapham, J.H. (1966) *Economic Development of France and Germany* (Cambridge: Cambridge University Press).

Clay, D.C. (1993) *Fighting an Uphill Battle: Demographic Pressure, the Structure of Land Holding and Land Degradation in Rwanda*, Department of Agricultural Economics, Michigan State University.

Cohn, Norman (1970 [1967]) *Warrant for Genocide* (London: Penguin Books).

Dadrian, Vahakn, N. (1998) 'The Determinants of the Armenian Genocide', Working paper GS 02, Genocide Studies Program, Yale Center for International and Area Studies, New Haven, 1998.

Dadrian, Vahakn, N. (2003 [1995]) *The History of the Armenian Genocide: Ethnic Conflict from the Balkans to Anatolia to the Caucasus* (New York: Berghahn Books).

de Sainte Croix, G.E.M. (1981) *The Class Struggle in the Ancient Greek World* (London: Duckworth).

de Zulueta, Felicity (2006) *From Pain to Violence: The Traumatic Roots of Destructiveness* (Chichester: John Wiley & Sons).

Defourneaux, Marcelin (1971) *Daily Life in Spain in the Golden Age* (New York: Praeger).

Deutscher, Isaac (1959) *The Prophet Unarmed: Trotsky, Volume 2, 1921–1929* (Oxford: Oxford University Press).

Dicks, Henry V. (1972) *Licenced Mass Murder: A Socio-Psychological Study of Some SS Killers* (London: Chatto/Heinemann for Sussex University Press).

Dobyns, Henry F. (1966) 'Estimating Aboriginal American Population: An Appraisal of Techniques with a New Hemispheric Estimate', *Current Anthropology*, 7.

Dobyns, Henry (1983) *Their Numbers Become Thinned: Native American Population Dynamics in Eastern North America* (Knoxville: University of Tennessee Press).

Docker, John (2008) *The Origins of Violence: Religion, History and Genocide* (London: Pluto Press).

Doyle, David Noel (2006) 'Scots Irish or Scotch-Irish?', in *Making the Irish American: History and Heritage of the Irish in the US*, edited by J.J. Lee and M.R. Casey (New York University Press).

Drinnon, Richard (1997) *Facing West: The Metaphysics of Indian-Hating and Empire-Building* (Norman: University of Oklahoma Press).

Easton, Lloyd D. and Guddat, Kurt H. (eds) (1967) *Writings of the Young Marx on Philosophy and Society* (New York: Anchor Books/Doubleday & Co.).

Ehrenreich, Barbara (1987) 'Foreword' to Klaus Theweleit, *Male Fantasies*, Vol. I (Minneapolis: University of Minnesota Press).

Elliott, J.H. (2002 [1963]) *Imperial Spain: 1469–1716* (London: Penguin).

Elliott, J.H. (2006) *Empires of the Atlantic World: Britain and Spain in America 1492–1830* (New Haven: Yale University Press).

Elliott, J.H. (2006) 'Contrasting Empires in History', *Today Magazine*, August.

Eltis, David (1993) 'Europeans and the Rise and Fall of African Slavery in the Americas: An Interpretation', *American Historical Review*, 98.5.

Engels, Friedrich (1953) 'Letter to Mehring, 14 July 1893', in K. Marx and F. Engels, *Selected Correspondence* (Moscow: Foreign Languages Publishing House).

Erikson, Erik (1963 [1950]) *Childhood and Society* (New York: W.W. Norton & Co.).

Fairbairn, W.R.D. (1994 [1952]) *Psychoanalytic Studies of the Personality* (New York: Brunner-Routledge).

Faulkner, Neil (2006) 'Crusade and Jihad in the Medieval Middle East', *International Socialism Journal*, 109.

Fenichel, Otto (1945) *The Psychoanalytic Theory of Neurosis* (New York: W.W. Norton).

Fenichel, Otto (1953) *The Collected Papers*, First Series (New York: WW. Norton).

Fenichel, Otto (1954) *The Collected Papers*, Second Series (New York: WW. Norton).

Fisk, Robert (1992) *The Hidden Holocaust* (London: Panoptic Productions).

Fisk, Robert (2005) *The Great War for Civilisation* (London: Fourth Estate).

Ford, Henry Jones (2006 [1915]) *The Scotch-Irish in America* (Massachusetts: Adamant Media Corporation).

Frenkel-Brunswik, Else (1954) 'Further Explorations by a Contributor to *The Authoritarian Personality*', in *Studies in the Scope and Method of The Authoritarian Personality* (Glencoe: Free Press).

Freud, Anna (1993 [1936]) *The Ego and the Mechanisms of Defence* (London: Karnac Books).

Freud, Sigmund (1940) *An Outline of Psychoanalysis* (London: The Hogarth Press).

Freud, Sigmund (1953) *Collected Papers*, Vol. 2 (London: The Hogarth Press).

Freud, Sigmund (1953 [1929]) *Civilisation and Its Discontents*, translated by J. Riviere (London: The Hogarth Press).

Freud, Sigmund (1977 [1905]) *Three Essays on Sexuality* (London: Pelican Freud Library).

Freud, Sigmund (1984 [1914]) *On Narcissism: An Introduction* (London: Pelican Freud Library).

Freud, Sigmund (1984 [1923]) *The Ego and the Id* (London: Pelican Freud Library).

Freud, Sigmund (1987 [1905]) *Three Essays on the Theory of Sexuality* (London: Pelican Freud Library).

Freud, Sigmund (1987 [1920]) *Beyond the Pleasure Principle* (London: Pelican Freud Library).

Freud, Sigmund (2001) *'Why War?'*, *Standard Edition*, Vol. 22 (London: The Hogarth Press).

Freud, Sigmund (2001 [1900]) *The Interpretation of Dreams*, *Standard Edition*, Vol. 4 (London: Vintage Books, The Hogarth Press).

Freud, Sigmund (2001) [1913–14]) *Totem and Taboo*, *Standard Edition*, Vol. 13 (London: The Hogarth Press).

Freud, Sigmund (2004 [1921]) *Mass Psychology and the Analysis of the 'I'* (London: Penguin Books).

Fromm, Erich (1942) *Fear of Freedom* (London: Routledge & Kegan Paul).

Fromm, Erich (1949) *Man For Himself* (London: Routledge & Kegan Paul).

Fromm, Erich (1949) 'Psychoanalytic Characterology and its Application to the Understanding of Culture', in S. Stansfeld Sargent and Marian W. Smith (eds), *Culture and Personality* (New York: Viking Press), reprinted in *Fromm Forum*, No. 12, 2008, pp. 5–10.

Fromm, Erich (1955) 'The Humanistic Implications of Instinctivistic "Radicalism"', *Dissent*, II. 4 (Autumn).

Fromm, Erich (1956) 'A Counter-Rebuttal', Dissent III, 1 (Winter).

Fromm, Erich (1956) *The Sane Society* (London: Routledge & Kegan Paul).

Fromm, Erich (1971) *The Crisis of Psychoanalysis* (London: Jonathan Cape).

Fromm, Erich (1974) *The Anatomy of Human Destructiveness* (London: Jonathan Cape).

Fromm, Erich (1984) *The Working Class in Weimar Germany: A Psychological and Sociological Study*, edited by W. Bonss (Leamington Spa: Berg Publishers).

Fromm, Erich (2004 [1963]) *The Dogma of Christ* (New York: Routledge).

Fromm, Erich (2011 [1968]) *The Revolution of Hope: Towards a Humanized Technology* (New York: Lantern Books).

Fromm, Erich and Maccoby, Michael (1970) *Social Character in a Mexican Village* (New Jersey: Prentice-Hall).

Frosh, Stephen (1987) *The Politics of Psychoanalysis: An Introduction to Freudian and Post-Freudian Theory* (London: Macmillan).

Frosh, Stephen (1991) *Identity Crisis: Modernity, Psychoanalysis and the Self* (London: Macmillan).

Frosh, Stephen (2009) *Hate and the Jewish Science: Anti-Semitism, Nazism and Psychoanalysis* (London: Palgrave-Macmillan).

Frosh, Stephen (2010) *Psychoanalysis Outside the Clinic* (London: Palgrave-Macmillan).

Funk, Rainer (2005) 'Violence in Our Time – Psychology and Religion', *Fromm Forum*, Vol. 9, pp. 12–16.

Funk, Rainer (2006) 'Foreword' to Erich Fromm, *Beyond the Chains of Illusion: My Encounter with Marx and Freud* [1962] (London: Continuum).

Funk, Rainer (2010) 'Living by the Manual: Ego-Oriented Social Character – Pathogenic Effects of Globalisation', *International Forum of Psychoanalysis*, Vol. 19, No. 2, pp. 84–91.

Funk, Rainer (2011) 'Erich Fromm and the Intersubjective Tradition', in *Fromm Forum*, (English Edition – ISBN 1437-1189) 15/2011, Tuebingen (Selbsverlag), pp. 60–4.

Geras, Norman (1983) *Marx and Human Nature: Refutation of a Legend* (London: Verso).

Geras, Norman (1998) *The Contract of Mutual Indifference: Political Philosophy After the Holocaust* (London: Verso).

Geras, Norman (1999) 'Marxists Before the Holocaust', in *The Legacy of Ernest Mandel*, edited by Glibert Achcar (London: Verso).

Gerth, Hans (1940) 'The Nazi Party: Its Leadership and Composition', *American Journal of Sociology*, XLV.

Gibson, Charles (1966) *Spain in America* (New York: HarperCollins).

Giddens, Anthony (1984) *The Constitution of Society: Outline of the Theory of Structuration* (Cambridge: Polity).

Gluckstein, Donny (1999) *The Nazis, Capitalism and the Working Class* (London: Bookmarks).

Goldman, Lucien (1968) 'Is There a Marxist Sociology?', introduced and translated by Ian Birchall, *Internationalism Socialism Journal* (Autumn).

Goldthorpe, John H., Lockwood, David, Bechhofer, Frank, Platt, Jennifer (1969) *The Affluent Worker in the Class Structure*, Vols. 1–3 (Cambridge: Cambridge University Press).

Gourevitch, Philip (2000 [1998]) *We Wish to Inform You That Tomorrow We Will Be Killed With Our Families* (London: Picador).

Gramsci, Antonio (1971) 'The Intellectuals', in *Selections from The Prison Notebooks*, edited and translated by Quinton Hoare and Geoffrey Nowell-Smith (London: Lawrence and Wishart).

Greenstein, Fred I. (1965) 'Personality and Political Socialisation: The Theories of Authoritarian and Democratic Character', *Annals of the American Academy of Political and Social Science* (September).

Greven, Philip (1977) *The Protestant Temperament: Patterns of Child-Rearing, Religious Experience and the Self in Early America* (Chicago: University of Chicago Press; New York: Alfred A Knopf).

Grinker, Roy R., and Spiegel, John P. (1945) *Men Under Stress* (Philadelphia: Blakiston).

Grosse, Scott (1994) *More People, More Trouble: Population Growth and Agricultural Change in Rwanda* (Ann Arbor: University of Michigan).

Grunberger, Bela (1964), 'The Anti-Semite and the Oedipal Conflict', *International Journal of Psychoanalysis*, 45.

Haney, C., Banks, C. and Zimbardo, P. (1973) 'Interpersonal Dynamics in a Simulated Prison', *International Journal of Criminology and Penology*, 1.

Hanke, Lewis (1969) *Indians and Spaniards in the New World: A Personal View* (Salt Lake City: University of Utah Press).

Hanke, Lewis (2002 [1949]) *The Spanish Struggle for Justice in the Conquest of America* (Dallas: Southern Methodist University Press).

Harman, Chris (1982) *The Lost Revolution: Germany 1918 to 1923* (London: Bookmarks).

Harman, Chris (1986) 'Base and Superstructure', *International Socialism Journal*, 32.

Hatzfeld, Jean (2005) *Machete Season: The Killers in Rwanda Speak* (New York: Farrar, Straus and Giroux).

Heberle, Rudolf (1945) *From Democracy to Nazism* (Baton Rouge: Louisiana State University Press).

Henderson, W.O. (1962) 'Germany's Economic Development, 1871–1914', Part 2 of Chapter II of *A Short History of Germany 1815–1945* by E.J. Passant (Cambridge: Cambridge University Press).

Hilberg Raul (1985) *The Destruction of the European Jews* (New York: Holmes & Meier). (Original three volumes published by Quadrangle Books, Chicago, 1961).

Hill, Christopher (1964) *Society and Puritanism in Pre-Revolutionary England* (London: Secker & Warburg).

Hinshelwood, R.D. (1991) *A Dictionary of Kleinian Thought* (London: Free Association Books).

Horkheimer, Max (2002 [1968]) 'Authority and the Family', in *Critical Theory: Selected Essays* (New York: Continuum).

Human Rights Watch (1999 and 2003), World Reports: Burundi, Rwanda, Sudan.

Innes, Hammond (1972) *The Conquistadors* (London: Book Club Associates).

Issawi, Charles (1980) *The Economic History of Turkey: 1800 to 1914* (Chicago: University of Chicago Press).

Jacoby, Russell (1983) *The Repression of Psychoanalysis* (Chicago: University of Chicago Press).

Jacoby, Russell (1997) *Social Amnesia: A Critique of Contemporary Psychology* (New Jersey: Transaction Publishers).

Jaimes, M. Annette (1990–91) 'The Stone Age Revisited: An Indigenist View of Primitivism, Industrialism and the Labor Process', *New Studies on the Left*, XIV.3.

Jaimes, M. Annette (ed.) (1992) *The State of Native America: Genocide, Colonization and Resistance* (Boston: South End Press).

Jakubowski, Franz (1990) 'Ideology and Superstructure', in *Historical Materialism* (London: Pluto Press).

James, Oliver (2008) *The Selfish Capitalist: Origins of Affluenza* (London: Vermillion, Ebury Publishing).

James, Oliver (2010) *Britain On the Couch* (London: Vermillion, Ebury Publishing).

John F. Walzer (1976) 'A Period of Ambivalence', in *The History of Childhood*, edited by Lloyd de Mause (London: The Souvenir Press).

Jones, Ernest (1993) *The Life and Work of Sigmund Freud* (London: Pelican Books).

Jones, Larry Eugene (1972) '"The Dying Middle": Weimar Germany and the Fragmentation of Bourgeois Politics', *Central European History*, 5.

Jorg, Friedrich (2006) *The Fire: The Bombing of Germany 1940–1945* (New York: Columbia University Press).

Kamen, Henry (2004) *Empire: How Spain Became a World Power: 1492–1763* (New York: Perennial, HarperCollins).

Kamen, Henry (2005) *Spain 1469–1714: A Society of Conflict* (London: Longman).

Kater, Michael (1983) *The Nazi Party: A Social Profile of Members and Leaders, 1919–1945* (Oxford: Blackwell).

Kay, Jeanne (1984) 'The Fur Trade and Native American Population Growth', *Ethnohistory*, 31.4.

Keeley, Lawrence (1996) *War Before Civilisation: The Myth of the Peaceful Savage* (Oxford: Oxford University Press).

Kelly, Douglas M. (1947) *22 Cells in Nuremberg* (London: W.H. Allen).

Kenny, Kevin (2009) *Peaceable Kingdom Lost* (Oxford: Oxford University Press).

Kershaw, Ian (1983) *Popular Opinion and Political Dissent in the Third Reich* (Oxford: Oxford University Press).

Kershaw, Ian (1998) *Hitler: 1889–1936, Volume 1, Hubris* (London: Penguin Books).

Kershaw, Ian (2007) *Fateful Choices: Ten Decisions That Changed the World 1940–1941* (London: Penguin).

Kettenacker, L. (1985) 'Social and Psychological Aspects of the Fuhrer's Rule', in *Aspects of the Third Reich*, edited by W.H. Koch (London: Macmillan Education Ltd.)

Keysers, Christian, and Gazzola, Valeria (2009) 'Expanding the Mirror: Vicarious Activity for Actions, Emotions and Sensations', in *Science Direct, Current Opinion in Neurobiology*, available online at www.sciencedirect.com.

Kicza, John E. (2004) 'First Contacts', in *A Companion to American History*, edited by Philip J. Deloria and Neal Salisbury (Malden, MA: Blackwell).

Kiernan, Ben (2004) 'The First Genocide: Carthage, 146 BC', *Diogenes* (August).

Kiernan, Ben (2007) *Blood and Soil: A World History of Genocide and Extermination From Sparta to Darfur* (New Haven: Yale University Press).

Klein, Janet (2007) 'Conflict and Collaboration: Re-Thinking Kurdish-Armenian Relations in the Hamidian Period, 1876–1909', in *Identity and Identity Formation in the Ottoman World: Essays in Honor of Norman Itzkowitz* (Madison: University of Wisconsin Press).

Klein, Melanie (1975) 'Some Theoretical Conclusions Regarding the Emotional Life of the Infant' and 'The Psycho-Analytic Play Technique: Its History and Significance', in *Envy and Gratitude and Other Works* (New York: Delta).

Kohut, Heinz (1971) *The Analysis of the Self* (Chicago: University of Chicago Press).

Kohut, Heinz (1977) *The Restoration of the Self* (Chicago: University of Chicago Press).

Kohut, Heinz (1985) *Self Psychology and the Humanities: Reflections on a New Psychoanalytical Approach*, edited by C.B. Strozier (New York: W.W. Norton).

Konstan, David (2007) 'Anger, Hatred, and Genocide in Ancient Greece', *Common Knowledge*, 13.1.

Korsch, Karl (1970) *Marxism and Philosophy* (New York: Monthly Review Press).

Kovel, Joel (1981) *The Age of Desire* (New York: Pantheon Books).

Kovel, Joel (1988) *The Radical Spirit: Essays on Psychoanalysis and Society* (London: Free Association Books).

Kovel, Joel (1989) Interview by Sebastian Gardner and Richard Kuper, *Interlink Magazine*, 12 (May–June).

Krystal, Henry (1968) 'Clinical Observations on the Survivor Syndrome', in *Massive Psychic Trauma*, edited by Henry Krystal (New York: International Universities Press).

Kulcsar, I.S., Kulcsar, Shoshanna and Szondi, Lipot (1966) 'Adolf Eichmann and the Third Reich', in *Crime, Law and Corrections*, edited by R. Slovenko (New York: Thomas Publishing).

Kuper, Leo (2002), 'Genocide: Its Political Use in the Twentieth Century', in *Genocide: An Anthropological Reader*, edited by A.L. Hinton (Oxford: Blackwell).

Laclau, Ernesto (1971) 'Feudalism and Capitalism in Latin America', *New Left Review*, 67.

Landau, Jacob, M. (1996) *Pan-Turkism: From Irredentism to Cooperation* (Bloomington: Indiana University Press).

Lasch, Christopher (1979) *The Culture of Narcissism: American Life in an Age of Diminishing Expectations* (New York: W.W. Norton & Co.).

Laub, Dori (2002) *Can Psychoanalysis Enhance Historical Understanding of Genocide?* (Genocide Studies Program, Yale University).

Lemaire, Anika (1977) *Jacques Lacan* (London: Routledge & Kegan Paul).

Lemarchand, Rene (1995) 'Rwanda: The Rationality of Genocide', *Issue: A Journal of Opinion*, 23.2.

Lemkin, Raphael (2002) 'Genocide', in *Genocide: An Anthropological Reader*, edited by A.L. Hinton (Oxford: Blackwell).

Levene, Mark (2005) *Genocide in the Age of the Nation State, Volume 1, The Meaning of Genocide* (London: I.B. Tauris & Co. Ltd.).

Lewis, Bernard (2002) *The Emergence of Modern Turkey* (Oxford: Oxford University Press).

Lewis, Raphaela (1971) *Everyday Life in Ottoman Turkey* (New York: Dorset Press).

Leyburn, James (1962) *The Scotch-Irish: A Social History* (Chapel Hill: University of North Carolina Press).

Lichtman, Richard (1982) *The Production of Desire: The Integration of Psychoanalysis into Marxist Theory* (New York: The Free Press).

Linden, Ian (1977) *Church and Revolution in Rwanda* (Manchester: Manchester University Press).

Lipset, S.M. (1960) *'Fascism' – Left, Right and Center* (London: Heinemann).

Lockhart, James (1984) 'Social Organisation and Social Change in Colonial Spanish America', in *The Cambridge History of Latin America, Volume 2: Colonial Latin America*, edited by L. Bethell (Cambridge: Cambridge University Press).

Loewenberg, Peter (1971) 'The Psychohistorical Origins of the Nazi Youth Cohort', *American Historical Review*, 76.

Loomis, Charles P. and Beegle, J. Allen (1946) 'The Spread of German Nazism in Rural Areas', *American Sociological Review*, 11.

Lozowick, Yaacov (2000) *Hitler's Bureaucrats: The Nazi Security Police and the Banality of Evil* (London: Continuum).

Lukács, Georg (1971 [1932]) *History and Class Consciousness* (London: Merlin Press Ltd.).

McAfee, W. and Morgan, V. (1981) 'Population in Ulster, 1660–1760', in *Plantation to Partition: Essays in Ulster History in honour of J.L. McCracken*, edited by Peter Roebuck (Belfast: Blackstaff Press).

Maccoby, Michael (1982) 'Social Character vs. The Productive Ideal: The Contribution and Contradiction in Fromm's View of Man', *Praxis International*, 2.1.

McKenzie, Robert (1968) *Angels in Marble* (London: Heinemann).

MacMullen, Ramsey (2003) *Feelings in History* (California: Claremont, Regina Books).

Mahler, Margaret (1979) *The Selected Papers of Margaret S. Mahler, M.D.: Infantile Psychosis and Early Contributions* (Maryland: Aronson).

Malinowski, Bronislaw (1927) *Sex and Repression in Savage Society* (London: Routledge & Kegan Paul).

Mamdani, Mahmood (2001) *When Victims Become Killers: Colonialism, Nativism, and the Genocide in Rwanda* (Princeton: Princeton University Press).

Mancall, Peter C. (1998) 'Native Americans and Europeans in English America, 1500–1700', in *The Oxford History of the British Empire, Volume 1, The Origins of Empire*, edited by Nicholas Canny (Oxford: Oxford University Press).

Mann, Michael (2004) *Fascists* (Cambridge: Cambridge University Press).

Mann, Michael (2005) *The Dark Side of Democracy: Explaining Ethnic Cleansing* (Cambridge: Cambridge University Press).

Maquet, Jacques and Jerome, Pierre (1954) *Le Système des Relations Sociales dans le Rwanda Ancien* (Tervuren: MRCB).

Marcuse, Herbert (1956) *Eros and Civilisation* (London: Routledge & Kegan Paul).

Marcuse, Herbert (1956) 'A Reply to Erich Fromm', *Dissent*, III.1 (Winter).

Marx, Karl (1961 [1867]) *Capital, Volume 1* (Moscow: Foreign Publishing House).

Marx, Karl (1961 [1845]) *Theses on Feuerbach*, in K. Marx and F. Engels, *Selected Works, Volume 2* (Moscow: Foreign Languages Publishing House).

Marx, Karl (1962) *Preface to the Critique of Political Economy*, in K. Marx and F. Engels, *Selected Works, Volume 1* (Moscow: Foreign Languages Publishing House).

Marx, Karl (1962) *The Bourgeoisie and the Counter-Revolution*, Second Article, December 1848, in K. Marx and F. Engels, *Selected Works, Volume 1* (Moscow: Foreign Languages Publishing House).

Marx, Karl (1962 [1851]) *The Eighteenth Brumaire of Louis Bonaparte*, in K. Marx and F. Engels, *Selected Works, Volume 1* (Moscow: Foreign Languages Publishing House).

Marx, Karl (1973 [1953]) *Grundrisse* (London: Penguin Books in association with New Left Review).

Marx, Karl and Engels, Friedrich (1965 [1845]) *The German Ideology* (London: Lawrence & Wishart).

Mattaus, Jurgen (2004) 'Operation Barbarossa and the Onset of the Holocaust, June–December 1941', in Christopher Browning, *The Origins of the Final Solution: The Evolution of Nazi Jewish Policy, September 1939–March 1942* (Lincoln: University of Nebraska Press and Yad Vashem, Jerusalem).

Mayer, Arno (1988) *Why Did The Heavens Not Darken?* (New York: Random House).

Mayer, Hans Eberhard (1992), *The Crusades* (Oxford: Oxford University Press).

Mead, Margaret (1971 [1928]) *Coming of Age in Samoa: A Psychological Study of Primitive Youth for Western Civilisation* (London: Penguin Books).

Mead, Margaret (2002 [1935]) *Sex and Temperament in Three Primitive Societies* (London: HarperCollins).

Mears, E.G. (2004), *Modern Turkey: An Economico-Political Interpretation 1908–1924* (New York: Macmillan).

Meggitt, M. J. (1962) *Desert People: A Study of the Walbiri Aborigines of Central Australia* (Chicago: University of Chicago Press).

Meisenhelder, Thomas (2006) 'From Character to Habitus in Sociology', *Social Science Journal*, 43.

Milgram, Stanley (1963) 'Behavioural Study of Obedience', *Journal of Abnormal and Social Psychology*, 67.

Miller, Alice (1986 [1979]) 'Depression and Grandiosity as Related Forms of Narcissistic Disturbances', in *Essential Papers on Narcissism*, edited by A. Morrison (New York: New York University Press).

Miller, Alice (1987) *The Drama of Being a Child* (London: Virago).

Miller, Alice (2002 [1983]), *For Your Own Good: The Roots of Violence in Child-Rearing* (New York: Farrar, Straus & Giroux).

Mitchell, Juliet (ed.) (1987) *The Selected Melanie Klein* (New York: The Free Press).

Molière (2004) *The Miser* (London: Nick Hern Books).

Mommsen, Hans (1991) *From Weimar to Auschwitz: Essays in German History* (Cambridge: Polity Press).

Morgan, Edmund S. (1966 [1944]) *The Puritan Family: Religion and Domestic Relations in Seventeenth-Century New England* (New York: Harper & Row).

Morner, Magnus (1967) *Race Mixture in the History of Latin America* (Boston: Little Brown).

Morton, A.L. (1965 [1938]) *A People's History of England* (London: Lawrence & Wishart).

Nash, Gary B. (1974) *Red, White and Black: The Peoples of Early North America* (New Jersey: Prentice Hall).

Newbury, Catherine (1989) *The Cohesion of Oppression: Clientship and Ethnicity in Rwanda, 1860–1960* (New York: Columbia University Press).

Newbury, Catherine and Newbury, David (1995) 'Identity, Genocide and Reconstruction in Rwanda', Paper presented at the European Parliament Conference.

Niewyk, Donald L. (2001) *The Jews in Weimar Germany* (New Jersey: Transaction Publishers).

Oliver, Charles (2005) 'They Shaped America But Did They Make It More Free?', www.reason.com (July).

Ollman, Bertell (1979) *Social and Sexual Revolution: Essays on Marx and Reich* (London: Pluto Press).

Orwell, George (1984 [1937]) *The Road to Wigan Pier* (London: Penguin).

Osborn, Reuben (1965) *Marxism and Psychoanalysis* (London: Barrie & Rockliff).

Pagden, Anthony (1990) *Spanish Imperialism and the Political Imagination: Studies in European and Spanish-American Social and Political Theory* (New Haven: Yale University Press).

Pagden, Anthony (1995) *Lords Of All the World* (New Haven: Yale University Press).

Paker, Murat (2010) 'Turkish-Armenian Conflict in the Context of the Dominant Political Culture in Turkey: A Psycho-Political Enquiry' (manuscript sent to the author).

Parker, Theodore (2005 [1865]) *Collected Works, Volume X: Critical Writings* (London: Trubner & Co).

Peckham, Howard, and Gibson, Charles (eds) (1969) *Attitudes of Colonial Powers Toward the American Indian* (Salt Lake City: University of Utah Press).

Pilbeam, D. (1970) *The Evolution of Man* (London: Thames and Hudson).

Prunier, Gerard (1995) *The Rwanda Crisis: History of a Genocide* (London: Hurst & Co.).

Ramsauer, E.E. (1957) *The Young Turks: Prelude to the Revolution of 1908* (Princeton: Princeton University Press).

Reich, Wilhelm (1961 [1933]) *Character Analysis* (New York: Pocket Books).

Reich, Wilhelm (1966 [1929]) 'Dialectical Materialism and Psychoanalysis', *Studies on the Left*, 6.4.

Reich, Wilhelm (1970 [1933]) *The Mass Psychology of Fascism* (New York: Farrar, Straus & Giroux).

Reiche, Reimut (1968) *Sexuality and Class Struggle*, translated by David Fernbach (London: New Left Books).

Reid, James (1993) 'Social and Psychological Factors in the Collapse of the Ottoman Era, circa 1780–1918', *Journal of Modern Hellenism*, 10.

Reid, James (2000) *Crisis of the Ottoman Empire: Prelude to Collapse 1839–1878* (Stuttgart: BL Franz Steiner Verlag).

Reid, James (2002 [1999]) 'Philosophy of State-Subject Relations', in *Studies in Comparative Genocide*, edited by Levon Chorbajian and George Shirinian (London: Macmillan UK).

Remini, Robert V. (1985) *The Revolutionary Age of Andrew Jackson* (New York: Harper & Row).

Richards, Barry (1984) 'Schizoid States and the Market', in *Capitalism and Infancy: Essays on Psychoanalysis and Politics*, edited by Barry Richards (London: Free Association Books).

Rickert, John (1986) 'The Fromm-Marcuse Debate Revisited', *Theory and Society*, 15.

Roazen, Paul (1969) *Freud: Political and Social Thought* (London: Hogarth Press).

Robinson, Paul (1974) 'Cleaning Up Freud', Review of Erich Fromm's *Anatomy of Human Destructiveness*, *Partisan Review*, 41.

Robinson, Paul A. (1990) *The Freudian Left* (New York: Cornell University Press).

Rose, Jacqueline (1993) 'Why War?', in *Why War? – Psychoanalysis, Politics, and the Return to Melanie Klein* (Oxford: Blackwell).

Rose, Jacqueline (2004) 'Introduction' to new edition of Sigmund Freud, *Mass Psychology and the Analysis of the 'I' and Other Writings* (London: Penguin Books).

Rose, Jacqueline (2007) *The Last Resistance* (London: Verso).

Rustin, Michael (1982), 'A Socialist Consideration of Kleinian Psychoanalysis', *New Left Review*, 131.

Saint-Saens, Alain (ed.) (1999) *Sex and Love in Golden Age Spain: Part 1, The Demand for Pleasure* (New Orleans: University Press of the South).

Sale, Kirkpatrick (2006) *Christopher Columbus and the Conquest of Paradise* (London: Tauris Parke Paperbacks).

Schaffner, Bertram (1948) *Father Land: A Study of Authoritarianism in the German Family* (New York: Columbia University Press).

Schneider, Michael (1975) *Neurosis and Civilisation: A Marxist/Freudian Synthesis* (New York: Seabury Press).

Schweitzer, Arthur (1977 [1964]), *Big Business in the Third Reich* (Bloomington: Indiana University Press).

Service, E.R. (1966) *The Hunters* (New Jersey: Prentice Hall).

Seve, Lucien (1975 [1968]) *Marxism and the Theory of Human Personality* (London: Lawrence & Wishart).

Shaw, Martin (2007) *What Is Genocide?* (Cambridge: Polity Press).

Slotkin, Richard (1973) *Regeneration Through Violence: The Mythology of the American Frontier 1600 to 1860* (Norman: University of Oklahoma Press).

Soper, Kate (1995) *What Is Nature?* (Oxford: Blackwell).

Spero, Patrick (2011), 'The Landscape of Life on the Mid-Atlantic Frontier', *American History* (March).

Spicer, Edward H. (1969) *Political Incorporation and Cultural Change in New Spain: A Study in Spanish-Indian Relations* (Salt Lake City: University of Utah Press).

Spinden, J.H. (1928), 'The Population of Ancient America, Anthropological Report', *Geographical Review*, 18.4.

Stannard, David (1992) *American Holocaust: The Conquest of the New World* (Oxford: Oxford University Press).

Staub, Ervin (1986) 'A Conception of the Determinants and Development of Altruism and Aggression: Motives of the Self and the Environment', in *Altruism and Aggression, Biological and Social Origins*, edited by C. Zahn-Waxler, E.M. Cummings and R. Ianotti (Cambridge: Cambridge University Press).

Staub, Ervin (1989) *The Roots of Evil: The Origins of Genocide and Other Group Violence* (Cambridge: Cambridge University Press).

Stedman-Jones, Gareth (1977) 'Society and Politics at the Beginning of the World Economy', *Cambridge Journal of Economics*, 1.

Stiffarm, Leonore A. with Phil Lane, Jnr. (1992) 'The Demography of Native North America: A Question of American Indian Survival', in *The State of Native America: Genocide, Colonization and Resistance*, edited by M. Annette Jaimes (Boston: South End Press).

Stone, Lawrence (1977) *Family, Sex and Marriage in England 1500–1800* (London: Penguin).

Stone, Lawrence (1987) 'Puritanism', in *The Past and the Present Revisited* (London: Routledge & Kegan Paul).

Storr, Anthony (1991) *Human Destructiveness* (London: Penguin).

Strachey, John (1965) 'Introduction' to Reuben Osborn, *Marxism and Psychoanalysis* (London: Barrie & Rockcliff).

Streit, C. (1994) 'Wehrmacht, Einsatzgruppen and Anti-Bolshevism', in *The Final Solution: Origins and Implementation*, edited by D. Cesarani (London: Routledge).

Suhnaz, Yilmaz (2007), 'In Pursuit of Elusive Glory: Enver Pasha's Role in the Pan-Islamic and Basmachi Movements', in *Identity and Identity Formation in the Ottoman World: A Volume of Essays in Honor of Norman Itzkowitz*, edited by Baki Tezcan and Karl K. Barbir (Madison: University of Wisconsin Press).

Sweezy, Paul (1964 [1942]) *The Theory of Capitalist Development* (New York: Monthly Review Press).

Tannenbaum, Frank (1946) *Slave and Citizen: The Negro in the Americas* (New York: Random House).

Tawney, R.H. (1926) *Religion and the Rise of Capitalism* (London: John Murray).

Theweleit, Klaus (1987/1989 [1977]) *Male Fantasies, Volumes 1 and 2* (Minneapolis: University of Minnesota Press).

Thompson, E.P. (1963) *The Making of the English Working Class* (London: Gollancz).

Traverso, Enzo (1995) *The Jews and Germany: From the 'Judeo-German Symbiosis' to the Memory of Auschwitz* (Lincoln: University of Nebraska Press).

Traverso, Enzo (1999) *Understanding the Nazi Genocide* (London: Pluto Press).

Trotsky, Leon (1966) *Literature and Revolution* (Ann Arbor: University of Michigan Press).

Trotsky, Leon (1975 [1926]) *Culture and Socialism* (London: New Park Publications).

Trotsky, Leon (1981) *The War Correspondence of Leon Trotsky: The Balkan Wars 1912–13* (New York: Pathfinder).

Uvin, Peter (1997) 'Prejudice, Crisis and Genocide in Rwanda', *African Studies Review*, 40.2.

Van Every, Dale (1966) *Disinherited: The Lost Birthright of the American Indians* (New York: William Morrow & Co.).

Verwimp, Philip (2003) *An Economic Profile of Peasant Perpetrators of Genocide: Micro-Level Evidence from Rwanda* (Genocide Studies Program, Yale University).

Vidal, Herman (ed.) (1989) *Cultural and Historical Grounding for Hispanic and Luso-Brazilian Feminist Literary Criticism* (Minneapolis: University of Minnesota Press).

Volkan, Vamik (1994) *The Need to Have Enemies and Allies. From Clinical Practice to International Relations* (Northvale: Jason Aronson).

Waite, Robert G.L. (1993 [1977]) *The Psychopathic God: Adolf Hitler* (New York: De Capo Press).

Waller, James (2007) *Becoming Evil: How Ordinary Men Commit Genocide and Mass Killing* (Oxford: Oxford University Press).

Weber, Max (1958 [1930]) *The Protestant Ethic and the Spirit of Capitalism* (London: Unwin University Books).

Weeks, Jeffrey (1985) *Sexuality and Its Discontents* (London: Routledge & Kegan Paul).

White, Richard (1991) *The Middle Ground: Indians, Empires, and Republics in the Great Lakes Region, 1650–1815* (Cambridge: Cambridge University Press).

Winnicott, Donald (1975) 'Aggression in Relation to Emotional Development', in *Through Pediatrics to Psychoanalysis*, edited by M. Masuds and R. Khan (London: Hogarth Press).

Wolf, Ernest (2002 [1988]) *Treating the Self: Elements of Clinical Self Psychology* (New York: The Guilford Press).

Wolfenstein, Eugene (1993) *Psychoanalytic Marxism, Groundwork* (London: Free Association Books).

Wollheim, Richard (1973) *Freud* (London: Fontana Press).

Young, Robert M. (1993) 'Psychoanalysis and the Other: Psychopathology and Racism',

Conference Paper, Oxford, available at www.human-nature.com/rmyoung/papers.

Young, Robert M. (1994) *Mental Space* (London: Process Press).

Young, Robert M. (1996) *Whatever Happened to Human Nature?* available at www. human-nature.com/rmyoung/papers.

Zimbardo, Philip (1972) 'Pathology of Imprisonment', *Trans-Action*, 9.

Zinn, Howard (2001) *A People's History of the United States* (New York: Perennial, HarperCollins).

Žižek, Slavoj (1989) *The Sublime Object of Ideology* (London: Verso).

Žižek, Slavoj (2005) 'Neighbours and Other Monsters: A Plea for Ethical Violence', in *The Neighbour: Three Inquiries in Political Theology*, by Slavoj Žižek, Eric Santer and Kenneth Reinhard (Chicago: University of Chicago Press).

Žižek, Slavoj (2008) *Violence: Six Sideways Reflections* (London: Profile Books Ltd.).

Index

Aborigines, 10

Adler, Alfred, 42

Adorno, Theodor, 20, 47, 48, 49, 77, 201, 251n33, 255n45, 256n53, 277n124

Africa, 16, 33, 130, 132–4, 175, 212, 228

Agriculture, 115, 116, 127–9, 133, 134, 143, 147, 162, 168, 233, 237, 245

Ahmad, Feroz,163–5, 169, 170, 271n32, 271n37, 272n36, 272n41, 272n43, 272n47, 272n57, 272n62, 272n64, 272n68, 272n69

Albania, 159, 166, 167, 175, 178

Alienation, 7, 8, 30, 31, 44, 45, 57, 61, 65, 78, 79, 86–9, 93, 94, 98, 100, 135, 178, 203, 207, 248

Altemeyer, Bob, 20, 21, 22, 77, 252n34

Althusser, Louis, 32

Aly, Gotz, 213, 217, 279n205, 280n210, 280n211, 280n230

America (North), 3, 111–56, 200, 221

Amherst, Lord, 113

Anasazi, 128

Anatolia, 159, 163

Anderson, Benedict, 253n101

Anglo-American, 114, 115, 134, 135

Anthropology, 29, 33, 45, 59, 185

Anti-Apartheid Movement, 184

Anti-Semitism, 48, 185–221

Arabs, 166, 168

Archaeology, 128, 129

Archer, Margaret, 4, 258n2

Arendt, Hannah, 24, 184, 252n53, 278n147, 279n206, 280n208, 280n214

Aristotle, 34

Armenia, 1, 2, 3, 10, 13, 26, 36, 119, 158–81, 240, 241

Army, 16, 42, 114, 119, 138, 145, 158, 162, 164, 165, 167, 168, 169, 170, 173, 175, 176, 177, 178, 179, 199, 205, 212, 215–18, 223, 224, 231–41

Aryanisation, 219

Assimilation, 72, 77, 111, 115, 119, 123, 124, 127, 129, 130, 133, 134, 141, 142, 151, 157, 174, 175, 181, 182, 245

Attachment theory, 25, 49, 50, 52, 53, 62, 63, 101, 244

Auschwitz, 25, 120, 183, 184, 204, 214

Australia, 10, 130

Austria, 42, 159, 164, 211, 244

Authoritarian personality, 8, 13, 20–3, 42, 47, 48, 49, 53, 66, 73, 74, 77, 83, 84, 105, 107, 127, 135, 142, 147, 151, 156, 179, 181, 182, 200, 201, 207, 208, 210, 221, 242, 246

Authoritarianism, 96, 144, 202, 219, 242, 243

Aztecs, 76, 113, 123, 124, 132

Balakian, Peter, 270n1, 270n3, 272n80, 273n81, 274n120, 274n135

Balkan wars, 159, 164, 167, 170, 172

Balint, Michael, 46

De Balzac, Honore, 77

Banality of evil, 184

Bandura, Albert, 22

Bankruptcy, 159

Banks, 187, 188, 189, 191, 196, 219

Barbarossa, Operation, 210, 212, 214, 215, 216

Baron-Cohen, Simon, 101, 263n55

Bartov, Omer, 210, 279n187

Bauer, Yehudi, 210, 279n189

Baumann, Zygmunt, 184, 218, 274n3, 274n4

Bavaria, 194

Bedouins, 175

Belgium, 222, 224–6, 228, 229, 230, 242, 243

Benjamin, Jessica, 96

Benjamin, Walter, 6, 250n26

Bennassar, Bartolome, 140, 144, 268n158, 268n159, 269n178

Bentham, Jeremy, 31

Berkhofer, Robert F, 116, 136, 149, 265n29, 267n135

Berman, Marshall, 77, 260n82

Big Business (German), 188, 189, 190, 197, 200, 201, 202, 207

Biological determinism, 39, 40

Bion, Wifred, 15, 251n6

Bismarck, 197

Blackburn, Robin, 129, 131, 132, 266n68, 267n117, 267n118

Blackbourn, David, 197, 198, 201, 277n118

Bloxham, Donald, 271n7, 271n8

Boas, Franz, 185

Bohm, Tomas, 243, 244, 283n91

Bolshevism, 186, 200, 212, 215, 218

Bosnia, 14, 16, 164, 222

Bourdieu, Pierre, 64

Bourgeoisie, 7, 15, 43, 77, 82, 89, 135, 137, 162, 163, 197

Bowlby, John, 49, 50, 256n54, 256n56

Brazil, 115, 132

Breitman, R., 280n213

Breuer, Josef, 5

Britain, 22, 124, 125, 143, 159, 196, 197, 221

Browne, Robert, 146

Browning, Christopher, 26, 209, 211, 212, 214, 216, 218, 252n52, 279n180, 279n181, 279n182, 270n183, 279n185, 279n191, 279n192, 279n194, 279n195, 279n196, 279n197, 279n198, 279n199, 279n200, 279n201, 279n202, 279n203, 279n204, 280n207, 280n209, 280n212, 280n215, 280n218, 280n217, 280n221, 280n222, 280n223, 280n239, 280n240

Bulgaria, 159, 164, 166, 173, 178

Bullock, Alan, 275n35, 278n137

Bureaucracy, 139, 140, 142, 144, 161, 165, 169, 170, 179, 181, 184, 197, 200, 204, 211, 217, 219

Burrin, Phlippe, 216, 280n228

Burundi, 222, 229, 231, 234, 237, 240

Butler, Judith, 47, 56, 57, 60, 61, 255n42, 258n134, 258n141, 258n145

Cahokia, 129

Calderon, Pedro, 144

California, 47, 111, 118, 134

Callinicos, Alex, 31, 32, 57, 60, 185, 217, 252n94, 257n115, 257n116, 258n130, 275n17, 179n188, 280n236, 280n237

Calvinism, 149, 153

Cambodia, 9

Canetti, Elias, 260n46

Catholic Church, 42, 125, 127, 130, 139, 140, 142, 144, 146, 150, 194, 225, 226, 227, 230, 231, 232, 238

Capitalism, 1, 7, 15, 30, 31, 32, 35, 42, 44, 35, 59, 60, 65, 66, 75, 80, 81, 82, 87, 89, 90, 91, 93, 95, 98, 100, 101, 102, 103, 105, 106, 112, 126, 145, 147, 150, 151, 153, 157, 162, 183, 186, 187, 189, 191, 196, 198, 200, 210, 248

Capitulations, 159, 160, 161, 166

Caribbean, 133

Carthage, 34, 35, 36

Castration complex, 66

Cato, 34, 35

Caucasus, 159, 175, 181

Central America, 120, 121

Cervantes, Miguel de, 145

Character (structure), 4, 6, 8, 10, 23, 28, 32, 34, 35, 36, 42, 43, 44, 45, 47, 50, 53, 56, 63, 64, 65, 67, 68–76, 84, 86, 88, 90, 92, 105, 107, 127, 135, 142, 144, 146, 147, 150, 151, 156, 178, 179, 181, 182, 193, 201, 202, 243, 244, 245, 246, 247

Charles I (King of England), 154

Charles II (King of England), 142

Charles V (King of Spain), 142

Charny, Israel, 14, 251n4

Cherokee, 116, 117

Chickasaw, 116

Childers, Thomas, 194, 195, 276n77, 276n79, 276n80, 276n85, 276n86

Chile, 120

China, 17, 233

Choctaw, 116

Churchill, Ward, 124, 264n16, 266n93

Circassians, 178, 179

Civil war, 234, 235, 236, 237, 239, 240, 241, 244

Clapham, J. H., 276n93

Class, 4, 13, 14, 20, 22, 30, 53, 65, 67, 69, 80, 83, 85, 86, 89, 107, 142, 145, 150, 157, 159, 176, 210, 234, 241, 247, 248

ruling class 35, 36, 64, 65, 66, 82, 83, 84, 90, 91, 101, 102, 103, 105, 140, 141, 144, 146, 185, 188, 197, 200

upper class 96, 139, 144, 168, 169, 185, 186, 205, 207, 208

middle class 3, 14, 20, 67, 70, 74, 75, 78, 82, 83, 84, 86, 87, 105, 153, 161, 167, 169, 181, 185, 186, 187, 188, 189, 190, 191, 192, 193, 194, 195,

196, 197, 200, 201, 202, 203, 204,
206, 207, 208, 210, 221, 239, 240,
248

lower middle 83, 86, 87, 193, 194, 195,
200, 201, 202, 203, 207, 208, 209,
248

working class 7, 42, 70, 77, 82, 83, 84,
90, 96, 97, 100, 113, 163, 164, 186,
187, 188, 189, 192, 193, 194, 195,
197, 199, 202, 205, 207, 208, 209,
210

lower class 169, 239

Classicide, 17

Cohn, Norman, 204, 278n145

Colonialism, 9, 10, 14, 20, 113, 114, 115,
116, 122, 124, 125, 126, 129, 130,
132, 133, 135, 136, 138, 140, 143,
149, 151, 152, 222, 223, 224, 225,
226, 227, 229, 230, 233, 235, 236,
239, 240, 241, 243, 245, 247

Columbus, Christopher, 111, 120, 121,
136, 139, 146

Commissar order, 216

Commodification, 10, 80, 89, 92, 93, 94,
95, 101, 135, 179, 245

Communism, 16, 21, 40, 190, 192, 195,
204, 205, 215, 229

Comprador, 245

Condensation, 57

Congo, 227

Conquistadores, 121, 140, 142

Conscription, 160, 161, 162

Cortes, Hernando, 113, 122, 139

Cossacks, 178

Creek (Native Americans) 116, 119

Crete, 162, 164

Crimean war, 159

Crisis, 1, 2, 3, 5, 15, 21, 22, 26, 29, 49,
106, 107, 135, 150, 154, 164, 171,
172, 173, 175, 176, 177, 181, 189,
195, 196, 200, 201, 208, 231, 233,
235, 237, 244

Cromwell, Oliver, 147

Crusades, 9, 35, 36

Cuba, 133

Cultural construction (worldview), 24

Dadrian, Vahakn, 175, 273n193,
273n119, 274n123, 274n129

Darwin, Charles, 4, 27

Death drive (Thanatos), 38, 39, 46, 49,
53, 54, 55, 59, 62, 72

Deep South (USA), 74, 117

Defense mechanisms, 21, 50, 51, 52

Defourneaux, Marcelin, 144, 268n176

Dehumanisation, 179

Delawares, 124, 125

Democracy, 7, 13, 88, 112, 117, 118,
129, 150, 167, 188, 189, 191, 228, 229

Deportation, 17, 114, 117, 118, 119, 158,
175, 179, 181, 211, 212, 213, 214,
215, 216, 218

Desire, 97–8

Destructiveness, 53, 54, 55, 56, 63, 64,
65, 71, 72, 73, 91, 99, 100, 101, 103,
107, 151, 157, 176, 179, 182, 184,
201, 203, 216, 220, 244, 246, 247

Desublimation, 66

Deutscher, Isaac, 249n15

Dialectics, 85, 106

Dickens, Charles, 77

Dicks, Henry, 203, 204, 278n141,
278n142, 278n143, 278n144, 278n146

Diseases, 1, 15, 111, 113, 114, 120, 128,
133, 158

Division of labor, 92, 127, 184, 223

Dobyns Henry, 111, 114, 129, 264n3,
265n20

Docker, John, 37, 254n122

Dostoevsky, Fyodor, 77

Doyle, David Noel, 155, 270n240

Dresden (bombing of), 18

Drinnon, Richard, 148, 269n203

Durkheim, Emile, 64

Dutch, 131, 143, 144, 154

Dwight, Timothy, 149

Eder, M. D., 248, 284n2

Egypt, 162

Ehrenreich, Barbara, 205, 278n153

Eichmann, Adolf, 184, 204, 211, 213,
214, 220

Einsatzkommando, 25, 215

Einstein, Albert, 62

El Saffar, Ruth, 145, 269n181, 269n182,
269n183

Elections, 163, 167, 188, 189–95, 227–9

Elliot, J. H., 122, 129, 130, 137, 139,
140, 266n66, 266n69, 267n109,
268n138, 268n139, 268n175

Eltis, David, 134, 267n131

Empire, 36, 42, 76, 115, 120, 121, 122, 124, 126, 129, 132, 139, 142, 158, 172, 174, 178–82, 219

Engels, Friedrich, 4, 5, 77, 249n12, 249n14, 253n90, 253n91, 257n117, 257n118, 259n33, 261n99, 263n51, 277n98

Engermann, S., 132

England, 142, 146, 150, 151, 153, 156

Enlightenment, 4, 43

Epidemics, 111, 113, 114, 120

Ethnocide, 16

Ethnicity, 1, 9, 13, 14, 17, 42, 48, 67, 78, 104, 125, 155, 168, 175, 176, 213, 222, 230, 231, 232, 234, 235, 237

Ethnic cleansing, 13, 14, 16, 17, 37, 111, 112, 115, 116, 119, 127, 130, 133, 134, 176

Erikson, Erik, 79, 261n89

Eros, 38, 39, 54, 86

Eugenics, 185

Evolutionary biology, 27

Exploitation, 75, 101, 102, 122, 135

Extermination, 116, 120, 149, 170, 204, 212, 216, 217, 220, 222, 245

Fairbairn, W. R. D., 46, 54, 255n37, 257n58

Family, 3, 4, 5, 6, 8, 15, 24, 29, 38, 43, 45, 49, 56, 59, 65, 66, 68, 73, 78–80, 86, 90, 91, 96, 98, 105, 106, 138, 145, 147, 151, 156, 172, 174, 177, 178, 190, 196, 200, 201, 203, 206, 208, 221, 237, 241, 243, 248

Famine, 17, 103, 114, 154, 155, 208, 233

Fascism, 7, 20, 22, 47, 64, 96, 192, 194, 201, 204

Faulkner, Neil, 35, 36, 254n117

Fenichel, Otto, 5, 53, 105, 249n20, 257n94, 257n100

Feud, 174, 177

Feudalism, 3, 30, 35, 36, 42, 59, 63, 74, 76, 80, 84, 98, 105, 106, 112, 121, 122, 126, 135, 136, 137, 139, 140, 142, 146, 147, 153, 162, 167, 197, 199, 221, 226, 229, 236, 240

First World War, 3, 4, 6, 38, 55, 74, 105, 161, 163, 170, 175, 181, 186, 196, 200, 201, 203, 204, 221

Fisk, Robert, 191, 270n2, 274n128

Ford, Henry Jones, 152, 270n229, 270n229, 270n230

Foreclosures, 189

France, 116, 113, 116, 124, 125, 131, 132, 135, 140, 143, 159, 162, 174, 197, 211, 218, 221, 227

Frank, Hans, 212

Freikorps, 204, 205

Frenkel-Brunswik, Else, 255n48

Franco-Prussian War, 196

Frank, Andre Gunder, 126

Frankfurt School, 7, 8, 21

Franklin, Benjamin, 116

Friedlander, Saul, 200

Freud, Anna, 50, 71, 73, 88, 177, 265n65, 240n58

Freud, Sigmund, 4, 5, 6, 8, 15, 21, 38–48, 50, 54, 55, 58, 59, 62, 63, 64, 66, 67, 78, 86, 88, 89, 90, 91, 92, 95, 98, 104, 105, 106, 147, 151, 179, 182, 246, 247, 248, 249n8, 251n9, 254n1, 254n1, 254n2, 254n3, 254n3, 254n4, 254n5, 254n6, 254n7, 254n8, 254n9, 254n11, 257n95, 258n149, 261n95, 262n12

Fromm, Erich, 5, 7, 15, 23, 28, 40, 48, 50, 51, 54–6, 63, 64, 68, 83, 85, 86, 88, 89, 90, 91, 95, 96, 97, 99, 100, 101, 102, 103, 105, 144, 145, 150, 151, 173, 179, 181, 200, 202, 207, 242, 245, 247, 249n19, 250n28, 251n8, 252n49, 253n110, 254n9, 256n73, 256n75, 258n150, 259n15, 259n19, 259n20, 259n21, 258n25, 259n34, 260n50, 260n52, 260n54, 260n59, 260n63, 260n67, 261n103, 262n118, 262n121, 262n123, 262n124, 263n31, 263n40, 263n48, 264n73, 269n179, 274n133, 277n119, 277n119, 278n133, 284n104

Friedrich, Jorg, 280n233

Frosh, Stephen, 6, 39, 46, 47, 48, 60, 61, 78, 249n22, 255n40, 255n47, 256n78, 258n128, 258n133, 261n87

F-Scale, 21, 47

Functionalist, 2, 210, 214, 218, 220

Funk, Rainer, 71, 72, 260n50

Galton, Francis, 185

Gates, Bill, 58

Genocide (definition of), 1, 2, 3, 4, 5, 6, 7, 9, 10, 13, 14, 15, 16, 17, 18, 19, 20, 24, 25, 26, 27, 29, 32, 34, 35, 36, 37, 52, 53, 55, 59, 62, 69, 70, 72, 77, 80, 99, 100, 101, 104, 106, 107, 111, 112, 115, 116, 117, 118, 119, 120, 122, 124, 125, 127, 130, 134, 136, 151, 157, 158, 162, 167, 169, 170, 171, 176, 177, 179, 181, 182, 183, 184, 203, 214, 215, 220, 222, 236, 237, 238, 239, 240, 241, 243, 248

Genocide Convention (1948), 1, 2

Genovese, Eugene, 132

Georgia, 152

Geras, Norman, 30, 31, 32, 99, 184, 185, 252n93, 274n3, 274n14

Germany, 3, 7, 14, 22, 23, 24, 33, 55, 65, 65, 74, 77, 83, 84, 105, 135, 159, 162, 174, 183, 185, 186–221, 222, 224, 227, 242

Gerth, Hans, 192, 275n54

Ghettoisation, 213, 214, 216

Gibson, Charles, 114, 265n21

Gidddens, Anthony, 251n21

Gluckstein, Donny, 185, 186, 274n18, 275n34

Goebbels, Josef, 23

Goldman, Lucien, 85, 261n113

Gourevitch, Philip, 242, 281n1, 283n88

Gramsci, Antonio, 99, 263n50

Great Depression, 3, 105, 188, 189, 190, 196, 200, 221

Great Leap Forward, 17

Greece, 1, 9, 29, 34, 36, 37, 50, 105, 159, 160, 163, 164, 166, 168, 175

Greco-Turkish War, 175

Greenstein, Fred, 48, 49, 255n46

Greven, Philip, 269n199, 281n257

Grinker, Roy, 273n106

Grunberger, Bela, 208, 279n176

Guilt, 25, 41, 46, 50, 52, 73, 101, 148, 149, 173, 177, 178, 204, 208, 245

Guntrip, Harry, 46

Gypsies (Roma), 1, 177, 183

Habyarimana, Juvenal, 231, 232, 234, 235, 238, 239, 244

Hamitic hypothesis, 226

Hamlet, 104

Hanke, Lewis, 126, 127, 142, 146, 266n62, 266n87, 269n188

Harman, Chris, 259n33, 279n186

Hatzfeld, Jean, 240, 243, 244, 245, 251n11, 281n2, 283n71, 283n75, 283n93, 283n94, 283n97, 283n98, 283n99, 283n102, 284n103, 284n105

Heberle, Rudolf, 194

Hegel, G. W. F., 3, 85

Henderson, W. O., 196, 277n94, 277n95, 277n96, 277n97

Heraclitus, 57

Herzegovina, 164

Heydrich, Reinhard, 212, 213, 215, 216, 220

Hilberg, Raul, 217, 218, 274n1, 280n236

Hill, Christopher, 147, 260n80, 269n193

Himmler, Heinrich, 190, 211, 212, 213, 214, 217, 218

Hispaniola, 111, 120, 121, 139

Hitler, Adolf, 14, 23, 71, 188, 200, 202, 203, 210, 211, 213, 214, 215, 216, 218, 219, 220

Hobbes, Thomas, 40, 41, 43, 58, 98

Hoess, Rudolf, 25

Hohokam, 128

Holocaust (Nazi), 2, 3, 10, 19, 36, 119, 171, 183, 197, 210, 221, 241

Holocaust, 119, 127, 136

Holocaust survivors, 177

Homosexuals, 1, 21, 183

Horkheimer Max, 8, 201, 250n40, 277n124

Human nature, 4, 23, 32, 38, 43, 67, 81, 91, 97, 99, 106, 247

Hungary, 218

Hutus, 13, 222–49

Incas, 120, 132

Ideal types, 18, 74

Identification, 41, 59

Identification with the aggressor, 50, 71, 73, 177

Ideology, 4–8, 14, 18, 22, 48, 60, 64–8, 75, 81, 82, 83, 84, 86, 90, 91, 96, 99, 107, 112, 116, 119, 132, 134, 136, 141, 142, 144, 146, 168, 175, 183–7, 236, 240, 242, 247

IG Farben, 217

Imperialism, 35, 36, 37, 46, 113, 127, 140, 146, 159, 179, 200

Industrialisation, 159, 161, 187, 196, 197, 199

Indonesia, 16

Innes, Hammold, 268n136, 268n137, 268n143

Inquisition (Spanish), 140, 145

Instinct, 4, 8, 27, 38, 39, 40, 41, 42, 43, 44, 45, 46, 48, 49, 53, 54, 55, 59, 62, 63, 65, 66, 67, 89, 90, 93, 95, 97, 100, 218, 247, 248

Intentionality, 2, 18

Intentionalists, 2, 210, 214, 218

Intermarriage, 125

Intersubjectivity, 58, 72

Introjection, 50, 205

Irrationality, 4, 6, 9, 10, 16, 17, 20, 32, 34, 35, 36, 43, 48, 77, 103, 104, 107, 112, 120, 129, 134, 136, 157, 171, 183, 217, 218, 219, 240, 241

Ireland, 13, 130, 135, 152, 154, 155, 156

Irregulars, 177, 178

Israel, 14

Issaswi, Charles, 161, 162, 271n6, 271n7, 271n9, 271n14, 271n28

Italy, 135, 137, 159, 166, 167, 221

Jacoby, Russell, 8, 83, 87, 250n38, 256n53, 257n93, 261n101, 262n122

Jackson, Andrew, 117, 119

Jaimes, Annette, 128, 129, 136, 267n96, 267n100

James, Oliver, 7, 81, 250n28, 261n97, 264n72

James II (King of England), 154, 155

James, William, 173

Japan, 49, 162, 221

Jekyll and Hyde, 91

Jefferson, Thomas, 112, 116, 118

Jews, 1, 2, 17, 23, 26, 35, 48, 53, 118, 140, 144, 146, 159, 160, 167, 168, 177, 180, 183–221, 240, 241

Jones, Ernest, 249n13

Jones, Larry, 187, 191, 196, 275n29, 275n30, 275n52, 276n92

Jung, Carl, 84

Junkers, 196, 197, 199

Just war, 143

Kafka, Franz, 78

Kamen, Henry, 136, 139, 140, 266n67, 268n142

Kant, Immanuel, 23, 57, 252n50

Kardiner, Abraham, 64

Kater Michael, 192, 193, 195, 201, 275n334, 276n59, 276n70

Kattenacker, I., 203, 278n140

Kaye, Jeanne, 114, 133, 264n18

Kayibanda Gregoire, 230, 231, 236, 242

Keeley, Lawrence, 33, 250n46, 253n106, 257n102

Kelly, Douglas, 23, 252n51

Kenny, Kevin, 113, 151, 155, 264n9, 265n28, 267n126, 270n217, 270n246

Kentucky, 117, 152

Kernberg, Otto, 80

Kershaw, Ian, 183, 184, 195, 203, 215, 220, 274n2, 276n78, 276n89, 276n91, 278n136, 281n251, 281n252, 281n253

Kiernan, Ben, 18, 19, 33, 34, 121, 168, 180, 190, 249n11, 251n24, 253n105, 265n58, 271n25, 272n61, 272n63, 273n136, 275n45, 275n47

Kigali conference, 222

King Philip's War, 149

Klein, Janet, 170, 171, 273n83

Klein, Melanie, 4, 8, 41, 42, 48, 49, 53, 55, 59, 63, 72, 73, 97, 98, 105, 151, 182, 205, 206, 243, 246, 247, 278n161

Kohut, Heinz, 50, 51, 77, 79, 179, 203, 220, 256n71, 256n79, 278n134, 278n135, 281n254, 281n255

Konstan, David, 253n107, 253n112

Korsch, Karl, 7, 8, 250n32

Kovel, Joel, 6, 8, 80, 81, 84, 97, 98, 249n23, 261n96, 253n39

Krystal, Henry, 177, 273n110

Krupp, 217

Kubandwa, 225

Ku Klux Klan, 21

Kulaks, 9, 17

Kuper, Leo, 1, 129n3

Kurds, 160, 170, 171, 175, 178

Labour (forced), 226, 227, 233, 236

Labour movement, 66, 166, 187, 190, 197, 200, 207

Labour (power), 30, 42, 213, 219, 233

Labour process, 30, 31, 81, 89, 92, 93, 94, 96, 132, 157, 147, 247

Lacan, Jacques, 58, 59, 60

Laclau, Ernesto, 126, 266n86

Landau, Jacob, 272n79

Landlords, 112, 138, 154, 155, 162, 168

Language, 20, 31, 56, 57, 58, 59, 60, 86, 99, 100, 104, 117, 118, 127, 143, 146, 156, 166, 174, 223

Laplanche, Jean, 47, 62, 63

Las Casas, Bartolome de, 121–2, 123, 127, 132, 139, 142, 265n57

Lasch, Christopher, 79, 261n86

Latin America, 124, 125, 126, 127, 129, 131, 134

Laub, Dori, 3, 249n6, 250n25

Laud, Archbishop, 150

Lebensraum, 18

Lemaire, Anika, 258n124

Lemarchand, Rene, 283n76

Lemkin, Raphael, 1, 2, 16, 249n2

Levene, Mark, 4, 19, 20, 249n10, 251n26

Lewis, Bernard, 162, 163, 164, 166, 167, 271n7, 271n34, 272n272n40, 272n46, 272n48, 272n50, 272n52, 272n58

Lewis, Raphaela, 172, 271n20, 271n21, 271n22, 273n91, 273n82

Leyburn, James, 153, 270n223, 270n224, 270n225

Liberalism, 2, 4, 39, 40, 42, 164–7, 170, 183, 189, 190, 191

Libya, 159, 164, 166

Lichtman, Richard, 7, 8, 30, 43, 44, 83, 84, 90, 101, 105, 250n33, 252n84, 252n87, 255n25, 261n109, 263n58, 264n69

Linden, Ian, 282n38, 282n39

Lipset, Seymour Martin, 194, 275n36, 275n38, 276n73, 276n74, 276n76

Locke, John, 143

Lockhart, James, 125, 126, 266n85

Loewenberg, Peter, 203, 278n138

Long Depression, 161

Love, 68, 70, 71, 72, 73, 83, 85, 86, 87, 91, 95, 96, 97, 99, 100, 119, 141, 142, 148, 208

Lozowick, Yaacov, 284n9, 274n10

Lukacs, Georg, 3, 6, 8, 42, 45, 249n7, 250n27, 254n21, 255n36

Maccoby, Michael, 51, 69, 72, 74, 75, 76, 77, 85, 91, 141, 144, 150, 181, 245, 256n73, 256n75, 259n25, 259n29, 259n31, 260n54, 260n59, 260n69, 261n100, 261n111, 262n13, 268n163, 268n165, 269n179, 269n215, 274n142, 274n133, 284n104

Macedonia, 165, 169, 175

MacMullen, Ramsay, 4, 249n11

Madagascar plan, 211, 212, 218

Mahler, Margaret, 205, 206, 278n162

Makrygiannes, General Yannis, 177

Malinowski, Bronislaw, 43, 45, 255n24

Mamdani, Mahmood, 223, 225, 229, 233, 234, 238, 239, 240, 242, 281n6, 281n7, 281n8, 281n11, 281n12, 281n13, 281n19, 281n20, 282n21, 282n22, 282n24, 282n26, 292n28, 292n29, 282n29, 282n30, 282n31, 282n32, 282n35, 282n40, 282n41, 282n42, 282n43, 282n46, 282n49, 282n54, 282n55, 282n56, 282n59, 283n61, 283n62, 283n63, 283n64, 283n72, 283n86

Mannheim, Karl, 84

Mann, Michael, 9, 13, 14, 17, 32, 37, 115, 116, 118, 129, 130, 168, 176, 179, 184, 192, 193, 195, 204, 238, 239, 249n1, 250n44, 250n1, 251n5, 253n100, 265n22, 265n25, 265n26, 265n35, 265n42, 267n107, 272n67, 273n195, 274n8, 274n13, 275n55, 276n60, 276n65, 276n169, 278n149, 281n3, 283n60

Mao, 17

Maquet, Jean-Jacques, 242

Marcuse, Herbert, 7, 53, 54, 63, 66, 67, 86, 87, 105, 257n92, 261n115, 261n116

Marketing orientation, 70, 71, 105

Marx, Karl, 3, 4, 5, 8, 23, 30, 38, 57, 58, 75, 77, 81, 85, 92, 94, 96, 97, 98, 99, 100, 103, 106, 135, 161, 179, 197, 249n12, 252n86, 252n88, 252n90, 252n91, 252n92, 252n95, 252n96, 257n118, 259n33, 260n65, 261n99, 262n15, 263n51, 283n30, 277n98

Marxism, 3, 4, 5, 6, 7, 8, 10, 13, 23, 28, 29, 47, 49, 60, 64, 66, 69, 94, 183, 192, 201, 247, 248

Massacre, 16, 17, 32, 34–7, 103, 128, 134, 142, 149, 151, 158, 162, 170, 171, 179, 209, 222, 231, 234, 236, 238

Mass media, 66, 68, 96

Mass murder, 9, 16, 32, 209, 215

Masochism, 51, 71, 72, 74, 96, 100, 107, 201

Matriarchy, 59

Mather, Cotton, 142
Mather, Increase, 142
Matthaus, Jurgen, 280n219, 280n220
Mayer, Arno, 215, 216, 280n227
Mayer, Hans Eberhard, 35, 254n118
McKenzie, Robert, 260n79
Mead, Margaret, 45, 255n33
Mears, E.G., 271n16
Megalomania, 219
Methodism, 77, 83
Mexico, 68, 69, 74, 76, 111, 113, 115,
    118, 120, 121, 123, 124, 127, 128,
    133, 139, 142
Meggitt, M. .J., 33, 253n102
Miller, Alice, 51, 52, 179, 203, 245,
    256n72, 256n80
Millet (system), 160
Milgram, Stanley, 28, 252n75
Military, 7, 14, 15, 16, 17, 35, 36, 78,
    105, 107, 114, 116, 123, 124, 126,
    130, 138, 139, 152, 154, 157, 160,
    161, 163, 166, 167, 170–81, 192,
    213–16, 217, 218, 222–4, 229, 237,
    240, 241, 243.
Militarism, 2, 49
Mills, C. Wright, 64
Militias, 239
Mitchell, Juliet, 255n38
Milton, John, 154
Missionaries, 116, 123, 124, 130, 135,
    138, 142, 225, 227
Modernity, 19, 77, 78, 183, 184, 203
Mode of production, 30, 35, 45, 69, 76,
    87, 89, 90, 126, 1141, 157, 161, 245,
    247
Moliere, 77, 260n81
Mommsen, Hans, 185, 204, 210, 211,
    216, 217, 218, 219, 274n15, 275n29,
    278n151, 279n188, 280n226, 280n229,
    280n241, 280n241, 280n243, 280n244,
    280n245, 280n246, 281n247, 281n248,
    281n249, 281n250
Money, 35, 83, 89, 90, 92–, 112, 161
Moors, 136, 138, 139, 143, 144
More, Thomas, 143
Morgan Edward, 5, 151, 269n216
Moriscos, 143
Morner, Magnus, 122, 266n
Morton, A. L., 269n189, 269n191
Moscow, 215, 216

MRND (mouvement revolutionaire Nationale
    pour le Developpement), 232
Museveni, Yoweri, 235
Muslims, 57, 136, 140, 142–6, 158–63,
    165, 166, 167, 171, 175, 179
'Myth of the peaceful savage', 33

Napoleonic wars, 199
Narcissism, 43, 50, 51, 52, 73, 79–80, 99,
    100, 144, 179, 203, 206, 220, 245
Nash, Gary B, 111, 115, 125, 128, 129,
    130, 131, 134, 264n6, 264n13,
    265n23, 266n94, 267n97, 266n102
Nationalism, 2, 26, 52, 162, 166, 170,
    175, 180, 188, 228
National Resistance Army (NRA), 235
Native Americans, 1, 9, 10, 20, 36,
    111–56, 222, 241
Nazis, 1, 2, 3, 9, 10, 13, 14, 19, 20, 22,
    23, 24, 26, 36, 47, 49, 53, 55, 65, 103,
    105, 167, 171, 177, 180, 183–221, 239,
    241, 248
Necrophilia, 71
Neanderthal, 33
New Guinea, 45
Newbury, Catherine, 236, 282n27,
    282n53
Newbury, David, 236, 282n27, 282n53
Neurosis, 5, 15, 32, 38, 42, 65, 78, 89,
    90, 92, 104
Nicaragua, 120
Niewyk, Donald, 75n33
Normality, 23
Nuremburg trials, 1, 23

Object relations school, 8, 41, 44, 46–9,
    54, 60, 62, 72, 78–9, 97, 98, 105, 206,
    247
Obote, Milton, 235
Oedipus complex, 42, 45, 104, 145, 204,
    206, 208
Oedipus Rex, 104
Oliver, Charles, 152, 154, 270n218
Ollman, Bertell, 65, 258n6
Oriental despotism, 161
Orwell, George, 67, 96, 259n17, 263n39
Osborn, Reuben, 8, 250n42
Ottomans, 20, 158–81

Pagden, Anthony, 142, 143, 268n164

Paker, Murat, 180, 271n4, 271n30,
    274n125
Papen, Chancellor Franz Von, 195
Paramilitaries, 239
Paranoia, 20, 23, 50, 156, 162, 170, 179,
    180, 202, 203, 219
Paranoid-schizoid position, 73, 105, 136,
    243
Parker, Reverend Edward, 152
Parker, Theodore, 268n167
Pasa, Kamil, 166, 167, 170
Pasa, Sevket, 170
Pasha, Enver, 168, 179, 180
Pasha, Suleyman, 172, 173
Pasha, Said, 170
Pasha, Valentine Naker, 173, 178
Pavlov, Ivan, 5
Peasantry, 9, 17, 43, 69, 74, 76, 82, 126,
    135, 138, 139, 147, 162, 168, 171,
    186–91, 199, 222–32, 236, 239, 240,
    242, 245, 246, 248
Penn, William, 127
Pennsylvania, 115, 116, 124, 152
Performance principle, 54
Personality, 4, 8, 20, 22, 29, 42, 46, 48,
    51, 68, 70, 71, 75, 79, 81, 82, 86, 89,
    91, 95, 103, 106, 158, 173, 207, 219
Pequots, 128, 142, 149
Peru, 115, 120, 130
Petty-bourgeoisie, 20, 192, 193, 194, 195,
    197, 198, 201
Pilgrims, 128
Pinter, Harold, 78
Plantation, 122, 123, 132, 136
Plunder, 33, 35, 36, 115, 130, 177, 213
Pilbeam, D., 33, 252n104
Pol Pot, 9
Poland, 13, 26, 135, 209, 211, 212, 213,
    217, 218, 221
Politicide, 16
Popper, Karl, 21
Portugal, 124, 125, 130, 131, 142
Post-Traumatic Stress Disorder (PTSD),
    176, 178
Postmodernism, 4, 9
Powhatan, 129
Presbyterians, 154, 156
Preston, David, 113
Productivity, 33, 36, 132, 133
Projection (projective identification), 20,
    23, 46, 48, 50, 53, 73, 75, 105, 107,

136, 148, 149, 151, 156, 173, 180,
    182, 195, 203, 208, 220, 241, 242,
    246, 247, 248
Propaganda, 164, 183, 188, 191, 219,
    235, 236
Protestantism, 89, 125, 144, 147, 148,
    155, 216, 225
Prunier, Gerard, 224, 225, 228, 229, 230,
    238, 239, 241, 242, 243, 251n23,
    281n9, 281n10, 281n14, 281n15,
    281n16, 281n17, 282n25, 282n33,
    282n35, 282n36, 282n37, 282n44,
    282n45, 282n27, 282n48, 283n65,
    283n66, 283n67, 283n68, 283n69,
    283n70, 283n73, 283n74, 283n77,
    283n78, 283n79, 283n85, 283n87,
    283n90, 283n101
Psychiatry, 14
Psychoanalysis, 4–8, 13, 15, 20, 22, 27,
    40, 43–9, 51, 53, 55, 60, 61, 64, 67,
    75, 81, 86, 90, 96, 97, 100, 104, 105,
    149, 177, 180, 186, 200, 201, 203,
    204, 2205, 208, 210, 220, 243, 247
psychological reductionism, 6, 22
Psychologism, 208
psychology, 2–9, 10, 14, 15, 18, 19, 22,
    24, 27, 28, 32, 40–9, 52, 54, 55, 59,
    63, 65, 68, 69, 71, 73, 75, 77, 78, 82,
    85, 87, 89, 90, 92, 96, 100, 101, 103,
    105, 106, 112, 136, 141, 145, 151,
    157, 171, 172, 174, 176, 180, 181,
    182, 195, 200, 201, 203, 204, 208,
    217, 218, 219, 241, 242, 245, 246
Pueblo, 123, 124, 128
Puritans, 113, 115, 128, 135, 136, 146,
    147, 148, 149, 150, 151, 155, 156,
    157, 248

Quakers, 115, 116, 152

Racism, 18, 19, 52, 112, 113, 116, 119,
    127, 129, 133, 134, 136, 151, 157,
    168, 185, 204, 216, 230, 242, 243
Ramsauer, E. E., 168, 272n66, 274n132
Rationality, 1, 4, 6, 9, 10, 16, 19, 22, 25,
    29, 32, 35, 36, 30, 41, 42, 43, 63, 89,
    90, 91, 103, 112, 121, 129, 136, 143,
    146, 157, 183, 184, 185, 217, 220, 248
Rationalizations (psychological), 26, 35,
    179
Rationalisation (industrial), 196

Rearmament, 200
Reed, John, 84
Reich, Wilhelm, 7, 48, 53, 54, 55, 64, 65, 66, 67, 77, 83, 88, 89, 105, 145, 201, 242, 250n30, 255n22, 257n91, 257n103, 258n5, 259n11, 277n121, 277n126, 277n131
Reiche, Reimut, 8, 66, 259n13, 284n2
Reid, James, 162, 171, 172, 174, 176, 177, 179, 271n26, 273n87, 273n88, 273n108, 273n111, 273n117, 273n118, 274n121
Reification, 70, 92, 94, 95
Religion, 85, 140, 141, 144, 147, 159, 160, 164, 175, 208, 223, 225
Remini, Robert, 119
Repression (political), 90, 165, 176, 230
Repression (sexual), 65, 66, 78, 89, 90, 95, 147, 148, 151, 248
Resistance, 84, 96, 97, 118, 124
Richards, Barry, 90, 262n6
Rickert, John, 86, 87, 250n31, 258n3, 261n114, 261n117, 262n119
Right-Wing Authoritarianism (RWS), 21, 48
Roazen, Paul, 41, 254n16
Robinson, Paul, 54, 85, 257n97, 261n112, 277n132
Rome, 34, 35, 36, 105, 126
Roman law, 125
Romania, 218
Rorschach tests, 22, 23
Rose, Jacqueline, 6, 40, 41, 249n9, 250n24, 254n10, 258n149
Royal Air Force, 217
Rumelia, 165, 166
Rustin, Michael, 46, 255n39
Russia, 7, 17, 64, 84, 159, 162, 170, 171, 172, 173, 175, 178, 180, 181, 182, 186, 204, 208, 210, 212, 213, 214, 215, 216, 218, 220, 221, 239
Russian revolution, 7, 64, 84, 186
Rwanda, 1, 3, 16, 20, 222–8
Rwandan Patriotic Front (RPF), 232, 235, 236, 237, 239, 240, 241, 244

Sadism, 23, 28, 54, 56, 71, 73, 96, 100, 120, 134, 173, 174, 201, 209, 220
Sadomasochosm, 96, 106, 203, 209
de Saint-Croix, G.E.M., 34, 253n111
Sale, Kirkpatrick, 111, 264n4, 268n148

Samuels, Andrew, 8, 250n43
Sartre, Jean-Paul, 29
Schaffner, Bertram, 206, 207, 279n167, 279n168, 279n169, 279n170, 279n171, 279n172
Schneider, Michael, 8, 15, 42, 43, 80, 89, 91, 93, 94, 95, 210, 250n42, 251n10, 254n17, 255n22, 262n1262n8, 262n14
Schutzstaffel (*SS*), 22, 25, 188, 203, 204, 209, 212, 213, 219
Schweitzer, Arthur, 186, 187, 191, 192, 193, 195, 275n20, 275n28, 275n32, 275n37, 275n39, 275n53, 276n58, 276n69
Science, 4, 31, 85, 99, 116, 185, 248
Scotland, 153–6
Scots-Irish, 135, 136, 151–7, 248
Second World War, 1, 18, 47, 75, 183, 220
Seminoles, 116
Serbia, 159
Serge, Victor, 84
Service, E. R., 33, 250n45, 252n103
Sexuality, 5, 7, 24, 31, 38, 40, 41, 42, 45, 48, 53, 54, 59, 62, 67, 72, 79, 86, 89–91, 95, 105, 125, 141, 147, 148, 176, 204, 205
Shaw, Martin, 2, 16, 17, 18, 249n5, 251n12
Siberia, 213
Skinner, B. F., 28
Slavs, 177
Slavery, 33–7, 63, 103, 105, 111, 113–18, 120–7, 131–4, 139, 230, 242
Slotkin, Richard, 149, 150, 269n204, 269n213
Smallpox, 113, 114, 120
Smith, D. N., 24
Smith, R. W., 264n7
Social psychology, 20, 41, 47, 86
Socialization, 72
Soper, Kate, 102, 263n63
South Carolina, 133
Spero, Patrick, 264n10
Spicer, Edward H., 122, 123
Society of Muhammed, 164
Sociology (explanation), 9, 13, 14, 16–19
Sokoloff, K., 132
Sombart, Werner, 190
Southampton University, 2
Soviet Union, 212, 213, 216, 217, 218

Spain, 18, 113, 120, 121, 123, 125, 126, 127, 130, 136–44, 145, 146

Spanish America (colonies), 113–15, 118, 120–3, 129, 130, 131

Spinden, J. H., 267n99

Splitting, 23, 52, 53, 105, 209

SPD (German Social Democratic Party), 192

Spicer, Edward, 266n61

Spinden, J. H., 129

Srebenica, 16, 222

Stalin, 5, 9, 16, 17

Stannard, David, 120, 121, 125, 128, 134, 148, 249n4, 264n1, 264n2, 265n38, 266n60, 266n89, 266n92, 267n132, 268n166, 269n202

Star Chamber, 150

State feudalism, 126, 142

Staub, Ervin, 171, 181, 252n73, 256n86, 271n7, 271n23, 273n85, 273n86, 274n132

Stedman-Jones, Gareth, 197, 277n99

Stone, Lawrence, 105, 147, 148, 264n71, 269n192, 269n194, 269n197

Storr, Anthony, 101, 104, 263n61

Story of O, The, 96

Straub, Ervin, 27

Strauss, S., 281n3

Streit, C., 280n218

Sturmabteilung (SA), 203, 209

Subjectivity, 2, 4–9, 15–18, 44, 47, 49, 56, 58, 64, 67, 85, 94–6, 98, 99, 105, 183, 218, 221

Sublimation, 53, 66

Sultan, 161, 162, 163–8, 169, 173, 180, 181

Sweezy, Paul, 93, 262n15, 262n23

Symbiotic, 72, 100

Tannenbaum, Frank, 131, 267n112, 267n113

Tanzania, 234

Tanzimat reforms, 174

Tawney, R. H., 89, 146, 269n192

Taxes, 118, 121, 160, 161, 199, 224, 226, 233

Technology, 31, 128, 184

Tennessee, 152

Theweleit, Klaus, 71, 204, 206, 208, 220, 259n45, 260n37, 278n154, 278n155, 278n156, 278n157, 278n158, 378n159,

278n160, 278n163, 278n164, 278n165, 281n256

Thompson, E. P., 77, 83, 96, 260n80, 261n102

Thomson, Charles, 266n80

Thucydides, 37

Tompson, Benjamin, 149

Tories, 195

Totalitarian, 232

Trail of tears, 117

Trade unions, 44, 49, 82, 84, 91, 91, 96, 187, 190, 200

Traverso, Enzo, 184, 252n53, 274n5, 274n6, 274n6, 280n238

Treaty of Lausanne, 166

Treaty of Versailles, 188, 190, 200

Treblinka, 209

Tribal society, 9, 30, 33, 39, 41, 45, 56, 59, 80, 98, 103, 105, 106, 113–16, 118, 124–30, 132, 133, 145, 149, 171, 179

Trotsky, Leon, 5, 17, 84, 164, 248, 249n17, 249n18, 271n34, 284n

Troy, 34, 35, 36

Turkey, 1, 13, 158–81

Tutsis, 13, 26, 222–49

Uganda, 227, 229, 233, 234, 235

Ukraine, 17

Ulster, 152, 153, 154, 155

Unconscious, 5, 7, 21, 22, 38, 42, 43, 44, 47, 48, 52, 59, 60, 65, 69, 71, 72, 73, 76, 77, 79, 81, 82, 84, 85, 86, 88, 89, 90, 94, 95, 98, 100, 104, 105, 145, 148, 149, 151, 157, 173, 177, 208, 220, 232, 243, 244, 247, 248

Unemployment, 189, 192–4, 199, 200

United Nations, 228, 229, 234, 238

United States, 111, 113, 117, 118, 129, 131, 135, 159, 196, 197, 216

USAID (US Agency for International Development), 237

Uvin, Peter, 241, 283n80, 283n81, 283n82, 283n84, 284n84

Van Every, Dale, 117, 135, 265n31, 265n34

Vega, Lope de, 144

Vendetta, 174

Vienna, 159, 219

Vietnam Solidarity Movement, 184

Vigilantism, 174, 175, 177, 178, 179, 231